SO-ALB-104

Integrated Curriculum and
Developmentally Appropriate Practice

SUNY Series, Early Childhood Education: Inquiries and Insights
Edited by Mary A. Jensen

Integrated Curriculum and Developmentally Appropriate Practice

Birth to Age Eight

Edited by
Craig H. Hart, Diane C. Burts,
and Rosalind Charlesworth

STATE UNIVERSITY OF NEW YORK PRESS

$40—

Published by
State University of New York Press, Albany

© 1997 State University of New York

For information, address State University of New York Press,
State University Plaza, Albany, N.Y., 12246

Production by Cathleen Collins
Marketing by Theresa Abad Swierzowski

Library of Congress Cataloging in Publication Data

Integrated curriculum and developmentally appropriate practice : birth
    to age eight / edited by Craig H. Hart, Diane C. Burts, and Rosalind
    Charlesworth.
        p.   cm. — (SUNY series, early childhood education)
    Includes bibliographical references and index.
    ISBN 0-7914-3359-5 (alk. paper). — ISBN 0-7914-3360-9 (pbk. :
alk. paper)
    1. Early childhood education—United States—Curricula.   2. Child
development—United States.   3. Curriculum planning—United States.
4. Interdisciplinary approach in education—United States.
I. Hart, Craig H., 1957–   .   II. Burts, Diane C., 1947–   .
III. Charlesworth, Rosalind.   IV. Series.
    LB1139.4.I58   1997
    372.21—dc20   96-28735
                                                                          CIP

10 9 8 7 6 5 4 3 2 1

This volume is dedicated to the original commission that developed the 1987 developmentally appropriate practice guidelines, the 1997 revision committee, and the editors of both publications. It is also dedicated to the many graduate students and teachers who have worked with us over the years and helped us formulate our view of developmentally appropriate practices. Gratitude is extended to our families who have generously supported us in this work.

Contents

Figures

Tables

Foreword

One of the fundamental premises of early childhood education is the concept of the "whole child." Early childhood educators frequently speak of "whole child philosophy" as one of the important underlying principles of developmentally appropriate practice. Awareness of and respect for the whole child are important in thinking about our practices—that is, our ways of teaching. A holistic approach to early childhood education requires attention not only to what we know about child development and its implications for how to teach, but also to the content of the curriculum—what to teach and when, how to assess what children have learned, and how to adapt curriculum and instruction to children's individual strengths, needs, and interests.

This broader definition of "whole child philosophy" is clearly the organizing principle of this book. The editors, who are researchers who have studied the effects of developmentally appropriate teaching practices on children's success in school, begin by framing this book so as to give sufficient attention to all the critical aspects of early childhood curriculum. A research-based foundation is provided for this framework. The book continues with Suzanne Krogh's excellent summary of what we know about development and the implications for teaching and learning in early childhood.

Part 1 follows, thoroughly covering the content of the early childhood curriculum, addressing each discipline area in detail while also demonstrating its connections to the other areas of the curriculum. To teach in developmentally appropriate ways, teachers must have an understanding of the key concepts and tools of inquiry that characterize each discipline. The national curriculum standards, cited throughout this book, provide a basic framework from which teachers can build this understanding. But unless adults are able to help children make connections across disciplines, the matrix of curriculum standards will become overwhelming for teachers and children alike.

Young children are meaning makers. The quest for better and deeper understanding of the elements of the world and the attempt to make meaning is characteristic of early childhood. Unfortunately, the traditional subject matter curriculum, separated by disciplines, leaves children responsible for making all the connections. As more and more content is added to the curriculum, a choice must be made: We can add slimmer versions of everything, thus necessitating rote learning, or we can identify a coherent set of understandings that are broader and more likely to generate new learning. The best strategy, clearly applied by the authors in this book, is to begin with the discipline frameworks and identify the connections, the ways that curriculum can be integrated and made more meaningful for learners. Integrated curriculum is the answer to achieving coverage of the curriculum while also promoting meaningfulness.

So part 1 provides important pieces of the "whole" that need to be integrated—an overview of the content of the curriculum and the ways it can be taught. But more information is needed if the well-qualified early childhood teacher is to adequately adapt the curriculum for individual children and in various contexts. Part 2 addresses each of these important issues—assessment, individualization, diversity, and partnerships with parents and colleagues—in greater detail.

A definite strength of this "curriculum" book is the attention given to social development and guidance. Too often these topics are addressed in separate courses or even using a set of isolated behavioral strategies that are not connected to the overall approach. Clearly, the development of the whole child includes social development. Early childhood teachers know that discipline is not something to be handled so that they can get on with teaching the curriculum; the development of socially competent, self-disciplined members of a community of learners is a primary goal of the early childhood curriculum that must be an integral part of the program.

General knowledge of curriculum content and appropriate ways of teaching are not enough to ensure developmentally appropriate practice. Teachers must also understand individual children's strengths, needs, and interests and ways of adapting curriculum and teaching. Inclusion of children with special needs obviates the need for individualized educational plans, but such individualization should not be limited to those with identified disabilities or special abilities. Likewise, developmentally appropriate curriculum must be meaningful and effective in diverse social and cultural contexts. Achieving the goals of individually and culturally appropriate curriculum and teaching requires that ongoing assessment be integrated with teaching and learning. Because young children do not come with résumés, such assessment can only be done with the full involvement of families. Part 2 addresses each of these topics in detail.

Good early childhood teachers must know many things—the children they teach, the curriculum content, how to assess children's learning, and how to adapt the curriculum to ensure the successful progress of individuals and groups. But good teaching is more than knowing each of these separate topics of information. Good early childhood teachers must know how to make connections across each of these dimensions, how to integrate their own knowledge so as to use it effectively to teach children.

The challenge that early childhood teachers face—to integrate curriculum so as to make it meaningful for children—parallels the challenge faced by early childhood teacher educators—to develop teachers who can make connections across the discrete elements of the early childhood knowledge base. This book will be a valuable resource for helping integrate the early childhood teacher education curriculum as well as the curriculum for young children.

Sue Bredekamp

CHAPTER ONE

Integrated Developmentally Appropriate Curriculum

From Theory and Research to Practice

CRAIG H. HART
DIANE C. BURTS
ROSALIND CHARLESWORTH

The National Association for the Education of Young Children (NAEYC) published its position paper on developmentally appropriate practice in early childhood programs in 1987 (Bredekamp, 1987); since then, it has become the most influential document guiding the field of early childhood education today. The document stemmed from developmental theories about how young children think and learn (Bredekamp & Rosegrant, 1992). These guidelines have prompted practitioners to modify their classroom practices and researchers to empirically examine the effects of developmentally appropriate and inappropriate classroom practices on the development of young children from birth through age 8. The document has also generated much interest with thoughtful, sometimes "lively," discourse. Some professionals have questioned the conceptual base and breadth of developmentally appropriate practice and have encouraged a reconceptualization of the construct (e.g., Bloch, 1992;

1

Fowell & Lawton, 1992; Jipson, 1991; Kessler, 1991a, 1991b; Lubeck, 1994; Lubeck, 1996; Walsh, 1991). This discourse has been healthy for the profession.

The position paper was designed to indicate current knowledge and thinking in the field; NAEYC has revised the guidelines to reflect not only new knowledge but new political trends as well (Bredekamp & Copple, 1997). Changes addressed some concerns expressed and should help clarify misconceptions about the concept. One of the major changes was an expanded definition of "developmentally appropriate" to more clearly portray the relationship among age, culture, and individual determinants of development. Vignettes illustrate the process of professional reflection that occurs in making decisions about developmentally appropriate practice (Bredekamp, 1995).

The purpose of this introductory chapter is to briefly (1) introduce readers to the concept of developmentally appropriate practice, (2) overview the recent debate on developmentally appropriate practice, and (3) discuss research findings to date concerning the efficacy of developmentally appropriate curriculum. Probably one of the most challenging areas for practitioners is translating the integrated curriculum guidelines that are a part of developmentally appropriate practice into classroom applications. It is hoped that this volume will go far in helping not only theorists, researchers, and practitioners understand integrated curriculum, but in promoting practical applications of the concept for teachers and parents as well.

Developmentally Appropriate Practice

Many child development and early childhood education professionals have expressed concerns that the increasing emphasis on formalized instruction for young children that is being pulled down from the upper grades is creating undue stress for young children and undermining opportunities for them to reach their full potential. This theme has been echoed by many in the field who argue that academic skill-based instruction is out of step with the developmental needs of young children (e.g., Charlesworth, 1985, 1989; Elkind, 1986; Hirsh-Pasek & Cone, 1989; Piccigallo, 1988; Schweinhart & Weikart, 1988). For instance, David Elkind (1986) has warned that increased stress levels followed by negative motivational, intellectual, and social consequences may likely ensue as a result of developmentally inappropriate classroom practices. In light of these concerns and theory promoting the view that children construct knowledge in an active rather than a passive manner in the context of interactions with materials, peers, and adults (e.g., Piaget, 1952; Erikson, 1963; Vygotsky, 1978), guidelines for matching curriculum with how it is believed young children think and learn have been formalized (see Bredekamp & Rosegrant, 1992; Hyson, in press; Krogh, this volume, for theoretical review).

In contrast with developmentally inappropriate practices (DIP), the child-centered perspective offered by developmentally appropriate practices (DAP) stresses that the child needs to be the primary source of the curriculum. As Williams (1994) states: "It is through observation of emerging physical, social, emotional, and cognitive capabilities in children's natural activity that teachers can discover the content and form of activities to foster children's growth across developmental domains" (p. 157). This, coupled with knowledge of cultural nuances and normative child development, should go far in constructing a tailored curriculum that meets the needs of all children, regardless of age, gender, disabilities, socioeconomic status, or race (e.g., Bredekamp & Rosegrant, 1992; Escobedo, 1993; Hale, 1992; Stremmel, chapter 14, this volume; Dugger-Wadsworth, chapter 13, this volume). DAP teachers provide options for children rather than expecting all children to always be doing the same thing at the same time. By facilitating child learning experiences with nondirective, mediating, and directive teaching approaches that are based on cues from the child, the likelihood of adjusting for individual differences is increased (Bredekamp & Rosegrant, 1992).

Our interpretation of the NAEYC guidelines for developmentally appropriate practice as set forth by Bredekamp (1987) is that the extremes of DIP and DAP are defined and that there is a continuum from one extreme to the other (cf. Marcon, 1994). Recent research by Stipek, Daniels, Galluzzo, and Milburn (1992) and Charlesworth, Hart, Burts, Mosley, and Fleege (1993b) lends credence to this perspective. On one extreme, DIP attempts to pour in knowledge through lecture and other whole-group activities. Rather than being in a facilitator role, the teacher disseminates knowledge through more formal, direct-instructional means. Thus, "learning" occurs through workbook/worksheets, seatwork, and rote drill/practice activities that focus on discrete skills which must be completed by all children at once within an inflexible time frame.

Developmentally inappropriate classrooms are characterized by varying degrees of the following practices. The curriculum is compartmentalized into the traditional content areas (math, science, social studies, etc.), with no attempts to integrate across these domains through relevant and meaningful child hands-on activities. Moreover, little opportunity is allowed for children to move around the room, make choices, and actively explore a carefully crafted learning environment full of concrete experiences. The curriculum is also typified by an overreliance on punishment and extrinsic reward systems and the use of standardized assessment tests. Little attention is given to individual differences among children.

In contrast, developmentally appropriate practice as defined in the guidelines emphasizes the whole child (physical, social, emotional, and cognitive) while taking into account gender, culture, disabilities, and other factors that require varied applications of curriculum to meet both group and individual child needs and learning styles. For example, Charlesworth et al. (1993b) noted in a recent study measuring the developmental appropriateness of kindergarten teachers that DAP classrooms were all different and varied in the methods used to implement DAP. Moreover, activities were conducted in such a way in DAP classrooms that both African American and European American children were drawn into them. However, how children participated in these activities varied. Children were allowed to participate in ways that met their individual needs and learning styles. Teachers were flexible in modifying the course of activities while taking individual child differences into account. Interestingly, less stress-related behavior was observed during many of the activities administered in DAP classrooms when compared with similar but differently administered using "one-fits-all" approaches to activities occurring in DIP classrooms (Abshire, 1990; Burts et al., 1992; Charlesworth et al., 1993b).

The DAP curriculum is also designed as an interactive process utilizing activities that are relevant and meaningful for young children (e.g., Knapp, Shields, & Turnball, 1995). Rather than being taught in isolation, curriculum areas (e.g., science, math literacy, social studies) are integrated in the context of these activities (Jones & Nimmo, 1994; Krogh, 1995). The environment provides opportunities for active exploration and concrete, hands-on experiences. Positive guidance techniques are used, and children have opportunities to make choices. Learning through dramatic and other forms of play is also valued and facilitated by teachers in both indoor and outdoor settings (cf. Hart, 1993).

Motivation for learning in a DAP classroom is derived from children's natural curiosity and desire to make sense of their world. The curriculum is not an inflexible, prescriptive method; rather it is intended to be a framework that is adaptable to each individual group of children (Taylor, 1995). It is flexible and provides for a variety of different structures that meets both age group and individual, child-specific needs. Once the environment is set up, developmentally appropriate teachers actively facilitate interactive child-centered learning, using direct and indirect instruction as appropriate (e.g., Bredekamp & Rosegrant, 1992; Kostelnik, 1992; Stipek, 1994). How this all works is illustrated in the chapters that follow. It should be noted at the outset that such a curriculum is best facilitated by having at least two teachers in the classroom (e.g., a teacher and an aide). However, developmentally appropriate practices were implemented in classrooms with only one teacher that were part of the LSU studies described by Charlesworth et al. (1993a).

Developmentally Appropriate Practices Debate

Although few child developmentalists, reconceptualists, and early childhood professionals would argue that an overemphasis on academic skill-based instruction is in the best interest of young children, a growing number of scholars express concern that the framework of developmentally appropriate practice as currently conceptualized is too limited. It has been argued that the NAEYC guidelines set forth in the Bredekamp (1987) document promoting DAP based on child development research and theory is problematic in many ways. Many of the controversial points are thoughtfully explored in two recent edited volumes (Kessler & Swadener, 1992; Mallory & New, 1994). Presenting our view of all the criticisms regarding the construct of DAP is beyond the scope of this chapter. Many of them have already been discussed at length elsewhere (see Charlesworth et al., 1993a). In short, although we are not in agreement with many of the concerns, it is our view that questioning the construct of DAP has fostered valuable and constructive debate over what should best constitute theoretical and philosophical underpinnings for developmentally appropriate practice. This will ultimately lead to the strengthening of the construct in areas where it might be lacking.

Specifically, it has been argued that DAP does not meet the needs of culturally and otherwise diverse populations, thus perpetuating social inequity to the advantage of the dominant classes (Lubeck, 1994). It is stated (1) that DAP does not include considerations of family and social contexts (Kessler, 1991a; Ludlow & Berkeley, 1994); (2) that the ideology "is too narrowly conceived to address the range of problems faced by ethnic, racial, and linguistic minority children and families" (Lubeck, 1994, p. 30); (3) that DAP is heavily biased toward European American middle-class values (Jipson, 1991; O'Loughlin, 1992); and (4) that DAP relies too heavily on the contributions of child development theory and research to the exclusion of the important influences of gender, politics, culture, and history (e.g., Bloch, 1991, 1992; Graue, 1992; Kessler & Swadener, 1992; Lubeck, 1996; Stott & Bowman, 1996).

In response to these types of criticisms, Bredekamp (1991) has reminded us that normative data and theory on child development are not the sole basis for NAEYC's definition of appropriateness. Thus, child development should not be the only consideration in programming for young children. Moreover, some of the basic foundations for criticisms against using child development theory as a basis for DAP are currently in question (e.g., Lourenco & Machado, 1996). Another dimension of appropriate practice is that of "individual appropriateness" (p. 202). This requires attention to individual and cultural differences. Knowledge of the culture and values of individual children as well as those of the family and community are also important sources for curriculum development (Bredekamp & Rosegrant, 1992). It has been further argued, however, that the way culture is considered in determining individual appropriateness "misses the essential point" (Lubeck, 1994, p. 34) and that the current construct of DAP maintains social inequity, giving the dominant classes an advantage. In our view, empirical data at hand are not supportive of this latter perspective. We now turn to the research literature that we believe supports our view.

Research Support for Developmentally Appropriate Practice

Before directly addressing the equity issue, it would be important to review the research on DAP in general. Although findings are not entirely supportive of DAP, the weight of evidence appears to favor the approach (cf. Bredekamp & Copple, 1997; Frede, 1995). Research involving several different samples suggests that both preschool and kindergarten-age children who attend less developmentally appropriate classrooms exhibit about twice the levels of stress-related behaviors when compared with those in more developmentally appropriate programs (Burts et al., 1990; Burts et al., 1992; Hart et al., in press; Love, Ryer, & Faddis, 1992).

Attendance in academically focused preschool and kindergarten classrooms that have been identified as low-quality and/or more developmentally inappropriate has yielded a further pattern of consistent findings. Children enrolled in such classrooms have been found to display more negative academic achievement (Bryant et al., 1994; Frede & Barnett, 1992; Mantzicopoulos & Neuharth-Pritchett, 1995; Marcon, 1993), behavioral (Mantzicopoulos & Neuharth-Pritchett, 1995; Marcon, 1994), and motivational outcomes (Hirsh-Pasek, 1991; Stipek et al., 1995) when compared with children attending more child-initiated/DAP programs. Moreover, the general thrust of findings from these studies suggests that it is children who attend more child-centered/DAP programs who perform better in all of these domains. Achievement findings favor DAP curriculum approaches, even when compared with programs that enact mixed curriculum models (Marcon, 1992, 1994).

Postkindergarten follow-up studies into the early and middle elementary school years are also telling. Findings suggest that less developmentally appropriate preschool and kindergarten classroom experiences are linked to: poorer academic achievement; lower work habit grades; more distractibility; and less prosocial/conforming behavior during the early grade school years. In contrast, attendance in DAP programs appears to be linked with overall positive benefits in terms of later achievement and behavioral outcomes in elementary school for children from varying backgrounds (Burts et al., 1993; Charlesworth et al., 1993a; Hart, Charlesworth, Burts & Dewolf, 1993; Larsen & Robinson, 1989; Marcon, 1994).

Other findings, however, have indicated some positive benefits for children in DIP programs. Stipek and colleagues have found that children in programs that emphasized basic skills had higher scores on a letters/reading achievement test (Feiler, 1994; Stipek, 1993; Stipek et al., 1995) and had better classroom work habits (i.e., effort while working on tasks, utilization of classroom resources, asking for help) than children in more child-centered programs (Feiler, 1994). These results, coupled with those mentioned above, have led some to conclude that while there may be some advantages in the use of didactic programs, they may come with costs for children's motivational factors (Stipek et al., 1995).

Equity in Outcome Variables

With regard to the equity issue, findings from our research program, though far from conclusive, suggest that developmentally appropriate curriculum based on child development research and theory promotes equity in developmental outcomes, at least when considering African American and European American male and female children from socioeconomically diverse backgrounds. Our concurrent (Burts et al., 1990, 1992a; Hart et al., in press) and prospective, longitudinal research program has targeted children who attended DAP and DIP preschool and kindergarten classrooms (summarized in Charlesworth et al., 1993a).

Specifically, our findings have indicated that classrooms typified by varied applications of DAP curriculum to meet diverse child needs (as described above) reduce stress to a supportive level. These classrooms also appear to provide strong foundational experiences for males and females from different racial and socioeconomic backgrounds, thus minimizing inequitable outcomes. Regarding the stress studies cited above, children who appeared to be most adversely affected by DIP classrooms were males, low-SES children, and African Americans. In contrast, all children (regardless of SES, racial background, or gender) in DAP classrooms exhibited less stress-related behavior as a function of this curriculum type (Burts et al., 1992; Hart et al., in press).

With regard to academic achievement findings, no differences in California Achievement Test scores have been found between higher- and lower-SES children from DAP kindergarten classrooms. Moreover, children in DAP kindergarten classrooms scored no differently on this test than children in DIP kindergarten classrooms (Burts, Charlesworth,

& Fleege, 1991). These results also suggested that children from DAP classrooms were performing on par one with another, notwithstanding standardized assessments are not deemed developmentally appropriate and have been found to induce high levels of stress-related behavior in kindergarten-age children (Fleege et al., 1992). In contrast, higher-SES children in DIP classrooms were found to score better than lower-SES children in DIP classrooms (see Charlesworth et al., 1993a). This follows past research indicating standardized test scores favor high-SES children (cf. Alexander & Entwisle, 1988; Patterson, Kupersmidt, & Vaden, 1990; Shakiba-Nejad & Yellin, 1981), but suggests that this may be the case only in DIP classrooms during the early childhood years.

Additional findings suggest DAP classroom settings may be beneficial for low-income African American children. Marcon (1992, 1994) found both short- and long-term gains (through grade 4) for disadvantaged children who attended child-initiated (DAP) preschool and kindergarten classrooms. These children outperformed those from similar backgrounds in both academically directed programs (DIP) and mixed programs (DAP and DIP) in academic, social, and physical skill domains. Using measures of achievement and preacademic skills, Bryant et al. (1994) recently obtained similar short-term results for Head Start African American children, favoring DAP over DIP classrooms, even after controlling for the quality of home environment. Other studies also lend support to such findings (cf. Hirsh-Pasek, Hyson, & Rescorla, 1990; Mantzicopoulos, Neuharth-Pritchett, & Morelock, 1994).

Along similar lines, research by Weikart and Schweinhart (1986, 1991) showed positive long-term sociobehavioral gains for disadvantaged children at age 15 who were randomly assigned to a child-initiated (DAP) versus a teacher-controlled, direct instruction-oriented preschool program (DIP). Moreover, children from the more child-centered program showed additional lasting gains through age 27 (Schweinhart, Barnes, & Weikart, 1993). In contrast, recent evidence indicates that children who attended the direct instruction program (as compared with those who participated in the child-centered program) were more likely to have had more work and criminal related problems in adulthood (Schweinhart & Weikart, in press).

In our own longitudinal research program targeting children who attended DAP and DIP kindergarten classrooms, we have noted gains for all children, regardless of SES and racial background, who attended DAP as opposed to DIP classrooms (see Charlesworth et al., 1993a). Specifically, whereas higher-SES and European American children appear to do equally well in achievement and behavior whether they attended DIP or DAP kindergartens, lower-SES and lower-SES African American children appear to gain an equal advantage with regard to better academic achievement if they had a DAP kindergarten experience (Charlesworth et al., 1993a). Lower-SES students from DAP kindergartens have continued to hold this gain into the early primary grades when compared with those from DIP classrooms (Burts et al., 1993; Charlesworth et al., 1993a).

Additional findings (as referred to earlier) by Stipek et al. (1995) have indicated that enrollment of economically disadvantaged and middle-class preschoolers and kindergartners in DAP classrooms was associated with positive outcomes on measures of motivation. Specifically, when compared to children in DIP programs, children in DAP programs rated their abilities significantly higher, had higher expectations for success on academic tasks, evidenced more pride in their accomplishments, showed less dependency on adults for permission and approval, and claimed to worry less about school. Program effects appeared to be the same for both preschool and kindergarten children whether they were from economically disadvantaged or middle-class backgrounds.

Equity in Activity Type Participation

There are also data that suggest that children from diverse backgrounds may all similarly benefit not only from DAP but have more opportunities for equal access to developmentally appropriate activities in DAP classrooms (although DAP curriculum administration is varied somewhat across DAP classrooms to meet individual child needs). As will be seen, a cautious interpretation of the extant data indicates that foundational experiences necessary for building skills through appropriate experiences appear less available to low-SES and African American children in DIP classrooms. Such does not appear to be the case in DAP classrooms.

It has been suggested that minority children (relative to the predominant European American middle class) may be directed by some teachers into more conformance-oriented activities in teacher-directed group settings. This is because many teachers and parents believe that is what these children need to be successful in the predominant culture (e.g., Delpit, 1988, 1995; Goldenberg, 1994; Knapp & Shields, 1990; Lubeck, 1994; Pine & Hilliard, 1990; Powell, 1994; Stipek, 1993; Stipek & Byler, in press). Recent research further indicates that parents with low incomes and relatively poor education are more likely to endorse structured, basic skills-oriented programs for young children (Rescorla et al., 1990; Stipek et al., 1992). This literature also suggests that teachers may select, prioritize, and expose children to instructional strategies based on what teachers perceive as the children's capacity and need to profit from these strategies. Capacity and need are based on the teachers perceptions of culture, SES factors, and parental expectations. For example, factors such as home background and parental pressure have been found to be weighted into teacher decisions regarding the type of reading curriculum exposure for older children (Haller & Waterman, 1985; Reutzel & Cooter, 1996) and the structural degree of skills-based programs for younger children (Stipek & Byler, in press).

Greater exposure to conformance-based activities may be particularly difficult for African American children, even though such approaches may be viewed by minority cultures as a means for helping their children succeed in the mainstream culture (Delpit, 1988). Compared with their European American counterparts, past research indicates that African American children tend to thrive more on people-oriented activities where freedom, variation, and novelty abound (Charlesworth, 1996). Because of this, Hale (1981, 1992) stresses that for successful learning to occur, African American children need a more physically active, socially oriented environment to support their high energy level.

Tentative results of our studies including African American children indicate that this more active, socially oriented environment was not occurring in DIP kindergarten classrooms. In contrast, DAP teachers appeared to strike a balance between these culture-specific needs and group practices in ways that maximized opportunities for all children, regardless of racial background. For example, our data show that African American children in DIP kindergarten classrooms were observed less frequently participating in group story and music activities and more frequently in whole-group, waiting, and teacher-directed transitions when compared with their European American counterparts in the same classes (Burts et al., 1992).

Of particular concern was accompanying qualitative data indicating that these African American children appeared to be funneled (Abshire, 1990) more into whole-group, waiting, and group-managed transitional activities where there was greater teacher control over their high activity level. Not surprisingly, quantitatively higher levels of stress-related behavior were observed for these African American children in DIP classrooms during whole-group, waiting, and group-managed transitional activities (Burts et al., 1992). No such activity type differences or stress manifestation differences within activity type were found between African American and European American children in DAP classrooms.

In short, the developmentally inappropriate curriculum appeared to foster racial inequity by not providing more experiences that were adaptable to the interaction and learning styles of African American children and that were balanced in ways that would meet needs of the whole group regardless of racial background (cf. Delpit, 1988; Kessler, 1992). Such did not appear to be the case in DAP classrooms.

Similar findings have been obtained regarding SES. In the Burts et al. (1992) sample, lower-SES children had tendencies to be less involved in developmentally appropriate activities than higher-SES children. These findings were extended in a separate sample of preschool-age children (Hart et al., in press). Lower-SES children were found to participate in more conformance-oriented waiting and academically oriented workbook/worksheet activities in teacher-directed small-group settings. This, coupled with their lesser involvement in other classroom activities involving group story, music, and center activities (when offered in DIP classrooms), suggests that these children did not have as much access to developmentally appropriate classroom activities when they were available. In contrast, no significant activity type participation differences were found in this sample between higher- and lower-SES children in DAP classrooms.

Research Summary

Taken together, these child outcome and activity participation findings indicate that an integrated curriculum that is part of a DAP classroom experience may indeed meet the needs of a diverse population and promote equality rather than inequity. By taking into account cultural, SES, and gender differences, the studies reviewed above indicate that all children benefit from similar types of developmental experiences that vary according to the "age" and "individuality" of the children (Bredekamp, 1987). Based on the evidence at hand, it appears that the universal child development-based guidelines as currently portrayed by DAP coupled with culture-specific understandings have substantial positive merit in the early education of young children (Bredekamp & Copple, 1997). This is not to imply that reconceptualists have ever suggested that inequities may or may not occur in DIP classrooms. The data simply illustrate that, contrary to what would be expected from arguments about inequity promoted by DAP, no significant racial/SES activity participation or concurrent/ longitudinal child outcome differences as a function of SES or race have been found for children with DAP experiences. In contrast, data appear to suggest that such inequity is promoted by DIP classroom experiences.

Notwithstanding, these conclusions based on the extant data that have been deemed supportive of our view should be treated with caution for several reasons. First, none of the studies reviewed above were designed specifically to assess the equity issue. Thus, causal relationships between curriculum and equity cannot be certain. Second, outcome variables addressed in these studies could have different meanings depending on their sociocultural context. Third, although findings have been remarkably similar across different samples, most of these studies do not take into account possible confounding family background characteristics of the child (e.g., parenting styles, patterns of family functioning, etc.). Fourth, only European American and African American children of varying socioeconomic backgrounds have been studied in this regard. There is no guarantee that these findings will translate to other groups. Fifth, the mechanisms by which all of this may be happening are not clearly understood. No simultaneous beliefs data from DAP and DIP teachers about what type of curriculum activities they perceive children from different backgrounds might need were collected in our studies mentioned above.

Outline of the Volume

With this research background in mind and our biases clearly stated, we now turn to an overview of what is ahead. In this volume we have attempted to bring together a group of scholars and practitioners who not only understand and can implement developmentally appropriate practices, but who can take their own content area specialty and integrate it with others.

In order to maintain a degree of uniformity across the volume a format was suggested for structuring the chapters (occasionally, content areas necessitated variation from the prescribed format). First, each chapter is grounded in the framework for integrated developmentally appropriate curriculum outlined by Krogh (chapter 2, this volume). Second, research-based developmental trends for each curriculum content area (e.g., math, science, social studies) are covered from infancy/toddlerhood through grade 3. Third, tables and figures are included in most chapters for quick and easy reference to important points each author makes. Fourth, explicit examples of integrated curriculum activities involving each content area for infants/toddlers, ages 3–5, and ages 6–8 are included. These examples demonstrate how each curriculum area is connected to others (e.g., math, science, art, music, social studies, literacy, social development, etc.) Fifth, sample webs are included in each curriculum content area chapter that illustrate how curriculum can be integrated across content domains. Some chapters are longer and more in-depth than others, reflecting varied degrees of diversity and/or bulk of research and content that are available within each of the designated areas that are directly related to young children. Finally, each content area's national standards are related to DAP. These sections complement the more in-depth content standards/DAP discussions in the second volume of *Potentials* (Bredekamp & Rosegrant, 1995).

This volume is organized into two major parts. Part 1 deals with specific curriculum areas (i.e., mathematics, science, art, music, social studies, language arts, physical activities) and how they can be integrated across these areas in developmentally appropriate classrooms. Part 2 addresses selected topics and special issues that are integral to developmentally appropriate practice and an integrated curriculum.

Chapter 2, "How Children Develop and Why It Matters: The Foundation for the Developmentally Appropriate Integrated Early Childhood Curriculum," by Suzanne Krogh lays the foundation for the volume. Krogh provides a definition of developmentally appropriate practice as established by the National Association for the Education of Young Children (NAEYC). She then presents an overview of some of the predominant theoretical perspectives on child development that are influencing the field of early childhood education. She describes how these perspectives relate to curriculum creation and integration. Suggestions of ways the curriculum can be integrated through the use of thematic studies and webbing are presented. Krogh concludes with four questions critical to the design and implementation of an integrated curriculum in developmentally appropriate classrooms.

In her chapter, "Mathematics in the Developmentally Appropriate Integrated Curriculum" (chapter 3), Rosalind Charlesworth begins with the current view of mathematics instruction based on theoretical and research foundations and direction from professional societies. She suggests ways that the immersed model and webbed model presented in chapter 2 can be used to meet mathematics standards through developmentally appropriate instruction. Resources and materials that can be used to assist the early childhood professional in instituting a developmentally appropriate integrated mathematics program are included. A brief description of appropriate assessment that evolves from instruction is also provided.

In chapter 4, Karen Lind focuses on science in the integrated curriculum. She describes how the early childhood curriculum can be built on constructivism and developmental foundations. Lind highlights the importance of development and warns that if the science content is not appropriate for the cognitive capactiy of the children at different stages of their development, scientific misconceptions, including alternative or naive understandings, will occur. Inquiry-oriented instruction is discussed, and strategies and processes that encourage children to think using inquiry are presented.

In her chapter on "Music in the Developmentally Appropriate Integrated Curriculum" (chapter 5), Susan Kenney explores some common misconceptions about music knowledge using examples of music development in other cultures. She states that "music may be the most used and the least understood of all subjects in early childhood curriculum." In her discussion of the theoretical foundations of developmental music instruction, she focuses on the works of Jean Piaget and Howard Gardner. With the idea that music is a basic intelligence available to all human beings, Kenney presents typical music behaviors for various ages and suggests teaching strategies appropriate for each developmental level. She describes how music can be integrated with other subjects in the curriculum while at the same time helping children develop musical behaviors and musical knowledge.

Chapter 6 deals with integrating physical activities with the other curriculum areas. V. Gregory Payne and Judith Rink begin by defining a physically educated person, highlighting five major focus areas. They proceed by clarifying what is meant by a developmental perspective in physical education. Motor development from birth to 8 years is presented with emphasis on infant reflexes, voluntary movements, and fundamental movement. Payne and Rink note that motor development of most prekindergarten children has received little attention, and most early childhood programs do little more than provide for naturalistic experiences. Appropriate content and structure for developmentally appropriate integrated early childhood programs are addressed.

In chapter 7, "Social Studies in the Integrated Curriculum," Carol Seefeldt begins with an example that illustrates how *not* to create a meaningful, integrated curriculum. While the "very definition of social studies conveys the integrative nature of the field," the all-encompassing nature of the social studies also brings disorder. Seefeldt describes how learned societies have provided frameworks that serve to bring order to the field. She focuses on three of the social studies—history, geography, and economics. She then presents key concepts in these areas and examples of how they can be interwoven to present an integrated curriculum that serves to enhance the total development of the young child.

Cynthia Colbert begins chapter 8 on the visual arts by discussing two philosophical positions held by many adults concerning art instruction with young children. The noninterventionist view holds that children should have little interference from adults. Those who take the opposing view believe that children need instruction in creating work or discussing the work they have created. Colbert continues with an overview of how children's artistic abilities develop. In discussing the issue of integration with other curriculum areas, Colbert emphasizes that while the visual arts are an excellent vehicle for integrating the curriculum, the integrity of the discipline (i.e., visual arts) must be maintained. She provides examples of how to take trivial activities that are sometimes labeled as "art" and modify them so they become meaningful art experiences.

The final chapter in part 1 (chapter 9), "Integrating Literacy Learning for Young Children: A Balanced Literacy Perspective," was written by D. Ray Reutzel. Reutzel describes the stages of reading and writing development and then makes a comparison between the two. Later in the chapter, he describes a model he developed for balanced literacy classrooms based on recent literacy environmental research. In the final portion of his chapter, he describes elements of a balanced literacy program and presents examples of developmentally appropriate instructional practices focusing on reading and writing to, with, and by children.

The remainder of this volume focuses on other topics and issues integral to the integrated developmentally appropriate curriculum. Topics in part 2 include social development, guidance, assessment practices, students with disabilities, diversity and the multicultural perspective, informal learning in the home, and parents and administrators.

In chapter 10, "Social Development and Behavior in the Integrated Curriculum," Michele DeWolf and Joan Benedict state that "socialization is the common thread that ties the entire curriculum together." They present an eclectic approach to viewing children's social development based on the models/theories of Bandura, Piaget, Dodge, Rubin, and Erikson. DeWolf and Benedict highlight children's social skill development from infancy to age 8 and present activities adults can do to encourage social development during these years. Later in the chapter they explore the family and school as contexts for supporting social development. The indirect and direct ways families influence peer relations and the ways schools impact children's social (and academic) competence through enhancement of play, peer relationships, classroom organization, and teacher–child relationships are discussed.

The adoption of a developmentally appropriate, integrated curriculum has implications not only for classroom activities but also for the way practitioners guide, direct, manage, control, and influence children's behaviors. Marion Hyson and Shawn Christiansen address the issue of "Developmentally Appropriate Guidance and the Integrated Curriculum" in chapter 11. They present a historical perspective on the guidance of young children, noting that consensus has not been reached concerning the goals of guidance nor about the best ways to implement those goals. Hyson and Christiansen discuss three areas of theory and research—early emotional development, motivation, and sociomoral understanding and prosocial behavior—which have implications for establishing guidance strategies consistent with a developmentally appropriate, integrated curriculum. They highlight some of the unique guidance challenges that face practitioners using the integrated approach and present ways these challenges can be dealt with.

Another issue related to the integrated curriculum in developmentally appropriate classrooms is that of assessment. Alternative forms of assessment have become more popular partly as a means of implementing developmentally appropriate practices in classrooms and as an avenue for integrating assessment with curriculum. In chapter 12, Pamela Fleege provides an overview of assessment as defined by NAEYC using assessment snapshots to help the reader better visualize the integration of instruction and assessment. Fleege describes various methods of assessment and how assessment can be accomplished with different age children. Suggestions for teachers and/or schools developing an assessment plan are included, along with resources available to those beginning an assessment project.

One of the most timely topics related to developmentally appropriate practice and the integrated curriculum is that of working with children with disabilities. In chapter 13, Donna Dugger-Wadsworth presents some of the similarities and differences between early childhood education (ECE) and early childhood special education (ECSE). She explores the controversy between ECE and ECSE focusing on four primary issues. Dugger-Wadsworth explains how developmentally appropriate practice can be incorporated into an early childhood special education curriculum. Throughout the chapter she points out the importance of resolving issues related to working with families and with personnel from other disciplines who may have different knowledge and theoretical perspectives.

Andrew Stremmel addresses the highly complex and political issue of multicultural education in chapter 14, "Diversity and the Multicultural Perspective." As a basis for his arguments, Stremmel draws on the constructivist perspectives of Piaget and Vygotsky and on feminist epistemology to form his sociocultural framework. He begins with an examination of children's awareness of diversity and moves to a discussion of perspectives about multicultural education. He then addresses how to provide developmentally appropriate and culturally sensitive curriculum and how to prepare teachers to be caring and responsive to the needs of diverse children.

Parents play a major role in children's development and cannot be overlooked in the developmentally appropriate integrated early childhood curriculum. Chapter 15, "Integrating Home and School: Building a Partnership," presents two avenues for integrating home and school in ways that can facilitate optimal child development. In this chapter,

Jean Larsen and Julie Haupt remind us that early childhood educators have a responsibility to assist parents in fulfilling their role as the child's first and most important teacher in the home through parent education and training efforts. Parents also need to be involved in the child's school. Research literature illustrating what works and practical ways to facilitate parents as partners in the education process are reviewed and expanded upon.

The full benefits of developmentally appropriate practice will not be realized without the support of teachers, administrators, and parents. Making the change from a less developmentally appropriate approach to more developmentally appropriate classroom practices is an involved process. Julia Haupt and Margaret Ostlund address this process in the final chapter of this volume (chapter 16), "Educating Parents, Administrators, and Teachers about Developmentally Appropriate Practices." They assert that teachers are in a unique position to influence the parents they serve and the other teachers and administrators they work with. Haupt and Ostlund provide specific strategies for nurturing the change process for each of these groups.

In sum, this volume describes many ways to implement an integrated developmentally appropriate curriculum by touching on all areas of a child's development. Advances in our understanding of how children's growth and development are enhanced by developmentally appropriate practices is just beginning. It is hoped that this volume will provide a springboard for future research on and applications for the integrated curriculum approach to facilitating optimal child development during the early childhood years.

References

Abshire, S. (1991). *A study of developmentally appropriate and developmentally inappropriate kindergarten classrooms: Activity types and experiences.* Unpublished master's thesis, Louisiana State University, Baton Rouge.

Alexander, K.L., & Entwisle, D.R. (1988). Achievement in the first 2 years of school: Patterns and processing. *Monographs of the Society for Research in Child Development, 53.*

Bloch, M.N. (1991). Critical science and the history of child development's influence on early education research. *Early Education and Development, 2,* 95–108.

Bloch, M.N. (1992). Critical perspectives on the historical relationship between child development and early childhood education research. In S. Kessler & B.B. Swadner (Eds.), *Reconceptualizing the early childhood curriculum: Beginning the dialogue* (pp. 3–20). New York: Teachers College Press.

Bredekamp, S. (1987). *Developmentally appropriate practice in early childhood programs serving children from birth through age 8.* Washington, DC: National Association for the Education of Young Children.

Bredekamp, S. (1991). Redeveloping early childhood education: A response to Kessler. *Early Childhood Research Quarterly, 6,* 199–209.

Bredekamp, S. (1994). The competence of entry-level early childhood teachers: Teachers as learners. In S.G. Goffin & D.E. Day (Eds.), *New perspectives in early childhood teacher education: Bringing practitioners into the debate.* New York: Teachers College Press.

Bredekamp, S. (1995, November). *Developmentally appropriate practice.* Seminar presented at the annual conference of the National Association for the Education of Young Children, Washington, DC.

Bredekamp, S., & Copple, C. (Eds.). (1997). *Developmentally appropriate practice in early childhood programs: Revised.* Washington, D.C.: National Association for the Education of Young Children.

Bredekamp, S., & Rosegrant, T. (Eds.). (1992). *Reaching potentials: Appropriate curriculum and assessment for young children* (Vol. 1). Washington, DC: National Association for the Education of Young Children.

Bredekamp, S., & Rosegrant, T. (Eds.). (1995). *Reaching potentials: Appropriate curriculum and assessment for young children* (Vol. 2). Washington, DC: National Association for the Education of Young Children.

Bryant, D.M., Burchinal, M., Lau, L.B., & Sparling, J.J. (1994). Family and classroom correlates of Head Start children's developmental outcomes. *Early Childhood Research Quarterly, 9,* 289–309.

Burts, D.C., Charlesworth, R., & Fleege, P.O. (1991, April). *Achievement of kindergarten children in developmentally appropriate and developmentally inappropriate classrooms.* Paper presented at the biennial meeting of the Society for Research in Child Development, Seattle, WA.

Burts, D.C., Hart, C.H., Charlesworth, R., & Kirk, L. (1990). A comparison of frequencies of stress behaviors observed in kindergarten children in classrooms with developmentally appropriate versus developmentally inappropriate instructional practices. *Early Childhood Research Quarterly, 5*, 407–23.

Burts, D.C., Hart, C.H., Charlesworth, R., Fleege, P.O., Mosley, J., & Thomasson, R.H. (1992). Observed activities and stress behaviors of children in developmentally appropriate and inappropriate kindergarten classrooms. *Early Childhood Research Quarterly, 7*, 297–318.

Burts, D.C., Hart, C.H., Charlesworth, R., DeWolf, D.M., Ray, J., Manuel, K. & Fleege, P.O. (1993). Developmental appropriateness of kindergarten programs and academic outcomes in first grade. *Journal of Research in Childhood Education, 8* (1), 23-31.

Charlesworth, R. (1985). Readiness: Should we make them ready or let them bloom? *Daycare and Early Education, 12* (3), 25–27.

Charlesworth, R. (1989). Behind before they start? *Young Children, 44* (3), 5–13.

Charlesworth, R. (1996). *Understanding child development* (4th ed.). Albany, NY: Delmar.

Charlesworth, R., Hart, C.H., Burts, D.C., & DeWolf, M. (1993a). The LSU studies: Building a research base for developmentally appropriate practice. In S. Reifel (Ed.), *Advances early education and day care: Perspectives on developmentally appropriate practice* (Vol. 5, pp. 3–28). Greenwich, CT: JAI.

Charlesworth, R., Hart, C.H., Burts, D.C., Mosley, J., & Fleege, P.O. (1993b). Measuring the developmental appropriateness of kindergarten teachers' beliefs and practices. *Early Childhood Research Quarterly, 8*, 255–76.

Delpit, L.D. (1988). The silenced dialogue: Power and pedagogy in educating other people's children. *Harvard Education Review, 58*, 78–95.

Delpit, L.D. (1995). *Other people's children: Cultural conflict in the classroom*. New York: New Press.

Elkind, D. (1986). Formal education and early childhood education: An essential difference. *Phi Delta Kappan, 67*, 631–36.

Erikson, E. (1963). *Childhood and society.* New York: Norton.
Escobedo, T.H. (1993). Curricular issues in early education for culturally and linguistically diverse populations. In S. Reifel (Ed.), *Advances in early education and day care: Perspectives on developmentally appropriate curriculum* (Vol. 5, pp. 213–46). Greenwich, CT: JAI.
Feiler, R. (1994, April). The effects of different instructional approaches on young children's cognitive and social-motivational outcomes. In D. Stipek (Chair), *Reconceptualizing the debate on appropriate early childhood education.* Symposium presented at the annual meeting of the American Educational Research Association, New Orleans, LA.
Fleege, P.O., Charlesworth, R., Burts, D.C., & Hart, C.H. (1992). Stress begins in kindergarten: A look at behavior during standardized testing. *Journal of Research in Childhood Education,* 7, 20–26.
Fowell, N., & Lawton, J. (1992). An alternative view of appropriate practice in early childhood education. *Early Childhood Research Quarterly,* 7, 53–73.
Frede, E.C. (1995). The role of program quality in producing early childhood program benefits. In R.E. Behrman (Ed.), *The future of children: Long-term outcomes of early childhood programs* (Vol. 5). Los Altos, CA: The Center for the Future of Children.
Frede, E.C., & Barnett, W.S. (1992). Developmentally appropriate public school preschool: A study of implementation of the High/Scope curriculum and its effects on disadvantaged children's skills at first grade. *Early Childhood Research Quarterly,* 7, 483–99.
Goldenberg, C. (1994, April). Rethinking the means and goals of early literacy education for Spanish-speaking kindergartners. In D. Stipek (Chair), *Reconceptualizing the debate on appropriate early childhood education.* Symposium presented at the annual meeting of the American Educational Research Association, New Orleans, LA.
Graue, M.E. (1992). Meanings of readiness and the kindergarten experience. In S. Kessler & B.B. Swadner (Eds.), *Reconceptualizing the early childhood curriculum: Beginning the dialogue* (pp. 62-92). New York: Teachers College Press.
Hale, J. (1981). Black children: Their roots, culture, and learning styles. *Young Children,* 36 (2), 37–50.

Hale, J.E. (1992). An African-American early childhood education program: Visions for children. In S. Kessler & B. B. Swadener (Eds.), *Reconceptualizing the early childhood curriculum: Beginning the dialogue* (pp. 205–26). New York: Teachers College Press.

Haller, E.J., & Waterman, M. (1985). The criteria of reading group assignments. *The Reading Teacher, 28,* 772–81.

Hart, C.H. (Ed.). (1993). *Children on playgrounds: Research perspectives and applications.* Albany, NY: State University of New York Press.

Hart, C.H., Burts, D.C., Durland, M.A., Charlesworth, R., DeWolf, M., & Fleege, P.O. (in press). Stress behaviors and activity type participation of preschoolers in more and less developmentally appropriate classrooms: SES and gender differences. *Journal of Research in Childhood Education.*

Hart, C.H., Charlesworth, R., Burts, D.C., & DeWolf, M. (1993, March). *The relationship of attendance in developmentally appropriate or inappropriate kindergarten classrooms to first and second grade behavior.* Paper presented at the biennial meeting of the Society for Research in Child Development, New Orleans, LA.

Hirsh-Pasek, K. (1991). Pressure or challenge in preschool? How academic environments affect children. In L. Rescorla, M.C. Hyson, & K. Hirsh-Pasek (Eds.), *New directions in child development. Academic instruction in early childhood: Challenge or pressure?* (No. 53, pp. 39–46). San Francisco: Jossey-Bass.

Hirsh-Pasek, K., & Cone, J. (1989, April). *Hurrying children: How does it affect their academic, social, creative, and emotional development?* Paper presented at the biennial meeting of the Society for Research in Child Development, Kansas City, MO.

Hirsh-Pasek, K., Hyson, M., & Rescorla, L. (1990). Academic environments in preschool: Do they pressure or challenge young children? *Early Education and Development, 1,* 401–23.

Hyson, M.C. (in press). Theory: An analysis. In S. Reifel (Ed.), *Advances in early education and day care: Theory into practice.* Greenwich, CT: JAI.

Jipson, J. (1991). Developmentally appropriate practice: Culture, curriculum, connections. *Early Education and Development 2,* (2), 120–36.

Jones, E., & Nimmo, J. (1994). *Emergent curriculum.* Washington, DC: National Association for the Education of Young Children.

Kessler, S.A. (1991a). Early childhood education as development: Critique of the metaphor. *Early Education and Development, 2,* 137–52.

Kessler, S.A. (1991b). Alternative perspectives on early childhood education. *Early Childhood Research Quarterly, 6,* 183–97.

Kessler, S.A. (1992). The social context of the early childhood curriculum. In S. Kessler & B.B. Swadener (Eds.), *Reconceptualizing the early childhood curriculum: Beginning the dialogue* (pp. 21–42). New York: Teachers College Press.

Kessler, S., & Swadener, B.B. (Eds.). (1994). *Reconceptualizing the early childhood curriculum: Beginning the dialogue.* New York: Teachers College Press.

Knapp, M.S., & Shields, P.M. (1990). Reconceiving academic instruction for the children of poverty. *Phi Delta Kappan, 71,* 753–58.

Knapp, M.S., Shields, P.M., & Turnbull, B.J. (1995). Academic challenge in high-poverty classrooms. *Phi Delta Kappan, 76,* 770–76.

Kostelnik, M.J. (1992). Myths associated with developmentally appropriate programs. *Young Children, 47* (4), 17–23.

Krogh, S.L. (1995). *The integrated early childhood curriculum* (2nd ed.). New York: McGraw-Hill.

Larsen, J.M., & Robinson, C. (1989). Later effects of preschool on low-risk children. *Early Childhood Research Quarterly, 4,* 133–44.

Lourenco, O., & Machado, A. (1996). In defense of Piaget's theory: A reply to 10 common criticisms. *Psychological Review, 103* (1), 143–64.

Love, J.M., Ryer, P., & Faddis, B. (1992). *Caring environments: Program quality in California's publicly funded child development programs.* Portsmouth, NH: RMC Research Corporation.

Lubeck, S. (1996). Deconstructing "child development knowledge" and teacher preparation. *Early Childhood Research Quarterly, 11,* 147–67.

Lubeck, S. (1994). The politics of developmentally appropriate practice: Exploring issue of culture, class, and curriculum. In B.L. Mallory & R.S. New (Eds.), *Diversity and developmentally appropriate practices* (pp. 17–43). New York: Teacher College Press.

Ludlow, B.L. & Berkeley, T.R. (1994). Expanding the perceptions of developmentally appropriate practice: Changing theoretical perspective. In B.L. Mallory & R.S. New (Eds.), *Diversity and developmentally appropriate practices* (pp. 107–18). New York: Teachers College Press.

Mallory, B.C. & New, R.S. (Eds.). (1994). *Diversity and developmentally appropriate practices.* New York: Teachers College Press.

Mantzicopoulos, P.Y., Neuharth-Pritchett, S., & Morelock, J. B. (1994, April). *Academic competence, social skills, and behavior among disadvantaged children in developmentally appropriate and inappropriate classrooms.* Paper presented at the annual meeting of the American Educational Research Association, New Orleans, LA.

Mantzicopoulos, P.Y., & Neuharth-Pritchett, S. (1995, April). *Classroom environments, parental involvement, and children's school achievement and adjustment: Two-year results from a Head Start early school transition demonstration program.* Paper presented at the annual meeting of the American Educational Research Association, San Francisco, CA.

Marcon, R.A. (1992). Differential effects of three preschool models on inner-city 4-year-olds. *Early Childhood Research Quarterly, 7,* 517–30.

Marcon, R.A. (1993). Socioemotional versus academic emphasis: Impact on kindergarteners development and achievement. *Early Child Development and Care, 96,* 81–91.

Marcon, R.A. (1994). Doing the right thing for children: Linking research and policy reform in the District of Columbia public schools. *Young Children, 50* (1), 8.

O'Loughlin, M. (1992, September). *Appropriate for whom? A critique of the culture and class bias underlying developmentally appropriate practice in early childhood education.* Paper presented at the Conference on Reconceptualizating Early Childhood Education: Research, Theory, and Practice, Chicago.

Patterson, C.J., Kupersmidt, J.B., & Vaden, N.A. (1990). Income level, gender, ethnicity, and household composition as predictors of children's school-based competence. *Child Development, 61,* 485–94.

Piaget, J. (1952). *The origins of intelligence in children.* New York: International Universities Press.

Piccigallo, P.R. (1988). Preschool: Head start or hard push? *Social Policy, 45–48.*

Pine, G.J, & Hilliard, A.G. (1990). Rx for racism: Imperative for America's schools. *Phi Delta Kappan, 71, 593–600.*

Powell, D.R. (1994). Parents, pluralism, and the NAEYC statement on developmentally appropriate practices. In B.C. Mallory and R.S. New (Eds)., *Diversity and developmentally appropriate practices* (pp. 166–82). New York: Teachers College Press.

Rescorla, L., Hyson, M., Hirsh-Pasek, K., & Cone, J. (1990). Academic expectations of mothers of preschool children: A psychometric study of the educational attitude scale. *Early Education and Development, 1, 165–84.*

Reutzel, D.R., & Cooter, R.B., Jr. (1996). *Teaching children to read* (2nd ed.). Englewood Cliffs, NJ: Prentice Hall.

Schweinhart, L.J., Barnes, H.V., & Weikart, D.P. (1993). The High Scope Perry preschool study through age 27. *Monographs of the High/Scope Educational Research Foundation.* Ypsilanti, MI: High/Scope.

Schweinhart, L.J., & Weikart, D.P. (1988). Education for young children living in poverty: Child-initiated learning or teacher-directed instruction? *The Elementary School Journal, 89, 213–25.*

Schweinhart, L.J., & Weikart, D.P. (in press). *The High/Scope curriculum comparison study through age 23. Early Childhood Research Quarterly.*

Schweinhart, L.J., Weikart, D.P., & Larner, M.B. (1986). Consequences of three preschool curriculum models through age 15. *Early Childhood Research Quarterly, 1, 15–45.*

Shakiba-Nejad, H., & Yellin, D. (1981). *Socioeconomic status, academic achievement, and teacher response* (Report No. 022 355). Stillwater, OK: Oklahoma State University. (ERIC Document Reproduction Service No. ED 231 754).

Stipek, D.J. (1993). Is child-centered early childhood education really better? In S. Reifel (Ed.). *Advances in early education and day care: Perspectives on developmentally appropriate practice* (Vol. 5, pp. 29–52). Greenwich, CT: JAI.

Stipek, D. (1994). *Reconceptualizing the debate on appropriate early childhood education.* Symposium presented at the annual meeting of the American Educational Research Association, New Orleans, LA.

Stipek, D., & Byler, P. (in press). *Early childhood education teachers: Do they practice what they preach? Early Childhood Research Quarterly.*

Stipek, D., Feiler, R., Daniels, D., & Milburn, S. (1995). Effects of different instructional approaches on young children's achievement and motivation. *Child Development, 66,* 209–23.

Stipek, D., Daniels, D., Galluzzo, D., & Milburn, S. (1992). Characterizing early childhood education programs for poor and middle-class children. *Early Childhood Research Quarterly, 7,* 1–19.

Stipek, D., Milburn, S., Clements, D., & Daniels, D. (1992). Parents' beliefs about appropriate education for young children. *Journal of Applied Developmental Psychology, 13,* 293–310.

Stott, F., & Bowman, B. (1996). Child development knowledge: A slippery base for practice. *Early Childhood Research Quarterly, 11,* 169–83.

Taylor, B.J. (1995). *A child goes forth: A curriculum guide for preschool children,* (8th edition). Englewood Cliffs, NJ: Merrill-Prentice Hall.

Vygotsky, L.S. (1978). *Mind in society: The development of higher psychological processes.* Eds. and Trans. M. Cole, V. John-Steiner, S. Scribner, & E. Souberman. Cambridge, MA: Harvard University Press.

Walsh, D.J. (1991). Extending the discourse on developmentally appropriateness: A developmental perspective. *Early Education and Development, 2,* 109–19.

Weikart, D.P., & Schweinhart, L.J. (1991). Disadvantaged children and curriculum effects. *New Directions For Child Development, 53,* 57–64.

Williams, L.R. (1994). Developmentally appropriate practice and cultural values: A case in point. In B.L. Mallory & R.S. New (Eds.), *Diversity and developmentally appropriate practices* (pp. 155–65). New York: Teachers College Press.

CHAPTER TWO

How Children Develop and Why It Matters

*The Foundation for the Developmentally Appropriate
Integrated Early Childhood Curriculum*

SUZANNE LOWELL KROGH

This chapter lays the foundation for those following through a description of developmentally appropriate practice (DAP), an overview of early childhood development, a description of the relationship of development to the integrated curriculum, and the relationship of DAP and the integrated curriculum. It is the intent of this book, *Integrated Curriculum in Developmentally Appropriate Classrooms*, to build on the work of the National Association for the Education of Young Children (as will be described shortly) by establishing a foundation from what is known about child development and then providing readers with an integrated approach to curriculum creation. In the chapters that follow, each curricular area is dealt with in turn. Here, we take a general view of development and its relation to curriculum integration.

By the time young children enter kindergarten or 1st grade the majority of them have accomplished most or all of the following: the ability to speak one language or more in complete sentences and with an intuitive awareness of the entire structure of its grammar; the ability to sit, stand, walk, run, hop, throw and catch a ball, ride a three-wheeled vehicle, climb structures taller than they are and jump down safely from them; negotiate their emotional/social place in the world with an array of family members and friends, many or most of whom are bigger and older than they are; and gain, at the least, an intuitive understanding of addition, subtraction, multiplication, division, and geometry. Often all of this is accomplished without the benefit of preschool or even kindergarten. As well, some young children, again often without the benefit of formal instruction, learn a second or even third language, begin to read and/or write, master the use of a two-wheeler, and can apply their mathematical understanding to formal problem solving.

Once they have accomplished all this, we welcome children to their formal education with the hope that they will, in the words of The National Education Goals for America 2000 (1991), "start school ready to learn." Yet it is apparent that children have already made inroads into even the formal school curriculum. For example, language, mathematics, social issues, and physical education have all just been described as part of the natural learning of the early years. Often when adults mentally peer down at children and judge them as "ready" (or "not ready") to learn, they are defining learning in terms of their adult view: desks placed in neat rows, children well scrubbed and facing the front of the room, everyone on the same page at the same time, the teacher unquestionably in charge. Adults who possess this "peer down" view of learning (and historically they have been in the majority) seem to dismiss much of the almost miraculous early childhood acquisition of knowledge and skills in favor of regarding the child new to school as a blank slate or empty pitcher to be filled. Then, when children attempt to alter and adapt their natural modes of learning to the more rigid adult model, but cannot perform to adult expectations, these same adults choose to fault the children rather than the system.

It is this historically prevalent view of teaching, learning, and blame placing that led the National Association for the Education of Young Children (NAEYC) to devote considerable resources, during the 1980s, to gathering support for and finally publishing a comprehensive statement of what should be the proper approaches to the teaching and learning of young children. *Developmentally Appropriate Practice in Early Childhood Programs Serving Children from Birth through Age 8* (Bredekamp, 1987) was the first major publication (recently revised,

Bredekamp & Copple, 1997). Others have followed, including a volume intended to "operationalize" or "make meaningful" the first: *Reaching Potentials: Appropriate Curriculum and Assessment for Young Children* (Bredekamp & Rosegrant, 1992) and a volume making the connection between developmentally appropriate practice and the standards developed by professional organizations in the content areas (Bredekamp & Rosegrant, 1995). These volumes present the most up-to-date knowledge on how children develop and then explain how and why this matters to early education. There is little that NAEYC recommends that looks like the traditional, adult-centered model of formal teaching and learning. Instead, there is a recognition and acceptance of the way children naturally develop and learn with a recommendation that much of their schooling be based on and inspired by this natural development. As the second volume states, there is, among many national organizations representing the subject area disciplines,

> a growing consensus that the traditional scope and sequence approach to curriculum, with its emphasis on drill and practice of isolated academic skills, does not reflect current knowledge of human learning. . . . Specifically, these national organizations call for schooling to place greater emphasis on active, hands-on learning; conceptual learning that leads to understanding, along with acquisition of basic skills; meaningful, relevant learning experiences . . . and a broad range of relevant content, integrated across traditional subject-matter divisions. (Bredekamp & Rosegrant, 1992, pp. 10–11)

Within this philosophical preference, there is still acceptance by NAEYC of a diversity of approaches to teaching and learning. As indicated in the statement just quoted, one approach that is highly favored for its comfortable affinity with today's understanding of child development is integration of the curriculum.

Developmentally Appropriate Practice: A Definition

This term, sometimes abbreviated "DAP," came to the fore with the publication of the first NAEYC volume (Bredekamp, 1987) and continues in the revision (Bredekamp & Copple, 1997). According to its authors, there are three dimensions to the concept of developmental appropriateness: age, individual growth patterns, and cultural factors.

Age appropriateness draws on the theories of those who posit universal stages of human development, particularly as applied to the first nine years of life. Not just cognitive, but physical, social, and emotional stages are considered. It is important for teachers to have knowledge of children's development in all these areas and use what they know as "a framework from which [they] prepare the learning environment and plan appropriate experiences" (p. 2).

Individual and cultural appropriateness takes into account each child's own growth patterns, personality, learning styles, family background, and culture. The challenge for teachers is to create curricula that match each child's developing abilities while also providing the right level of challenge and interest.

What Is Known about Child Development

Skillful, knowledgeable teaching cannot take place if the teacher lacks child development information. There are at least four ways in which this information can be used in planning the curriculum: (1) it provides theoretical perspectives on how and why children behave; (2) it gives normative guidelines to help teachers determine what children can do and understand; (3) it offers chronologically based data showing when children can be expected to reach various milestones of development; and (4) it provides perspectives on the development of individual children and differences between cultures (Bredekamp & Rosegrant, 1992, p. 68).

Theory and research related to child development are themselves in a never-ending state of development. Views change across both time and geography as different periods of history and different cultures, with their own definitions of reality, influence philosophies and even the outcomes of "values neutral" research. A view that has gained increasing acceptance in a number of cultures and countries during much of this century is that of constructivism.

The name most intimately tied to this theory is that of its originator, Jean Piaget, Swiss biologist, psychologist, observer of child development, epistemologist, and highly original thinker whose research findings have fueled decades of discussion and further research throughout much of the world. His contemporaries tended to view child development in one of two general ways. The first view, with its philosophical roots in the seventeenth-century writings of John Locke, was that of the child as a blank slate, waiting and receptive to whatever the environment might write on it. *Behaviorism* is an important twentieth-century evolution of this view. It ascribes primary importance to the influence of the environment on young children's learning. This includes the teacher, both as controller of the environment and as a part of the environment itself. In the 1960s, when the federal government provided substantial support to the development of early childhood programs for disadvantaged children, curriculum and instructional approaches were developed based on this view of learning. These experiments inspired models that emphasized direct instruction as the primary method of teaching.

The second view, with its philosophical roots in the eighteenth-century writings of Jean Jacques Rousseau, regarded children more as plants with biologically predetermined growth patterns and needing only a bit of skillful nurturing for successful development. *Maturationism* is the most popular twentieth-century term that describes this approach. It is demonstrated in the use of both developmental kindergartens for those children identified as "not ready" for kindergarten and of transitional kindergartens for children who are deemed not maturationally "ready" for 1st grade and in the views of those who object to pushing children too soon into the rigors of formal schooling. The work of Arnold Gesell in the first half of this century was influential in creating these views. His institute at Yale University developed norms for children's development that are still widely used in so-called readiness assessment programs.

Both behaviorism and maturationism are still accepted today by many educational leaders and practitioners. Behaviorism leads rather naturally to the traditional view of teaching as direct instruction with a carefully sequenced set of prescribed materials and goals. Maturationism leads quite naturally to a more hands-off approach to teaching, with much dependence on informality and play as appropriate teaching techniques.

Piaget did not reject either of the views in their entirety, feeling that each had something important to offer. To some extent, he argued, the environment does "write on" the child's intellectual structure. And, to some extent, play and playing around with ideas are important for gaining real understanding of materials and ideas. And, finally, there is plenty of evidence that a child's biology determines much of his or her development, both physically and intellectually. Here, however, Piaget took issue with these historical views of development. He believed that children are not passive recipients of environmental influences, nor do they lack power over their entire biology. Rather, they interact with these elements in their lives, thereby constructing their own intellects.

Today, many, even most early childhood specialists look to this more complex view of the child while still relying on some of the contributions of the earlier views. Chronological norms, for example, have been provided by the "child as plant" researchers and are useful guidelines if not consulted with slavish acceptance. The research on direct instruction that has been carried on by the "child as blank slate" adherents has contributed a vast array of successful teaching, management, and discipline techniques.

A major contribution of Piaget's constructivist approach has been the delineation of cognitive and social/moral stages of development. While research subsequent to Piaget's has pointed up occasional inaccuracies in the stages when viewed across cultures and over time, and when different research methods or materials are used, these stages still offer much guidance for curriculum development (cf. Lourenco & Machado, 1996).

Briefly, there are four stages in the child's development from birth to early adulthood. The sensorimotor period covers the first two years in which the physical senses and motor activities form the basis of the infant's cognitive development. From the beginning of the child's third year, the preoperational period takes over for the next five or six years; at this time, children become able to use one thing to symbolize another, a critical step in the progress toward abstract understandings and school learning. The third stage, the concrete operational period, lasts throughout the elementary school years. During this time, children gradually decenter their attention from themselves, learning to see things from others' points of view in both the cognitive and social sense. They learn to reason more logically and understand their learning more fully, as long as concrete objects are present in reality or in their thoughts. Finally, the formal operational stage begins to appear at about age 11 and extends through early adulthood. Its hallmark is the ability to think abstractly in a systematically logical way.

Progress through these stages begins with the development of organized patterns of behavior called *schemata*. The infant's simple reflexes become coordinated with each other; chance actions and new actions are experimented with.

To achieve movement from one stage to the next, children engage in both *accommodation* and *assimilation,* two cognitive processes that complement and coincide with each other. The former refers to the process of learning something totally new. It may be necessary to alter old understandings to make it part of the intellectual structure. Assimilation is not as rigorous as accommodation, for new information can be assimilated into the old. These two processes enable the child to achieve cognitive *equilibration* that provides a place for each new bit of knowledge the child constructs. From Piaget's perspective, this kind of learning is playful, and can even be defined as play.

One last aspect of Piagetian theory that relates directly to educational interactions with young children is that of *heteronomy* and *autonomy.* The young child is, to a great extent, heteronomous or dependent on the authority of others when making cognitive and social decisions. It is a mark of maturity to make decisions autonomously, based on a personal conviction and some self-assurance. It is important for teachers to realize that the more practice children have in making decisions of their own the more quickly they will develop their autonomous capabilities.

A somewhat different view of constructivist development was proposed by Lev Vygotsky. His ideas on child development were sufficiently threatening to the authorities in the Soviet Union that his publications were suppressed and untranslated until the mid-1950s. In addition, Vygotsky became ill and died in 1934 at age 38, thus cutting short an emerging body of research in psychology, education, and psychopathology. Despite these setbacks, Vygotsky's work has become fairly well known in recent years, providing a useful complement to Piaget's.

While Piaget's theory of development stresses what happens within the individual, Vygotsky's theory is sociocultural, emphasizing socially constructed knowledge. It is through dialogues with others, both adults and peers, that children learn. The support provided by adults or more advanced peers is referred to as *scaffolding.*

When his theory is applied to education, Vygotsky's notion of a *zone of proximal development* provides some direction for teachers of young children. This zone represents a body of knowledge, tasks, and skills that a child is just ready to reach with the help of others. Through guidance from adults and interactions with more mature peers, children move at their own pace and in their own way to higher levels of understanding. Vygotsky argued that such social interaction was more important to education than Piaget believed. He agreed with those who criticized Piaget for not taking "into account the importance of the social situation and milieu." Speaking of language development he said, "Whether the child's talk is more egocentric or more social depends not only on his age but also on the surrounding conditions" (1962, p. 23).

It is interesting to note the complementary views of Vygotsky and Piaget relative to play. For both of them, play was an activity critically important to children's learning and development. They agreed that representational (dramatic or pretend) play offered opportunities to develop the concept that one object can symbolize another. To Vygotsky, such play also gave children an opportunity to act out the rules of society, a development that could begin in the toddler years. From Piaget's perspective, the rules of society would first be learned in the elementary school years when games containing rules would become more prevalent in children's lives than simple dramatic play. In general, Vygotsky was more impressed than Piaget by the importance of social interactions. His concept of *intersubjectivity*, or shared understandings, is demonstrated in dramatic play when the necessary social give and take results in agreed upon rules of behavior or symbolic meanings.

Whatever the similarities or differences between the Piagetian and Vygotskian theories, the underlying view of both is of children actively constructing their own knowledge. Such a constructivist view of development favors a curriculum that requires much direction from the child and less from the teacher. Thus, the teacher's responsibility leans more toward setting up a suitable environment for learning and supporting children's interactions with it, and less toward taking charge in a direct or authoritarian mode. Later we shall see how this attitude toward teaching and learning leads toward a curriculum that integrates its subject matter.

First, however, let us take a look at a slightly different view of childhood. It has been formulated by a psychologist intimately familiar with constructivism and might even be termed *post-Piagetian*. This view holds that intelligence is multifaceted—that the human being actually possesses multiple intelligences. Howard Gardner (1993/ 1983), a developmental psychologist at Harvard University, proposed this theory as a way to "broaden conceptions of intelligence to include not only the results of paper-and-pencil tests but also knowledge of the human brain and sensitivity to the diversity of human cultures" (p. ix). Arguing that what Western culture sometimes defines as talents and skills should rightfully be deemed intelligences in their own right, Gardner includes the following "intelligences" in his list: linguistic, musical, logico-mathematical, spatial, bodily-kinesthetic, intrapersonal, and interpersonal. Following is a brief description of each intelligence as applied in the early years.

- *Linguistic intelligence.* The expression of early linguistic intelligence, Gardner suggests, is found in the kinds of words that children first say, the extent to which they mimic their elders, and the speed and skill with which they master the characteristics of language.
- *Musical intelligence.* Infants imitate singing and rhythmic structures just as they do spoken language. Experimental inventions continue until the preschool years, when songs from the child's culture then take precedence.
- *Logico-mathematical intelligence.* Gardner's view of this intelligence is primarily informed by the work of Piaget's stage theory. For example, the early preoperational preschooler learns to count but views it as mere rote activity; the older concrete operational child understands that numbers can be connected to counted objects, that they are numerical patterns, and that numbers represent sets.
- *Spatial intelligence.* Infants orient themselves to the size of their cribs and the distance to a hanging mobile. By the end of the sensorimotor period children can imagine an object or event without its physical presence. At the concrete operational level they can imagine how an object or scene would look from varying angles and sides
- *Bodily-kinesthetic intelligence.* The capacities to handle objects skillfully and to control one's bodily motions are at the core of this intelligence. As an example, reaching leads to grasping, which leads to passing an object to someone, which expands to grasping groups of objects, and, finally, to building structures.
- *Intrapersonal intelligence* and *interpersonal intelligence.* The first refers to the ability to understand one's self, the second to the ability to understand others. The basis of both, Gardner

believes, is the postbirth bond that develops between infant and mother.

Gardner's view of multiple intelligences is, in one sense, new in its acceptance by many in this culture, and at the same time old, being traceable to the ancient Greek appreciation of the varying facets of the mind. Certainly he demands that we think of intelligence more broadly than we ordinarily do in our culture. His view also demands of us a wider appreciation of child development as we gain greater respect for emerging capacities we have often referred to as simply skills or talents.

A Real-World Vignette

As a bridge between this discussion of child development and the integrated curriculum, let us take a side excursion into a preschool class for 3- and 4-year-olds. It is early morning and the children are straggling in accompanied by a parent or baby sitter. The teacher directs a string of informal activities (there is no requirement that anyone join in) so that children move in and out of the directed activities while spending time at outlying centers. Some of the activities engaged in during a one-hour period include the following:

- While the teacher leads the children in a song about a turtle, she helps them role play the motions of a real turtle, then leads a discussion of the day Candace brought in a turtle.
- During a song about various possible body positions, the teacher again leads role play, focusing on such terms as upside down, inside out, over, and under.
- While more music plays on a tape, the teacher welcomes new children and speaks with parents. Without her leadership, some children move to the centers while others stay and dance.
- One father stays with his son, who chooses a book on space travel. The father reads straight from the text, which is quite mature, but the boy asks questions about the sections he understands. One of the dancers "flies" over to them, leans over the father's shoulder, asks a question or two, then flies away.
- Two children leave the music area and take several stuffed animals into a house made of large cardboard boxes. Soon,

one of them begins to role play, correctly, the lives of the animals' real-life counterparts.

- Three children engage in clay art, rolling out and measuring against some agreed upon size, then rolling out again until they are content that the size is "right."
- One girl spends three or four minutes observing peacock feathers with a magnifying glass.
- A boy builds a high structure with plastic blocks, then experiments with rolling marbles from top to bottom.

Once the teacher has spoken with several parents and welcomed their children, she returns to the music area. Seeing that the children's interests have become more far-flung, she devotes herself to interacting informally with the children. The two children in the box house are asked if they remember how a fox, not represented in the stuffed animal collection, goes looking for food. The children immediately role play. The children working with clay are asked about their measuring techniques, and the introduction of two sticks, one long and one short, is suggested for more accurate measurement. This is of interest to just one girl, and others gather around to watch her as she tries it. The teacher passes by the girl with the peacock feather, giving her a quick little shoulder pat, and moves on to the boy with the block tower. She asks if he has tried rolling the marbles from various sides of the structure. He has and explains the results to her. She then returns to the music area, gets the attention of the entire group, reminds them that this is their weekly swimming morning, and asks that they clean up and prepare to go to the pool. Despite the varying activities, the mood has been rather quiet. It is still early morning and some of the children seem a bit sleepy. The cleanup is orderly, quiet, and happy, and the children are soon ready to leave for the pool.

While the activities in this classroom have great variety to them, they are still part of an overall plan. The class had spent several weeks studying the lives and habits of a number of animals; the play of the children in the box house and the turtle role play were fantasy with a strong base in scientific knowledge. Another theme of study had been that of movement and its causes; the boy rolling marbles was expanding on what he had learned. Other centers, such as clay and music, were present because of the teacher's commitment to including full representation of the curriculum during free time. Let us see how this real-life vignette takes into account what is known about child development and connects it to the integrated curriculum.

Since the children have all demonstrated cognitive and physical development that appears to be within normal range, curriculum planning can make use of the norms established by maturationist researchers and the stages posited by Piaget. Nevertheless, no collection of children can be expected to develop in all areas at the same rate; and no single child will perform in a predictable fashion on a given day or retain the same interests over a given period of time or announce in advance that a new stage of understanding is about to be reached on a given topic. Thus, this teacher has chosen to reject a behaviorist curriculum that expects group goals and schedules. She has chosen instead a combination of play and facilitated informal activities. Children are permitted to choose activities, but she asks leading questions or suggests directions that will enhance their understanding or even lead it into new territory.

During much of the school year, this teacher's curriculum is held together by a series of thematic studies. On this particular morning, the class is taking a break between themes; thus, some old, familiar materials which, in themselves, do not necessarily depend on thematic study for their existence have been brought out. In addition, materials from two previous themes—animals and moving things— have been retained and some children have chosen them. The teacher plans these nontheme days as carefully as she does the more structured ones, making sure that the entire subject matter curriculum is covered in some way, that there are activities at various cognitive and physical levels, and that there is a good balance of free choice play and opportunities for her to encourage academic growth. Soon, she knows, the children will be ready and excited to focus on a new theme.

The teacher in this preschool chooses her themes carefully to cut across the curriculum. For example, during the animal unit there were observations of real animals in their habitats (science); songs and dances about how animals live (music, movement); counting games using stuffed animals (math); stories read and chanted aloud and plenty of books for browsing (reading, language); and opportunities to create animal forms in clay (art).

This teacher also chooses her themes with an eye to developmental appropriateness. The study of animals was based on the interest that many of the children brought with them. Candace, for example, had spent several months in Australia and came back with stories about reaching inside a kangaroo's pocket and being befriended at the beach by a dolphin. Another child brought his new pet hamster to school. The enthusiasm of the class for learning more about animals presented a natural opportunity to the teacher.

Less obvious was the choice of movement as a theme. While a few of the boys had expressed interest in zooming toy cars around the room and both sexes fought over the available tricycles, there was no apparent natural interest in or understanding of movement as a focus of study. However, the teacher is aware that simple, observational physics is a subject area that is developmentally appropriate for preschool children. She observed the activities the children already enjoyed such as cars and tricycles and built the curriculum from there.

This description of a preschool classroom is, no doubt, fairly typical of a quality experience in a U.S. early education center. A somewhat more focused model has evolved in recent decades in Italy and is beginning to influence curricular practices in some American early childhood settings as well. With more than thirty preschool and infant care centers, the city of Reggio Emilia, located in north-central Italy, has become an international leader with its approach to integrating the curriculum. In Reggio Emilia schools, the curriculum is not established in advance, but "emerges in the process of each activity or project and is flexibly adjusted accordingly" (Gandini, 1993, p. 4). Both the teachers and the children contribute to this emergent curriculum, as they join together to construct knowledge. Key to this model is the *project*, which may be long- or and short-term and which provides the real focus to the curriculum. Topics for projects may emerge from children's interests and questions or they may come directly from the teachers' understanding of the children's need to know.

What about the Primary Grades?

While all but the behaviorists tend to agree that informal learning and a cross-discipline curriculum are almost universally appropriate for the preschool years, this preference often disappears when children in the primary grades, or even kindergarten, are considered. Yet if the norms of the maturationists and the stages of the constructivists are even close to correct, then this sort of learning is important for the older children as well.

One writer who studied the classrooms of several primary teachers committed to integrating their curricula noted that "integrating a curriculum around a theme allows children of different ages and stages to work together in a group as well as to practice skills at different levels" (Cushman, 1990, p. 32). Developmentally, such a preference for group work is totally applicable to the elementary years, when children move from a focus on themselves to their interactions with others, most notably their peers. The same author describes ways in which these primary teachers achieve broad curriculum coverage through integration. For example, "children practice language skills as they read about the theme and write about it; they measure and graph its component parts using math and science skills. Social studies material like history and geography is all tied in; and the whole class takes field trips together around the theme, practicing social skills along the way" (p. 32). A growing number of specialists in early education share Cushman's enthusiasm for informal learning and an integrated curriculum in the primary grades. While schools often find themselves pressured to continue the more rigid, traditional approach, research focused on developmental appropriateness indicates more and more the need to rethink this view.

Developmentally Appropriate Practice: Guidelines for *Best* Practice

Implications of the NAEYC view of developmentally appropriate practice lead to some guidelines regarding *best* practice:

- The curriculum reflects children's natural learning, which does not take place in narrowly defined subject areas, but is integrated across all areas of development: physical, emotional, social, and cognitive.
- Curriculum planning is based on teachers' observations of individual appropriateness and knowledge of age appropriateness.
- Adult-established concepts of success and completion are rejected in favor of a prepared environment that fosters active

involvement in the exploration of interactions with both materials and other people (both adults and peers).

- In developmentally appropriate practice, learning activities and materials are provided that are relevant to young children because they are concrete and real.
- Since the children in a single classroom can represent a wide range of interests and abilities, despite a possibly narrow range of ages, curriculum and practices should cover a wider range of developmental levels than those represented by the group.
- Curriculum, activities, and materials do not remain static once they have been created. Rather, teachers observe their children's progress and adjust the difficulty, complexity, and challenge of each activity as appropriate.

These guidelines do not suggest a curriculum that is prescribed, lockstep, and predetermined. They do not indicate that children control the classroom or that teachers do not teach. They do not reject the idea of goals and objectives. And they do not suggest that child development is the only justification for appropriate practice, although it is of primary importance (Bredekamp & Rosegrant, 1992; Bredekamp & Copple, 1997).

These guidelines do seek to address two basic problems: "the 'early childhood error' (inadequate attention to the content of the curriculum) and the 'elementary error' (over attention to curriculum objectives, with less attention to the individual child)" (Bredekamp & Rosegrant, 1992, p. 3). They do indicate the need to take into account each child's total growth and a broad spectrum of interests. And they do strongly suggest movement toward learning that is inherently meaningful to children, and based on their interests rather than on adult definitions of academics. Thus, moving from a traditional view of subject-specific curriculum to a more integrated approach is a natural step.

The Integrated Curriculum and Its Relationship to DAP

A major goal of the second NAEYC volume (Bredekamp & Rosegrant, 1995) is to help early childhood practitioners engage children in learning that is meaningful to them, using activities that are "mindful" rather than mindless. The idea is to enable children "to make sense of what they are learning and to connect their experiences in ways that lead to rich conceptual development" (p. 29). Too much curriculum today, it is argued, touches on topics briefly then, goes on to the next rushed and unconnected subject, always with the assumption that, if a topic has been covered, it has been learned.

While the goal for providing guidelines to developmental appropriateness is the achievement of meaningfulness, the strategy for accomplishing this state is, according to the authors, the integrated curriculum. They state that "the interrelatedness of developmental domains virtually dictates an integrated approach to programming. . . . The human brain is a pattern detector; it functions most effectively when processing meaningful information. Integrated curriculum, therefore, works because it makes maximum use of the brain's capacity for learning" (p. 37). While curriculum integration has long been held in high regard by early childhood educators, it is only in recent years that this approach has been discovered by curriculum planners to be appropriate for older children and even adults. Fogarty (1991) notes that a number of models have emerged, including

- *Nested*: Multiple skills are incorporated within one focus topic
- *Shared*: Two subject areas with overlapping concepts are team taught
- *Threaded*: Major concepts such as multiple intelligences or social skills are threaded throughout various subjects
- *Sequenced*: Topics are rearranged and sequenced to coincide with each other
- *Immersed*: The learner chooses an area of interest and incorporates curricular areas within it
- *Webbed*: A theme of interest is webbed to curriculum content and subject areas

The latter two models are most commonly found in early childhood settings. The immersed model has its counterpart in the early childhood *project approach* (Katz & Chard, 1989), in which children spend extended periods of time researching, at their developmentally appropriate level, a project of intense interest to them. The webbed model (Krogh, 1995) also focuses on areas of children's interest, usually regarded as a theme or, more loosely, a strand. In the preschool observation described earlier, the animal theme incorporated most of the traditional subject matter curriculum. A few of the activities have already been mentioned. Using them as a starting point, the teacher

FIGURE 2.1
Content Area Web for Animal Theme

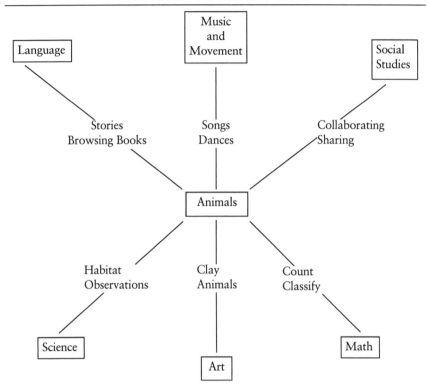

might create a web that looks like figure 2.1. It would be immediately apparent that social studies had not yet been incorporated, and this observation could be taken into account as more activities were added.

This would be a starting place for determining what subject areas will receive coverage and which might be focused on more intensively in a subsequent unit or at other times of the day. In addition, a second web might be created to determine what developmental needs are being met by the unit of study and which require more attention, either through adding other activities or finding other opportunities outside the unit. In figure 2.2 we see that a need for this particular theme is to incorporate activities that include a regard for emotional development. Possibly the addition of some social studies activities would help this come about.

FIGURE 2.2
Developmental Needs Web for Animal Theme

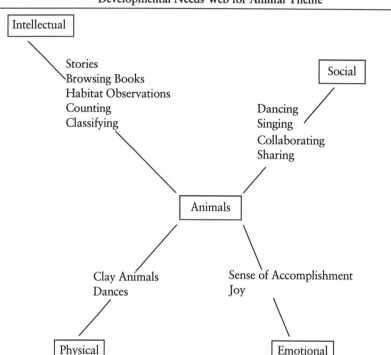

The use of both types of web provides a planning tool and a post-planning check to answer two critical questions that should be raised when planning a developmentally appropriate integrated curriculum: (1) Have all areas of the curriculum been incorporated to the extent that is important for my class at this time? (2) Does this theme unit provide for my children in all areas of their development? The visual nature of the webs answers these questions quite effectively.

It is the teacher's knowledge of development and subsequent delivery of these curriculum plans that can then answer two other critical questions: (1) Are the activities at a comfortable yet challenging level of interest for the age I am teaching? (2) Is there sufficient variety in the activities to take into account the wide array of abilities and interests of the individuals in my class?

Summary

This chapter has laid the foundation for those that follow. The guidelines for developmentally appropriate practice published by the National Association for the Education of Young Children are described and defined. An overview of development from birth through age 8 is presented. The major historical elements that led to the current focus on the developmentally appropriate integrated curriculum are described. The theoretical views of Piaget and Vygotsky have been delineated as the major elements underlying the point of view that guides this volume. Gardner's theory of multiple intelligences is included as providing an important element in curriculum planning. Finally, a real-life example is presented along with brief descriptions of the major models for integration.

Four critical questions relate to the important issues raised in this chapter and by the NAEYC guidelines. The first issue is the need to respect the entire curriculum, to bring all subject areas into the center of the classroom in a way that has meaning for young children's learning. The second issue is the need for a concern with all areas of child development. The temptation is often to focus on the cognitive, instead of considering the whole child. Age appropriateness is an important third consideration when planning the curriculum and individual appropriateness the fourth important consideration. In each case, the zone of proximal development must continually be sought and incorporated in learning activities for young children.

As you delve into the rest of this book, try to keep these four issues in mind. They are central to our discussion of the integrated curriculum in developmentally appropriate classrooms.

References

Bredekamp, S. (Ed.). (1987). *Developmentally appropriate practice in early childhood programs serving children from birth through age 8*. Washington, DC: National Association for the Education of Young Children.

Bredekamp, S., & Rosegrant, T. (Eds.) (1992). *Reaching potentials: Appropriate curriculum and assessment for young children*

(Vol. 1). Washington, DC: National Association for the Education of Young Children.

Bredekamp, S., & Copple, C. (Eds.). (1997). *Developmentally appropriate practice in early childhood programs: Revised.* Washington, DC: National Association for the Education of Young Children.

Bredekamp, S., and Rosegrant, T. (Eds.) (1995). *Reaching potentials: Appropriate curriculum and assessment for young children* (Vol. 2). Washington, DC: National Association for the Education of Young Children.

Cushman, K. (1990). The whys and hows of the multi-age primary classroom. *American Educator,* vol. 14, 28–39.

Fogarty, R. (1991). *How to integrate the curricula.* Palatine, IL: IRI/Skylight.

Gandini, L. (1993). Fundamentals of the Reggio Emilia approach to early childhood education. *Young Children, 49* (1), 4–8.

Gardner, H. (1983). *Frames of mind.* New York: Basic Books.

Katz, L., & Chard, S. (1989). *Engaging children's minds: The project approach.* Norwood, NJ: Ablex.

Krogh, S. (1995/1990). *The integrated early childhood curriculum.* New York: McGraw-Hill.

Lourenco, O., & Machado, A. (1996). In defense of Piaget's theory: A reply to 10 common criticisms. *Psychological Review, 103* (1), 143–64.

National Education Goals for America 2000, The. *From America 2000: An education strategy.* (1991, revised). Washington, DC: U.S. Department of Education.

Piaget, J., & Inhelder, B. (1969). *The psychology of the child.* New York: Basic Books.

Vygotsky, L. (1962). *Thought and language.* Cambridge, MA: MIT.

PART ONE

Integrating across Curriculum Areas

CHAPTER THREE

Mathematics in the Developmentally Appropriate Integrated Curriculum

ROSALIND CHARLESWORTH

S.L. Krogh has described the principal components and concepts of developmentally appropriate practice (DAP) (Bredekamp, 1987; Bredekamp & Copple, 1997; Bredekamp & Rosegrant, 1992), multiple intelligences, and the integrated curriculum (Krogh, 1995). The primary criteria for developmental appropriateness are *age appropriateness, individual appropriateness* and *cultural appropriateness*. DAP is defined as including an integrated curriculum based on children's natural interests, allowing for construction of concepts through exploration of concrete materials, and adjusting to the diversity in our society relative to culture, gender, learning styles, and exceptionalities. Gardner's theory of multiple intelligences (1993/ 1983) places mathematics in the area of *logico-mathematical intelligence* as initially studied by Piaget. However, in planning instruction, logico-mathematics intelligence should be integrated with the other areas of intelligence in order to reach children through their strongest areas for learning. As quoted by Krogh from Bredekamp and Rosegrant (1992, p. 37) "the interrelatedness of developmental domains virtually dictates an integrated approach to programming."

51

This chapter opens with a brief description of the current view of mathematics for young children as defined by the National Association for the Education of Young Children (NAEYC) in the DAP guidelines and by the National Council of Teachers of Mathematics (NCTM) in its position statement and standards. The next part of the chapter is a brief explanation of the theoretical foundations of mathematics education. In the following section, suggested directions for instruction as indicated by research are reported. Documentation as to what young children know about mathematics and how children learn mathematics is summarized. The reader is directed to models congruent with the research. How the classroom and curriculum can be organized for developmentally appropriate integrated mathematics instruction is explained. Examples of activities, themes, units, and projects are included. Finally, suggestions are made for integrating mathematics assessment with instruction.

The Goals and Standards for Mathematics Today

According to the NAEYC guidelines (Bredekamp, 1987; Bredekamp & Copple, 1997), mathematics begins with exploration of materials such as building blocks, sand, and water for 3-year-olds. For 4- and 5-year olds,

> Learnings about math, science, social studies, health, and other content areas are all integrated through meaningful activities such as those when children build with blocks; measure sand, water, or ingredients for cooking; observe changes in the environment; work with wood and tools; sort objects for a purpose; explore animals, plants, water, wheels, and gears; sing and listen to music from various cultures; and draw, paint and work with clay. (Bredekamp, 1987, p. 56)

For 5- through 8-year-olds, "the goal of the math program is to enable children to use math through exploration, discovery, and solving meaningful problems. Math activities are integrated with other relevant projects, such as science and social studies" (Bredekamp, 1987, p. 71). If a textbook is required the teacher's edition may be used as a guide, but instructional practices should focus on the use of manipulatives and games and student-constructed problem solutions.

The National Council of Teachers of Mathematics (NCTM) published three sets of standards for mathematics: *Curriculum and Evaluation Standards for School Mathematics* (NCTM, 1989), *Professional Standards for Teaching Mathematics* (NCTM, 1991), and *Assessment Standards for School Mathematics* (NCTM, 1995). These three volumes set forth developmentally appropriate practice for teaching K–12 mathematics. The curriculum standards emphasize five goals for students:

1. Learning to value mathematics
2. Becoming confident of one's own ability
3. Becoming a mathematical problem solver
4. Learning to communicate mathematically
5. Learning to reason mathematically

In 1991 NCTM published a position statement, *Early Childhood Mathematics Education* (NCTM, 1991), which opens as follows: "The National Council of Teachers of Mathematics believes that early childhood mathematics education, for young children aged 3–8, should be developmentally appropriate" (NCTM, 1994–95, p. 16). In line with the NAEYC guidelines NCTM advocates that mathematics knowledge is constructed through "exploration and interaction with materials and people" (ibid., p. 16). NCTM also emphasizes flexible planning that fits the children's developmental levels and interests and recognizes cultural and ethnic diversity. NCTM lists several aims for early childhood mathematics instruction:

- Acknowledge and build on children's accumulated knowledge by including children's experiences, language, and relevant real-world contexts.
- Incorporate active and interactive learning.
- Offer opportunities for children to develop and expand language acquisition while structuring, restructuring, and connecting mathematical understandings.
- Be concept and problem solving oriented. . . . Mathematics concepts should be integrated with other subject areas, making use of natural connections wherever they occur.
- Develop children's confidence in their mathematical abilities.
- Include ongoing assessment. . . . Evaluation strategies such as observations, interviews, and portfolios give evidence of children's thinking processes and their understanding of concepts.

The position statement concludes: "Developmentally appropriate early childhood mathematics instruction should meet the needs of individual learners at different stages of readiness by considering the influences of cultural backgrounds, prior experiences, learning styles, and cognitive abilities" (ibid., p. 17).

More recently NCTM published a position statement on interdisciplinary learning for pre-K–4 (1995). The statement was prepared by a task force that included members from six major professional associations in addition to NCTM: the International Reading Association, National Council for the Social Studies, National Council of Teachers of English, National Science Teachers Association, and the Speech Communication Association. This statement promotes the view that the curriculum should build on children's natural curiosity and problem-solving capabilities and that it should be interdisciplinary. Finally, the NCTM 1995 Yearbook describes how mathematics can be connected across the curriculum (House, 1995). The mathematics standards have been directly connected to developmentally appropriate practice by Richardson and Salkeld (1995).

The Theoretical Foundations of Mathematics Instruction

The theoretical foundations of mathematics instruction lie in the *constructivist approach* inspired initially by the work of Jean Piaget (Cobb, 1994; Davis, Maher, & Noddings, 1990; Kamii, 1982; Simon, 1995a, 1995b; Steffe & D'Ambrosio, 1995). From the Piagetian view mathematics is lodged in the area referred to as logicol-mathematical knowledge. This area of knowledge includes relationships and constructs (i.e., same and different, more and less, number, classification, etc.) that are needed to make sense out of the world and to organize the variety of information that is met during everyday activities. Logico-mathematical knowledge is closely tied to the physical knowledge area. Physical knowledge is the type of knowledge that focuses on objects in the environment and their characteristics (i.e., color, weight, size, texture, and other features that can be learned and identified through observation and are physically intrinsic to the object). The Piagetian constructivist view places the major focus on the child, and the child's inner maturation and spontaneous discoveries. The emphasis is on children as intellectual explorers, making their own discoveries and constructing knowledge independently (Charlesworth & Lind, 1995a).

More recently, the work of Lev Vygotsky has become influential as an underpinning to mathematics learning and teaching (Cobb, 1994). Vygotsky recognized the importance of developmental factors but in addition emphasized the importance of environmental factors. He believed that people developed mental tools just as they developed physical tools such as knives, spears, vehicles, and the like. The mental tools are used to aid in mastery of the individual's behavior. He viewed speech as the most important tool because it enables the child to interact socially and also facilitates the child's thinking. For Vygotsky writing and numbering were also critical mental tools. According to Vygotsky good teaching is presenting material that is a little ahead of development. Children might not fully understand at first but they will understand with appropriate scaffolding provided by more mature learners. This region for possible instruction and learning is the zone of proximal development (ZPD). The foundation for instruction is laid by the concepts constructed independently and spontaneously by children. The teacher's responsibility is to identify each student's ZPD and provide developmentally appropriate instruction. The teacher can assess if the right zone has been identified by the response of the students. They will respond with enthusiasm, curiosity, and active involvement if the instruction is lodged in their current ZPD. Vygotskians are especially concerned with children reaching their full potential (Charlesworth & Lind, 1995a).

There has been some argument among mathematics educators as to whether the Piagetian constructivist view of the individual in control of constructing knowledge or the Vygotskian sociocultural approach with the more mature learner supporting the construction of knowledge is the best guide for shaping mathematics instruction (Cobb, 1994; Davis, Maher, & Noddings, 1990). Cobb (1994) makes a case for the complementary nature of the two views, suggesting that "each of the two perspectives, the sociocultural and the constructivist, tells half of a good story, and each can be used to complement the other" (p. 17). By combining both approaches mathematics educators can take into account the students' learning through meaningful tasks (constructivist theory) in schools that account for student diversity (sociocultural theory). "Teachers . . . have to act with wisdom and judgment by continually developing ways to cope with dilemmas in particular situations. . . . we [researchers] [should] give up the quest for an acontextual, one-size-fits-all perspective" (Cobb, 1994, p. 19).

Research: Mathematics Concept Development, Knowledge, Strategies and Effective Instructional Practices

Mathematics education research includes a growing body of studies that focus on young children: what they know about mathematics and how they learn to think mathematically in meaningful ways. This section includes a review of some of that research, describes how mathematics concept development and acquisition and instruction can be described in everyday settings, and suggests some formats that can be used to guide the development of a developmentally appropriate integrated mathematics curriculum.

An Overview of Mathematics Education Research

Hiebert and Carpenter (1992) reviewed theory and research on learning and teaching for understanding. First they discussed learning with understanding. "One of the most widely held and accepted ideas within the mathematics community is the idea that students should understand mathematics" (p. 65). Hiebert and Carpenter pointed out that research and implementation efforts in mathematics have attempted to learn about and promote mathematical understanding. However, it has been difficult to design school environments that successfully achieve the goal of promoting student understanding. They define understanding as the situation where a mathematical idea or procedure is part of an internal mental network. The number and the strength of connections determine the degree of understanding. Understanding is not present to any great degree when mathematics is learned as isolated skills and procedures. Understanding grows as networks grow through increases in connections through reorganizing of previously developed connections.

Classroom activities that build connections are characterized by using a variety of materials and situations and by the presence of a great deal of social interaction. A variety of materials and settings provides for generalization. Social interaction gets the students' attention and focuses it on shared mathematics experiences. The association of language and concrete materials in a social setting with exchange of ideas between students and teacher focuses attention on many relevant ideas and factors and makes it more likely that students will construct the relationships that teachers intend for them to construct. Associations with written symbols can be developed in the same kind of context (Hiebert & Carpenter, 1992).

When a new topic is first met by students they should have the opportunity to construct their own relationships and share them with their peers and their teacher. This approach is in contrast to the drill-and-practice approach used to store discrete bits of information. Understanding helps students remember. Memory is not just passive storage of discrete bits of information but is a construction and reconstruction process. New knowledge that is connected to old knowledge is remembered better than knowledge learned in discrete, isolated pieces. Understanding reduces the amount of information that must be remembered and enhances transfer to other situations and problems. Beliefs about mathematics are also influenced by understandings: "Many students believe that mathematics is mainly a matter of following rules, that it consists of mainly symbols on paper, and that the symbols and rules are disconnected from other things they know about mathematics" (Hiebert & Carpenter, 1992, p. 77). This is in contrast to the possibility that if students could make a network of mathematical connections they might view mathematics as a cohesive body of knowledge (Hiebert & Carpenter, 1992).

A long-standing argument in mathematics education focuses on the debate over conceptual knowledge versus procedural knowledge: Is it more important to understand mathematics or to have precise mathematical skills? Hiebert and Carpenter (1992) define conceptual knowledge as knowledge that is understood through strongly connected networks with rich relationships. They define procedural knowledge as a series of actions that are only connected to each other in a sequence. Both kinds of knowledge are necessary in order to have mathematical expertise. There are data that support developing meaning (understanding) before efficiency (using the most competent procedures). The problem that develops when efficient procedures are stressed is that they are practiced until perfect. They become fixed and prevent an individual from stepping back and reflecting on the problem situation in an alternative way (Hiebert & Carpenter, 1992).

Some mathematics education researchers have focused on mathematics learned outside of school, in the home and community, compared with mathematics learned in school. There is some evidence that mathematics learned in school may enhance what has been learned outside of school, but it is not clear why some students make the connection and some do not. It seems that prior knowledge should influence what students learn and how they perform. Another important factor is development. Younger children connect information in ways that differ from those of older children (Hiebert & Carpenter, 1992).

After discussing learning for understanding, Hiebert and Carpenter (1992) address the issue of teaching mathematics for understanding. They examine how instruction should be designed to help students build connections. They describe the two major frameworks for instruction that have developed in mathematics: the bottom-up and the top-down approaches. The bottom-up approach focuses on making connections with prior knowledge. The top-down approach focuses on how to get students from the novice to the expert level. Examples are included in table 3.1. The current curriculum reform movement (NCTM, 1989) focuses on the bottom-up strategy, using problems in familiar contexts. "The implication is that learning situations should be embedded in authentic problem situations that have meaning for the students" (Hiebert & Carpenter, 1992, p. 81). There is a danger in the top-down method that connections with what the students already know will be missed. In the bottom-up instructional procedure students invent their own computational systems before being shown the most efficient method. This way they draw on what they already know and make connections that can then provide an understanding of what underlies the application of an algorithm to the problem. To sum up, problems are explored before explicit instruction is given so that students connect old knowledge to new knowledge. Hiebert and Carpenter (1992) point out that assessment of bottom-up instruction requires more concrete authentic assessment methods than are used with conventional top-down instruction.

A review of research on the organization of the mathematics classroom by Nickson (1992) shows that student roles vary depending on the teacher's beliefs. Mathematics taught in a formal linear fashion following the textbook promotes a passive attitude on the part of students and causes them to accept mathematics as an abstract subject that has little, if any, connection to other subjects or to real life. Students view mathematics as a subject with right or wrong answers and concentrate on being correct. In classrooms where instruction is based

TABLE 3.1
Examples of Top-Down and Bottom-Up Approaches to Instruction

Concept: The number 12 can be divided into a variety of subsets.
Top-Down: Today we are going to learn which numbers divide equally into 12. Here is a sheet with the 12's listed. Study each one and write it five times. Tomorrow I will give you a quiz.
Bottom-Up: Teacher reads the story *The Doorbell Rang* by P. Hutchins (1986, Greenwillow, NY). Each time more visitors come, she asks the children to predict how many cookies there will be for each child. During the work period each child counts out twelve counters, representing twelve cookies. The teacher tells them to figure out how many cookies each person would get if there were one, two, three, four, six, or twelve people who had to share. Teacher reviews with them the ways they can show their solutions (with counters, with drawings, or with writing). What if there were five, seven, eight, nine, ten, or eleven? The children report on what they find out.

on a belief in the social construction of knowledge, students feel free to try out different solutions and challenge each other and the teacher. Their role in learning is an active one.

This brief overview demonstrates that the current movement toward teaching for understanding and bottom-up instruction fits the developmentally appropriate paradigm. In the following sections research directed at young children's learning and instructional methods that work with young children is addressed.

Development of Mathematical Knowledge and Strategies: What Young Children Know and Can Learn

If we want children to understand mathematics we need to find out what they know and what, developmentally, they are capable of knowing. Table 3.2 outlines the development of mathematics concepts and skills during early childhood. These concepts and skills emerge gradually and continue to be refined throughout early childhood and beyond. Infants are busy observing the world around them and assimilating information. They are multisensory in their explorations as they look, listen, taste, and touch (Charlesworth, 1996; Charlesworth & Lind, 1995a). As they grow and develop into toddlerhood their ability to move about increases their interests and methods of

TABLE 3.2
Emergence of Mathematical Concepts and Skills During Piaget's Periods

Sensorimotor Birth–2	Preoperational 2–6 or 7	Concrete Operations 6 or 7–11 years
Observation	Classification	Abstract whole
Problem solving	Comparing	number operations
	Counting	Fractions
One-to-one	Parts and	Number facts
correspondence	wholes	Place value
Number	Math language	Geometry
Shape	Ordering	Measurement with
Spatial	Informal measurement	standard units
sense	Graphing	Statistics
	Number symbols	
	Sets and symbols	
	Concrete whole number	
	operations	

approaching problems. In their natural play they begin to gain concepts of one-to-one correspondence, number, shape, and size. By the time children move from the sensorimotor into the preoperational period they have constructed a cache of informal mathematical knowledge (Charlesworth, 1996; Charlesworth & Lind, 1995a).

Ginsburg and Baron (1993) reviewed research relative to young children's construction of mathematics. Preschool children have a natural curiosity regarding mathematical events. They spontaneously construct knowledge about concepts such as more and less and develop basic ideas about addition and subtraction. Through informal experiences they build up a storehouse of mathematical knowledge. When they enter school and meet formal mathematics they find it is difficult, and many are not very successful.

According to Ginsburg and Baron (1993) research has shown that children as young as 2 or 3 years old can understand simple addition and subtraction using concrete objects. By age 4 children can usually add the amounts in two small sets of concrete objects by "counting all." That is, if given a set of three and a set of two they will count all the object ("one, two, . . . five"). Eventually they realize that they can "count on." That is, they can take the group of three and count on— "four, five." This is a legitimate means of adding but is not acceptable in a conventional classroom. Eventually many young children develop the ability to do these simple calculations mentally. This same developmental sequence has been found to cut "across boundaries of culture, race and class" (p. 8).

Instructional Research: How Children Learn Mathematics

Ginsburg and Baron (1993) believe that the research supports that young children, even preschoolers, are ready to learn mathematics through informal experiences but not in the formal, written, rote manner that is traditional in most classrooms. In numerous cultures that have been studied young children have been observed to learn mathematics through handling and counting objects found in their natural environment.

Ginsburg and Baron (1993) suggest that formal mathematics instruction should build on children's informal knowledge. They propose that the most "useful approach should involve stimulating young children's spontaneous mathematical interests and activities in the natural environment and helping them enrich and supplement their informal mathematics" (p. 9). For example, they suggest that teachers of 4- through 7-year-olds could frequently have their students record information on graphs such as the number of buttons on their clothing each day. After data are collected for a week the teacher and students can examine the graphs, analyze and compile the information, and discuss their findings. This type of activity provides opportunities to apply counting skills, concepts of more and less, and classification concepts.

When it is time to introduce formal mathematics teachers should build on children's informal knowledge. Ginsburg and Baron (1993) provide an example using the learning of the meaning of the equals sign (=) to show how children reconstruct what teachers try to teach. In this case the teacher tried to teach an abstract verbal rule to the effect that "=" indicates that there is the same amount on the left and on the right. Contrary to what the teacher was trying to teach, the 1st graders viewed the "=" sign as an action symbol meaning time to add or the answer comes next rather than as indicating the equality of two sides of an equation. Rather than rejecting these responses the teacher should accept them as normal constructions but also demonstrate that there are other placements for "=" such as $3 + 2 = 5$, $5 = 2 + 3$, and $5 = 5$ that all indicate equality. Ginsburg and Baron (1993) suggest making a bridge to the formal definition using a balance beam. Through this experience children can see equivalence in a concrete setting and the teacher can assess whether students are ready to understand what "=" means.

Jensen (1993) identified the following themes that sum up what research on early childhood recommends for classroom instruction (p. xv):

- Build on children's strengths and informal strategies; treat them as able, valuable members in a community of learning.
- Use a "good" question or problem to motivate interest in a particular topic or to introduce new concepts.
- Focus on language and communication of ideas in early childhood math classes, both in spoken and written formats.
- Encourage connections among the various content areas; much that is important in mathematics involves bridges among related knowledge fields.
- Use alternate assessment strategies for a truer picture of children's actual mathematical ability.
- Change classroom dynamics through cooperative groupings, classes of heterogeneous ability levels, and new technologies.

Mathematics Concept Acquisition and Instruction: Application of the Research

Charlesworth and Lind (1995a, unit 2) describe three ways that children acquire mathematics concepts: through naturalistic, informal, and structured experiences. These can be described as follows:

Naturalistic	Children interact with the environment, constructing knowledge as they explore the objects and people available to them
Informal	Children engage in naturalistic activities during which an adult may offer a suggestion, ask a question, or make a comment
Structured	Children are involved in preplanned activities that the teacher structures

As we move from naturalistic, to informal, to structured activities we move from the child totally in control of learning, to the child selecting the activity with some adult intervention, to the adult providing some preplanned materials and/or guiding the children through a preplanned sequence of experiences. Provided with all three types of experiences children encounter a variety of instruction from free exploration to teacher-structured activities.

The focus of instruction in mathematics today is problem solving (Charlesworth & Lind, 1995a, chapter 3). Problems are no longer defined as the patterned, decontextualized type conventionally found in traditional mathematics textbooks but as authentic problems that are relevant to real life. Skinner (1990, p. 1) offers the following definition of a problem:

> A problem is a question that engages someone in searching for a solution.

Problem solving begins with naturalistic and informal problems such as:

- How many children are in our class today? How many boys? How many girls? How many people?
- Be sure that you take enough crackers so that everyone at your table gets four.
- Do you want a big helping of mashed potatoes or a small helping?
- Be sure your block building is no more than six blocks high.
- Do more children like chocolate or strawberry ice cream?
- If there are six children at your table and three glasses, how many more do you need? How do you know?

Skinner (1990) presents contrived problems to her 5-year-old students to get them started. Once children learn to meet the challenge of problem solving, they construct their own dictated problems. By age 7 Skinner's students were writing their own problems. Students can build their communication abilities by sharing and discussing solutions. They can work independently or in groups. The teacher serves as a facilitator and a guide.

Frameworks That Can Be Used as Guides for Developmentally Appropriate Integrated Instruction

A number of instructional frameworks have been developed that can be used to guide the development of an integrated, developmentally appropriate curriculum (i.e., Bodrova & Leong, 1996; Charlesworth & Lind, 1995a and b; DeVries & Kohlberg, 1987/1990; Gardner, 1991; Katz & Chard, 1989; Krogh, 1995; Moll 1990; Raines, 1995; Raines & Canady, 1990; Wasserman, 1990). Charlesworth and Lind (1995) focus specifically on mathematics and science. DeVries and Kohlberg (1987/1990) present the overall constructivist approach to instruction while Moll's volume (1990) presents a number of authors' descriptions of applications of Vygotsky's theory to education. Bodrova & Leong (1996) provide an overview of the Vygotskian approach to Early Childhood Education. Gardner (1991) relates his theory of multiple intelligences to the school setting. Katz and Chard (1989) describe how to adopt the project approach that builds on students' interests. Krogh (1995) presents each of the major content areas as a focus for integrated instruction. Raines (1995) and Raines and Canady (1990) use whole language as the focus for integrating all the content areas. Wasserman (1990) describes a program for building an integrated curriculum using primary children's natural inclination to explore materials and ideas.

Integrating through Themes, Units, and Projects

In chapter 2 of this volume Krogh described two models for integration that are most frequently found in early childhood settings: the *immersed model* and the *webbed model*. The immersed model is one where one or more learners select a project for study and integrate a variety of curricular areas as the project area is studied. With the webbed model an area of interest is mapped out in a weblike pattern to form an interconnected theme that incorporates multiple areas of the curriculum. Both types of curricular organization are being used increasingly in mathematics instruction. Both of these approaches afford opportunities to meet the mathematics standards through developmentally appropriate instruction.

Integrated Classroom Instruction

Integrated classroom instruction naturally follows from the standards that focus on communications, connections, and reasoning.

Curriculum that meets these standards can be implemented through thematic units that integrate mathematics with science, social studies, language arts, art, music, and movement (Charlesworth & Lind, 1995a). Integration can be accomplished by focusing on a theme or topic (i.e., ecology, classification, number sense, spatial sense, time, measurement, or a piece of literature), deciding on the important concepts associated with the topic, or developing a plan through brainstorming a web. The thematic web, like a spider web, includes a central focus point from which ideas grow in several directions like the spokes of a wheel. The spokes could be the major curriculum areas (Krogh, 1995) with various activities for each area growing out of the spokes. The areas in the mathematics standards (NCTM, 1989) could also serve as spokes (Piazza, Scott, & Carver, 1994; Workman & Anziano, 1993). Concepts within the theme may also be used as spokes. Figure 3.1 depicts an example of a web that was designed for a child–adult workshop that focused on an overview of integrated preprimary mathematics. Each of the spokes depicts examples of mathematics activities as they could relate to each of the major content areas. Note that some activities appear on more than one spoke. In tables 3.3 and 3.4 some of the resources available for guiding integration are listed.

Integrating Assessment and Instruction

Assessment in the developmentally appropriate mathematics program should be done using methods that meet the NCTM and NAEYC assessment standards, including the most recent (NCTM, 1995). Children should be assessed relative to what they know and how they think using methods that are integral to teaching. Referring to the assessment of young children,

> methods should consider the characteristics of the students themselves. . . . At this stage, when children's understanding is often closely tied to the use of physical materials assessment tasks that allow them to use such materials are better indicators of learning. (NCTM, 1989, p. 202)

Assessment data should be collected through observations and interviews as children engage in mathematics problem solving and

FIGURE 3.1
Mathematics Focused Web

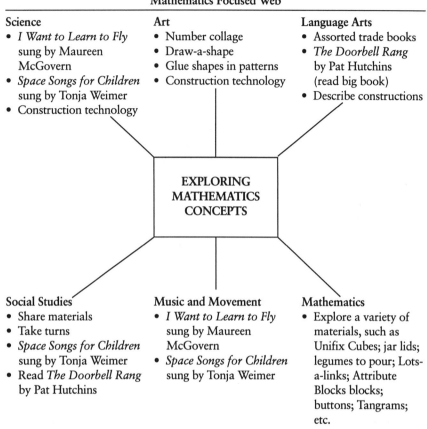

Science
- *I Want to Learn to Fly* sung by Maureen McGovern
- *Space Songs for Children* sung by Tonja Weimer
- Construction technology

Art
- Number collage
- Draw-a-shape
- Glue shapes in patterns
- Construction technology

Language Arts
- Assorted trade books
- *The Doorbell Rang* by Pat Hutchins (read big book)
- Describe constructions

EXPLORING MATHEMATICS CONCEPTS

Social Studies
- Share materials
- Take turns
- *Space Songs for Children* sung by Tonja Weimer
- Read *The Doorbell Rang* by Pat Hutchins

Music and Movement
- *I Want to Learn to Fly* sung by Maureen McGovern
- *Space Songs for Children* sung by Tonja Weimer

Mathematics
- Explore a variety of materials, such as Unifix Cubes; jar lids; legumes to pour; Lots-a-links; Attribute Blocks blocks; buttons; Tangrams; etc.

investigations, not through timed arithmetic fact tests (Bellin, 1990). Observations and interviews should be recorded as anecdotal records or on checklists describing expected performance in the areas listed in table 3.2. Teacher and children should collaborate on putting together portfolios of children's work to show progress during the year. Work may be documented with drawings, paintings, problems developed, photos or sketches of constructions (made from blocks and other manipulatives), graphs, and the like (Charlesworth & Lind, 1995a, unit 4; Piazza, Scott, & Carver, 1994; Sgroi et al., 1995; Webb, 1993).

TABLE 3.3
Selected Resources for the Integrated Developmentally
Appropriate Mathematics Curriculum

There are a multitude of topics and themes that can be the focus for the integrated mathematics curriculum.

General Resources

Edwards (1990)	Units formed around topics as diverse as dragons and the zoo.
Baker & Baker (1991)	Environmental mathematics
Katz & Chard (1989)	Projects growing out of student interests
Raines & Canaday (1990)	Integrated into a whole-language program for kindergarten
Charlesworth & Lind (1995b)	Integrated in a primary whole-language program
Burk, Snider & Symonds (1988a, 1988b)	provides activities for seasonal themes directed at the kindergarten and primary levels
Robins (1994)	Cooking as a focus for integrating themes
Stone & Russell (1990)	Mathematics activities that focus on a family theme
Jones & Nimmo (1994)	Emerging themes in a child care center
Harcourt (1988)	A Series of thematic units

Literature-Focused Resources

Thiessen & Matthias (1992)	Provides an extensive annotated bibliography of children's books with mathematics concepts
Whitin & Wilde (1992)	Describes how books can enrich learning of mathematics concepts and skills
Burns (1992)	In-depth focus on mathematics emerging from children's literature
Welchman-Tischler (1992)	In-depth focus activities that emerge from selected pieces of children's literature

TABLE 3.4
A Selected List of Support Resources from Periodicals

Charlesworth, R. (1988). Integrating math with science and social studies. *Day Care and Early Education, 15* (4), 28–31. (preschool/kindergarten)

Conaway, B., & Midkiff, R.B. (1994). Connecting literature, language, and fractions. *Arithmetic Teacher, 41* (8), 430–33. (pre-K–primary)

Gable, W. (1995). Try an integrated unit on symmetry. *Teaching K–8, 25* (4), 46–47. (1st grade)

Greenberg, P. (1993). How and why to teach all aspects of preschool and kindergarten math naturally, democratically, and effectively (for teachers who don't believe in academic programs, who do believe in educational excellence, and who find math boring to the max)—Part 1. *Young Children, 48* (4), 75–84. (pre-K–K)

Greenberg, P. (1994). How and why to teach all aspects of preschool and kindergarten math naturally, democratically, and effectively (for teachers who don't believe in academic programs, who do believe in educational excellence, and who find math boring to the max)—Part 2. *Young Children, 49* (2), 12–18, 88. (pre-K–K)

TABLE 3.4 (*continued*)
A Selected List of Support Resources from Periodicals

Jaberg, P. (1995). Assessment and Geraldine's blanket. *Teaching Children Mathematics, 1* (8), 514–17. (1st grade)

Karp, K. (1994). Telling tales: Creating graphs using multicultural literature. *Teaching Children Mathematics, 1* (2), 87–91. (primary)

Lamphere, P. (1994). Investigations: All about our class. *Teaching Children Mathematics, 1* (1), 28–34. (pre-K–6)

Mason, M., & Lloyd, A.K. (1995). Ramona and the fruit flies: An interdisciplinary approach. *Teaching Children Mathematics, 1* (6), 388–92. (3rd grade)

McMath, J., & King, M.A. (1994). Using picture books to teach mathematical concepts. *Day Care and Early Education, 21* (3), 18–22. (pre-K–K)

Mills, H. (1993). Teaching math concepts in a K–1 class doesn't have to be like pulling teeth—But maybe it should be! *Young Children, 48* (2), 17–24.

Perlmutter, J.C., Bloom, L., & Burrell, L. (1993). Whole math through investigations. *Childhood Education, 70* (1), 20–24.

Piazza, J.A., Scott, M.M., & Carver, E.C. (1994). Thematic webbing and the curriculum standards in the primary grades. *Arithmetic Teacher, 41* (6), 294–98. (primary)

Schneider, S. (1995). Links to literature: Scrumptious activities in the stew. *Teaching Children Mathematics, 1*, 549–52. (multi-age primary)

Smith, J. (1995). A different angle for integrating mathematics. *Teaching Children Mathematics, 1* (5), 288–93. (3rd grade)

Smith, J. (1995). Threading mathematics into social studies. *Teaching Children Mathematics, 1* (7), 438–44. (3rd grade)

Van Scoy, I.J., & Fairchild, S. H. (1993). It's about time! Helping preschool and primary children children understand time concepts. *Young Children, 48* (2), 21–24.

Ward, C.D. (1995). Meaningful mathematics with young children. *Dimensions of Early Childhood, 23* (2), 7–11.

Whitin, D.J. (1994). Literature and mathematics in preschool and primary: The right connection. *Young Children, 49* (2), 4–11.

Whitin, D.J., Mills, H., & O'Keefe, T. (1994). Exploring subject areas with a counting book. *Teaching Children Mathematics, 1* (3), 170–74. (1st grade)

Workman, S., & Anziano, M.C. (1993). Curriculum webs: Weaving connections from children to teachers. *Young Children, 48* (2), 4–9. (pre-K–primary)

Young, C., & Maulding, W. (1994). Mathematics and Mother Goose. *Teaching Children Mathematics, 1* (1), 36–38. (pre-K–3)

Summary/Conclusions

The current view of mathematics instructional practices is congruent with the concepts underlying the developmentally appropriate integrated curriculum. Both the NAEYC and NCTM goals and standards promote an integrated curriculum and practices that emphasize exploration, the process of mathematics rather than the one-correct-answer end product, and the inclusion of concepts and skills that are both individually and age appropriate. Both use a constructivist theoretical view as support for practice, aligned with both Piaget and Vygotsky. A growing body of research in early childhood mathematics supports the standards and teaching for understanding using a bottom-up approach. With the advent of modern technology being able to apply traditional algorithms to paper-and-pencil computation is no longer necessary. Children can be encouraged to construct their own problem-solving methods (Burns, 1994). A constructivist approach to mathematics instruction leaves space for integrating mathematics into the other content areas and providing a curriculum that builds on students' cultural backgrounds and interests (Tate, 1994).

A wealth of resources and materials is available to provide ideas for instituting a developmentally appropriate integrated mathematics program. The major problem is providing teachers with the knowledge and the vehicles for change. In order to join the reform movement teachers must have beliefs about how children learn that are congruent with a constructivist view of teaching. Teachers who learned mathematics in the traditional memorization and drill-and-practice paradigm have difficulty revising their belief structures (i.e., Battista, 1994; Merseth, 1993; Schifter & Fosnot, 1993). While some change will come about through the current intensive teacher inservice education programs, much of the change will have to emanate from the new teachers who experience teacher education programs where the faculty model the type of instructional practices they expect their students to use in the future and where they have the opportunity to use constructivist, developmentally appropriate, integrated approaches to mathematics instruction.

References

Baker, A., & Baker, J. (1991). *Counting on a small planet*. Portsmouth, NH: Heinemann.

Battista, M.T. (1994). Teacher beliefs and the reform movement in mathematics education. *Phi Delta Kappan, 75*, 462–70.

Bellin, S.V. (1990). What good are timed arithmetic fact tests? *Principal*, 63–63.

Bodrova, E., & Leong, D.J. (1996). *Tools of the mind*. Englewood Cliffs, NJ: Merrill/Prentice-Hall.

Bredekamp, S. (Ed.). (1987). *Developmentally appropriate practice in early childhood programs serving children from birth to age 8*. Washington, DC: National Association for the Education of Young Children.

Bredekamp, S., & Copple, C. (Eds.). (1997). *Developmentally appropriate practice in early childhood programs, Revised*. Washington, DC: National Association for the Education of Young Children.

Bredekamp, S., & Rosegrant, T. (Eds.). (1992). *Reaching potentials: Appropriate curriculum and assessment for young children*. Washington, DC: National Association for the Education of Young Children.

Burk, D., Snider, A., & Symonds, P. (1988a). *Box it or bag it mathematics: Kindergarten teachers resource guide*. Portland, OR: The Math Learning Center.

Burk, D., Snider, A., & Symonds, P. (1988b). *Box it or bag it mathematics: First–second grade teachers resource guide*. Portland, OR: The Math Learning Center.

Burns, M. (1992). *Math and literature (K–3)*. Sausolito, CA: Math Solutions Publications. (Distributed by Cuisinaire Company of America, White Plains, NY)

Burns, M. (1994). Arithmetic: The last holdout. *Phi Delta Kappan, 75*, 471–76.

Charlesworth, R. (1996). *Understanding child development* (4th ed.). Albany, NY: Delmar.

Charlesworth, R., & Lind, K.K. (1995a). *Math and science for young children* (2nd ed.). Albany, NY: Delmar.

Charlesworth, R., & Lind, K.K. (1995b). Whole language and the mathematics and science standards. In S. Raines (Ed.), *Whole language across the curriculum: Grades 1, 2, and 3* (pp. 156–78). New York Teachers College Press.

Cobb, P. (1994). Where is the mind? Constructivist and sociocultural perspectives on mathematical development. *Educational Researcher, 23* (7), 13–20.

Davis, R.B., Maher, C.A., & Noddings, N. (Eds.). (1990). Constructivist views on the teaching and learning of mathematics. *Journal for Research in Mathematics Education Monograph, 4*.

DeVries, R., & Kohlberg, L. (1987/1990). *Constructivist early education: Overview and comparison with other programs.* Washington, DC: National Association for the Education of Young Children.

Edwards, D. (1990). *Maths in context: A thematic approach.* Portsmouth, NH: Heinemann.

Gardner, H. (1991). *The unschooled mind.* New York: Basic Books.

Gardner, H. (1993/1983). *Frames of mind.* New York: Basic Books.

Ginsburg, H.P., Baron, J. (1993). Cognition: Young children's construction of mathematics. In R.J. Jensen (Ed.), *Research ideas for the classroom: Early childhood mathematics* (pp. 3-21). Reston, VA: National Council of Teachers of Mathematics.

Harcourt, L. (1988). *Explorations for early childhood.* Menlo Park, CA: Addison-Wesley.

Hiebert, J., Carpenter, T.P. (1992). Learning and teaching with understanding. In D.A. Grouws (Ed.), *Handbook of research on mathematics teaching and learning* (pp. 65-97). New York: Macmillan.

House, P.A. (Ed.). (1995). *1995 Yearbook: Connecting mathematics across the curriculum.* Reston, VA: National Council of Teachers of Mathematics.

Jensen, R.J. (Ed.). (1993). *Research ideas for the classroom: Early childhood mathematics.* Reston, VA: National Council of Teachers of Mathematics.

Jones, E., & Nimmo, J. (1994). *Emergent curriculum.* Washington, DC: National Association for the Education of Young Children.

Kamii, C. (1982). *Number in preschool and kindergarten.* Washington, DC: National Association for the Education of Young Children.

Katz, L.G., & Chard, S.C. (1989). *Engaging children's minds: The project approach.* Norwood, NJ: Ablex.

Krogh, S.L. (1995). *The integrated early childhood curriculum* (2nd ed.). New York: McGraw-Hill.

Merseth, K.K. (1993), How old is the shepherd? An essay about mathematics education. *Phi Delta Kappan, 74,* 548–58.

Moll, L.C. (Ed.). (1990). *Vygotsky and education.* Cambridge: Cambridge University Press.

NCTM (National Council of Teachers of Mathematics). (1989). *Curriculum and evaluation standards for school mathematics.* Reston, VA: Author.

NCTM (National Council of Teachers of Mathematics). (1991). *Professional standards for teaching mathematics.* Reston, VA: Author.

NCTM (National Council of Teachers of Mathematics). (1994–95). *1994–95 Handbook: NCTM goals, leaders, and positions.* Reston, VA: Author.

NCTM (National Council of Teachers of Mathematics). (1995). *Assessment standards for school mathematics.* Reston, VA: Author.

Nickson, M. (1992). The culture of the mathematics classroom: An unknown quantity? In D.A. Grouws (Ed.), *Handbook of research on mathematics teaching and learning* (pp. 101–14). New York: Macmillan.

Piazza, J.A., Scott, M.M., & Carver, E.C. (1994). Thematic webbing and the curriculum standards in the primary grades. *Arithmetic Teacher, 41* (6), 294–98.

Position statement on interdisciplinary learning: Pre-K–4. (1995). *Teaching Children Mathematics, 1* (6), 386–87.

Raines, S.C. (Ed.). (1995). *Whole language across the curriculum: Grades 1, 2, and 3.* New York: Teachers College Press.

Raines, S.C., & Canady, R.J. (1990). *The whole language kindergarten.* New York: Teachers College Press.

Richardson, K., & Salkeld, L. (1995). Transforming mathematics curriculum. In S. Bredekamp & S. Rosegrant (Eds.), *Reaching potentials: Transforming early childhood curriculum and assessment* (Vol. 2, pp. 23–42). Washington, DC: National Association for the Education of Young Children.

Robins, D. (1994). *The kids around the world cookbook.* New York: Kingfisher.

Schifter, D., & Fosnot, C.T. (1993). *Reconstructing mathematics education: Stories of teachers meeting the challenge of reform.* New York: Teachers College Press.

Sgroi, L.A., Gropper, N., Kilker, M.T., Rambusch, N.M., & Semonite, B. (1995). Assessing young children's mathematical understandings. *Teaching Children Mathematics, 1* (5), 275–77.

Simon, M.A. (1995a). Reconstructing mathematics pedagogy from a constructivist perspective. *Journal for Research in Mathematics Education, 26,* 114–45.

Simon, M.A. (1995b). Elaborating models of mathematics teaching: A response to Steffe and D'Ambrosio. *Journal for Research in Mathematics Education, 26,* 160–62.

Skinner, P. (1990). *What's your problem?* Portsmouth, NH: Heinemann.

Steffe, L.P., & D'Ambrosio, B.S. (1995). Toward a model of constructivist teaching. *Journal for Research in Mathematics Education, 26,* 145–59.

Stone, A., & Russell, S.J. (1990). *Used numbers, counting: Ourselves and our families.* Palo Alto, CA: Dale Seymour.

Tate, W.F. (1994): Race, retrenchment, and the reform of school mathematics. *Phi Delta Kappan, 74,* 477–84.

Thiessen, D., & Matthias, M. (Eds.). (1992). *The wonderful world of mathematics.* Reston, VA: National Council of Teachers of Mathematics.

Wasserman, S. (1990). *Serious players in the primary classroom.* New York: Teachers College Press.

Webb, N.L. (Ed.). (1993). *Assessment in the mathematics classroom: NCTM 1993 yearbook.* Reston, VA: National Council of Teachers of Mathematics.

Welchman-Tischler, R. (1992). *How to use children's literature to teach mathematics.* Reston, VA: National Council of Teachers of Mathematics.

Whitin, D.J., & Wilde, S. (1992). *Read and good math lately?: Children's books for mathematical learning, K–6.* Portsmouth, NH: Heinemann.

Workman, S., & Anziano, M.C. (1993). Curriculum webs: Weaving connections from children to teachers. *Young Children, 48* (2), 4–9.

CHAPTER FOUR

Science in the Developmentally Appropriate Integrated Curriculum

KAREN K. LIND

The waves of reform in science education leave no doubt that science is understood to be a process of finding out and a system for organizing and reporting discoveries. Passé is the notion that science is the memorization of facts. Science is viewed as a way of thinking and working toward understanding the world. More than ever before, educators agree that preschool and elementary science is an active enterprise. This agreement can be seen in the national standards for science education as well as the guidelines of professional organizations in early childhood education and major science and science education organizations.

As any scientist knows, the best way to learn science is to do science. This is the only way to get beyond dry facts to the real business of asking questions, conducting investigations, collecting data, and looking for answers. With young children this can be best accomplished by examining natural phenomena that can be studied over time. Children need to have a chance to ask and answer questions do investigations, and learn to apply problem-solving skills. Active, hands-on, student-centered inquiry should be at the core of good science education.

This chapter describes how the early childhood science curriculum can be built on the foundation of constructivism and developmental

75

foundations laid by Krogh in chapter 2 of this volume. An understanding of the major reform efforts in science education and the relationship of these efforts to science in the early childhood classroom are discussed and an overview of the current view of teaching and learning science in the early years is presented, with emphasis on the importance of selecting science content that matches the cognitive capacities of students at different stages of their development. The teaching of science through inquiry is discussed, and strategies and processes that encourage children to think in this way are presented.

National Standards in Science Education Today

A national consensus is evolving around what constitutes effective science education. This consensus is reflected in two major national reform efforts in science education that impact the teaching and learning of young children: the National Research Council's (NRC) *National Science Education Standards* (1996) and the American Association for the Advancement of Science's (AAAS) *Project 2061* (1989), which has produced *Science for All Americans* (1989) and *Benchmarks for Science Literacy* (1993). With regard to philosophy, intent, and expectations, these two efforts share a commitment to the essentials of good science teaching and have many commonalities, especially regarding how children learn and what science content students should know and be able to understand within grade ranges and levels of difficulty. Although they take different approaches, both the AAAS and NRC efforts align with the National Association for the Education of Young Children guidelines for developmentally appropriate practice (Bredekamp, 1987; Bredekamp & Copple, 1997; Bredekamp & Rosegrant, 1992) as discussed by Krogh (chapter 2, this volume) and the National Council for the Teaching of Mathematics guidelines presented by Charlesworth (chapter 3, this volume). The national reform documents are based on the idea that active, hands-on, conceptual learning that leads to understanding, along with the acquisition of basic skills, provides meaningful and relevant learning experiences. These documents also emphasize and reinforce Oakes's (1990) observation that all students, especially underrepresented groups, need to learn scientific skills such as observation and analysis that have been embedded in a "less-is-more" curriculum that starts when children are very young.

The American Association for the Advancement of Science's Project 2061 (the name is derived from the date of the next return of Halley's Comet) first report is *Science for All Americans* (1989). As the title might indicate, its focus is not only on those who will become the next generation of scientists, but on a scientific understanding for all. It is argued that scientific understanding of the world is required to solve problems and live in a complex world.

The AAAS report describes the knowledge, skills, and attitudes that students should possess as a result of their science experiences. *Science for All Americans* recommends the following:

1. Instructional methods based on classroom activities that engage students with science and teachers who help students actively construct meaning
2. A view of science as an activity and process, as well as a body of knowledge
3. A focus on developing higher-order problem-solving skills, rather than rote memorization
4. The development of students' scientific skills, scientific attitudes, and ability to make connections between science and other disciplines and between science and the real world

The AAAS initiative, Project 2061 (1989), constitutes a long-term plan to strengthen student literacy in science, mathematics, and technology. Using a "less-is-more" approach to teaching, Project 2061 recommends that educators use six major themes that occur again and again in science to weave together the science curriculum: models, scale, evolution, patterns of change, stability, and systems and interactions. Although aspects of all or many of these themes can be found in most teaching units, *models and scale, patterns of change, and systems and interactions* are the themes considered most appropriate for younger children.

The second AAAS Project 2061 report, *Benchmarks for Science Literacy* (1994), categorizes the science knowledge all students need to possess at all grade levels. The report is not in itself a science curriculum, but it is a useful resource for curriculum developers.

The recently released *National Science Education Standards* (NSES) (1996) were coordinated by the National Academy of Science's National Research Council (NRC) and were developed with the major professional organizations in science and individuals with expertise germane to the process of producing the standards. The document presents and discusses the standards that provide criteria to be used by educators and others making decisions and judgments in six major components: (1) Science Teaching Standards, (2) Standards for the Professional Development of Teachers, (3) Assessment in Science Education, (4) Science Content Standards, (5) Science Education Program Standards, and (6) Science Education System Standards.

The *National Science Education Standards* are directed to all who have interests, concerns, or investments in improving science, education, schools, and society. A major goal is improving science education and ultimately achieving higher levels of scientific literacy for all students. The document intends to provide support for the integrity of science in science programs by presenting and discussing criteria for the improvement of science education.

The Theoretical Foundations of Science Instruction

The theoretical foundation of science instruction is grounded in the constructivist approach found in the work of Jean Piaget. This theoretical foundation can also be seen in the current science education reform movements, where the more traditional view of the student absorbing knowledge has shifted to one of the student constructing knowledge, interpreting and understanding new content, and linking new knowledge to existing knowledge in a meaningful way. Research from both the cognitive sciences and science education has guided understanding of how children learn science. Much of this understanding of how and when the development of basic concepts takes place comes from research based on Piaget's theory of how concept development occurs (DeVries & Kohlberg, 1987/1990; Driver, Guesne, & Tiberghein, 1985; Kamii & DeVries, 1978; Osborne & Freyberg, 1985).

The major view of the constructivist approach is to place the emphasis on individual children as intellectual explorers, making their own discoveries and constructing knowledge (Charlesworth & Lind, 1995a). In science, teaching for conceptual change, or "teaching for understanding" as it is frequently called, requires different strategies from those found in many traditional classrooms. Instead of memorizing science facts, students are encouraged to use the inquiry process. Science education researchers find that this is best done within a developmentally appropriate context that progressively increases in conceptual depth and complexity as students advance through the grades and throughout life. The assessment of prior knowledge is thought to be key to this process. Researchers such as Mestre (1991), citing Resnick (1987), Von Glaserfeld (1989), and others, caution that if we as educators do not take students' prior knowledge into consideration, it is likely that the message we think we are sending will not be the message received.

The emphasis in science education is not as much on children discovering everything for themselves as it is on relating new knowledge both to previously learned knowledge and to experiential phenomena so that students can build a consistent picture of the physical world. This can be reflected in science teaching in several ways. For example, when the students in a 2nd grade class show an interest in learning more about a nearby wooded area an integrated project based on studying animals and plants that are found in the woods begins when questions are asked to elicit prior knowledge. Children are asked to contribute to a class chart labeled "What Do We Know?" by asking the following questions:

- What do you think of when you hear the word "woods"?
- Has anyone been to a woods or a forest?
- What plants and animals did you see?
- What did you hear and smell?

The activity continues by discussing familiar stories such as "Little Red Riding Hood" and drawing a picture of a woods. Reading a story such as *The Apartment House Tree* by Bette Killion, brainstorming lists and ideas about animals and plants that live in the woods, and listing things that children say they want to learn about the woods further sets the stage for learning, as seen in the following example. "Things We Want to Learn" might include questions about how plants and animals live in the woods, keep dry in the rain, or a variety of other questions about animal protection.

In this way, prior knowledge is assessed and learning experiences can be modified to meet student needs. After completing a series of lessons, individual "What Did We Learn?" responses can provide an opportunity for whole-class reflection as well as individual portfolio opportunities.

The views of Piaget's approach and Vygotsky's sociocultural approach, as discussed by Charlesworth in chapter 3, do not differ on the major aspects of constructivist theory as applied to science learning. Today many educators find that a combination of both Piaget and Vygotsky provides a foundation for instruction that follows the child's interests and enthusiasms while at the same time providing an intellectual challenge (Charlesworth & Lind, 1995a).

Research: Science Concept Development, Knowledge, Strategies and Effective Instructional Practices

This section of the chapter presents an overview of major areas of research that are of value to teaching, learning, and integrating science with young children. The discussion begins with a major area of concern for science educators. If the science content is not appropriate for the cognitive capacity of students at different stages of their development, scientific misconceptions (alternative or naive understandings) will occur. Research in the areas of inquiry-based teaching and hands-on, process-oriented curriculum are presented.

Science Content and Cognitive Capacity: Avoiding a Mismatch

Although evidence of developmental stages of learning (Piaget, 1969) is considered a major contribution from research to the teaching and learning of science, these developmental stages are not always taken into account when designing science curriculum and experiences for young children. If students are to learn science and become scientifically literate, science content and science experiences must be appropriately chosen to match the cognitive capacities of students at different stages of their development (Lowery, 1989, 1992). The importance of this match can be seen in research by Cowan (1978), who reports that mismatching content and developmental levels (e.g., expecting 1st grade students to understand the movements of the Earth's crust) leads to misconceptions and frustrations for teacher and student. Mismatches such as this tend to cause teachers to resort to telling the information because the content cannot be conceptualized by the child. Children's thinking is often reduced to simple memorization and accepting ideas because they are told rather than learned. As Covington and Berry (1976) and Brophy (1983) found, the results of mismatched content and cognitive capacity levels are: (1) students are not able to extend, apply, or interpret deeper meanings of the content; (2) interest and positive attitudes toward science are likely to diminish. The implication from the research is that the content to be learned must always be within the realm of possibility for the student to comprehend it.

Both the AAAS *Benchmarks* and the *National Science Education Standards* consider the match between appropriate science content and cognitive capacity important enough to provide guidance for grade level-appropriate science content. *Benchmarks* (1995), for example, presents the appropriate science content of "Position and Motion of Objects" for grades K–2 and grades 3–5 as follows:

Benchmarks, 4F, p. 89, grades K–2
   The way to change how something is moving is to give it a push or a pull.
Benchmarks, 4F, p. 89, grades 3–5
   Changes in speed or direction of motion are caused by forces. The greater the force is, the greater the change in motion will be. The more massive an object is, the less effect a given force will have.

Research in Scientific Misconceptions

A prominent feature of research in thinking is the study of student misconceptions in science. These are not merely errors in calculations or misapplication of strategies. They are ideas that are based on individual misconceptions or incorrect generalizations that are consistent with the student's general understanding. For this reason they form powerful barriers that must be overcome before new concepts can be learned. For example, misconceptions can be seen in children's ideas about light and shadows that have been an area of interest and were initially studied by Piaget (1930), DeVries (1986), and Feher and Rice (1987). Young children think of a shadow as an object or substance and that light is the agent that causes the object to form or that allows people to see the shadow, even when it is dark.

The current interest in the study of science concept learning owes much to the work of Novak (1977). This line of research and the clinical methods used employ Piagetian tasks to explore children's explanations for natural phenomena. Since this work, a large number of studies related to a wide range of topics in the science curriculum have now been reported, reviewed, and summarized by many researchers, including Eylon and Linn (1988), Osborne and Freyberg (1985), and Confrey (1990).

Although most of the misconception research focuses on elementary and middle school children, younger subjects fall within the age group reported in some of the studies. Studies of students' conceptions are especially valuable because they point out common misconceptions. For example, Howe, in her 1993 synthesis of misconception literature, reports studies by Erickson (1979) who, in a study of elementary children (K–6), showed that the younger children do not differentiate between heat and temperature and think of heat and cold as substances that flow in and out of bodies.

In the life sciences, an example of conceptual development involving concepts of living and nonliving things can be seen in children's explanations of what it means to be alive. Early work by Piaget (1965) and a replication by Laurendeau and Pinard (1962) found that, at an early age, children believe that all things are alive. At a later age, children believe that moving objects such as a bicycle or cloud are alive in contrast to a tree, which stays in one place. The research literature on this concept is extensive and has been significantly augmented by numerous researchers such as Carey's (1986) series of studies investigating 4-, 6-, and 10-year-olds understandings of living things, animals, and human body functions. Expected and significant differences were found among the understandings of each age group.

Achieving the necessary match between science content and cognitive capacity is essential to learning. The extent of the literature is too broad to be covered in depth in this chapter. It is recommended that the *Benchmarks* and *Standards* be used as basic tools in avoiding a mismatch between content and cognitive capacity. Additional useful information is provided by Pfundt and Duit (1991), who have compiled a useful bibliography for additional research on students' conceptions in science. This bibliography documents and categorizes research and contains about two thousand citations from the literature. More than 70 percent of the published papers about students' conceptions in science listed were concerned with topics related to the physical science settings such as the Earth, energy and motion, and the structure of matter. Available literature on students' understanding of topics related to the physical sciences are reviewed in Driver, Guesne, and Tiberghein (1995). Although there is little research available on student understanding about the universe, the ideas "the sun is a star" and "the Earth orbits the sun" appear counterintuitive to elementary school students (Vosniadou & Brewer, 1992) and lend support to the idea of the phenomenological approach to studying science with young children. Further information on matching science content with cognitive capacity can be found by accessing the suggested research literature and national reform documents.

Teaching Science to Young Children through Inquiry

A major area of interest in science education research is the teaching of science through inquiry. The national reforms in science education and research findings overwhelmingly endorse the concept of teaching science through inquiry. The U.S. Department of Education and the National Science foundation (1992) endorse mathematics and science curricula that promote active learning, inquiry, problem solving, cooperative learning, and other instructional methods that motivate students.

The *Standards* state that science teaching must reflect science as it is practiced and that one goal of science education is to prepare students who understand the modes of reasoning of scientific inquiry and can use them. *Benchmarks* states specifically that students need to have many and varied opportunities for collecting; sorting and cataloging; observing; note taking and sketching; interviewing; polling; and surveying. Active learning is the beginning.

The *Standards* present inquiry as a step beyond process learning, such as observing, inferring, and experimenting. In inquiry, the process skills are required but students also must combine these skills with scientific knowledge as they use scientific reasoning and critical thinking to develop understanding. According to the *Standards*, engaging students in inquiry serves five essential functions:

- It assists in the development of understanding of scientific concepts.

- It helps students "know how we know" in science.
- It develops an understanding of the nature of science.
- It develops the skills necessary to become independent inquirers about the natural world.
- It develops the dispositions to use the skills, abilities, and habits of mind associated with science.

From a science perspective, inquiry-oriented instruction engages students in the investigative nature of science. As Novak (1977) suggested, inquiry is a student behavior that involves activity and skills, but the focus is on the active search for knowledge or understanding to satisfy curiosity.

Inquiry-oriented instruction is often contrasted with expository methods and reflects the constructivist model of learning often referred to as active learning. This is a position that is strongly held by science educators today. Osborne and Freyberg (1985) describe the constructivist model of learning as the result of ongoing changes in our mental frameworks as we attempt to make meaning out of our experiences.

There are a variety of strategies used to attempt to engage students in the active search for knowledge. Some advocate structured methods of guided inquiry; others advocate providing students with few instructions (Tinnesand & Chan, 1987); yet others promote the use of heuristic devices to aid skills development (Germann, 1991). Throughout the literature, inquiry always involves collection and interpretation of information in response to wondering and exploring.

Strategies That Encourage Inquiry

Students of all ages should experience science in a form that engages them in the active construction of ideas and explanations and enhances their opportunities to develop the skills of doing science. Fundamental abilities and concepts that underlie the Science as Inquiry Content Standard from the *Standards* (V-19–V-22) lay a groundwork for developing and integrating strategies that encourage inquiry.

There is basic agreement among scientists, science educators, and the professional science organizations on what abilities are needed to do scientific inquiry and have an understanding about scientific inquiry. In the early years, children can investigate materials and properties of common objects. They can focus on the process of doing investigations and develop the ability to ask questions. The following strategies are suggested by the *Standards*:

1. *Ask a question about objects, organisms, and events in the environment.* Children should be encouraged to answer their questions by seeking information from their own observations and investigations and from reliable sources of information. When possible, children's answers can be compared to what scientists already know about the world.

2. *Plan and conduct a simple investigation.* In the earliest years investigations are based on systematic observation. As children develop, they may design and conduct simple experiments to answer questions. However, the idea of a fair test necessary for experimentation may not be possible until the 4th grade. Types of investigations that are appropriate for younger children include describing objects, events, and organisms; classifying them; and sharing what they know with others.

3. *Employ simple equipment and tools to gather data and extend the senses.* Simple skills such as how to observe, measure, cut, connect, switch, turn on/off, pour, hold, and hook and simple instruments such as rulers, thermometers, magnifiers, and microscopes should be used in the early years. Children can use simple equipment and can gather data such as observing and recording daily weather conditions. Children can also develop skills in the use of computers and calculators.

4. *Use data to construct a reasonable explanation.* In inquiry, students' thinking is emphasized as they use data to formulate explanations. Even at the earliest grade levels, students learn what counts as evidence and judge the merits of the data and explanations.

5. *Communicate investigations and explanations.* Students should begin developing the abilities to communicate, critique, and analyze their work and the work of other students. This communication might be spoken or drawn as well as written.

Inquiry through Hands-on, Process-Oriented Curriculum

Hands-on, process-oriented instruction is well established as an effective teaching strategy. Studies of the effect of inquiry-oriented science curricula on student performance were synthesized by Shymansky, Hedges, and Woodworth (1990) in a reanalysis of an earlier meta-analysis of twenty-five years of primary research on the effect on student performance of activity-based, process-oriented elementary science programs (Shymansky, Kyle, & Alport, 1983). The criterion clusters used as dependent variables are science achievement, student perceptions, process skills, problem solving, related skills (reading, math computation, writing), and other performance areas (involving mostly studies of Piagetian task performance). The evidence is overwhelming that hands-on, process-oriented learning positively impacts teaching and learning in many curricular areas. (Refer to table 4.1 for basic science process skills appropriate for young children.)

TABLE 4.1
Basic Science Process Skills Appropriate for Birth–Age 8

1. *Observing*: Assimilating information in a multisensory manner such as looking at, tasting, biting, and handling an object. Observation is the basis for gathering information about objects or events.
2. *Comparing*: Using the senses to look at similarities and differences in real objects. Comparison begins when the child notices that objects can be big or small, long or short, light or heavy. In the primary grades, students begin to compare and contrast ideas, concepts, and objects.
3. *Classifying*: Grouping and sorting according to properties such as size, shape, color, use, and so on. By age 3 children sort and group to help organize play activities. Pre-K's sort their toys by color or shape and match them with one-to-one correspondence. Older children sort by pattern, then by size. Sorting by more than one characteristic is a higher-level process that most children cannot perform until they are in the 4th grade.
4. *Measuring*: Making quantitative descriptions either directly through observation or indirectly with a unit of measure. Descriptions move from comparison into more elaborate measurement, such as informal, nonstandard units.
5. *Communicating*: Communicating ideas, directions, and descriptions orally or in written form such as pictures, maps, graphs, or journals so others can understand what you mean.

Bredderman (1983) included three federally funded process-oriented elementary school science curricula in a national synthesis of research reports (see Science A Process Approach, based on Gagne, 1963, 1965; Science Curriculum Improvement Study, based on the Learning Cycle approach; and the Elementary Science Study). The analysis of fifty-seven studies and more than nine hundred classrooms indicates about a 14 percent improvement for the average student as a result of being in an activity-based program. Bredderman reports gains over traditional methods in a wide range of student outcomes at all grade levels. Gains were found for science content, science processes tests, and affective outcomes. Gains were also reported in creativity, intelligence, language, and mathematics. Disadvantaged students derived greater benefits than other students. The research on the learning effects of a particular program reflected the relative curricular emphasis of that program.

Hands-on Learning and Inquiry Learning

Hands-on science means just that—learning from materials and processes of the natural world through direct observation and experimentation. Direct experience, experimentation, and observation are sources of students' learning about science and are essential to learning. This hands-on learning begins in infancy with sensory stimulation that hones the infant's observational and discrimination skills and readies him or her for the more detailed explorations of toddlerhood. However, hands-on instruction alone does not constitute inquiry teaching. There is a substantial difference between an open-ended, problem-solving approach to an activity and an approach that is hands-on but does not encourage problem solving and inquiry. For example, one approach to teaching the concept that water expands when it freezes might be as follows:

a. Fill a plastic container with water.
b. Place the container in the freezer and have the children observe the condition of the water after a period of time.
c. Ask the children, What happened? How would you explain this?

Another way to approach this same concept may be to present the following challenge: "Can you prove at least three things that happen or don't happen to water when it freezes? Be prepared to share what you have discovered with others."

Both activities provide students with a teacher-selected topic and a hands-on experience. The first, however, offers only one strategy (a procedure) that can be used to demonstrate an already given solution (water expands). While this is a useful strategy, the second approach promotes inquiry because it requires students to first figure out what they observe happening or not happening to water when it freezes and then plan a way to convince someone else of their discovery.

Although both activities are hands-on, use process skills, and require physical manipulation of objects to gain an understanding of a science concept, only the second activity involves problem solving, from which inquiry is most likely to spring. By listening to students who are actively engaged in conceptual problem solving, the teacher will uncover many scientific misconceptions, which will provide instructional material for years to come.

Encouraging Inquiry through Problem Solving

The driving force behind problem solving is curiosity, an interest in finding out. Problem solving is not as much a teaching strategy as it is a student behavior. The challenge for the teacher is to create an environment in which problem solving can occur. An example of the encouragement of problem-solving behavior in a primary classroom can be seen in the following example.

After studying the movement and structure of the human body, the teacher adds a final challenge to the unit. The teacher asks the children to work with partners, poses the following situation, and asks each pair to come up with a solution to the problem: "You like to play video games, but your family is worried because your wrists seem to be hurting from the motion you use to play the games. Plan a solution to the problem, and role play the family discussion that might take place" (Charlesworth & Lind, 1995a; Lind, 1996).

The asking and answering of questions is what problem solving is all about. When the situations and problems that the students wonder about are perceived as real, their curiosity is stimulated and they want to find answers. This means a problem is some question or situation that is important to the students that gets attention, and student enthusiasm is focused on the search for a solution (Charlesworth & Lind, 1995b; Lind, 1996).

Problems should relate to, and include, the children's own experiences. From birth on, children want to learn and naturally seek out problems to solve. Problem solving through the prekindergarten years focuses on naturalistic and informal learning, which promotes explorations and discovery through experiences such as filling and emptying containers of water, sand, or other substances, observing ants, or racing toy cars down a ramp. In kindergarten and primary grades, a more structured approach can be instituted.

There is a remarkable degree of agreement in the professed beliefs of most science educators—that problem solving and reflective thinking play an important role in children's learning of science in school. Hurd (1989) summarized the findings of twenty-six national reports calling for reform in education, particularly curriculum and instruction in mathematics and science. Eighteen of the reports specifically describe problem solving in science as an educational objective.

Integration and Inquiry Learning through Inquiry

Integrating the Curriculum through Process Skills

The emphasis in process-oriented teaching and learning is how to obtain and understand information, not simply finding out what the information is. The minds-on part of instruction comes with dialogue, discussion, and making connections between scientific ideas.

There is a substantial overlap in the skills and activities that are associated with manipulative science and those associated with emergent literacy, conventional reading, mathematics, and social studies. The research presented in this chapter supports the view that science inquiry activities enhance skills in other areas of the curriculum.

Young children's understanding of mathematics and science grows from the development of some of the same fundamental concepts during early childhood. Charlesworth presents the sequence of emergence of these concepts and skills relative to Piaget's periods of development in chapter 3, (see her table 3.2). For further information, extensive explanation and integration of concepts and skills in mathematics and science and other subject areas are made by Charlesworth and Lind (1995a, 1995b).

Manipulative science activities, especially in the younger years, are identical to many of the basic skill activities taught in preschool, kindergarten, and primary programs as preparation for upper-level applications in reading and language arts, mathematics, and social studies. Research on the early science programs gave curriculum developers valuable information about those processes in science that worked with children. These processes were incorporated into the various subject area curricula and today there is a great overlap of actual learning activities of reading and language arts, mathematics, and social studies programs with science. Several emergent literacy basic concept programs are based on Science A Process Approach and were developed to take advantage of these findings.

Because of the overlap in learnings and activities, lessons that teach children the basic skills in several subjects simultaneously can be developed. In many instances, however, the teacher needs to help children make a transfer of learning. For example, the skill of "cause and effect" can be seen in a science and mathematics lesson when children are observing and measuring the bounce of various balls dropped from varying heights and making comparisons between the height of the bounce and the height from which the ball is dropped. In this form, the skill is not the same as reading a story or paragraph and comprehending the reading skill of "cause and effect." Some transfer of learning of the concept would have to be made. On the other hand, recording data through dictation, drawing, and/or writing provides opportunities to practice literacy and communication skills. Doing these activities in cooperative groups supports the learning of important social skills that are included in the social studies content.

There is impressive evidence that hands-on science programs aid in the development of language and reading skills. Some evidence indicates that reading achievement scores increase as a result of such programs. This statement is supported by the research evaluating the major science curricula and by other research.

Integrating Science in a Broad Theme

The integration of science and social studies is especially appropriate when both are taught as problem-solving activities. A recommended way to integrate is to base a lesson or unit on these two subjects by performing the related science and social studies investigations first and following these with the application of mathematics and language arts skills. Numerous activities may be used to integrate the subjects with music, drama, and art and to provide opportunities for creative explorations. The following examples describe appropriate science content integrated with other subject areas.

"Seeds, Seeds, Seeds"

One example of integrating around a science concept is shown in the planning web in figure 4.1. In this example the teacher's focus is on outcomes such as describing how seeds germinate and grow into plants and that seeds travel in several ways. First she identifies the main science concepts appropriate for the children's level of understanding. In this example, kindergarten and primary age children are the intended grade levels. Although younger children will not develop a full understanding of the science concepts, they can observe and compare their surroundings. After labeling the science concepts, the activities that will be used to teach the science concept are outlined and the subject integrations that will relate and reinforce those concepts are added.

The locating, mapping, and recording of changes in seeds and plants becomes an important focus of activity and provides many opportunities for all ages. The major science process skills in the unit are observing and comparing and the major applicable broader theme from Project 2061 is "Systems and Interaction."

"The Woods" as a Theme for Integration

The "Woods" unit is developed in response to 2nd grade children's fascination with plants and animals in the nearby woods. The children's interest centers around finding out about animals and plants and how

FIGURE 4.1
Web: Integrated Science Theme

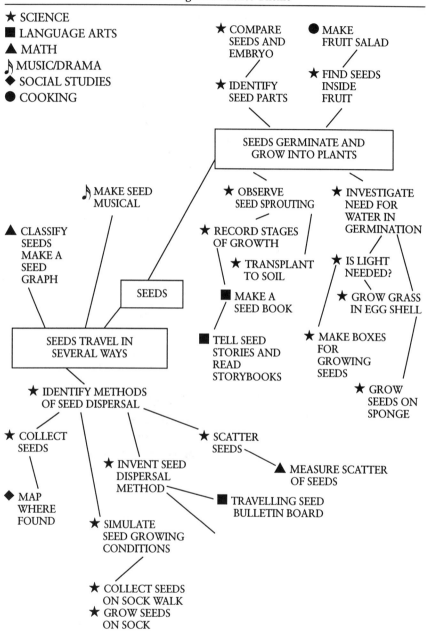

★ SCIENCE
■ LANGUAGE ARTS
▲ MATH
♪ MUSIC/DRAMA
◆ SOCIAL STUDIES
● COOKING

★ COMPARE SEEDS AND EMBRYO

● MAKE FRUIT SALAD

★ IDENTIFY SEED PARTS

★ FIND SEEDS INSIDE FRUIT

SEEDS GERMINATE AND GROW INTO PLANTS

♪ MAKE SEED MUSICAL

★ OBSERVE SEED SPROUTING

★ INVESTIGATE NEED FOR WATER IN GERMINATION

▲ CLASSIFY SEEDS MAKE A SEED GRAPH

★ RECORD STAGES OF GROWTH

★ TRANSPLANT TO SOIL

★ IS LIGHT NEEDED?

SEEDS

■ MAKE A SEED BOOK

★ GROW GRASS IN EGG SHELL

SEEDS TRAVEL IN SEVERAL WAYS

■ TELL SEED STORIES AND READ STORYBOOKS

★ MAKE BOXES FOR GROWING SEEDS

★ GROW SEEDS ON SPONGE

★ IDENTIFY METHODS OF SEED DISPERSAL

★ COLLECT SEEDS

★ SCATTER SEEDS

▲ MEASURE SCATTER OF SEEDS

★ INVENT SEED DISPERSAL METHOD

◆ MAP WHERE FOUND

■ TRAVELLING SEED BULLETIN BOARD

★ SIMULATE SEED GROWING CONDITIONS

★ COLLECT SEEDS ON SOCK WALK
★ GROW SEEDS ON SOCK

they protect and take care of themselves. A project focusing on plants and animals in the woods is a logical choice for integration of these learnings.

Woods are a small forest where a large number and variety of plants, trees, and animals are found. Because of this, the woods provides a rich environment for learning about the interdependence of plants and animals, how they protect themselves and obtain food, and how woodland plants scatter their seeds.

After listing the students' questions about the woods to planning, the teacher lists the appropriate science concepts so that scientific misconceptions are minimized. Then activities are designed that integrate skills and disciplines and assess learning. These lessons are structured around major science concepts, listed in table 4.2, and the idea that children are going to the woods to learn about animals and plants. The classroom can be constructed around the woods theme and decorated as the project progresses.

In order to maximize inquiry learning in the "Woods" project, children need to be provided with many opportunities to collect data, record information they gather from observations, and show it in a visual form, such as a graph, diagram, or chart. Children should be encouraged to think of ways to categorize plant and animal structures and describe their observations within these categories. For example, inquiry can be stimulated with some questions such as, "Do you see similarities in the animals?" "How are they the same?" "How are they different?" "In what ways are they like people?"

TABLE 4.2
"The Woods"

1. Comparing Animals
   a. Animals have different coverings and body parts that protect them from other animals and extremes in weather.
   b. Animals can be categorized according to what they eat.
   c. Animals are suited to where they live.

2. Comparing plants
   a. Plants protect themselves from weather and animals.
   b. Plants need light, air, and water to produce food.
   c. Plants scatter seeds in several ways.
   d. Plants are suited to their environment.

"In the Woods"

Begin the unit by brainstorming a "What Do I Know" and "What Do I Want to Learn" chart about plants and animals in the woods, as described earlier in the chapter. This assessment of prior knowledge should guide further unit planning. The following outline suggests integrations for the major science concepts listed in table 4.2:

1. Comparing Animals:

• *Animals have different body coverings and body parts that protect them from other animals and from extremes in weather.* Science activities can focus on the physical characteristics of animals and how the animals are protected from weather and danger, or how they obtain food.

In addition to science activities, cultural integrations can be included, such as discussion of the Dakota Sioux tale "How the Fawn Got Its Spots" in *Native American Animal Stories* by Joseph Bruchac. Language arts can be included by reading *Something Told the Wild Geese* by Rachel Field and writing short poems and descriptions of birds flying south for the winter.

• *Animals can be categorized according to what they eat.* Science activities focus on what different animals eat. Then choose a woods animal and make a menu for that animal. Playing a predator-and-prey game will add a further dimension to the concept and an art activity of making spider web designs will relate to most environments.

• *Animals are suited to where they live.* Have the children draw an animal that lives in the woods, describe how it survives in the woods, and write or dictate a story about the animal. The construction of a woods diorama in a shoebox will help in assessing student learning.

Read *This Is My House* by Arthur Dorros and discuss why the house is built that way. Compare different houses that people build (e.g., igloos, mud houses, log homes, brick, and straw and grass). Children may enjoy the play activity of creating a woods environment in the room by constructing a tree or other house and making appropriate cardboard plants and animals.

2. Comparing Plants:

• *Plants protect themselves from weather and animals.* Students will be curious about how plants protect themselves from weather and animals. Living plants can be used to explore ways that plants are protected. Have children use a magnifying lens to explore the bark of a tree and the fine hairs on plant leaves. The teacher asks, "How do you think the sharp spines on the holly leaves or the thorns of a rose stem protect the plant?"

Make a plant mobile of how a plant protects itself. An especially effective activity is to observe a tree periodically and record how it changes from season to season in a "tree journal."

• *Plants need light, air, and water to produce food.* Children can investigate the effects of space, light, and water on plant growth in a variety of ways. One activity that demonstrates the importance of light for a plant to grow suggests covering half a leaf on a plant with foil, then observing how lack of light causes part of the leaf to turn yellow after several days.

Mathematics can be emphasized by having students collect leaves. Trace around each leaf on inch or centimeter graph paper. Make an X on each square covered by more than half with the leaf and an O on each square covered by less than half. Count up the Xs to show the area the leaf has to soak up sunshine. Compare numbers. Then, paint pictures of leaves to record how leaf shapes might serve as the basis of a pattern.

• *Plants scatter seeds in several ways.* In addition to investigating the ways seeds are scattered, have children compare the number of seeds found in different fruits and vegetables. Make a bar graph on butcher paper and compare seeds. Students will enjoy reading the story of Johnny Appleseed by Steven Kellogg and writing, dictating, or illustrating their own versions of the story.

• *Plants are suited to their environment.* Arrange for the class to plant a tree in an area near the school or a nearby park. Children should take part in planning and discussing where they think the tree should be placed. After observing the planted tree the teacher might ask, "In what way is this tree suited to its environment?" "Are there any reasons why it should not grow here?" Children observations and differing opinions will start a lively brainstorming session. The class will want to follow the progress of the tree throughout the year and maybe longer.

Children may not know that the Chinese were one of the first cultures to make paper. They will enjoy making paper from old newspapers and then drawing pictures or writing on their paper. They could also compare paintings of plants and trees in outdoor scenes painted by artists in different geographic areas. They might also visit the woods and draw or paint a picture of what they observe.

3. Assessment Options:

The following assessment strategies are suggested. First, portfolios provide an opportunity to assess students' understanding and progress. Second, observation checklists allow the teacher to assess student performance and group skills frequently. Third, performance assessments provide information on concept understanding and the ability to plan and follow through on a project. Examples of performance assessments would be projects such as making a woodland diorama and telling a story about the plants and animals that live in the habitat or creating a poster about a tree, "This Is Our Home," and describing where the tree grows and drawing the animals that live there.

Regardless of the assessment options or combination of assessments selected for the "In the Woods" unit, the children's descriptions should reflect the characteristics of the plants and animals studied in the unit. In the natural world, shapes and structures of plants and animals all have their purpose in helping living things survive. Note the amount of detail students give in their discussions, drawings, journal entries, and other work.

For further information on issues related to assessment, refer to Hein (1990) and to Kulm and Malcom (1991). For strategies for assessment in science, refer to Hein and Price's (1994) book, *Active Assessment for Active Science*.

Summary

This chapter provides an overview of the philosophy, purposes, and recommendations of the major reform efforts in science education. The theoretical foundations of science instruction within these reforms are closely aligned with the foundations of constructivism and developmental learnings that are the hallmark of early childhood curriculum.

One major area of research that is of value to teaching, learning, and integrating science with young children is the possibility of a mismatch between science content and cognitive capacity. If the science content does not match the child's stage of development, scientific misconceptions and a diminished interest in science are likely to occur.

Another major area of science education research is the teaching of science through inquiry. Teaching strategies that promote active learning, hands-on experiences, inquiry, problem solving, and process-oriented curriculum are essential.

The teaching of science through an integrated approach is also crucial. There is a natural integration of fundamental concepts and process skills across content area. Strategies for integrating science focus on selecting projects of interest to the students and having them apply concepts and skills from other content areas. This chapter suggests integrating the curriculum through process skills, a science concept, broad themes, and problem-solving activities.

References

American Association for the Advancement of Science. (1989). *Science for all Americans: A Project 2061 report on literacy goals in science, mathematics and technology.* Washington, DC: Author.

American Association for the Advancement of Science. (1993). *Benchmarks in science literacy.* Washington, DC: Author.

American Association for the Advancement of Science. (1995). Common ground: Benchmarks and national standards. *2061 Today, 5* (1), 1–3.

Berk, L.E., & Winsler, A. (1995) *Scaffolding children's learning: Vygotsky and early childhood education.* Washington, DC: National Association for the Education of Young Children.

Bredderman, T. (1983). Effects of activity-based elementary science on student outcomes: A quantitative synthesis. *Review of Educational Research, 53* (4), 499–518.

Bredekamp, S. (Ed). (1987). *Developmentally appropriate practice in early childhood programs serving children from birth to age 8.* Washington, DC: National Association for the Education of Young Children.

Bredekamp, S., & Coppel, C. (Eds.). (1997). *Developmentally appropriate practice in early childhood programs: Revised.* Washington, DC: National Association for the Education of Young Children.

Bredekamp, S., & Rosegrant, T. (Eds.). (1992). *Reaching potentials: Appropriate curriculum and assessment for young children.* Washington, DC: National Association for the Education of Young Children.

Brophy, J. (1983). Conceptualizing student motivation. *Educational Psychologist, 18* (3), 200–215.

Brummet, C.R., Lind, K.K., Barman, C.R., DeSpezio, M.A., & Ostlund, K.L. (1995). The woods. In *Destinations in science.* Teachers Destinations Guide, Grade 2. Menlo Park, CA: Addison-Wesley.

Bybee, R.W., & Champagne, A.B. (1995). The national science education standards. *The Science Teacher, 62* (1), 40–45.

Carey, S. (1986). Cognitive science and science education. *American Psychologist, 41* (10), 1123–30.

Charlesworth, R., & Lind, K.K. (1995a). *Math and science for young children* (2nd ed.). Albany, NY: Delmar.

Charlesworth, R., & Lind, K.K. (1995b). Whole language and the mathematics and science standards. In S. Raines (Ed.), *Whole language across the curriculum: Grades 1, 2, and 3.* New York: Teachers College Press.

Confrey, J. (1990). A review of the research on student conceptions in mathematics, science and programming. In C. Cazden (Ed.), *Review of research in education* (pp. 3–56). Washington, DC: American Educational Research Association.

Covington, M., & Berry, R. (1976). *Self-worth and school learning.* New York: Holt, Rinehart & Winston.

Cowan, P.A. (1978). *Piaget with feeling.* New York: Holt, Rinehart & Winston.

DeVries, R. (1986). Children's conceptions of shadow phenomena. *Genetic, Social & General Psychology Monographs, 112* (4), 479–530.

DeVries, R., & Kohlberg, L. (1987/1990). *Constructivist early education: Overview and comparison with other programs.* Washington, DC: National Association for the Education of Young Children.

Driver, R., Guesne, E. & Tiberghein, A. (Eds.). (1985). *Children's ideas in science.* Philadelphia, PA: Open University Press.

Erickson, G. (1979). Children's conception of heat and temperature. *Science Education, 63* (2), 221–30.

Eylon, B.S., & Linn, M.K. (1988). Learning and instruction: An examination of four research perspectives in science education. *Review of Educational Research, 58* (3), 251–301.

Feher, E., Rice, K. (1987). Shadows and anti-images. *Science Education, 72* (5), 637–49.

Gagne, R.M. (1963). The learning requirements for inquiry. *Journal of Research in Science Teaching, 1.*

Gagne, R.M. (1965). *Psychological basis of science—A process approach. AAAS Miscellaneous Pub. 65–68.* Washington, DC: American Association for the Advancement of Science.

Germann, P.J. (1991). Developing science process skills through directed inquiry. *American Biology Teacher, 53* (4), 243–47.

Hein, G. (Ed.) (1990). *The assessment of hands-on elementary science programs.* Grand Forks, ND: Center for Teaching and Learning.

Hein, G.E. & Price, S. (1994). *Active assessment for active science.* Portsmouth, NH: Heinemann.

Howe, A.C. (1993). Science in early childhood education. In B. Spodek (Ed.). *Handbook of research on the education of young children.* New York: Macmillan.

Hurd, P.D. (1989). *Science education and the nation's economy.* Paper presented at the American Association for the Advancement of Science Symposium on Science Literacy. Washington, DC.

Kamii, C., & DeVries, R. (1978). *Physical knowledge in preschool education: Implications of Piaget's theory.* Englewood Cliffs, NJ: Prentice Hall.

Killion, B. (1989). *The apartment house tree.* New York: Harper & Row.

Kulm, G. & Malcom, S.M. (Eds.). (1991). *Science assessment in the service of reform.* Washington, DC: American Association for the Advancement of Science.

Laurendeau, M., & Pinard, A. (1962). *Causal thinking in the child.* New York: International Universities Press.

Lind, K. (1996). *Exploring science in early childhood: A developmental approach* (2nd ed.). Albany, NY: Delmar.

Lowery, L.F. (1989). *Thinking and learning.* Pacific Grove, CA: Critical Thinking Press.

Lowery, L.F. (1992). *The scientific thinking processes.* Berkeley, CA: Lawrence Hall of Science.

Mestre, J. (1991). Learning and instruction in pre-college physical science. *Physics Today, 44,* 56–62.

National Research Council. (1996). *National Science Education Standards*. Washington, DC: National Academy Press.

Novak, J. (1977). *A theory of education*. Ithaca, NY: Cornell University Press.

Oakes, J. (1990). *Lost talent: The under participation of women, minorities, and disabled persons in science*. Santa Monica, CA: The Rand Corporation.

Osborne, M., & Freyberg, P. (1985). *Learning in science: Implications of children's knowledge*. Auckland, New Zealand: Heinemann.

Pfundt, H., & Duit, R. (1991). *Bibliography: Students' alternative frameworks and science education*. Kiel, Germany: Institute for Science Education at the University of Kiel.

Piaget, J. (1930). *The child's conception of physical causality*. Totowa, NJ: Littlefield, Adams.

Piaget, J. (1960). *The language and thought of the child*. London: Routledge.

Piaget, J. (1965). *The child's conception of the world*. Totowa, NJ: Littlefield, Adams.

Piaget, J. (1969). *Psychology of intelligence*. Totowa, NJ: Littlefield, Adam.

Resnick, L.B. (1987). *Education and learning to think*. Washington, DC: National Academy Press.

Shymansky, J. A., Kyle, W.C., & Alport, J.M. (1983). The effects of new science curricula on student perfnrmance. *Journal of Research in Science Teaching, 20* (5), 387–404.

Shymansky, J.A., Hedges, L.V., & Woodworth, G. (1990). A reassessment of the effects of inquiry-based science curricula of the 60's on students' performance. *Journal of Research in Science Teaching, 27*, 127–44.

Smith, C., Carey, S., & Wiser, M. (1985). On differentiation study of the development of size, weight and density. *Cognition*, 177–237.

Smith, D., Neale, D. (19891. The construction of subject matter knowledge in primary science teaching. *Teaching and Teacher Education, 5* (1), 1–20.

Tinnesand, M., & Chan, A. (1987). Step 1: Throw out the instructions. *Science Teacher, 54* (6), 43–45.

U.S. Department of Education National Science Foundatinn. (1992). *Statement of Principles* (Brochure). Washington, DC: Author.

Von Glasersfeld, E. (1989). Cognition, construction of knowledge, and teaching. *Syntheses, 80*, 121–40.

Vosniadou, S., & Brewer, W. (1992). Mental models of the earth: A study of conceptual change in childhnod. *Cognitive Psychology, 24*, 535–85.

CHAPTER FIVE

Music in the Developmentally Appropriate Integrated Curriculum

SUSAN H. KENNEY

If we can explain music, we may find the key for all of human thought—failure to take music seriously weakens any account of the human condition. —Howard Gardner

Mrs. Jones invited the children to join with her as she began singing and doing the actions to "Eensy Weensy Spider." Most of the children attempted to imitate her movements and some joined in singing. Mrs. Jones was not only providing the children with a needed change of pace; she was also integrating music and movement with a study of spiders. But was Mrs. Jones' music lesson developmentally appropriate for the young children? Was the experience helping the children grow musically? Mrs. Jones, like most early childhood caregivers, believes music is fun and provides a needed change of pace, but because she knows very little about how children develop musically, she based her lesson on instinct and tradition rather than on an understanding of child development in music.

Building on the foundation laid by Krogh in chapter 2, this chapter explores ways of creating music curriculum based on how children learn. Krogh draws on publications of the National Association for the Education of Young Children (NAEYC) (Bredekamp, 1987; Bredekamp & Copple, 1997; Bredekamp & Rosegrant, 1992), that describe developmentally appropriate practice (DAP) in early childhood programs. The three dimensions of DAP are *age appropriateness* (which draws on theories of stages of human development and includes physical, social, emotional, and cognitive needs), *individual appropriateness* (individual growth patterns, personality, and learning styles) and *context* (culture and family background). Krogh summarizes theories of child development, explores multiple intelligences, and argues for integrated curriculum based on the interrelatedness of developmental domains. Teachers who understand stages of development, individual differences, and how the brain processes knowledge holistically will develop curriculum that engages children in meaningful processes through which they construct their own knowledge base. This chapter also discusses some misconceptions about musical aptitude, theoretical foundations of music education, current research about how young children learn music, and how to integrate music with other subjects.

Music may be the most used and least understood of all subjects in the early childhood curriculum; it is usually ignored as a talent for the select few or indulged as fun-time diversion. Musical illiteracy is all too often accepted as the norm. Howard Gardner, developmental psychologist at Harvard University, challenges such thinking. Gardner identifies music as one of seven basic human intelligences possessed by all normal individuals. Musical thinking requires the mind to behave in ways different from linguistic or mathematical thinking, and musical development is essential to the growth of the whole child. Helmut Moog, German researcher and educator, suggests that understanding music is as attainable for every child as is understanding speech and reading:

> Musicality . . . is not a special ability but is the application of general abilities to music. The same abilities which enable a person to distinguish differences between noises, . . . enable him also to distinguish similar differences in music. . . . The ability to experience music is just as firmly woven into the total fabric of potential human abilities as the potential for understanding speech, for reading, for motor skills, and so on. Therefore the achievements and effects of musicality can only be considered as part of the total structure of human abilities. (Moog, 1976, pp. 45–46)

Musical literacy should be the goal for every child, as is reading literacy. Music should be taught with the same diligence and attention as reading. We have a musically illiterate society because "we do not 'music' back to children the way we 'language' back to them" (Swanwick, 1988, p. 60). In other words, we have speakers and writers, but not "musicers"—a word coined by music philosopher David Elliot (1995) for those who compose or perform music. Think of how many sentences and paragraphs an infant hears by age 12 months compared to the number of songs or recorded symphonies the infant hears. We dote on tiny ones when they speak their first words and mimic back to them, but their first sung word may go unnoticed.

In American culture, as toddlers begin creating fascinating (to them) sounds with pots and pot lids, we chastise them for making a ruckus, sending the message that their natural interest in sound is bad. But in Africa, when a young Venda child bangs on a plate, an adult begins tapping a rhythm and makes music with the child (Blacking, 1990, p. 75). The expectation in the Venda culture is that all human beings are musically competent. Among the Anang of Nigeria, infants a week old are introduced to music and dance by their mothers. Fathers make small drums for their young children. By age 5, Anang children can sing hundreds of songs, play several percussion instruments, and perform dozens of intricate dance movements. Anthropologists who have studied the Anang claim never to have encountered a nonmusical member (Gardner, 1983). Examples such as these support Gardner's research and Moog's assertion that musicality "is not a special ability" but is as much a part of the human potential ability as is the potential for understanding speech, for reading, and for motor skills (Moog, 1976). All children are musical and their musical development is largely dependent on the musical environment they are provided from infancy.

While American culture often deprives infants and young children of adequate musical experiences, there is also a tendency to impose developmentally inappropriate formal musical instruction too soon. Because musical development begins in infancy, and the prekindergarten years may have the greatest impact on the musical development of the child (Gordon, 1988), some have concluded that formal instruction should begin in the preschool years, requiring children to adjust to a developmentally inappropriate, teacher-centered program of instruction. Such "training," based on adult expectations rather than children's natural ways of learning, may develop a narrow range of performance skills, but inevitably fails to provide a rich and creative musical experience that meets children's social, emotional, physical, and cognitive needs.

Recognizing the importance of developmentally appropriate musical experience, the Music Educators National Conference (MENC) recently published a position statement for teaching early childhood music. Table 5.1 contains a summary of MENC's beliefs concerning the musical learning of young children. The position statement of MENC also established guidelines to help early childhood caregivers plan appropriate curriculum (table 5.2). In response to the challenge of Goals 2000: Educate America Act, MENC has established criteria (see table 5.3) for creating curriculum that will help prepare children for the twenty-first century.

These documents, consistent with NAEYC's position statement on developmentally appropriate practice, reflect three basic principles:

• Age appropriateness, individual appropriateness, and context must be taken into account when planning music learning environments.
• Play is a primary vehicle for musical growth.

TABLE 5.1
MENC's Beliefs about Children's Musical Learning

1. All children have musical potential
2. Children bring their own unique interests and abilities to the learning environment
3. Very young children are capable of developing critical thinking skills through musical ideas
4. Children come to early childhood music experiences from diverse backgrounds
5. Children should expreience exemplary musical sounds, activities, and materials
6. Children should not be encumbered with the need to meet performance goals
7. Children's play is their work
8. Children learn best in pleasant physical and social environments
9. Diverse learning environments are needed to serve the developmental needs of many individual children
10. Children need effective adult models

Reprinted by permission from Music Educator's National Conference (MENC). *The school music program: A new vision* (p. 9) by MENC. Reston, VA: Author. Copyright 1994.

TABLE 5.2
MENC Curriculum Guidelines for Teaching Young Children

1. A music curriculum for young children should include many opportunities to explore sound through singing, moving, listening, and playing instruments as well as introductory experiences with verbalization and visualization of musical ideas.
2. The music literature included in the curriculum should be of high quality and lasting value, including traditional children's songs, folk songs, classical music, and music from a variety of cultures, styles, and time periods.
3. Play is the primary vehicle for young children's growth and developmentally appropriate early music experience should occur in child-initiated, child-directed, teacher-supported play environments.
4. The teacher's role is to create a musically stimulating environment and then to facilitate children's engagement with music materials and activities by asking questions or making suggestions that stimulate children's thinking and further exploitation.
5. Children also need group music time to experience the important social and musical aspects of sharing music and making music together.
6. Effective music teaching should
   a. support the child's total development—physical, emotional, social, and cognitive
   b. recognize the wide range of normal development in prekindergarteners and the need to differentiate their instruction
   c. facilitate learning through active interaction with adults and other children as well as with music materials
   d. consist of learning activities and materials that are real, concrete, and relevant to the lives of young children
   e. provide opportunities for children to choose from among a variety of music activities, materials, and equipment of varying degrees of difficulty
   f. allow children time to explore music through active involvement

Adapted and used, by permission, from Music Educators National Conference (MENC). *The school music program: A new vision* (pp. 9–10) by MENC. Reston, VA: Author. Copyright 1994.

- Every student should have access to a balanced, comprehensive, and sequential program of study in music.

The School Music Program (MENC, 1994a) and a related publication, *Opportunity-to-Learn Standards for Music Instruction: Grades PreK–12* (MENC, 1994b), identify kindergarten through grade 3 achievement standards and equipment standards for quality music programs.

TABLE 5.3
MENC Criteria for Creating Curriculum in Music

1. The music curriculum should be conceived not as a collection of activities but rather as a well-planned sequence of learning experiences leading to clearly defined skills and knowledge. The experiences should be challenging, but reflect the joy and personal satisfaction that are inherent in music. The purpose of studying music should be to enable young Americans to enhance the quality of their lives by participating fully in their musical culture.
2. The music should reflect the multi musical diversity of America's pluralistic culture and should be of the highest quality.
3. The curriculum should involve the students in improvisation and composition, as well as singing, playing instruments, and listening.
4. The curriculum should emphasize problem solving and higher-order thinking skills, taking students beyond the acquisition of facts toward the synthesis of knowledge.
5. Because effective learning is not subject to artificial boundaries traditionally separating subject matter in school, the music curriculum should emphasize relationships between the arts and disciplines outside the arts.
6. The music curriculum should utilize technology when appropriate in order to achieve objectives of music education.
7. Every school should develop valid and appropriate techniques for assessing student learning in music. Paper–pencil tests do not represent authentic assessment in music.

Adapted and used by permission from Music Educators National Conference (MENC). *The school music program: A new vision* (pp. 3–5) by MENC. Reston, VA: Author. Copyright 1994.

Theoretical Foundations for Developmental Music Instruction

The cognitive developmental approach, based on Piaget's study of young children's behaviors, has dominated the study of child development in recent years and stimulated research in how music is learned. Piaget concluded that individuals try to make sense of the world beginning in infancy, and through interaction with objects, they construct meaning. Through time and experience, children develop increasingly abstract and logical forms of thinking. Thus, similar sets of logical rules (stages) develop in all children. (An overview of the ages and stages are outlined by Krogh in chapter 2.)

Howard Gardner supports the idea that children construct their own meaning, but he challenges Piaget for focusing only on logical-rational thinking, giving scant attention to the thought processes of artists, writers, musicians, and athletes, or to intuition or creativity (Gardner, 1979). Gardner believes that musical thought processes are different from logical-rational thinking. Interacting with aesthetic objects, children not only construct patterns of thought, but experience new configurations of *feelings*. Or, as Bunting puts it, "musical rhythms and tensions seem to mirror the flow of feeling within us in a direct, non-verbal and non-illustrative way. Most of us would consider this music's most important quality and it is not a thinking process but a feeling one" (Swanwick, 1988, p. 65).

Gardner (1994) proposes three interactive systems:

- Making system: the learner produces or acts as a composer or performer
- Perceiving system: the learner becomes a discriminating listener
- Feeling system: the learner experiences affective responses

Development is a process in which the degree of interaction among the three systems gradually increases, and includes the acquisition and use of symbols.

According to Gardner, Piaget also neglects the content of children's thinking as a consequence of their environment. Gardner suggests that the environment may not be as neutral and passive as Piaget implies. Rather, the environment stimulates and suggests, actually shaping thought (Gardner, 1979).

Gardner's theory of multiple intelligences asserts there are at least seven different ways of processing information. Music is one of these discrete intelligences. (For a description of each intelligence, see Krogh, chapter 2.) Gardner defines melody, rhythm, and timbre as the core elements of music and suggests that the affective aspects of music might also be considered close to music's core (Gardner, 1983, p. 105). In fact, according to Gardner, affect may be the central puzzle surrounding music. We don't completely understand the emotional factors of music, but we know they exist, just as we know that the quality of love transferred by the care given to the child is important in building trust, security, and comfort. An understanding of these phenomena may eventually explain "the general qualities and states crucial in artistic activity" (Gardner, 1994, p. 97).

Piaget's and Gardner's works are important because they provide us with theories on which to base our teaching. From Piaget we learn that teachers do not teach children music; rather, children construct their own musical meaning and must pass through certain developmental stages. Gardner points out that children create musical knowledge differently from other kinds of information processing and that environments have significant impact on the quality and kind of thinking that takes place in the learner. Musical stages may be fewer and more influenced by environment than Piaget would suggest. More research needs to be done in order to fully know how children gain musical knowledge. However, the research that has been done gives enough information to guide teachers in preparing developmentally appropriate teaching experiences.

Research on Musical Development in Early Childhood

Musical development includes learning concepts about the basic components of music (melody, rhythm, timbre, and form) through musical behaviors or skills (singing, playing instruments, creating, moving, listening, and symbolizing musical sounds). All musical concepts and skills can and should be explored at all age levels, but in developmentally appropriate ways. For example, infants experience melodic high and low sounds through vocal play and listening to others sing, while 6-year-olds can describe high and low melodic directions and write notation for them. It is not possible to learn about the basic components without being involved in the musical skills and vice versa, although for discussion purposes it is helpful to separate them. Table 5.4 illustrates the relationship between musical behaviors and musical components. The blank boxes created by the matrix provide space for the caregiver to describe developmentally appropriate activities that children might do while experiencing ideas about the musical components.

An overall summary of what the research says about musical skill development and related conceptual awareness of music components will be outlined next, followed by a more detailed outline of the research and implications for developmentally appropriate practice.

Singing

The earliest "singing" occurs when infants respond to musical sounds, and has been termed "musical babble." This babbling is the precursor

TABLE 5.4
Musical Behaviors and Components

Music Components (including ideas to learn about each)	Music Behaviors				
	Sing	Play Inst./ Sound Exp.	Listen/ Move	Create/ Improvise	Verbalization/ Visualization (symbols)
Melody • up/down • high/low • steps/skips • pitches can sound at same time creating harmony					
Rhythm • long/short • steady beat • beats sounded or silent • beats strong or weak • combinations of long and short sounds create rhythm patterns					
Form • combinations of sounds form patterns called phrases, motives sections, etc. • patterns can be combined, repeated, constrasted, etc.					
Timbre • different sources produce different sounds • sources can be identified by their sound					

of spontaneous song (Moog, 1976), which begins around 18 months and develops over the second and third years. Initially, spontaneous songs seem to be nothing more than experimenting with pitch sounds. As spontaneous songs develop, they get longer and show signs of internal organization. Gardner calls these "outline songs" because they indicate that children have some awareness of the basic form of the song but have not filled in the melodic and rhythmic details. Outline songs are directly analogous to children's first drawings of people (the so-called tadpole man), which reveal their understanding of the human form but include no details (Hargreaves, 1986). Spontaneous songs are the most musically creative outputs of early singing development, and 4-year-olds' spontaneous songs show awareness of expression as they sing and play, changing speed, loudness, and other musical gestures that appear to emanate directly from the immediate feelings of the children. One child, for example, singing about the sunshine, used melodic melissma (many notes sung on one syllable) on the word "shine," with no apparent awareness, just an outpouring of her feelings at the moment (Swanwick, 1988). Spontaneous songs soon develop into what Moog calls potpourri songs, in which pieces of learned songs begin to appear. A child may be singing a free-flowing melody with nonsense words, for example, then add E I E I O from "Old McDonald."

By 28 months, toddlers sing the words of learned songs, usually with correct rhythm and melodic contour but not accurate melodic intervals. Children do not typically have a sense of tonality, and thus total pitch accuracy through a song, until around age 7 or 8. Hargreaves says this process from musical babble to accurate song production is precisely analogous to Piaget's account of the processes of assimilation and accommodation. The child's music babble is purely exploration and enjoyment of sound. The babble gradually turns into spontaneous songs, songs the child *assimilates* from the environment into his or her own reality as indicated by nonsense words, inaccurate rhythms, and melodic contours, but not exact pitches. As the child fills in more parts of the song, he or she begins to *accommodate* to the environmental songs, eventually singing standard tunes. The development of song acquisition is dependent on hearing many songs in the environment. The environment begins to influence song development at birth.

Five-year-olds know many songs but typically still do not sing with melodic accuracy for the entire song. Most research indicates that as 5-year-olds learn new songs, they first learn the words, followed by rhythm, then melodic contour, and finally intervals (Davidson, 1985; Moog, 1976). However, one study indicated that while children with less musical experience proceed in the order suggested, those from musical families tended to begin with melodic contour, followed by rhythm, followed by words (Kelley & Sutton-Smith, 1987). This study suggests that when children hear more music in their daily lives, they produce more musical responses at earlier ages.

Listening and Moving

Music is an aural art and perceptive listening is the essence of musical intelligence (McDonald & Simons, 1989). There is evidence that children hear music before birth (Shetler, 1989) and infants respond to musical sounds very early as demonstrated by vocal babbling and movement. Moog (1976) has done one of the most extensive studies on young children's musical behaviors and his findings on listening and movement behaviors of children from 6 months to 5.5 years are summarized here. Infants move in response to music and as they develop, swaying and bouncing become evident. Around 18 months, children move less and show more focused listening and their movements include spinning, clapping, tapping, and moving in larger spaces. By 3 years, greater coordination in movements is demonstrated and more use of arms independent from body, but children this age do not clap or march easily to the musical beat. Three-year-olds love to dance with others and to participate in singing games as do older children. From 4 to 6 years, spontaneous movements decline as children show an increase in clapping and marching to the beat. However, 5-year-olds can imitate rhythm patterns by chanting easier than by clapping, and 6-year-olds find it easier to imitate if they chant while clapping (Schleuter & Schleuter, 1985). Gilbert (1981) developed a test to measure motoric music skill development (MMST) and found that improvements were age-related, and that the gain of 4-year-olds on all five subtests (motor pattern coordination, eye–hand coordination, speed of movement, range of movement, and compound factors) was greater than that of 7-year-olds. Gilbert's research supports the claim that most fundamental motor patterns emerge by age 5 and that skills are merely stabilized beyond that point. Gilbert also noted that girls did better than boys on the motor pattern coordination, eye–hand coordination, and compound factors subtests. Providing many opportunities for movement and movement instruction at age 4, especially for boys, may have significant impact on musical expression when children are older. However, care should be taken not to demand that young children synchronize their clapping to the beat before they are ready.

Taste for music appears to develop early. Children as young as 6 months have shown affective responses to music and research indicates infants show a definite preference for beautiful music (Moog, 1976). Until age 4.5, children seem to like all kinds of music, but by age 5, preferences for certain kinds of music begin to surface, with popular music preferred (Peery & Peery, 1986). This is not surprising, considering that in most cases, children hear more popular music than any other kind. This preference becomes more established with age. Peery and Peery found that if children are exposed to classical music weekly, they maintain a preference for all kinds of music, even after age of 5, suggesting that children's listening values are influenced more by environment and teaching than by age.

Playing Instruments

In the first few months of life, infants begin to intentionally make sounds by hitting or kicking. They seem to be fascinated with sound and their ability to control it. As infants become mobile, they tap drums, xylophones, pots, and pans, their playing driven by motor energy and fascination with extremes in dynamic level. This is a time of exploration and experimentation (Swanwick, 1988). By 3, children begin to create patterns through repetition of ideas and by 5, steady beat emerges (Moog, 1976). Children around 5 years are also interested in "the right way" to play simple instruments as they become more conscious of social behaviors. Their compositions may be long and rambling on drums or xylophones and will often repeat a pattern several times before moving on. At 7 children are still interested in improvising melodies on instruments, and often attempt to end their creations on the tonal center (Kratus, 1985). Children use simple instruments as naturally as blocks or paints. They experiment with them in many ways and use the knowledge they gain to create expressive music (Moorhead & Pond, 1978). Children up to 8 years old still need many opportunities to freely explore playing simple percussion instruments.

Creating

Infants first create with music babble and sound play, and most all preschool music behaviors involve creative production. As children get older, their creating becomes more sophisticated. Swanwick (1988) defines compositions as the act of assembling music, and suggests that in order for composition to take place there must be "some freedom to choose the ordering of music, with or without notational or other forms of detailed performance instruction" (p. 60). In one study, Swanwick and his colleagues gave children ranging in age from 3 to 9 several different kinds of percussion instruments and asked them to make music. Their "compositions" were recorded and then studied. Swanwick found that children of 3 and 4 showed a keen interest in very soft and very loud sounds. They experimented with short and long sounds and fingers and fists on surfaces of drums. Their primary concern was with the tone and resonance of the instruments. Children 4 and 5 tended to create compositions that were influenced by the type of the instruments they explored. Tunes went up and down on the xylophone, for example, and trills resulted on the drum when mallets were bounced using two hands. Their interest in these effects led them to repeat musical fragments many times and to ramble. Four- and 5-year-olds begin to show signs of musical expression, especially in their songs. A child may make sounds on instruments to express feelings such as anger, by making loud sounds on the drum, but children this age do not typically use sound to represent something outside themselves such as thunder. Six-year-old compositions reveal the child's attempts to imitate conventional music patterns. Much of the creative spontaneity appears to be lost as children try to copy standard songs.

Another important study on creative music behaviors emphasizes the importance of free exploration, time, and quality instruments. Moorhead and Pond (1978) worked with children ages 2 through 6. The play space was furnished with several different instruments including drums of different kinds, gongs and xylophones, as well as a record library and machine to play the recordings. The children were free to explore at will along with the usual preschool equipment (blocks, paints, playhouse, etc.). Moorhead and Pond's research led them to some conclusions about the kind of environment necessary for creative acts to take place: (1) children need freedom and time to explore and make sounds appropriate to them; (2) if music is to become a language for children, they must not only hear it, but make it on their own by constant use, just as they do language; (3) creativity often occurs in spontaneous play activities; and (4) improvisation is the key to musical creative development.

Gardner (1991) believes that the products of children's early music play provide the "the roots of creativity" for adult creative production. "The tunes and dances of the young singer-dancer contain important aspects of adult human creativity in the arts." He suggests that the spontaneous creative behaviors go underground during "the literal years" of middle childhood, and that this is the time for "skill building" when children most appropriately acquire the competencies necessary for adult creative production. If the early years provide a rich environment for creative musical exploration, and the years of middle childhood provide rich opportunity for children to study and practice basic musical skills, the two will come together to produce adult compositions.

Developmentally Appropriate Practices

To meet the unique needs and interests of individual children, Andress (1995) suggests that appropriate early learning classrooms must provide three kinds of music environments:

1. Use music throughout the day to enhance the teaching of other subjects.
2. Provide special music centers where children are free to interact with musical materials, including instruments and recordings.
3. Provide adult-guided group music play where children come together to sing, play instruments, listen to, and learn about music in a cooperative setting.

Experiences in all three musical environments are important if the child is to have a well-rounded music education. The following is organized by age for convenience, although musical behaviors overlap age boundaries. Research concerning typical music behaviors for each age is given with suggested teaching strategies or environments appropriate for the developmental level.

The First Year—Pleasure and Mastery of Sound

Play is intrinsically bound up with all artistic activity (Swanwick, 1988). During the first year of life, musical play is characterized by the sheer pleasure of exploring and mastering the sound environment. Infants 5 days old have been shown to discriminate between pitches and rhythm patterns (Bridger, 1961), and be calmed by music in their environment (Brackbill et al., 1966). By one month, infants produce sounds that have melodic structures and rhythms, and 2-month-old infants can match pitch and melodic contour of songs sung by the mother (Papousek & Papousek, 1981; Kessen, Levine, & Wendrich, 1979). Infants as young as 3 months show a desire to manipulate and control sounds and seem to delight in the sounds they make (Papousek & Papousek, 1981). Noy (1968) suggests that because infants do not understand language, the first aural communication is not words, but sound, which consists of intensity, pitch, rhythm, and timbre, the basic components of music. In other words, language is music to the new-born. If music (including language) is a primary mode of communication between the child and mother in infancy, Noy believes that music will continue to be important in the child's emotional exchange with the world.

Active (as opposed to passive) music listening begins during the first 6 months of life and precedes active seeing. Remplein, a German writer on child development, calls the first 5 months of life an "age of listening" (Moog, 1976).

MUSICAL BEHAVIORS	APPROPRIATE PRACTICE
Singing	
Musical babbling occurs sometime during the first year, and is distinguished from nonmusical babbling in that it always occurs as a specific response to music. Babies explore a wide range of pitches, and by the 8th month, infants often try to join in singing with the caregiver (Moog, 1976; McDonald & Simons, 1989).	Sing many songs while cuddling, rocking, or facing the baby. Songs include lullabies, folk songs from the culture, and folk song games that involve patting the baby's hands, feet, back, or tummy to the rhythms of the music, such as "Patty Cake" or "Shoe the Little Horse." (See Forrai, 1988; Feierabend, 1986; and Thurman & Langness, 1986

Papousek and Papousek (1981) suggest that vocal imitation of the infant by the caregiver may be crucial in the development of vocal imitation and thus singing. A study by Kucenski showed that before age one, children can distinguish individual songs from their actions, suggesting that acquisition of songs may begin before babies learn to sing (McDonald & Simons, 1989). Singing is associated with pleasurable interaction with adults. Range of pitches has been recorded at more than three octaves in infant vocal play (Papousek & Papousek, 1981).

for collections of English folk songs and activities to use with infants and toddlers.) Honig (1995) also outlines singing activities and suggests using folk songs from other cultures. Listen to the musical vocal play of the infant, then imitate the sounds in conversation back to the baby. Describe the sounds with language. For example, in response to a high squeal, you might say, "You love to sing high, don't you? I can sing high, too." Chant nursery rhymes while gently bouncing the baby to the beat and rhythm patterns of the rhyme. Communicate to parents about this important time for their infant. Parent classes, newsletters, or tapes of folk songs and lullabies should be made available to parents so they can learn about the importance of singing with their infant.

Listening/Moving

By 8 months, infants initiate rhythmic movement responses to music (McDonald & Simon, 1989; Moog, 1976). Children's musical preferences are being formed at this time and are dependent on the kinds of music they hear.

Expose children to a wide variety of recorded music, including classics of the Western world and folk music from cultures around the world. Include choral as well as orchestral music, solo singers, unaccompanied singing, and solo instrumentalists. As music plays, gently rock, bounce, or dance with the baby or pat baby's hands or feet to the beat or rhythms of the music. Refrain from sudden loud sounds and movements that might frighten the infant. Consider playing classical music each time the baby goes to sleep. Find ways to communicate to parents about the importance of sharing recordings of great music with their infants.

Playing Instruments

Infants do not play instruments in the traditional sense, but they delight in making sounds by hitting, kicking, and shaking rattles and other sound-making objects (Papousek & Papousek, 1981).

Provide safe toys that make sounds children can control. Several rattles that make different sounds, bells attached to socks, or objects that hang from a mobile that make sounds when kicked or touched should be a part of the environment. Toys that make sounds without requiring the infant to touch them such as music boxes may stimulate the infant's listening, but do not allow the baby to control and manipulate the sounds.

Toddlers—Control and Imitation of Sound

As children enter their 2nd year, an important shift in musical growth occurs (Moog, 1976; Swanwick, 1988). Children begin to reproduce what they hear, moving from the delight of making sounds that dominated their musical behaviors the 1st year, to controlling sound. Toddlers are becoming more aware of past and future, which makes memory possible. Because music exists only in time, acquisition of memory is important in order for children to begin to sing songs. The toddler years are important for children to acquire many songs and to hear many different kinds of music, for the music that is heard and put in the memory becomes the material from which later musical creativity and understanding grow.

BEHAVIORS   APPROPRIATE PRACTICE

Singing

Sometime during the 2nd year, children begin to sing spontaneous, self-created songs (Moog, 1976) which continue to develop over the 2nd and 3rd years. This is one of the most creative times of musical expression in the young child. As toddlers continue to hear singing, they begin to incorporate parts of learned songs into their spontaneous singing play.

The vocal range of children's singing seems to depend on the vocal range of the caregiver. In other words, toddlers will make the sounds they continue to hear from low Ab to high G (Moog, 1976).

Children love rhythmic chant, poems, and rhymes and seem more interested in the flow of the words than in their meaning (Moog 1976).

Continue to sing songs to children. Sing old songs they already know, and new songs. Short folk songs from the culture with many repetitions encourage the child to begin to imitate the songs. Sing in the high range of the voice to encourage the child to develop full vocal range. As the child begins speaking, the lower part of the voice is used. If singing in the higher voice is not continued, the child may lose flexibility in the higher voice.

Chant nursery rhymes and poems while bouncing, patting, or rocking the child. Create centers where children are free to explore spontaneous singing as well as singing of songs they have heard (Kenney, 1989).

Provide opportunities for children to see music notation for the songs they sing, helping them understand that music can be represented by symbols.

Listening/Moving

Toddlers attempt to match their movements to the music rhythm,

In addition to moving with the child while singing and chanting swaying, rocking, or bouncing. These active movements do not last for long. As the children begin listening more intently, they become more still and their listening is more focused. When they do move, they show greater variety in their movements and seem to have a feeling for themselves in space as they twirl around filling an empty room (Hargreaves, 1986; Moog, 1976).

rhymes, play a variety of music, allowing child to move freely as the music plays. Also hold toddlers while swaying or dancing to music. As the child becomes more mobile, more open space is needed to allow freedom of movement. Include a wide variety of music, encouraging the child to express differences in fast or slow music by the way he or she moves. Respect the children who wish to listen without moving. Ask one child to walk, clap, or jump. Tap a drum, matching the rhythm of the child's movements. Begin to name instruments heard on recordings.

Playing Instruments

When playing instruments, children up to age 3 are driven by motor energy, showing fascination with extremes in dynamic levels. There is much exploration and experimentation with sound (Flohr, 1985; Swanwick, 1988).

Provide many sound sources for this age, including drums of various sizes and kinds; sounds made from wood such as xylophones, wood blocks, temple blocks, and slit drums; metal sounds such as glockenspiels, resonator bells, triangles, and cymbals; and sounds that rattle, such as maracas, guiros, sand blocks, and cabasa. If possible, include percussion instruments from different cultures such as gamelon from Bali, steel drum from Jamaica, etc. Help children understand the importance of taking care of instruments, but

allow time and freedom for
children to explore and
experiment (Kenney, 1995).
Encourage exploration by
labeling sounds the child makes
("You made a very loud sound")
and suggesting other possibilities
("I wonder if you could make a
fast sound that is very soft").
Build vocabulary by naming the
instruments and the kinds of
sounds children make (short,
long, loud, soft, fast, slow, high,
low, etc.).

Three-Year-Olds—Musical Doodling

Ross (in Swanwick, 1988) identifies the period beginning at age 3 and
continuing until around age 7 as the time when children master sound
structures and patterns from the culture. It is also, Ross explains, a time
characterized by "musical doodling," especially vocally. Spontaneous
and potpourri songs become longer and are incorporated into imaginative play. The variety in singing is a sign of lively intellectual activity and
is the result of past experiences with songs. This is the age when it
becomes apparent that children who have had singing and song games
in their environment during the first 3 years have a clear advantage over
other children. Moog's research shows that children who do not sing
parts of learned songs by age 3 did not have the opportunity or
encouragement to sing spontaneous songs at an earlier age.

BEHAVIORS	APPROPRIATE PRACTICE
	Singing
Spontaneous and potpourri songs become longer and more sophisticated. Children incorporate music and singing into imaginative play, using music to help form social	Sing many folk and traditional songs that contain repetitive patterns. Place musical materials in learning centers to stimulate singing. A bell placed on the table in the kitchen center may

relationships. They love singing and round games where they dance with others (Moog, 1976).

prompt a child to sing "Jingle Bells" while fixing dinner. "Jingle Bells" may develop into a lengthy potpourri song. Include songs with games and movements that allow children to play together, but do not expect children to understand rules. (See Richards 1985, for song game ideas.) Sing spontaneous songs in conversation with children, using their names and describing their activities (Andress, 1980; Honig, 1995). Include singing centers in the room with books, toys, and tapes of simple folk songs that encourage children to sing while they play (Kenney, 1989). Encourage children to use the high part of their voice by modeling singing using the higher voice. Keep parents informed about songs children are learning. Provide copies of songs in the book center to help children learn that music can be represented by symbols.

Listening/Moving

Physical responses decline as attentive listening increases. The variety of movements increases, but coordination does not seem to improve at this age (Moog, 1976). Echo clapping and marching are difficult for this age group (Frega, 1979; Rainbow, 1981), but children can imitate rhythms with their

Provide a listening center with a tape recorder children can start and stop themselves. Include recordings of many kinds of music. Invite children to walk, run, jump, and freeze as an adult accompanies the rhythm of the movements on a drum or piano. Play singing games with the children.

voice or rhythm sticks. Threes like to dance with others but may not initiate getting a partner. They love to participate in round dances and are more willing to participate in singing games than in games without music (Moog, 1976)

Invite musicians to play orchestral instruments for the children. Identify sounds of instruments as recorded music plays.

Playing Instruments

Three-year-olds continue to show great interest in sound and their ability to make it. Their motor energy becomes more controlled and they begin to create patterns through repetition of rhythmic ideas characterized by even rhythms. Some attempt to imitate patterns made by adults (Flohr, 1985).

Provide many opportunities for children to explore instruments. A music center that contains a few instruments is important during free play time (Kenney, 1989). Children enjoy playing imitative games with a caregiver who enters the play, models musical behaviors, then leaves them to explore on their own (Andress, 1980). Continue to explore ideas suggested for toddlers.

Four- and 5-Year-Olds—Taking on the Culture

As children enter their 5th year, they become more conscious of the correct way to sing songs from the environment. Most have a standard repertoire of nursery songs, but they do not yet sing entire songs with total pitch accuracy (Hargreaves, 1986). Davidson (1985) calls songs learned by children this age "first draft" songs because children have better command of the words, rhythm, underlying beat, and melody than younger children, but do not yet sing songs with tonal accuracy until the end of the 6th or into the 7th year. If they have not learned many songs prior to this time, they will tend not to sing (Moog, 1976). By age 5, music preferences are already formed (McDonald & Simons, 1989; Peery & Peery, 1986), but preferences can be changed when caregivers share love for different kinds of music. Children 4 and 5 are beginning to conceptualize ideas such as high–low, loud–soft, and so on when describing sounds, and can walk, jog, and gallop in response to musical cues. Spontaneous singing still occurs when children are engaged in child-centered play. Children are very interested in exploring percussion instruments such as temple blocks and xylophones and will produce long, rambling tunes as they explore extremes in pitch, patterns of rhythm, and repetition.

MUSICAL BEHAVIORS	APPROPRIATE PRACTICE

Singing

Spontaneous singing is more expressive, showing variations in speed and loudness, and comes from the immediate feelings of the child without prior planning (Swanwick, 1988). Pitches may extend two octaves in spontaneous songs. When singing learned songs, words and rhythm are correct, but pitch is inconsistent throughout the song (Moog, 1976). Children match pitches in learned songs from about D to A above middle C (McDonald & Simons, 1989). Children this age love to chant and can echo pitch patterns sung by the teacher. However, there is no correlation between echoing pitch patterns and maintaining a tonality when singing a song, which indicates these are separate skills in young children (Flowers & Dunne-Sousa, 1990).

Play vocal exploration games that help children locate the full extent of their vocal range. Imitate sirens, animal sounds, and other sounds. Encourage children to speak parts in stories such as The Three Bears, speaking very high for Baby Bear, low for Papa Bear, and so on (Kenney, 1989).
Continue to sing simple folk and traditional songs that contain repeated melodic patterns. Sing the songs in a range above middle C.
Exaggerate dynamics to express ideas. For example, sing lullabies softly to help the baby go to sleep. When singing about trains, begin softly as though the train is far away, then louder as the train gets closer.
Encourage musical problem solving by asking children to decide which dynamic level and speed would be most appropriate to create the appropriate effect.

Listening/Moving

Children show fewer spontaneous movements when listening to music than when younger, but the ability to clap in time to recorded music increases. It is still easier for 4- and 5-year-olds to clap to their own singing than to clap to recorded music. Children are showing a greater ability to echo clap and clap and march in time to music (Frega, 1979; Rainbow, 1981).

Four-year-olds still show preference for all kinds of music, but 5-year-olds prefer popular music if that is the music they have heard the most. However, taste is still developing and when an adult shows approval of listening to certain music, preference can be changed.

Play examples of many musical styles from many historical periods and many cultures. Play the same music several times so children become familiar with it. Remember this is an important time for establishing taste in music. Children will tend to love what they perceive the adults in their environment love. Set a model that will give the children a broad base of music preference. Invite children to perform locomotor movements that express rhythms played by an adult on piano or drums. (See Aronoff, 1992, for movement ideas.)

Listen to instruments and identify by sound. Provide opportunities for children to see real instruments as well as pictures.

Playing Instruments

As children approach 5, they are interested in learning how to play simple instruments. They enjoy improvising on instruments such as xylophones and drums. Their compositions tend to be long and rambling and will often repeat a rhythmic or melodic pattern several times before moving on in an arbitrary way to the next possibility. Steady beat begins to emerge when improvising, and so does a

Create a music center where children can practice playing instruments and have freedom to explore their own rambling compositions and steady beat. Include a variety of sounds. Caregivers need to move in and out of centers, modeling appropriate exploratory behaviors. Caregivers might also begin to label sounds the children make, using words such as high sounds, low, fast, slow, sense of tonality. Children this age can imitate exactly patterns given by an adult (Flohr, 1985).

steady beat, melody, and so on. Tap four-beat rhythm patterns and invite children to echo clap or play patterns on instruments. Burton and Hughes (1979) have identified several activities for guiding children's sound exploration and listening. Some children this age may enjoy writing down some of their compositions using their own ideas for written symbols.

Six-, 7-, and 8-Year-Olds—Embracing the Culture

The main developmental trend in music with children up to age 10 seems to be the increasing reflective awareness of the structures and patterns that characterize music and which are already in the child's experience. The progress from experiential knowledge to reflective knowledge does not take place all at once, and various aspects of musical awareness become evident in different children at different ages throughout the middle years of childhood (Sloboda 1985). Six-, 7-, and 8-year-old children still benefit from exploratory musical experiences as suggested for 5-year-olds, but many are developmentally ready for more reflective music study. Children should begin to use traditional music notation when singing and composing. A music specialist is an important part of the education team to direct musical development for these children.

BEHAVIORS

APPROPRIATE PRACTICE

Singing

Children are becoming more aware of tonality and many are matching pitches with more accuracy. Goetze discovered that some children who sing accurately alone do not sing accurately when in a group (Goetze, 1985).

Continue singing folk and traditional songs. Be supportive and encouraging, and give children opportunities to sing alone. Help children expand their singing range with activities as suggested for 4s and 5s. Sing

Children are very conscious of the "right" way to sing, and, they may not want to sing if they have not had a lot of singing experience. Singing range is from around middle C to high D, depending on experience (McDonald & Simons, 1989).

songs in range higher than speaking voice. Play many moving games while singing. The games provide physical energy and help children feel more comfortable singing. Encourage children to create their own ideas about how they would visually represent the song's melody or rhythm. This is also the time to help children learn to read and write standard notation. Consult with a music specialist for guidance in preparing sequential music lessons.

Listening/Moving

These children may not feel comfortable moving spontaneously when listening to music, but enjoy moving with teacher direction. Most can keep a beat when clapping with music. These children are growing in ability to skip and perform other locomotor movements and enjoy musical accompaniments to their moving. Children can also move in response to notation for the locomotor movements. Age and experience impact on children's ability to attend and to discriminate duration, loudness, rhythm patterns, pitch, and tonal patterns (Peery & Peery, 1987).

Play music of many kinds. Provide opportunities for children to hear all kinds of music in a joyful setting. Continue to have children walk, jog, skip, slide, or freeze to musical cues from piano or drum. After children have demonstrated their understanding of these rhythms, show charts with symbols for each (figure 5.1).

Discuss names of composers. Put on skits about the lives of composers and about people from different places as you sing and listen to their music. Encourage children to conduct the music. Help children notice patterns in the music, including parts that repeat. Help children identify instruments by their

FIGURE 5.1
Music Symbol Charts Representing Rhythms of Basic Locomotor Movements

sounds. Play listening games using a book like *Polar Bear Polar Bear* by Martin (1991). Make sounds with instruments hidden behind a box and let children guess the sound. (See Burton & Hughes, 1979, for more ideas.)

Playing Instruments

Children love to explore sounds and improvise on musical instruments. They can use instrument sounds to express ideas, but are also eager to learn "how to play" instruments.

Provide free time each week for children to explore instruments. Encourage compositions. Record the compositions, and encourage children to try to write down what they have played. Allow them to invent their own symbols for the sounds they make, and begin to help children understand

traditional notation. Consult a
music specialist for guidance in
creating sequential music
lessons.

Integrating Music in the Curriculum

The inclusion of music in the curriculum as a discrete way of thinking
and experiencing provides the learner with one more way to construct
knowledge. It gives the brain more data from which it will integrate
internally.

The next section of this chapter explores ways for integrating music
into each curriculum area. Two approaches will be explored: (1) how
lessons in subjects other than music can support musical development;
and (2) how music can support development in other curriculum
areas.

The most obvious way to integrate music into the curriculum is by
singing. Words in songs can reinforce almost any subject. Singing
about a subject such as trains is one way to use music in the curriculum. However, care must be taken to recognize that even young
children can and should be developing musical skills and understanding. When planning to use music in change to a lesson, the
teacher might ask in what way the lesson can support musical
development of the child. For example, if singing about a train, the
children might move to the beat while singing. By adding a "whistle"
sound to begin the song, the children could locate their higher singing
voice before actually singing. The "people train" might begin with a
few "choo-choo's" starting slow and gradually getting faster in
preparation for singing. The song then becomes not only a joyful way
to enhance learning about trains, but an opportunity to practice
feeling the beat, experiencing the concept of accelerando, and feeling
the high voice in the whistle. A web may help teachers plan ways to
incorporate musical behaviors into their lessons. The following webs
show ways to integrate musical behaviors (figure 5.2) or basic music
components (figure 5.3) with a typical theme. Ideally, a music or arts
specialist could be consulted to help with the planning so that each
music experience is developmentally appropriate.

FIGURE 5.2
A Theme Web Integrating Music Behaviors

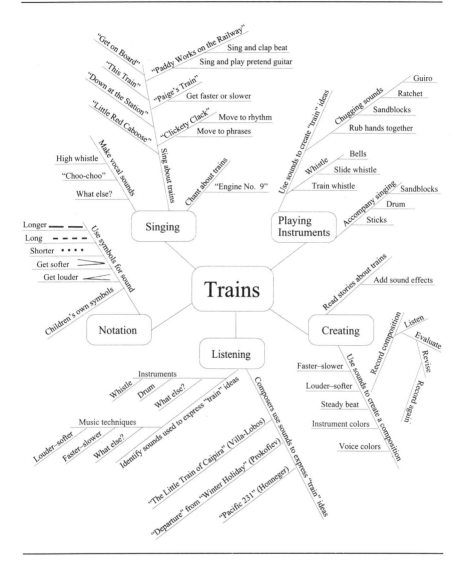

Another way of integrating music into the curriculum is to ask how music can support development in other curriculum areas. Many studies substantiate the notion that music experiences benefit other areas of personal, social, and intellectual development (Peery, 1993).

FIGURE 5.3
A Theme Web Integrating Music Components

MELODY	RHYTHM	FORM
• Hands can indicate whether a melody goes up or down or whether a sound is high or low • Hands can play tunes that go up or down on the xylophone. • Composers can write songs about hands. • You can write a song about hands.	• Hands can clap long and short sounds. • Hands can clap rhythm patterns. • Hands can play rhythms on many different instruments. • Hands can stop clapping on silent beats. • Hands can play steady beats. • Hands can play strong and weak beats in a pattern of three (strong, weak, weak; strong, weak, weak), or a pattern of four. • Hands can keep the beat while you sing. • Hands can conduct the music.	• Hands can play the drum during one part of the song, and play the triangle on another part of the song. • Jim's hands can create a pattern on the xylophone and Jill's hands can create a pattern on the drum. When Jim plays his part followed by Jill playing her part, they create a two-part song.

HANDS

TIMBRE	DYNAMICS
• Hands can make many different sounds. They can rub, tap, and clap in different ways. • What else can hands do? • Hands can make sounds on instruments made of metal or wood or drums. • Which sounds would your hands use to wake up a baby? which to imitate a train? which to express the wind? etc.	• Hands can make loud or soft sounds to express ideas. • Hands can make sounds that begin soft and get louder. Loud and soft sounds are used to express ideas. • How would you express the idea of rain with your hands? thunder? • Can you make the sounds of a rainstorm using your hands?

The material that follows may stimulate further thinking about the value of music for total child development and its importance in the integrated curriculum.

Music and Language

Songs carry language and actually intensify the rhythms and melodic structure of words, phrases, and sentences. Therefore, each time children hear or sing a song, they are experiencing vocabulary, phrase and sentence structures, and rhythmic and melodic flow of language. Hundreds of picture books containing songs are currently on the market. After children have learned a song by rote ("Old McDonald," for example), they can then "read" the words to the song in a picture book of the same name. Picture song books are an important addition to a book center. (For typical examples, see Aliki, 1968, 1986; Aylesworth & Christelow, 1990; Hale, 1984; Janovitz, 1991; Jones, 1989; and Peek, 1985.)

After learning a song such as "Eensy Weensy Spider," children might draw pictures of the events in the story, making a four-page book, one for each phrase (figure 5.4). The teacher could write the words to the song under each picture. Their books could be placed in the book center for other children to "read" and sing. Other songs that lend themselves to homemade books include, "This Old Man," "The Old Grey Cat" (in Andress, 1980), and "The Farmer in the Dell."

FIGURE 5.4
Picture Book of Song Phrases

Eensy Weensy Spider went up the water spout	Down came the rain and washed the spider out	Out came the sun and dried up all the rain	and the Eensy Weensy Spider went up the spout again

Drawing by Cornelia Liebscher

Because songs carry language, they are useful for studying parts of speech. When children know "Roll that Brown Jug Down to Town," invite them to change all the nouns in the song. *Jug* might be changed to *ball, town* to *the driveway, morning* to *winter.* Next change the adjectives, *brown* to *big, early* to *late.* Then work on the verbs. *Roll* might change to *throw.* The changes could go on and on. Children delight in the nonsense they might create or in the new story the song tells. Pictures could be drawn of their final version. Try this with other simple folk songs such as "The Farmer in the Dell" or "London Bridge." (For copies of songs suggested in this section, see Richards, 1985.)

Create new words to old favorites. When children have learned "Sally Go Round the Sun," invite them to make up a song about each class member using "Sally's" melody. Examples might include: *Bill climbed up a mountain, Bill climbed up a tree, Bill climbed up a flag pole, then fell and hurt his knee;* or *Janet slipped on the ice, Janet slipped on the snow, Janet slipped on the sidewalk, then fell and stubbed her toe.* Write the words, illustrate, then read. Richards (1975) has created a set of booklets using songs to explore language in this way.

Explore ways of expressing language ideas using instruments. For example, after reading *In the Small, Small Pond* (Fleming, 1993), encourage children to find instrument sounds to express the idea of the tadpole's "wiggle, jiggle," or the lobster's "claws crack, click clack." If possible, visit a pond and record the sounds heard there. Listen to them, then try to replicate the sounds with instruments or voices. A similar experience could be explored using *Music in the Night* (Wilson, 1993), or *We're Going on a Bear Hunt* (Rosen & Oxenbury, 1989).

Music and Math/Science

The obvious opportunity to integrate music with math is to sing counting songs. Many exist and can be found in most song collections. Especially delightful are the counting song picture books (see, for example, Adams, 1974, 1979; Aruego & Dewey, 1989; Conover, 1976; and McCracken & McCracken, 1989). Putting words to music seems to aid memory and add enjoyment to the counting games. But at a deeper level, music and math share some of the same features. Sound, the basis of music, is the result of vibrations at different frequencies. The pitch (or frequency) of sound is affected by the nature of the vibrating material and its mass (length, thickness, density). The vibrations can be heard when a resonating material is present. Young children can explore vibration by plucking the strings of a guitar, by striking a drum with a mallet (rice on the drum head will bounce when the drum head vibrates), or by buzzing their lips. Many exciting discoveries can be made with sound exploration centers. Books such as *Science Fun with Drums, Bells and Whistles* (Wyler, 1987) can lead to further science/music experimentation.

Math and music share other features. Music is a result of the organization of sound in time. It is composed of patterns that may repeat, be reversed, or create a sequence or series of patterns. Musical phrases are organized in very balanced ways so that if a musical statement is made, another of equal value follows. Beats recur in patterns of strong and weak, creating measures that children can feel as they sing or listen. Beats and measures may be counted for further mathematical practice. Beats may be subdivided into equal parts of two or three, and rhythmic patterns may include many or few sounds, but the number of sounds must always fit within the space of one beat, thus setting up a sort of equals sign. In the case of music, the number of sounds is always in relation to the passing of time. On one side of the equals sign is the beat, which indicates the amount of time. On the other side of the equals sign are any given number of sounds, which must be faster or slower to equal the same amount of time as the beat. Of course young children do not understand all of this, but they can *feel* these relationships.

Singing games often involve acting out mathematical ideas. For example, the folk song "Oats and Beans and Barley Grow" establishes sets of objects that can be reordered in the song, emphasizing the idea that while the order of things may change, the total number in the set does not. To play the game, place three pictures on the table. Invite children to point to them while singing. During the third line of the song, rearrange the three pictures, then change the word order for the last line of the song (figure 5.5). The game also provides opportunity to classify items that grow. For example, sing about flowers, trees, birds, etc.

The Kodaly method of music instruction (Choksy, 1988), which encourages children to learn to read what they hear, suggests processes that have mathematical implications. Children are asked to count the

FIGURE 5.5
Studying Sets in a Song

Oats and Beans and Barley

Oats and beans and bar - ley grow.

Oats, and beans and bar - ley grow.

Nor you, nor I, nor an - y - one knows

How oats and beans and bar - ley grow.

Dogs and cats and cows grow

Dogs and cats and cows grow

Nor you nor I nor anyone knows how   (*child rearranges pictures*)

Cats and cows and dogs grow

number of phrases in a song, to count the number of beats in a phrase, and to determine how many sounds occur during each beat. For example, when children can feel six phrases in "Twinkle, Twinkle Little Star," and four beats in each phrase, they can then count the number of sounds heard during each beat. Symbols such as heart shapes to represent beats and stars to represent the sounds per beat help reinforce what the children feel (figure 5.6).

Music and Social Studies/Social and Emotional Development

Group song games offer great opportunity for social awareness and development. The song part of the game provides a structure in which

FIGURE 5.6
Counting Beats and Sounds in Songs

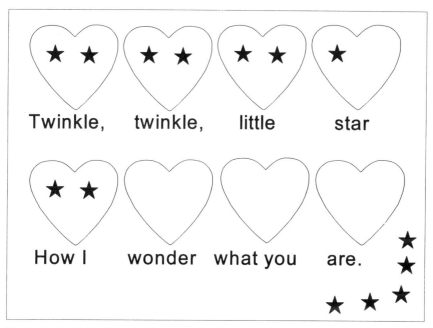

Tap the beat while singing to determine the number of beats (represented by hearts). Then listen to determine how many sounds occur on each beat. Put one star in the heart for each sound you hear.

to play. The games, depending on their complexity, provide opportunity for taking turns, working with partners, solving physical and social problems, creating rules when things aren't working well, touching, eye contact, leadership, stress release, and helping one another.

Folk songs from around the world help put children in touch with languages, behaviors, musical scales, and sounds from other cultures. Recordings of songs from other cultures are readily available and can be a part of every early childhood setting. Children can listen to songs, learn to sing them, and/or learn the games that may go with the folk songs.

Musicians might be invited into the classroom to perform and discuss their instruments. Children can write thank you notes to the visitors. A visit to an orchestra rehearsal might include the children interviewing the players and writing reports. The trip, including interviews, could be reported in a classroom newspaper.

Listening to orchestral music could lead to studying lives of great composers, where they lived, what they wore, what children did long ago, and so on.

Music and Physical Development

It is almost impossible for young children to hear music or to sing without moving. Music carries all the rhythms for locomotor movement. Walking, jogging, skipping, running, hopping, sliding, jumping can all be expressed in sound. The teacher might play any of these rhythms on a drum and invite children to match their movements to the drum. Or the teacher might ask a child to move and then match the drum to the movement. Children enjoy leading each other in such activities when a drum is placed in their play space after the teacher has demonstrated. In addition, many song games include locomotor movements as part of the game. Song games also explore small motor coordination, body parts, movement with partners, and movement in free space.

Recorded music provides children with opportunities to hear "the classics" while responding physically to waltzes, marches, slow sounds, fast sounds, loud sounds, and soft sounds. Children can practice "conducting" the orchestra and might enjoy conducting their own orchestra, if simple rhythm instruments are left in their place space.

When given the opportunity, children will organize their own orchestra, placing drum players together in one area, triangle players in another space, and wood block players next to the triangles. The orchestra players are practicing small motor coordination as they explore their instruments, and the conductor is gaining practice in coordinating movements. The opportunities for leadership and social development are obvious.

Summary

Music is a basic intelligence which is a part of all human beings. Musical thinking requires the mind to behave in ways different from logico-mathematical thinking, and musical development is therefore important for total child development. Musical literacy is possible and should be the goal for every child. Current thinking as outlined by MENC and research in the field suggests that music instruction should be developmentally appropriate, emphasizing age appropriateness as well as needs of individuals. Curriculum should include focus on musical behaviors (singing, listening, playing instruments, creating, and using musical symbols) as well as musical knowledge (built around concepts of melody, rhythm, timbre, and form). An environment that allows children freedom and time to construct their own musical knowledge is an environment that provides opportunity for individual expression of each unique child. Such an environment also encourages integration of music with other areas of children's play. Group music activities help children sense the social values of music, and also provide opportunities for caregivers to facilitate integration of music with other content.

This chapter began with Mrs. Jones and her kindergarten class. Was Mrs. Jones music lesson developmentally appropriate for the young children? Was this experience helping the children grow musically? The answer is both yes and no. Young children need to hear and sing the songs of our culture. Mrs. Jones was giving such an experience to the children. Preschoolers are anxious to copy songs and movements in their environment. Mrs. Jones was providing such an opportunity. In addition, Mrs. Jones was probably teaching more music than she thought. Had a music specialist been available as a resource person, she might have told Mrs. Jones that as the children copied the actions of the spider going up the spout, they were learning to move with the beat of the song. The actions of the song change with each phrase, so as the children went from the spider action to the rain falling to the sun coming up, they were responding to the different phrases in the song. Mrs. Jones was teaching the children about beat and formal structure in addition to helping children sing. And, of course, she was integrating music with her science lesson.

However, if Mrs. Jones' music lessons were always teacher-focused, with children doing as the teacher says, singing as the teacher sings, moving as the teacher moves, then she was not meeting all the developmental music needs of the children. If Mrs. Jones thought that the main purpose for music in preschool was for a change of pace or just to reinforce other subjects, then she would certainly not be meeting all of the musical needs of the children. Hopefully, Mrs. Jones realized that in addition to singing, children need experiences playing instruments, listening, and creating music, and that they need time and freedom to explore all kinds of sounds and movements and creative expression. Does Mrs. Jones have music centers in her room that allow children to explore sounds, listen, sing, create, and write their own music? Has she provided opportunities for children to express verbal ideas and stories with sound? Is she aware of the developmental music level of her class, and the unique experiences each child brings to class? Does she realize that the musical experiences of the preschool years build a foundation for later music study and therefore children need to learn many songs and recorded selections? Questions such as these may guide early childhood caregivers as they plan developmentally appropriate music lessons for young children.

References

Adams, P. (1974). *This old man.* Restrop Manor, England: Child's Play.

Adams, P. (1979). *There were ten in the bed.* [N.p.]: Child s Play.

Aliki. (1968). *Hush little baby.* New York: Macmillan.

Aliki. (1986). *Go tell Aunt Rhody.* New York: Simon & Schuster.

Andress, B. (1980). *Music experiences in early childhood.* New York: Holt, Rinehart, & Winston.

Andress, B. (1995). Transforming curriculum in music. In S. Bredekamp & T. Rosegrant (Eds.), *Reaching potentials: Transforming early childhood curriculum and assessment* (Vol. 2, pp. 99–108). Washington, DC: National Association for the Education of Young Children.

Aronoff, F.W. (1992). No age is too early to begin. In B.L. Andress & L.M. Walker (Eds.), *Readings in early childhood music education.* (pp. 51–57). Reston, VA: Music Educators National Conference.

Aruego, H., & Dewey, A. (1989). *Five little ducks.* New York: Crown.

Aylesworth, J., & Christelow, E. (1990). *The completed hickory dickory dock.* New York: Atheneum.

Blacking, J. (1990). Music in children's cognitive and affective development: Problems posed by ethnomusicological research. In F.R. Wilson, & F.L. Roehmann, (Eds.), *Music and child development* (pp. 68–79). St. Louis, MO: MMB Music.

Blakeslee, M. (Ed.). (1989). *Dance, music, theatre, visual arts: What every young American should know and be able to do in the arts.* Reston, VA: Music Educators National Conference.

Brackbill, Y., Adams, G., Crowell, D.H., & Gray, M.L. (1966). Arousal level in neonates and preschool children under continuous auditory stimulation. *Journal of Experimental Child Psychology, 4,* 178–88.

Bredekamp, S. (Ed.). (1987). *Developmentally appropriate practice in early childhood programs serving children from birth through age 8.* Washington, DC: National Association for the Education of Young Children.

Bredekamp, S., & Copple, C. (Eds.). (1997). *Developmentally appropriate practice in early childhood programs: Revised edition.* Washington, DC: National Association for the Education of Young Children.

Bredekamp, S., & Rosegrant, T. (Eds.). (1992). *Reaching potentials: Appropriate curriculum and assessment for young children.* Washington, DC: National Association for the Education of Young Children.

Bridger, W.H. (1961). Sensory habituation and discrimination in the human neonate. *American Journal of Psychiatry, 117,* 991–96.

Burton, L., & Hughes, W. (1979). *Music play: Learning activities for young children.* Menlo Park, CA: Addison-Wesley.

Choksy, L. (1988). *The Kodaly method* (2nd ed.). Englewood Cliffs, NJ: Prentice Hall.

Conover, C. (1976). *Six little ducks.* New York: Crowell.

Davidson, L. (1985). Preschool children's tonal knowledge. In J. Boswell (Ed.), *The young child and music: Contemporary principles in child development and music education* (pp. 25–40). Reston, VA: Music Educators National Conference.

Elliot, D.J. (1995). *Music matters: A new philosophy of music education.* New York: Oxford University Press.

Feierabend, J.M. (1986). *Music for very little people.* New York: Boosey & Hawkes.

Fleming, D. (1993). *In the small, small pond.* New York: Henry Holt.

Flohr, J.W. (1985). Young children's improvisation: Emerging creative thought. *The Creative Child Adult Quarterly,* 10, 79–85.

Flowers, P.J., & Dunne-Sousa, D. (1990). Pitch-pattern accuracy, tonality, and vocal range in preschool children's singing. *Journal of Research in Music Education,* 38, 102–14.

Forrai, K., with Sinor, J. (1988). *Music in preschool.* Budapest, Hungary: Corvina.

Frega, A.L. (1979). Rhythmic tasks with 3-, 4-, and 5-year-old children: A study made in the Argentine Republic. *Bulletin of the Council for Research in Music Education,* 59, 32–34.

Gardner, H. (1979). Developmental psychology after Piaget: An approach in terms of symbolization. *Human Development,* 22, 73–88.

Gardner, H. (1983). *Frames of mind.* New York: Basic Books.

Gardner, H. (1991). *To open minds.* New York: Basic Books.

Gardner, H. (1994). *The arts and human development.* New York: Basic Books.

Gilbert, J.P. (1979). Assessment of motoric music skill development in young children: Test construction and evaluation procedures. *Psychology of Music,* 7 (2), 3–12.

Gilbert, J.P. (1981). Motoric music skill development in young children: A longitudinal investigation. *Psychology of Music,* 9 (1) 21–25.

Goetze, M. (1985). Factors affecting accuracy in children's singing. Unpublished doctoral dissertation, University of Colorado, Boulder.

Gordon, E. (1988). Musical child abuse. *American Music Teacher,* 37 (5), 14–16.

Hale, S.J. (1984). *Mary had a little lamb.* New York: Holiday House.

Hargreaves, D.J. (1986). *The developmental psychology of music.* New York: Cambridge University Press.

Honig, A.S. (1995). Singing with infants and toddlers. *Young Children,* 50 (5), 72–78.

Janovitz, M. (1991). *Baa baa black sheep.* [N.p.]: Hyperion.

Jones, C. (1989). *Old McDonald.* Boston: Houghton Mifflin.

Kelley, L., & Sutton-Smith, B. (1987). A study of infant musical productivity. In J.C. Peery, I.W. Peery, & T.W. Draper (Eds.), *Music and child development* (pp. 35–53). New York: Springer-Verlag.

Kenney, S. (1989). Music centers: Freedom to explore. *Music Educators Journal, 76* (2), 32–36.

Kenney, S. (1995). The voice within. *Teaching Music, 2* (5), 36–37.

Kessen, W., Levine, J., & Wendrich, K.A. (1979). The imitation of pitch in infants. *Infant Behavior and Development, 2,* 93–99.

Kratus, J. (1985). *Rhythm, melody, motive, and phrase characteristics of children's original compositions.* Unpublished doctoral dissertation, Case Western Reserve University, Cleveland.

Martin, B., & Carle, E. (1991). *Polar bear, polar bear what do you hear?* New York: Henry Holt.

McCracken, R., & McCracken, M. (1989). *Five little speckled frogs.* Winnipeg, Canada: Peguis.

McDonald, D., & Simons, G. (1989). *Musical growth and development: Birth through six.* New York: Schirmer Books.

Moog, H. (1976). *The musical experience of the pre-school child.* (Trans. C. Clarke). London, England: Schott Music. (Original work published 1968)

Moorhead, G.E., & Pond, D. (1978). *Music for young children.* Santa Barbara, CA: Pillsbury Foundation for the Advancement of Music Education.

Music Educators National Conference (MENC). 1994a. *The school music program: A new vision.* Project director P. Lehman. Reston, VA.

Music Educators National Conference (MENC). 1994b. *Opportunity-to-learn standards for music instruction: Grades preK–12.* Task force chair P. Lehman. Reston, VA.

Noy, P. (1968). The development of music ability. *The Psychoanalytic Study of the Child, 23,* 332–47.

Papousek, M., & Papousek, H. (1981). Musical elements in the infant's vocalization: Their significance for communication, cognition, and creativity. *Advances in Infancy Research, 1,* 163–224.

Peek, M. (1985). *Mary wore her red dress.* New York: Houghton Mifflin.

Peery, J.C. (1993). Music in early childhood education. In B. Spodek (Ed.), *Handbook of research on the education of young children* (pp. 207–24). New York: Macmillan.

Peery, J.C. & Peery, I.W. (1986). Effects of exposure to classical music on the musical preferences of preschool children. *Journal of Research in Music Education, 34*, 24–33.

Peery, J.C., & Peery, I.W. (1987). The role of music in child development. In J.C. Peery, I.W. Peery, & T.W. Draper (Eds.), *Music and child development* (pp. 3–31). New York: Springer-Verlag.

Rainbow, E. (1981). A final report on a three-year investigation of rhythmic abilities of preschool aged children. *Bulletin of the Council for Research in Music Education, 66–67*, 69–73.

Richards, M.H. (1975). Tracks for Reading. Portola Valley, CA: Richards Institute.

Richards, M.H. (1985). *Let's do it again.* Portola Valley, CA: Richards Institute.

Rosen, M., & Oxenbury, H. (1989). *We're going on a bear hunt.* New York: Margaret K. McElderry Books.

Schleuter, S.L., & Schleuter, L.J. (1985). The relationship of grade level and sex differences to certain rhythmic responses of primary grade children. *Journal of Research in Music Education, 33* (1), 23–30.

Scott-Kassner, C. (1992). Research in music in early childhood. In R. Colwell (Ed.), *Handbook of research on music teaching and learning* (pp. 633–50). New York: Schirmer.

Shetler, D. (1989). The inquiry into prenatal musical experience: A report of the Eastman Project 1980–1987. *Pre- and Peri-Natal Psychology, 3*, 171–89.

Sloboda, J.A. (1985). *The musical mind: The cognitive psychology of music.* New York: Oxford University Press.

Swanwick, K. (1988). *Music, mind, and education.* New York: Routledge.

Thurman, L., & Langness, A.P. (1986). *Heartsongs.* Englewood, CO: Music Study Services.

Wilson, E., & Koontz, R.M. (1993). *Music in the night.* New York: Cobblehill Books.

Wyler, R. (1987). *Science fun with drums, bells, and whistles.* New York: Julian Messner.

CHAPTER SIX

Physical Education in the Developmentally Appropriate Integrated Curriculum

V. GREGORY PAYNE
JUDITH E. RINK

During the summer of 1996 the first Surgeon General's Report on Physical Activity and Well-Being was released. This document proclaimed that achieving moderate to vigorous levels of physical activity can make a significant difference in personal health and well-being. The level of activity does not need to be strenuous though more intense or longer bouts of activity can increase the benefit. The potential positive effects exist for all age groups and both genders and include reductions in heart disease, diabetes, blood pressure, colon cancer, depression and anxiety, and generally, less chance of dying prematurely. The report also indicated that physical activity also aids in weight control, builds and maintains the musculo-skeletal system, and improves psychological well-being.

Unfortunately, the Surgeon General also reported, that over 60 percent of adults in the United States are too sedentary to attain recommended amounts of physical activity with 25 percent not participating in any form of leisure time physical activity. Similar figures exist for younger Americans. Nearly half of people between the ages of 12 and 21 are not regularly vigorously active with this figure declining with age. In addition, during the four year period between 1991 and 1995 a

145

17 percent drop occurred in the number of students enrolled daily in high school physical education classes. All of these figures, according to a report, attest to the need for well designed programs in schools to increase physical activity through physical education. These programs can be effective in developing a strong base of physical activity early in life. Such a program can develop appreciation of physical activity early in life, when lifetime patterns are developed. Thus, the likelihood of being active throughout life is increased.

Similarly, in May 1995 a group of leading scientists from ten countries gathered to compile the evidence related to the effects of physical activity on health and well-being. As a result of that meeting, international consensus and summary statements were composed. In those statements, these experts proclaimed that physical activity reduces the incidence of coronary heart disease, stroke, hypertension, adult-onset diabetes mellitus, colon cancer, and maybe even breast cancer. Other factors positively affected by physical activity, according to these statements, include functional capacity, low back pain, osteoporosis, and general life quality. Psychosocial benefits can also be enhanced as physical activity was found to have a "moderate to large" effect on mild to moderate depression while generally positively impacting psychological well-being. Perhaps most important for this chapter, these experts also stated that physical activity is important at all stages of life from childhood through extreme old age" and "that schools should allocate adequate time to quality programs of physical activity, including physical education" (p. vii). Unfortunately, another finding from this same conference indicated that most adults in industrialized countries of the world fail to partake in sufficient physical activity to enable optimal health and that energy expenditure per individual seems to be declining (Consensus and Summary Statements, 1995).

As far as children are specifically concerned, a "Scientifically Documented Position Statement" on elementary school physical education was recently written by the California Governor's Council on Physical Fitness and Sports (1995). This document attests to the value of physical education at the elementary school level and its specific benefits in the areas of academic performance, general health, weight control, physical fitness, movement knowledge and motor skill development, self-esteem, stress management, and social development. This document has been endorsed by over fifty organizations, including the American Academy of Family Physicians; the American Academy of Podiatric Sports Medicine; American Academy of Pediatrics, California

District; American Cancer Society, California Division; American Heart Association, California; American Preventive Care Association; California Department of Aging; and the California Department of Education. In short, this position statement proclaims that a quality physical education program can enhance all aspects of human development (California Governor's Council on Physical Fitness and Sports, 1995).

Furthermore, Harter's theory of perceived competence posits that, when performance attempts become successful, the individual experiences a positive effect. This perception of successful competence motivates the individual to continue participation. Similarly, Harter's theory postulates that those individuals low in perceived competence will discontinue participation (Harter, 1978, p. 82). Thus, positive experiences early in life may have long-term, life-enhancing and -sustaining effects much later. To achieve positive attitudes toward movement at a young age proper instruction and practice are necessary. In other words, young children need a high-quality physical education program specifically designed for them. It must be "developmentally appropriate."

Developmentally Appropriate Physical Education

Like many disciplines, physical education has taken a special interest in creating developmentally appropriate activities for students. Recently, the Council on Physical Education for Children (COPEC) prepared a document entitled, *Developmentally Appropriate Physical Education Practice in Movement Programs for Young Children, Ages 3–5* (COPEC, 1994). This document was created following the model established by the National Association for the Education of Young Children (Bredekamp, 1987) and their series of position statements describing developmentally appropriate practices for children from birth to 8 years old. The document was thought to be necessary because of the increased interest in physical education programs at the preschool level. The intent was to assist educators of young children in making decisions concerning developmentally appropriate curriculum, content selection and presentation, curriculum and teaching evaluation, and curricular integration of movement activities (cf. Bredekamp & Copple, 1997).

In this document, COPEC (1994) strongly emphasized that a movement program primarily consisting of traditional games and dances would not optimally enhance the development of young children.

Quality physical education should be "developmentally and instructionally suitable for the specific children being served." In addition, developmentally appropriate physical education programs "recognize children's changing capacities to move and promote such change" (COPEC, 1992, p. 3). The orientation of these programs should be on development of motor skills and movement concepts that enhance psychological, physical, intellectual, and social development. Furthermore, the need for quality, daily movement programs is stressed. To achieve a satisfactory level of quality, programs must be "instructionally suitable," acknowledging the "changing capacities" of children's movement. To be developmentally appropriate, the program should be designed to accommodate each child's developmental status, previous experience in movement activities, physical fitness, skill level, body size, and age. COPEC (1994) further indicated that five premises are integral to the creation of movement programs. These premises are presented in table 6.1.

What Does "Developmental" Really Mean?

Fearing that the relatively sudden and intense interest in the term "developmentally appropriate" could render the term meaningless from overuse, the Motor Development Task Force (1994) of the National Association for Sports and Physical Education (NASPE) published a teaching guide. The purpose of this guide was to clarify what a "developmental perspective" in physical education means, and to explain how teachers can create lessons and programs that have such a perspective.

Development, according to the task force, is "about the changes in individuals across their lifespan" (Motor Development Task Force, 1994, p. 2). These changes are not simply a function of aging alone; for one to acquire motor skills certain prerequisite experiences, including instruction, must occur. This is not to suggest that movement develops solely as a result of life experience; one's genetic potential also plays a role. Thus, motor skill development is the result of an interaction between "nature" and "nurture."

For both growth and motor skill development, human change is characterized by six elements. It is qualitative, sequential, cumulative, directional, multifactorial, and individual. *Qualitative* implies that change means more than "just more of something." It also implies that something is different than before and, for children, maturity usually means that "more effective movement patterns" will be utilized.

TABLE 6.1
Five Integral Premises for the Creation of Movement Programs for Young Children*

1. **Three, 4- and 5-year-old children are different from elementary school-aged children.**
   Children this young are in the process of acquiring skill in fundamental movement patterns like running, throwing, and kicking. To assist children in this endeavor, they need wide-ranging experiences which facilitate fundamental motor skill development. Their teachers must be knowledgeable in the developmental process and understand that the rate of acquisition of these movement patterns is variable placing a premium of "teaching children, not activities." (COPEC, p. 5)

2. **Young children learn through interaction with their environment.**
   Thus, activities designed for children from three to five years old should be designed so children are actively, not passively, involved.

3. **Teachers of yound children are guides or facilitators.**
   They carefully monitor their students' behaviors and adjust the learning experiences accordingly to accommodate the individual student's needs. Emphasis should be placed on children solving problems, "making choices," and having sufficient time to explore in an active learning environment.

4. **Young children learn and develop in an integrated fashion.**
   Therefore, movement lessons for children of this age should emphasize physical and psychomotor objectives while incorporating aspects of intellectual and affective development.

5. **Planned movement experiences enhance play experiences.**
   In fact, when planned movement classes are interspersed with play to allow free practice and sufficient time to learn, children naturally show the greatest gains in motor skill development.

* The National Association for Sports and Physical Education has granted permission for the use of a number of excerpts from their publications. All of these publications have been fully referenced.

Sequential implies that a predictable ordering of skills exists. For example, children walk before they run. Knowing that motor skills evolve in a somewhat orderly sequence facilitates assessment. *Cumulative* suggests that initial motor behaviors serve as the rudiments for more advanced motor skills. Standing, for example, is a precursor to walking. *Directional* suggests that development may be progressive or regressive. For young children, the direction is usually progressive; however, following a period of disuse of a skill, regression may occur. *Multifactorial* implies that development is the result of an interaction of many factors working together. Standing requires sufficient balance and physical strength to hold the body upright. It also requires personal motivation and an environment (items in the household on which the child can pull up) conducive to leading up to the skill. Lastly, *individual* emphasizes the unique nature of change for each child. Though the sequence of change is fairly orderly and predictable, change rate varies considerably between individuals. This is clearly evident in the onset of independent locomotion—one child may begin walking as early as 9 months while another lags several months behind that pace (Motor Development Task Force, 1994).

Obviously an understanding of the term "development" is necessary in any attempt to create a developmentally appropriate physical education program or curriculum. However, according to the Motor Development Task Force (1994), one also needs to have a "developmental perspective." This implies that one continuously thinks in terms of what preceded or will follow a child's current level of movement ability. In addition, having a developmental perspective implies that emphasis is placed on aspects of the child's development beyond age because "development is age-related but not age-determined" (p. 5). While age is important it may not be as important as knowing where the child's "performance falls on the developmental continuum" (p. 5). For example, 3- or 4-year-old children may catch by turning their heads away from the ball and cradling the ball against their chest. Though these characteristics are somewhat immature, they are not wrong or inappropriate for a 3- or 4-year-old. To judge these behaviors as incorrect would be to apply an expectation of an older individual to the 3- or 4-year-old—a failure to apply a developmental perspective.

Defining a Physically Educated Person

In a document entitled *Outcomes of Quality Physical Education Programs* (1992), the National Association of Sports and Physical Education (NASPE) described a physically educated person. The five major focus areas of that definition are presented in table 6.2 with their accompanying outcomes.

In addition to the twenty outcome statements, seventeen to thirty benchmarks were created for each grade (K–12) level (NASPE, 1992). This information was the basis for the creation of the seven national standards for physical education that were recently published in a book entitled *Moving into the Future: National Standards for Physical Education* (NASPE, 1995). These standards were developed as an

TABLE 6.2
NASPE Definition of a Physically Educated Person

- **has learned the skills necessary to perform a variety of physical activities**

  1. . . . moves using concepts of body awareness, space awareness, effort and relationships.
  2. . . . demonstrates competence in a variety of manipulative, locomotor, and non-locomotor skills.
  3. . . . demonstrates competence in combinations of manipulative locomotor and non-locomotor skills performed individually and with others.
  4. . . . demonstrates competence in many different forms of physical activity.
  5. . . . demonstrates proficiency in a few forms of physical activity.
  6. . . . has learned how to learn new skills.

- **is physically fit**

  7. . . . assesses, achieves, and maintains physical fitness.
  8. . . . designs safe, personal fitness programs in accordance with principles of training and conditioning.

- **does participate regularly in physical activity**

  9. . . . participates in health enhancing physical activity at least three times a week.
  10. . . . selects and regularly participates in lifetime physical activities.

- **knows the implications of and the benefits from involvement in physical activities**

  11. . . . identifies the benefits, costs and obligations associated with regular participation in physical activity.
  12. . . . recognizes the risk and safety factors associated with regular participation in physical activity.
  13. . . . applies concepts and principles to the development of motor skills.
  14. . . . understands that wellness involves more than being physically fit.
  15. . . . knows the rules, strategies and appropriate behaviors for selected physical activities.
  16. . . . recognizes that participation in physical activity can lead to multi-cultural and international understanding.
  17. . . . understands that physical activity provides the opportunity for enjoyment, self-expression and communication.

- **values physical activity and its contributions to a healthful lifestyle**

  18. . . . appreciates the relationships with others that result from participation in physical activity.
  19. . . . respects the role that regular physical activity plays in the pursuit of life-long health and well-being.
  20. . . . cherishes the feelings that result from regular participation in physical activity.

extension, not a replacement, for the original twenty outcomes. In addition, the standards were intended to state "what a student should know as a result of a quality physical education program and be able to do" (NASPE, 1995, p. viii). The seven standards or competencies for physical education (K–12) are presented in table 6.3.

These standards were written to comply with the objectives of the National Education Standards Improvement Council, which was established to create criteria for the certification of content standards (NASPE, 1995). This council sought to ensure that standards were "internationally competitive, reflect the best knowledge about teaching and learning, and have been created through a broad-based, open adoption process" (NASPE, 1995, p. vi). The standards clearly indicate that physical education is much more than the traditional or stereotypical perception. They are also clear evidence that academic abilities and skill development are essential to a quality physical education program.

Motor Development from Birth to 8 Years

Creating a developmentally appropriate curriculum or program for children from birth to 8 years old is obviously contingent on having a developmental perspective, as discussed in the previous section of this chapter, and possessing a basic knowledge of the progressions in children's motor development. This section of the chapter describes the child's gradual progression from the subcortically controlled reflexes

---

TABLE 6.3
The Seven National Standards for Physical Education

---

1. Demonstrates competency in many forms and proficiency in a few movement forms.
2. Applies movement concepts and principles to the learning and development of motor skills.
3. Exhibits a physically active lifestyle.
4. Achieves and maintains a health-enhancing level of physical fitness.
5. Demonstrates responsible personal and social behavior in physical activity settings.
6. Demonstrates understanding and respect for differences among people in physical activity settings.
7. Understands that physical activity provides opportunities for enjoyment, self-expression, and social interaction.

---

of the first few weeks or months of life to the combining and varying of fundamental movements during early and middle childhood.

Infant Reflexes

For some months prior to birth and throughout the subsequent year, one of the most interesting forms of human movement appears. These movements are known as the infant reflexes. By definition, they are involuntary, subcortical, and stereotypical responses to a stimulus. Involuntary implies they are the product of the application of an external stimulus and do not happen as a result of a conscious effort. For example, in the palmar grasp reflex, one of the most well-known of all infant reflexes, applying pressure to the palm of the baby's hand during the first few months of life elicits a closing of the baby's fingers on the stimulated hand. This baby does not plan or think about creating the movement; it happens as a result of the appropriate stimulus being applied. The reflex is involuntary because it is subcortical. This means that the reflex occurs as a result of information being processed below the level of the cortex of the brain. When the hand is touched, as in the palmar grasp reflex, electrical impulses travel up the arm to the central nervous system. Though they may reach lower brain centers, like the brain stem, before being processed, they do not reach the higher levels, like the cerebral cortex, which is the processing center for most voluntarily produced movement. Stereotypical implies that these reflexes are the same upon repeated application of the same stimulus. Though a reflex may eventually dissipate following numerous applications of a stimulus, for the first several, the stimulus elicits the same movement over and over (Payne & Isaacs, 1995).

These reflexes are integral to life during infancy and beyond. Those reflexes known as the primitive reflexes impact the baby's survival by protection or nourishment (Barnes, Crutchfield, & Heriza, 1984). Examples of primitive reflexes are the sucking reflex where the baby sucks upon having the lips stimulated or the search reflex where the baby turns the head in the direction of the stimulation upon having the cheek or side of the face touched or stroked. Postural reflexes are believed to impact the development of later voluntary movements (Fiorentino, 1981). An example would be the crawling reflex. During the first few months of life babies make crawling-like movements when the bottoms of their feet are stroked with the body in a prone position. Most experts believe that this involuntary form of crawling, like all postural reflexes, provides "practice" that aids in attaining the later, voluntary form of the same movement (Payne & Isaacs, 1995).

Voluntary Movements of Infancy and Early Childhood

Infant reflexes are a dominant form of movement over the first few weeks of life, with many of them remaining up through the child's first birthday. However, over the course of that year the reflexes gradually diminish as voluntary movements become more pervasive. Voluntary movements are those that are created by a conscious effort and processed by the higher brain centers like the cerebral cortex. The first voluntary movements are extremely subtle, almost imperceptible actions like controlling the neck, head, and eyes. The first year of life, however, is one of remarkable developmental change as the baby comes under almost complete voluntary control by the end of the first year. This occurs as the higher brain centers gradually assume control.

These voluntary movements are often clustered into three major categories: the manipulatory, locomotor, and stability movements. Though the sequence of acquisition for these movements is quite pre-dictable for most children, the rate of acquisition may vary considerably.

Manipulatory movements are those involving the hands and arms, like reaching, grasping, and releasing. While many parents are well aware of the sequences and general timelines for development of loco-motion and stability, they are typically not so well informed concerning manipulation. Well over sixty years ago, the classic research of Halver-son (1931) nicely detailed the development of reaching and grasping development. Studying children from 16 to 52 weeks of age Halverson found a predictable developmental sequence for his subjects upon being presented with a one-inch red cube. Though Halverson eventually detailed ten specific stages of reaching and grasping development, three general steps seemed to emerge. At the most immature level of develop-ment, children simply swept the hand and arm backhand toward the object. This gradually evolved into a more mature sweep or scoop of the hand toward the object from a variety of directions. The last step was a direct reach similar to that seen in a mature reacher.

Locomotion includes those movements that enable the child to move from one point in space to another, like creeping and crawling with all of their variations. Prone locomotion obviously precedes upright forms, with the highly variable, somewhat inefficient, low-to-the ground form of crawling (popularly referred to as creeping) coming first at approximately 7 months of age. In this form of locomotion the arms are thrust forward awkwardly followed by an immediate flexion designed to create forward propulsion with the body being dragged or slid across the supporting surface. Slowly the legs become more involved as the body raises off the ground. By the 9th to 12th month of life, the more efficient elevated version of crawling may prevail. In this form of locomotion, the child is fully elevated on hands and knees in an increasingly efficient form of movement. In fact, many children who are capable of walking will regularly revert to crawling when necessary because of its efficiency over early walking attempts. Upright locomotion begins as early as 8 months when most children will walk with considerable assistance. Walking, or cruising, around furniture or other forms of hand-holds is often possible by 10 months of age, with full unassisted walking appearing around the end of the first year.

Stability, often referred to as postural control, includes a range of movements having to do with placing the body or its parts in a desired position. Examples include the head control, rolling over, sitting, and standing up. Minimal voluntary control of the head is often seen at approximately one month with complete head elevation occurring a month later. At 2 to 3 months the child can turn the head from left to right when prone and is able to elevate the head from a supine position by 5 months. Most children can also sit with a hand-hold at 5 months and sit unassisted by 8 months of age. Standing occurs slightly later, with assisted standing occurring at 9 to 10 months and unassisted standing developing by the end of the first year (Payne & Issacs, 1995).

Fundamental Movement

From the ages of approximately 2 through 7 years, the child's gross movement abilities begin to expand dramatically. This is particularly true of movements known as the fundamental locomotor and fundamental manipulative patterns. Examples of fundamental locomotor patterns are walking, running, jumping, galloping, skipping, and sliding. Examples of fundamental manipulative patterns include throwing, catching, striking, dribbling, kicking, and punting. All of these fundamental patterns are critical to future development because when they are combined and varied they can be used to create a vast repertoire of more complex movements. For example, combining walking and hopping can create skipping. Any number of the locomotor patterns can be combined to create even the most complex dances. Most forms of dance, including social, square, modern, and ballet, are composed of the fundamental movement patterns. This is also true of most sports. Baseball, basketball, track and field, to name a few, are sports that consist of combinations and variations of fundamental motor patterns. Thus, to perform these more complex activities competently, a relatively mature level of the fundamental patterns is required.

Unfortunately, too often children are not provided with the necessary instruction, opportunity, and practice to enable them to develop a sufficient level of ability in the fundamental patterns. According to Harter's model of perceived competence (1982), children are motivated to participate when their performance is successful. Similarly, children who are not successful in their performances will discontinue their involvement. Therefore, children fail to gain the health-related benefits of being physically active.

Like most movement, development in the fundamental movement patterns is predictable. Though all children are unique and vary considerably in their rate of movement acquisition, a fairly predictable sequence of development exists. Determining the child's current state of development is imperative for the creation of developmentally appropriate activities designed to enhance these abilities. Tools exist to assist in the assessment of children's developmental status. Two methods of evaluation for many fundamental motor patterns include the total body approach and the component approach. While each is designed to determine the developmental status of children's fundamental movement, the total body approach is simpler to administer and requires less detailed knowledge of the child's specific movement technique. For these reasons, many teachers who have a wide range of other educational responsibilities find this approach to be advantageous. The total body approach assumes that if a child is immature in several aspects of a fundamental movement pattern, then all components of the pattern will be immature. This is frequently not the case. While more difficult to apply, the component approach offers the advantage of providing more specific information concerning the child's development (Roberton & Halverson, 1984). It provides the teacher with sufficient information to determine the child's general developmental status while determining which aspects of the pattern may need special attention. More detailed information on these approaches and their advantages and disadvantages is available from a number of sources (Branta, Haubenstricker, & Seefeldt, 1984; Payne & Isaacs, 1995; Roberton & Halverson, 1984).

Physical Education in the Developmentally Appropriate Integrated Curriculum

Most experts on human movement who work with young children are strong advocates of student-directed approaches to curriculum and instruction. However, many early childhood movement programs become student-directed as a result of neglect rather than design. The motor development of most prekindergarten children has received little attention. Thus, gross motor experiences in early childhood education are often spontaneous and unplanned. What may appear to be a program designed to cultivate naturalistic experiences (letting the students naturally learn from their experiences on the playground) may be mislabeled as "education."

Most early childhood programs include equipment with limited potential to aid in the development of gross motor abilities. The potential of the environment to meet the diverse needs of children of different ages and needs remains static from month to month and year to year. Movement experiences are included as part of other activities, but clear evidence of a developmental sequence in the design of movement experiences is lacking. In these programs, movement experiences planned with the intent of being integrated with other curricular areas or as unique experiences rarely include any level of appropriate challenge for children.

Failing to include developmentally appropriate physical education results from several factors. First, many early childhood educators believe that gross motor skills simply unfold with free play. Second, many early childhood educators have no means through which they can determine what is appropriate motor content and may not know when and how to intervene to properly enhance children's movement abilities.

In the next sections, the issues of appropriate content and structure for early childhood programs are addressed. The national standards discussed earlier reflect a balanced program emphasizing the development of skill in moving, fitness, and cognitive and affective concerns related to physical activity. The young child's major developmental task is to learn to enjoy vigorous movement while learning to move well.

Therefore, the focus of content for young children in this chapter will be the development of movement skills. The national standards for physical education, while not addressing the toddler years, makes explicit the importance of participation in physical activity that results in positive affect. The fitness and motor skill competencies part of the school program cannot be accomplished unless children enjoy participation.

Movement Experiences/Physical Education in the Integrated Curriculum

The notion of integration of curriculum can be interpreted in several ways. Movement/physical education experiences can be integrated with other content experiences around a thematic center similar to leg of the spider (Krogh, this volume). Other curricular content can be integrated into learning experiences with primarily a physical education content emphasis, or physical education content can be used to support other content areas.

Although the ideal form of integration would be to design a learning experience that challenged a child in all curricular areas, what is most common in early childhood curricula is the use of movement in content experiences or themes that are primarily focused in other curricular areas. The integrated learning experience may use movement, but the nature of the movement experience is such that it may reinforce existing abilities but certainly not challenge most if not all children. For a learning experience to be truly integrated it must require students to use physical education content that is likewise developmentally appropriate. Content specialists are also particularly sensitive to the idea that much is taught "through" movement but little is taught about how to move. The following are relevant examples of integrating physical education into early childhood curricula. These examples are followed by specific ideas on how to make the movement experiences more developmentally appropriate for children.

Integration around a Theme

Finding themes that are rich in the potential to integrate many content areas at an appropriate developmental level is difficult for educators. In physical education, integrating activities for young children is probably easier than at any other age level. Because the young child can more easily communicate physically than verbally, experiences pretending to be things or processes or acting out ideas are fruitful avenues of integration that will develop expressive movement capabilities and control. If the child is challenged to move in different ways, to use more challenging forms of movement, and to move with increasingly higher levels of control, these integrated experiences have a greater potential to be developmentally appropriate from a physical education perspective. The examples that follow and those in table 6.4 illustrate some ways in which teachers can be more sensitive to the movement needs of children when developing themes.

Example: Acting out the role of community helpers (firefighters) **Discussion:** This activity holds great potential for enriching a child's movement knowledge. The goal here should be to increase the student's awareness and control of movement concepts related to speed, pathway, level, and direction of movement.
Making the experience more developmentally appropriate: How does fire move? Quick and darting, first here, then there. How can we move like fire? What happens when the firefighter puts water on the fire? It slowly dies and becomes steam. How does steam move?

Example: Moving from one place to another using locomotor movements **Discussion:** The movement goal here should be to increase the use of different locomotor patterns and to develop the ability to use the patterns with increasing

TABLE 6.4
General Guidelines for Using Movement Experiences in Integrative Ways

- Vary performance in locomotor skills
  - use different locomotor patterns
  - ask that the same locomotor pattern be done in different ways
- When using manipulative skills to project objects, ask that they be done faster and harder to promote the development of more mature patterns
- Require more control for body management skills; do not allow children to fling, throw, or collapse their weight
- Use the body more expressively; attend to the effort aspects of movement (light/strong, fast/low, direct/indirect)
- Use other parts of their body to perform skills; take advantage of the idea that the child does not have to do everything on their feet or with their hands

skill. Encouraging the use of different patterns and the use of those patterns at different speeds and direction as well as in different combinations becomes increasingly important as initial patterns are developed.

Making the experience more developmentally appropriate: Require children to use different locomotor patterns; to use a pattern in a different way (sideways or backwards); to do it quickly or slowly; to take one jump forward for every apple on your page and see how far across the room your jumps take you.

Integration of Other Areas into Physical Education

The teaching of movement experiences to young children provides many opportunities to integrate concepts critical to other content areas. Because movement is concrete and active in nature, critical concepts from other content areas such as shape, design, spatial awareness, math principals, or letters of the alphabet, are easily integrated into learning experiences. In addition, movement experiences are abundant with opportunities to help children be creative and develop problem-solving skills (see figure 6.1).

Example: **Math Concepts:** Experiences moving the body in relation to large equipment: moving into and out of hoops; moving over a rope; moving on and off a small piece of climbing equipment (tasks designated by the teacher and resolved by the student).

Math concepts can also be explored as students measure the distances of objects they send by either throwing or striking. For example, how far can you throw? They can also measure the size of play spaces or the balls themselves.

Weather Concepts: Experiences creating the movements of the wind, snow, storms, or lightning through movement. Each of these experiences is explored in terms of its movement potential.

wind: gentle or forceful, consistent or gusty direct or indirect movement through space

snow: gentle or gusty, moving from high to low how snowflakes make you feel (cold, warm, happy excited)

FIGURE 6.1
Web Integrating Physical Education with Other Content Areas

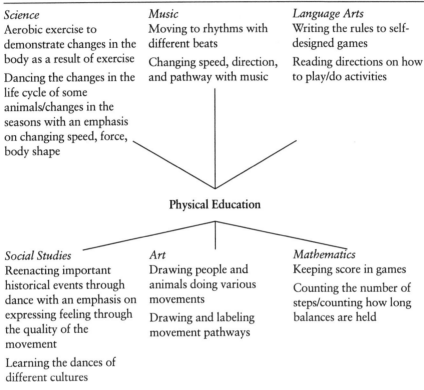

Science
Aerobic exercise to demonstrate changes in the body as a result of exercise

Dancing the changes in the life cycle of some animals/changes in the seasons with an emphasis on changing speed, force, body shape

Music
Moving to rhythms with different beats

Changing speed, direction, and pathway with music

Language Arts
Writing the rules to self-designed games

Reading directions on how to play/do activities

Physical Education

Social Studies
Reenacting important historical events through dance with an emphasis on expressing feeling through the quality of the movement

Learning the dances of different cultures

Art
Drawing people and animals doing various movements

Drawing and labeling movement pathways

Mathematics
Keeping score in games

Counting the number of steps/counting how long balances are held

Diversity: Diversity can first be explored with the concepts of individual differences in skill ability. Children will need to work with others of many abilities. Helping children understand and respect differences first emerges in cooperative relationships such as throwing and catching. One partner must recognize the ability level of the other and adapt his or her own performance to enable the partner to succeed.

One of the greatest challenges for teachers attempting to integrate movement experiences into the curriculum for young children is to make the movement experiences developmentally appropriate from one movement perspective to another (see table 6.5). Most physical educators and materials written for elementary physical education

TABLE 6.5
Integrating Movement with a Thematic Experience of How Things Grow

Setting. Students have been working on planting seeds and watching them grow. They have learned about needs for sunlight, water, and fertile soil. They have studies the best times for planting in their geographic area (seasons) and have measured their plant's growth (math). They have logged the progress of their plants (language arts) on a calendar they designed (art). They have also visited farms in the community. They are now going to create a dance that demonstrates the emergence of a seed into a plant.

The Task. The teacher explains that some of the children will be the seeds and some of the children will represent what the seed needs to grow. The dance can be done in a large group or in smaller groups of children. The teacher builds a story around the event and explores each of the parts with all of the children.

- What does a seed planted in the ground look like?
- How does rain move?
- How do the rays of the sun get to the seed/plant?

After the children decide which part they want to play they take a still pose to start the dance that represents their first positions.

The seed is planted in the soil. The students who are seeds become as *small* as possible and as *still* as they can.

The rain waters the seed. The students who are the rain move around a seed using *light* movements that move from *high to low*, dropping their magic on the seed.

When the rain stops the students who are rain withdraw from the seed and take a still pose until the next rain.

The sun is big, bright, strong, and everywhere around and over the seed making the seed feel good because it is getting what it needs to grow.

As the sun moves, the seed and small emerging plant follow the sun because the sun gives it what it needs.

As the seed grows to a medium level, it is watered again by the rain which beats it down slightly and makes it grow stronger.

The seed grows into a strong and tall plant stretching to the sky with the help of the sun and the rain.

emphasize three areas of content: manipulative skill, body management skill, and dance. The young child has no need for these to be distinguished. Children should be encouraged to dance with manipulative equipment and use that equipment as a part of locomotor and body management work. The following sections describe developmentally appropriate movement content that should be integrated into the curriculum for the young child. They are presented so that the teacher can make the addition of movement into integrated experiences more developmentally appropriate for children.

Sequencing Movement Expectations for Children— Learning How to Move

Many frameworks exist for designating and structuring movement content for young children. Most of the frameworks would include the following areas as critical dimensions of program development for movement experiences for young children:

- development of body awareness (exploring what the body and its parts can do)
- development of fundamental locomotor patterns (e.g., walk, run, hop, gallop, skip, slide)
- allowing opportunities to manage the weight of the body (e.g., climb, balance, hang, swing, support weight, roll)
- allowing opportunities to develop fundamental manipulative patterns (e.g., throw, catch, kick, strike with the body and external implements)

Each of these content dimensions is explored below in terms of its importance with guidelines for program development.

Development of Body Awareness

While the young child learns about the body from manipulating the body in relation to objects (large equipment and small equipment in relation to the body), preplanned learning experiences allowing the child to explore and use body parts in different ways can significantly enhance development of body awareness. Through age 5 the child will be finding and eventually labeling parts of the body. Through age 8 the child will be learning the function of body parts and an awareness of the body in space. Many of these experiences can be integrated with other aspects of the curriculum.

Examples: Moving different parts of the body to *music*; using different body parts to perform a task such as striking a balloon; bearing weight on different parts of the body; moving over, into, around, and onto different pieces of equipment in different ways on the feet and without using the feet.

Development of Fundamental Locomotor Patterns

From the time children learn to walk until about age of 7 they acquire new fundamental locomotor skills that will continually be refined and incorporated into complex motor skills for most of their lives. Opportunity-rich, naturalistic environments will facilitate the development of these patterns, which may also be enhanced and elicited by teacher-planned experiences and teacher involvement in individual responses.

Examples: Climbing, stepping, and jumping down from low equipment; moving over and around objects; moving on one or two feet and sideways and backwards; moving the feet to varied rhythms/music.

Locomotor patterns develop sequentially. Knowing the child's developmental status can help teachers make decisions about when, if, and how they should intervene. All fundamental locomotor patterns should be acquired by the age of 7 with rapid progress in control and diversity of these patterns from 5 to 8 years of age.

Development of Body Management Skills

The child's ability to manage the weight of the body is continuous from birth. The ability to balance and control the weight of the body in locomotor and nonlocomotor experiences develops as a result of opportunities to balance and move on a variety of body parts, climb, hang, swing, roll, and so on. The greater the variety of different experiences, the larger the potential for skill acquisition in this area.

Examples: Moving and balancing with different parts of the body as a base (e.g., two hands and one foot, elbows and knees, etc.); rolling down a hill or on a wedge-shaped mat; hanging from a bar or rings by the knees; jumping onto, moving along, and getting off a balance beam; sitting with no other body part touching a piece of equipment.

Development of the Ability to Use the Body as an Instrument of Expression

Movement experiences can be expressive with or without music. The young child's desire and ability to imitate and create (e.g., rhythmics, creative movement, movement to music) can be developed through opportunities to move creatively and freely to music as well as to create movements that express the child's imitation of characters or creation of movement through thought or feeling. The structure of experiences through toddlerhood should be primarily naturalistic, with teacher intervention to stimulate or reinforce responses. The older child can work with more structured movement ideas. However, programs should not emphasize rhythms that require children to perform complex combinations of locomotor patterns to music. (Guidelines for the integration of music with movement experiences are presented in table 6.6)

Examples: Playing music with a strong, clear, simple rhythm to which children can move freely; having children move different parts of their bodies to a rhythm; creating impressions of how different things move (e.g., animals, heavy equipment, tools, forces of nature); creating movements that express the movement qualities of different experiences (e.g., moving in molasses, walking on the moon, lifting off in a rocket).

Development of Fundamental Manipulative Patterns

The fundamental manipulative patterns (e.g., throwing, catching, and other forms of receiving, kicking, striking with the body and other implements, moving with objects) are gross movements basic to advanced and more specialized sports skills the child will want to ultimately develop. A major key to providing developmentally appro-

TABLE 6.6
Suggestions for the Integration of Music with Movement

Preschool students should be provided with unstructured opportunities to move to different kinds of music. They can be expected to do *their* dance. Too much structure is contraindicated.

Primary children should have opportunities to do the following:
- explore different ways to do various locomotor pattersn to even and uneven rhythms that have consistent and clear beats.
- explore the qualities of movement to short segments of music which clearly contrast sound that communicates different movement. Children can also use different body parts and body shapes; moving in different pathways, levels and directions; moving strong/light/fast/slow with direct/indirect use of space; moving with others in relationship to props (scarvesm elastic ropes, etc.)
- learn prepackaged dances with simple step pattersn, organization, etc. (Example: Jump Jim Joe)

priate experiences in this area is the selection of equipment. Equipment that is proportionate to the size and weight of the child is critical to developing appropriate patterns. Some ideas essential for developmentally appropriate programs include the following:

- Children can send objects (throw and strike) at advanced levels before they can receive objects (visual tracking of moving objects is not mature in this age group).
- Children can stop rolling objects before they can catch objects in the air.
- Objects to be caught or received (not appropriate for toddlerhood) should be light and soft (fleece, yarn, sponge, etc.) to prevent a fearful reaction to catching. *Note*: Many sponge balls are too light and will bounce out of the child's grasp.
- Mature forms of striking and throwing can be developed at an early age if children have the opportunity to throw, strike, or hit with maximum force production (as hard as they can without concern for object control), if the equipment is the appropriate size and weight, and if objects to be struck or hit are stationary.

Control of receiving objects in simple conditions will begin for most children at age 5 or 6. Because the young child cannot control the object in this process, asking the child to do things with maximum force may create some managerial problems in an instructional setting. However, providing these opportunities in the context of throwing, catching, or striking with minimal insistence on control is critical.

Examples: Hitting a large whiffleball with a small plastic golf club; throwing a tennis ball or bean bag as far as possible; catching a rolling ball from a sitting position; striking a balloon with a homemade nylon stocking and coat hanger racket; kicking a stationary plastic ball as far as possible.

The Structure of Learning Experiences— Developmentally Appropriate Practice

One of the significant questions with which physical educators struggle is how much structure learning experiences should have to be considered developmentally appropriate. Some form of continuum describing teacher-controlled/direct teaching at one end and student controlled/indirect teaching at the other appears to exist. In discussing the teaching of mathematics, Charlesworth (this volume) described three levels of potential structure of curricular experiences:

- Naturalistic experiences that allow children to interact with their environment
- Informal experiences that are naturalistic, with adults taking the opportunity to intervene when necessary
- Structured experiences that are planned by the teacher

Most experts would agree that programs for young children should be conducted with an emphasis on naturalistic experiences. As children pass from toddlerhood to early childhood teachers should increase their tendency to intervene and conduct more structured experiences with students. Teachers should also recognize that an environmental design approach is effective only if it elicits movement experiences that are flexible enough to meet the changing needs of developing children. High-quality physical education programs include those that elicit appropriate movement experiences from the participants. Although the student may be having a naturalistic experience, the teacher has spent a great deal of time planning the environment. Effective teachers of physical education intervene to change the conditions of the environment to make it developmentally appropriate and intervene to improve the children's responses. Knowing when and how to intervene is essential to the effective teaching of children. Effective teachers of physical education will also teach movement directly, providing models of effective patterns for children to follow. The need for and distribution of more teacher intervention and more highly structured experiences should increase as children age. This intervention and the nature of the intervention are dependent on sensitive and caring teachers knowing their subject matter and the individual child.

Summary

Clear and considerable scientific evidence exists to support the idea that physical education is important in the education of the young child (Consensus and Summary Statements, 1995). Benefits include enhancement of academic performance and general health, weight control, physical fitness, movement knowledge and motor skill, self-esteem, stress management, and social development (California Governor's Council on Physical Fitness and Sports, 1995). However, for the benefits to be optimal, this education must be developmentally appropriate with an orientation on development of motor skills and movement concepts. Programs for young children must be based on several important premises: Very young children are different from elementary school aged children and learn in an integrated fashion through interacting with their environment; teachers are guides or facilitators; and planned movement experiences enhance play experiences (COPEC, 1994).

Physical education programs for young children should also maintain a developmental perspective. Such a perspective recognizes that children are undergoing constant change. In the area of growth and motor skill development, that change is qualitative, sequential, cumulative, directional, multifactorial, and individual. A clear understanding of the term "developmental" is necessary to having a developmental perspective where one continuously thinks in terms of what preceded or will follow the child's current level of ability (Motor Development Task Force, 1994).

Recent work by NASPE has led to a definition of a physically educated person. A physically educated person "has learned the skills necessary to perform a variety of physical activities; is physically fit; does participate regularly in physical activity; knows the implications of and the benefits from involvement in physical activity; and values physical activity and its contributions to a healthful lifestyle" (NASPE, 1992). This definition subsequently led to the composition of seven national standards for physical education (NASPE, 1995).

To ensure that young children become physically educated an understanding of development from birth to 8 years of age is integral. Throughout the first year of life infant reflexes are exhibited. These movements, like a sucking or palmar grasp reflex, are involuntary yet may be the foundation for later voluntary movements. Throughout the first two years of life the voluntary movements of infancy and early childhood are prominent. Included are early attempts at reaching and grasping, rolling, sitting, standing, creeping, crawling, and even precursors to walking. From 2 to 7 years of age fundamental movements begin to emerge. Included are such movements as walking, running, skipping, throwing, catching, kicking, and striking.

Despite increasing understanding of these developmental trends, physical education programs for young children are often not developmentally appropriate. With some preplanning and an understanding of a developmental perspective, the program can become developmentally appropriate and even integrated with other curricular areas. Enriching lessons of this type can also be planned around a theme. Critical dimensions of most movement programs for young children would include development of body awareness; development of fundamental loco-motor patterns; allowing opportunities to manage one's own body weight; and development of fundamental manipulative patterns.

References

Barnes, M.R., Crutchfield, C.A., & Heriza, C.B. (1984). *The neuro-physiological basis of patient treatment*, vol. 2, *Reflexes in motor development*. Atlanta: Stokesville.

Branta, C., Haubentstricker, J., & Seefeldt, V. (1984). Age changes in motor skills during childhood and adolescence. In R.L Terjung (Ed.), *Exercise and sports sciences review*. New York: Macmillan.

Bredekamp, S. (1987). *Developmentally appropriate practices in early childhood programs: Serving children from birth through age 8*. Washington, DC: National Association for the Education of Young Children.

Bredekamp, S. & Copple, C. (Eds.). (1997). *Developmentally appropriate practice in early childhood programs: Revised*. Washington, DC: National Association for the Education of Young Children.

California Governor's Council on Physical Fitness and Sports. (1995). *Elementary school physical education: A scientifically documented position statement*.

Consensus and Summary Statements from Physical Activity, Health, and Well-being International Scientific Consensus Conference. (1995). *Research Quarterly for Exercise and Sport, 66*, ii–viii.

Council on Physical Education for Children. (1992). *Developmentally appropriate physical education practices for children*. Reston, VA: American Alliance for Health, Physical Education, Recreation, and Dance.

Council on Physical Education for Children. (1994). *Developmentally appropriate movement programs for young children ages 3–5*. Reston, VA: American Alliance for Health, Physical Education, Recreation, and Dance.

Fiorentino, M.R. (1981). *Reflex testing methods for evaluating C.N.S. development.* Springfield, IL: Thomas.

Gallahue, D.L. (1995). Transforming physical education curriculum. In S. Bredekamp & T. Rosegrant (Eds.), *Reaching potentials: Transforming early childhood curriculum and assessment.* Washington, DC: National Association for the Education of Young Children.

Halverson, H.M. (1931). An experimental study of prehension in infants by means of systematic cinema records. *Genetic Psychology Manuscripts, 10,* 107–286.

Harter, S. (1978). Effectance motivation reconsidered: Toward a developmental model. *Human Development, 21,* 34–64.

Harter, S. (1982). The perceived competence scale for children. *Child Development, 53,* 87–97.

Motor Development Task Force (National Association for Sports and Physical Education). (1994). *Looking at physical education from a developmental perspective: A guide to teaching.* Reston, VA: American Alliance for Health, Physical Education, Recreation, and Dance.

National Association for Sports and Physical Education. (1992). *Outcomes of quality physical education programs.* Reston, VA: American Alliance for Health, Physical Education, Recreation, and Dance.

National Association for Sports and Physical Education. (1995). *Moving into the future; National standards for physical education—A guide to content and assessment.* St. Louis: Mosby.

Payne, V.G., & Isaacs, L. (1995). *Human motor development: A lifespan approach.* Mountain View, CA: Mayfield.

Physical activity and health: A report of the Surgeon General (1996). U.S. Department of Health and Human Services, Centers for Disease Control and Prevention, National Center for Chronic Disease Prevention and Health Promotion and The President's Council on Physical Fitness and Sports.

Roberton, M.A., & Halverson, L.S. (1984). *Developing children— Their changing movement.* Philadelphia: Lea & Febiger.

CHAPTER SEVEN

Social Studies in the Developmentally Appropriate Integrated Curriculum

CAROL SEEFELDT

"Integrate your curriculum," the shiny, colorful brochure read, "with over 700 pages of seasonal activity sheets, make-and-do projects, and reproducible patterns" (IBC, 1994). Based on the claim that an integrated curriculum was important for children's success, the advertisement, filled with "hundreds of festive fall activities for October," "a cornucopia of teaching projects" for November, and "more great teaching ideas for the merry, merry month of May," promised to unify the curriculum, whether in a child care center, kindergarten, or primary grade.

An integrated curriculum is not only important for children's learning, but necessary. Research and theory support the fact that young children, who are whole, integrated beings, learn best through a curriculum that is also whole and integrated (Cobb, 1994; Dewey, 1944; Piaget & Inhelder, 1969). Recognizing the need for an integrated curriculum Bredekamp and Rosegrant state that "the interrelatedness of developmental domains virtually dictates an integrated approach to programming" (1992, p. 37).

But hundreds of reproducible activity sheets, packaged patterns, and make-and-do projects are not the way to create a meaningful, integrated curriculum that supports children's learning, growth, and development. Instead of using seven hundred activity sheets to integrate the curriculum, today's teachers use themes and topics revolving around the social studies that stem from children's social world and how it got that way (Jarolimek & Parker, 1993).

The Social Studies

The social studies, those studies that give primacy to the growth of the social individual and to understanding the complex world in which we live (Cuffaro, 1995), can serve to integrate the curriculum. The very definition of social studies conveys the integrative nature of the field. The social studies are defined as:

> The study of political, economic, cultural, and environmental aspects of societies of the past, present, and future. Designed to equip children with the knowledge and understanding of the past necessary for coping with the present and planning for the future, the social studies enable children to understand and participate effectively in their world and explain their relationships to other people, and to social, economic, and political institutions. (NCSS, 1989, p. 15)

This definition of the social studies, while broad and all encompassing, illustrates the potential of the social studies to integrate the early childhood curriculum (see also figure 7.1).

The social studies, in order to integrate the curriculum, must be grounded in the principles of developmentally appropriate practices (DAP) (Bredekamp, 1987; Bredekamp & Copple, 1997; Bredekamp & Rosegrant, 1992). DAP (Bredekamp, 1987) emphasizes learning as an interactive process, stating that:

- Curriculum planning is based on teachers' observations and recordings of each child's special interests and developmental progress (p. 3).
- Teachers prepare the environment for children to learn through active exploration and interaction with adults, other children, and materials (p. 3).
- Learning activities and materials should be concrete, real, and relevant to the lives of young children (p. 4).

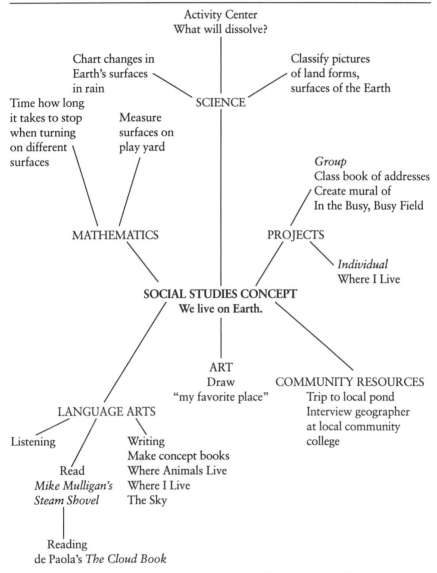

FIGURE 7.1
Social Studies as the Integrator

Activity Center
What will dissolve?

Chart changes in
Earth's surfaces
in rain

Classify pictures
of land forms,
surfaces of the Earth

Time how long
it takes to stop
when turning
on different
surfaces

SCIENCE

Measure
surfaces on
play yard

Group
Class book of addresses
Create mural of
In the Busy, Busy Field

MATHEMATICS

PROJECTS

Individual
Where I Live

SOCIAL STUDIES CONCEPT
We live on Earth.

ART
Draw
"my favorite place"

COMMUNITY RESOURCES
Trip to local pond
Interview geographer
at local community
college

LANGUAGE ARTS

Listening

Writing
Make concept books
Where Animals Live
Where I Live
The Sky

Read
Mike Mulligan's
Steam Shovel

Reading
de Paola's *The Cloud Book*

- Teachers provide a variety of activities and materials; they increase the difficulty, complexity, and challenge of an activity as children are involved with it and as they develop understanding and skills (p. 5).
- Adults are prepared to meet the needs of children who exhibit unusual interests and skills outside the normal developmental range (p. 4).

Beginning with an overview of frameworks designed to organize the social studies, this chapter describes children's understanding of concepts considered key to three disciplines of the social studies. How children gain these concepts through their own activity and experiences with their social world is included. The chapter concludes with an illustration of how the field of geography can serve to integrate the curriculum.

At the same time the all-encompassing nature of the social studies serves to integrate the curriculum, it also brings disorder. With its breadth, the field of the social studies lacks coherence, focus, and organization. To bring order to the field, several professional associations have presented frameworks for social studies education. The National Council for the Social Studies (NCSS), the National Council for Social Studies in the Schools (NCSSS), and the California State Board of Education (CSBE) have each developed position statements defining and organizing the social studies.

NCSS suggests that a planned K–12 social studies curriculum can be developed systematically and organized around key concepts in the study of geography, history, and economics. This plan is organized to include the processes and skills of social living as well.

Proposing a history-centered social studies curriculum, the CSBE organizes the field around the study of history. By organizing the social studies around the discipline of history, beginning during the period of early childhood, children will gain an "understanding of their own history, appreciate political and cultural diversity, and understand the economic and sociological realities of a rapidly changing world" (CSBE, 1989, p. xi).

"Breadth and depth," states NCSSS (1989, p. viii), "must co-exist . . . so that wide scanning and deep deliberation, knowing, and valuing, can all occur." Presenting a core of knowledge from history, geography, economics, and the humanities, NCSSS also believes they have designed a unifying and coherent framework for social studies in the schools.

These frameworks do have the potential to bring order to the social studies. The guidelines enable teachers to bring intellectual integrity to the social studies curriculum. Bruner (1960), writing of the need for intellectual honesty, advocated the use of key concepts. A framework of concepts key to a discipline would offer the potential for "simplifying information, for generating new propositions, and for increasing the manipulability of a body of knowledge" (p. 41).

Thinking in terms of key concepts may have first been suggested by Lucy Sprague Mitchell (1934). Mitchell described how key concepts from the field of geography could unify the social studies curriculum. By matching the key concepts to children's cognitive development, Mitchell believed, the study of geography could be made meaningful for children of any age. Starting with infancy and ending with the 12-year-old, Mitchell specified the interests, drives, orientation, and tools of children, and matched these with key concepts from geography. Then she wrote,

> To clarify my own thinking in working out a geography curriculum for children from four through thirteen, I made myself a sort of chart in which on one side, in progressive stages of development, I entered the interests which children showed, in their environment, the geographic relations which they had discovered, the kind of symbols they used in their play and art, in space relations, human geography and natural phenomena. I entered the practical school procedures which had developed from the children's maturity levels along with these various lines and in particular the maps they had made and used. (p. 17)

Today, each subject area discipline of the social studies has identified concepts key to its discipline. Table 7.1 displays a summary of these key concepts.

Bringing Key Concepts and Children Together

Identification of concepts key to a discipline is only one step in planning an integrated, meaningful social studies curriculum. The next is to understand what children already know about these concepts, and to identify and plan experiences that will extend and expand children's understanding.

TABLE 7.1
Key Concepts in History, Geography, and Economics

Key Concepts in History
  Time—The study of history is time-oriented.
  Change—As time passes, things change.
  Continuity of Life—Even though things change, there is continuity to the human experience.
  The Past—History is the study of the past.

Key Concepts in Geography
  The Earth is the Place We Live—The earth is covered with land and water and is part of the solar system.
  Direction and Location—Maps are a tool for locating self in space.
  Relationships within Places—Humans interact on the Earth.
  Spatial Interactions—There are patterns of movement of people, products, and information.
  Regions—Regions are manageable units on which to build knowledge of the world and study current events.

Key Concepts in Economics
  Scarcity and Decision Making—The wants of people everywhere are unlimited, but resources are limited. People must make decisions about their wants and needs.
  Producers and Consumers—Production is, to some extent, designed to meet the unlimited wants of consumers.
  Using Money and Barter—Money is used to purchase goods.

Admittedly, children's existing concepts are incomplete and inaccurate. Five-year-old Lauren's aunt came to visit her. The aunt said, "Oh, Lauren, I forget to bring you something, but I'll mail it to you." About an hour after her aunt had left, Lauren ran to the mailbox, only to be disappointed to find no gift waiting for her. Lauren had a concept of time and mail, but they were only beginning concepts.

It would be unlikely, however, for children to gain conventional concepts without this foundation of everyday, personal concepts (Pintrich, Marx, & Boyle, 1993). Vygotsky called these beginning concepts embryonic. He explained that although they stemmed from children's everyday experiences, they were critical to the development of accurate, conventional, or scientific concepts. "An everyday concept clears the path for the scientific concept. . . . It creates a series of structures necessary for the evolution of a concept's more primitive, elementary aspects, that give it body and vitality. Scientific concepts grow down through spontaneous concepts; spontaneous concepts grow upward through scientific concepts" (Vygotsky, 1986, p. 109).

Teachers might ask themselves a series of questions based on those Spodek (1977) suggested. These will help them gain an understanding of children's existing knowledge, as well as how to make concepts considered key to social studies disciplines meaningful to children.

1. *From this body of knowledge, what holds meaning for this group of children and for each individual child?*

What are children interested in? What has meaning to them? Obviously asking children to memorize historic dates or the capitals of states has little meaning for young children. These facts are abstract, and unrelated to children's daily lives.

2. *What aspects of this concept or content can be introduced to children through their own firsthand experiences or through community field trips?*

Children, as all humans, learn through experiences. Children should not be asked to memorize historic dates, but they might be able to take a walk to a historic marker in the community or start charting their own stories.

3. *What ideas or understanding do children have of this content?*

If only we were wise, we would look at the world through little children's eyes! As adults, we forget how new children are to this world, and how meaningful and exciting the here-and-now world is to children.

One teacher, implementing a unit on fire safety, asked children to tell her everything they knew about firefighters. Children had little to say, but as she probed, she found that most of the children believed firefighters started fires. She was then able to plan experiences to correct children's existing knowledge and expand their embryonic understandings (see table 7.2).

4. *How can the concept be integrated with what children have already experienced or learned?*

Learning does not occur in a vacuum or isolation chamber. Learning is whole and united. When planning meaningful social studies think of how one experience builds on another and how each experience is connected to another. Lauren's teacher, hearing of her experience with the mail, read stories about mail, took children to the school office to identify all the machines and the way people communicated with each other, and took a trip to a nearby post office. She set up numbered mailboxes in the room so children could write to each other, and then had children write themselves letters, address envelopes, and mail them. With eager anticipation, the children counted the days until they

TABLE 7.2
Interviewing Children

Teachers can ask children individually:
"Tell me everything you know about . . . "
Probing, teachers can ask children to:
- show them
- dance
- draw or paint a picture about the concept

Going deeper, teachers can ask children:
"Why did you say that?"
"Why else do you know?"
"Why do you suppose . . . ?"
"What would happen if . . . ?"

received their letters. In doing so, the teacher integrated reading, writing, mathematics (finding numbered mail boxes, addressing envelopes), economics (purchasing stamps), and a field trip into one social studies experience.

5. What does the novice learner, such as a child, need to learn now?

Do 4-, 5-, or even 7- or 8-year-olds really need to know the capital of their state or the names of planets in the solar system? No—because none of these facts can be used by children. What do children need to know about their state or the solar system? What is the most elementary idea of a given social studies concept that will be useful to children?

Fortunately, researchers and authorities have determined the nature of children's basic understandings of history, geography, economics, and other disciplines comprising the social studies. Reviewing this research and theory offers guidelines in creating an integrated social studies curriculum.

History

History, believed to be the integrator of the social studies, is of great interest to young children. Who hasn't heard a child ask for just one more story "about the olden days, when I was little, really little"? But history is a time-oriented discipline that deals with abstract and complicated concepts of change, the continuity of life, and the past, and children have limited understanding of each of these concepts.

Even though they are interested in the immediate past, the question of how to introduce these concepts to young children remains.

By beginning with what children already understand of concepts key to the study of history, teachers have a foundation on which to plan meaningful experiences with history. An understanding of children's intuitive sense of time, change, and the continuity of life informs teachers and guides their selection of learning activities (see table 7.3).

Time

"Is today tomorrow?" asked Aletha, skipping into the child care center. Aletha's teacher had told her the day before in response to her numerous questions about when they would go to the pumpkin patch that "tomorrow is the day we will go" (Seefeldt, 1975). Children's concepts of time are intuitive and embryonic. Young children have little concept of conventional time, nor will they be ready for instruction in time until well over 7 or 8 years of age (Vukelich & Thornton, 1990).

Five-year-olds begin to understand temporal units of time such as day, date, and calendar time, and can orient themselves in time, associating time with an external event. "It is day; the sun is shining."

TABLE 7.3
Time Concept Development

Sensorimotor 0–2	*Preoperational* 2–6/7	*Concrete* 6/7–10
Observes, follows routines	Ideas of time are personal and subjective	Utilizes clocks, watches to tell time
By age 2, aware of day/night	Measures time with arbitrary units	Ready for instruction in time concepts
Attends to environment	By age 5, some understanding of time units such as day	Conventional concepts will not develop until formal operational period—age 12+
	Recalls past, plans for future	
	By age 5, can sequence events of a day and use time words	

They will not, however, be able to understand conventional concepts of time until they are young adolescents, when they can understand operational time that requires logical thought and involves understanding relations of succession and duration (French, 1989; Piaget, 1971).

Still, young children are receptive to learning about time, if their learning is based on the cyclical, recurring, and sequential events of their day and life (Dunfee, 1970). Even though routines in an early childhood program are flexible, they occur with a regularity children can depend on. Talking about routines and labeling them with time words children can first respond to, and then use themselves, teaches children about time. Around 1st grade or so, children can begin to utilize clocks and watches to keep track of time (Patrirarca & Alleman, 1987).

Meaningful opportunities to measure time also occur in early childhood programs (see figure 7.2). Regardless of whether the goal of cooking is to introduce children to mathematics concepts of measurement or scientific concepts that matter changes, the experience offers

FIGURE 7.2
Experience with Time in the Integrated Curriculum

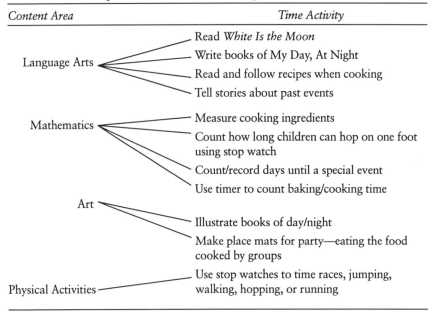

Content Area	Time Activity
Language Arts	Read *White Is the Moon*
	Write books of My Day, At Night
	Read and follow recipes when cooking
	Tell stories about past events
Mathematics	Measure cooking ingredients
	Count how long children can hop on one foot using stop watch
	Count/record days until a special event
	Use timer to count baking/cooking time
Art	Illustrate books of day/night
	Make place mats for party—eating the food cooked by groups
Physical Activities	Use stop watches to time races, jumping, walking, hopping, or running

children the opportunity to measure time. They can set timers and measure the time it takes for bread or their gingerbread people to finish baking, the applesauce to cook, or the pudding to set.

Timers can also be used to measure the time it takes for specific activities. Children might use stop watches to measure how many minutes it takes them to get ready to go out to play or the time it takes to clean up. A 1st grade class, intrigued with stop watches, began to measure how long they could jump rope without missing, hop on one foot, and complete a relay race. The seconds and minutes it took to accomplish a large number of activities were charted, and books were written about the passage and measurement of time. Thus social studies became integrated with the language arts, mathematics, and physical education.

Calendars are used as well, but only as they are functional and of immediate use to children. No child learns concepts of time by watching a teacher count the number of days they have been in school, or by finding all of the days of the week beginning with a letter "T." Nor do they need to spend the first twenty minutes of every day from preschool through the primary grades listening to a teacher talk about how many days children have been in school, or saying the names of the days of the week or months of the year while pointing to charts or calendars. But children do gain an understanding of calendar time when they count and record the days before a special event or the days that have passed since a birthday. By anticipating a coming event, children are learning to think of the future and to set goals. Thus, the simple act of using a calendar to record special events becomes a meaningful planning experience.

Reading to children is another way to increase their understanding of time concepts, but is reading to children a language arts activity or a part of the social studies? Obviously reading to children is an integrated act in itself. There are many wondrous books that bring children in touch with the power and beauty of language, as well as expose them to concepts of time. The sounds and patterns of the language of Greeley's *White Is the Moon* (1990) are enjoyed by children of any age and introduce even the youngest to the fact that time passes and is measured. Martin's *Good Morning, Good Night* (1968) is suited for the youngest of children, while Martin's *Knots on a Counting Rope* (1968) can be utilized by primary age children to increase their awareness of how time has been measured in the past.

Change

As time passes, things change. If children are to gain a sense of history, they must understand concepts of change. For young children whose thought is dominated by perception, however, change is a difficult concept for them to gain (Seefeldt, 1993b). Because children under the age of 8 or so have limited ability to conserve, changes that occur with the passage of time must appear as magical and unrelated to logic as any other change they experience.

Without an understanding of change, children are even unsure of the constancy and continuity of their own lives. Children under 5 years of age are uncertain of the stability of their own gender (Slaby & Frey, 1975). Nor do they understand the changes that occur with illness and death.

Aging and death, to young children, appear as events that can occur suddenly, either as the result of contagion or immanent justice. "Don't touch him," commanded a 5-year-old to her 7-year-old brother who was talking with an elderly man. "You might catch it [old age] if you get too close to him." "I won't die for a long, long time," bragged a 4-year-old child, explaining "because I'm always good" (Galper et al., 1980).

Change is a part of children's life, however, and these changes are the basis for introducing children to concepts of change. Children themselves change. They grow, learn new skills, lose teeth, and get their hair cut. Their moods change—one moment they are happy, the next in tears. And their families change—babies are born, people move away, and others die. Elkind (1981) suggests that these naturally occurring changes are the beginning of the study of change and history.

Children get the opportunity to keep track of the changes that occur in their lives through integrating evaluation strategies with concepts of time (see figure 7.3). In a portfolio, children and teachers keep samples of children's work; notes by both children and teachers about important events, their feelings, and accomplishments; and other information about children's growth, change, and progress (Grace & Shores, 1992). Kindergarten and primary teachers have found the practice of involving children in parent conferences around the portfolio useful. During parent-teacher conferences, teachers ask children to first go over the portfolio with their parents, describing their work, progress, and growth. Then the teacher, parent, and child discuss the child's progress. Teachers ask the child to tell their parent what they liked

FIGURE 7.3
Change in the Integrated Curriculum

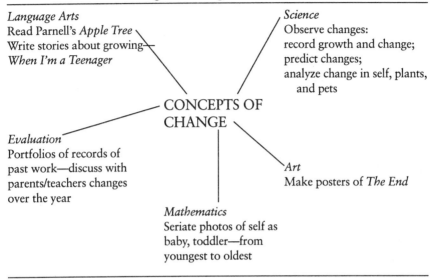

Language Arts
Read Parnell's *Apple Tree*
Write stories about growing
When I'm a Teenager

Science
Observe changes:
record growth and change;
predict changes;
analyze change in self, plants,
and pets

CONCEPTS OF
CHANGE

Evaluation
Portfolios of records of
past work—discuss with
parents/teachers changes
over the year

Art
Make posters of *The End*

Mathematics
Seriate photos of self as
baby, toddler—from
youngest to oldest

best about an event of special import, how they have changed, and what they plan to work on during the coming months (thus integrating the concepts of change with those of time).

Literature also supports focus on the changes that occur in children's lives. One teacher read A. A. Milne's poem "The End," (Milne, 1924), which begins with a child saying he was just begun when only one and concludes with him saying he will be clever as clever when 6. After reading the poem the children began a study of how much they had changed since they were one. They seriated baby photos of themselves and wrote their own poems about what they could do when one, 2, and so on. A poster for their door was painted illustrating the changes that had occurred during the first six years of their life.

Continuity of Life

Continuity is another abstract history concept, and one that appears limited in young children. For children under the ages of 7 or 8, time is discontinuous. It can appear to stop with any partial motion. This is why adults are believed to have stopped aging, or why a tree is thought to age if it still grows, but not otherwise. Only with the introduction of operational time will duration and the changes that occur with the passage of time be understood as a continuous flux (Acredo & Schmid, 1981). Still, the concept that life is continuous, that there is continuity to the human experience, is an important one. Margaret Mead (1970) suggested that children need the living presence of at least three generations to build an awareness of the continuity of human life.

Elders can be invited to volunteer or visit classrooms. They might teach children how they played a game familiar to the children when they were young. One grandmother taught the children to play "Cootie" by drawing the cootie, one part at a time, instead of assembling the cootie with plastic parts. The children decided they enjoyed drawing their own imaginative cootie more than simply putting plastic parts together, and at the same time felt a sense of security knowing that things stay the same even though changes do occur.

The Past

To understand the past children must be able to comprehend that the present is but a single moment in a continuous process. Temporal sequencing concepts, such as before and after, tomorrow and yesterday, or those that require only that children position two points in time, are generally not accurately understood prior to age 7 or 8 (Friedman, 1990).

Then, too, to understand the past children must also be able to store and retrieve memories. The literature on children's memory development is vast and readily available (Brainerd et al., 1990). Despite the differing theories on memory development, this literature documents the fact that children under the age of 7 or 8 have problems with storage as well as retrieval of memories. The process of being able to recall the past is based on a changing operational structure that continually governs and transforms what has been stored (Piaget & Inhelder, 1969).

To introduce children to concepts of the past, a 1st grade teacher often used a calendar at the end of the day instead of the beginning. Reflecting on what they had learned, enjoyed, and accomplished during the day, children recorded special activities and events on a large calendar, drawing pictures of their activities in a blank space under each day.

These calendars were then posted in the coatroom, where children continued reflecting on their past as they took off or put on their coats throughout the year. Children used math concepts as they counted the days and months that had passed, as well as predicted what they would do in the future. By reflecting on their past, children were gaining more than simple concepts from the study of social studies. They were gaining a sense of self-competence, of self-esteem as they thought about the things they had learned, the events they had enjoyed, and the things they were yet to do and learn.

Literature can make the past meaningful to young children. For children under the age of 3 or so, books about their day or what they did in the morning, in the evening, or on a walk are sufficient to introduce them to the past. Preschool children over 4 or 5 years old enjoy hearing stories of children who lived in the past, such as Clifton's *All Us Come Cross the Water* (1973) or Levinson's *Watch the Stars Come Out* (1989). Books such as these enable children to learn important ideas about the past as well as begin to understand the profound fact that although change is always a constant, there is a continuity to human life on this planet.

Geography

Geography is not the study of disconnected, static facts, or locating places on a map, but an understanding of, and an appreciation for the physical and cultural environment in which we live. Knowledge of geography provides a sense of place and relationship in time to historical and current events (NCSSS, 1989).

Study of geography, said Lucy Sprague Mitchell (1934), begins unofficially at birth. The infant first attends to and experiments with the qualities of things, including her own body, distance, weight, size, color, texture, etc. Teachers of young children build on children's beginning experiences with geography and children's understandings of key concepts in the field, including the Earth, direction and location, and relationships within places.

TABLE 7.4
Geography Skills

Sensorimotor 0–2	Preoperational 2–6/7	Concrete 6/7–10
Attends to qualities of things; self, Earth, sky Moves in Space	Moves on Earth Orients self in a given space, like in a room Represents world in building and drawing Draws rough maps, can find treasures with rough map Begins orientation to distance	8+, still having difficulty with left and right Still confused about relating directions 12+, understands cardinal directions

Earth—The Place We Live

Children are close to the Earth. They walk on and dig in it, yet their concepts of the Earth are primitive. Preoperational thinking dominates their ideas about it (see table 7.4). Piaget was told when he asked young children how the Earth was made that "All stones have been made by builders out of the earth and the earth is broken stone"; "Mountains made themselves so we can ski" (1965, p. 207). Determining that children thought the Earth was created either by people or itself, and often for children's own use, Piaget labeled this stage of thinking as *artificialism*. Animistic thought, the belief that anything that moves, as well as the idea that many things have the potential to move, also appears to influence children's ideas of the Earth as the place we live.

The concept that the Earth is a nearly round sphere and is a part of the solar system is clearly beyond that of young children. Nor is a complete and accurate understanding of the facts of the rotation of the Earth and revolution around the sun possible until late adolescence (Piaget, 1965).

Nevertheless, as Mitchell (1934) illustrated, it is during the early years of life that the foundations for later geographic learning are built. Therefore teachers ask themselves, "What have these children learned through their own experiences about the Earth?" "What do they understand of the natural phenomena—the action of the earth forces, how water runs down a hill, the effects of growth of plants and animals?" Based on their answers, teachers plan firsthand as well as meaningful vicarious experiences to extend children's embryonic understandings of the Earth.

Firsthand experiences include trips into the neighborhood and community. Walking field trips are taken frequently to explore different surfaces of the Earth, land forms, or to observe how humans change their land. Art activities are called for after explorations into the community (see figure 7.4). Children might create murals to represent their experiences. One teacher gave a committee the task of painting the bottom of a large sheet of mural paper green, to represent the Earth, and the top blue. All children drew, and then cut out and pasted on either the Earth or the sky of the mural, something they had noted—birds, trees, houses, planes—on a recent excursion into their community.

FIGURE 7.4
Geography—The Integrative Power of a Field Trip

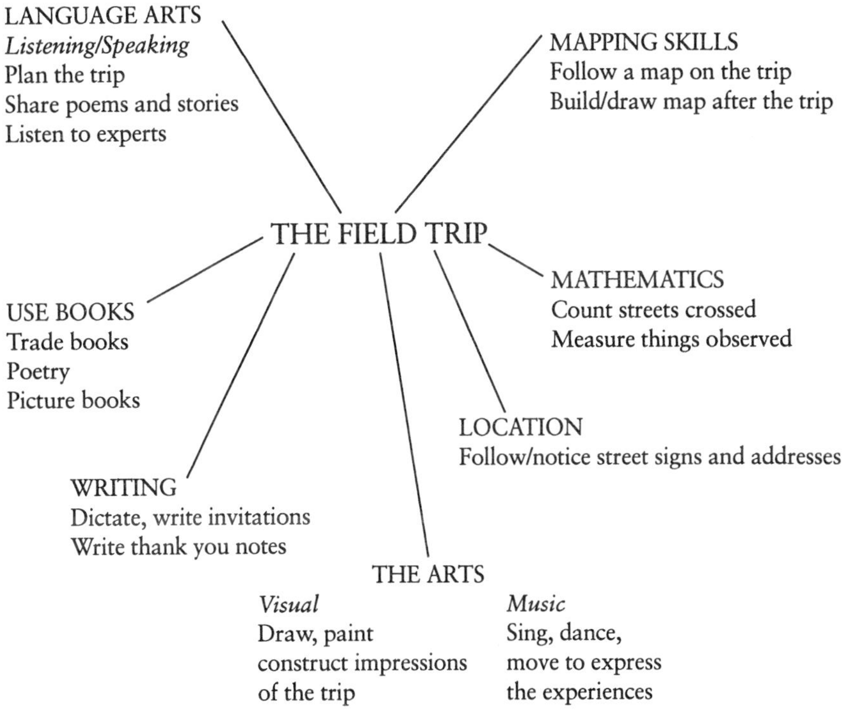

LANGUAGE ARTS
Listening/Speaking
Plan the trip
Share poems and stories
Listen to experts

MAPPING SKILLS
Follow a map on the trip
Build/draw map after the trip

THE FIELD TRIP

USE BOOKS
Trade books
Poetry
Picture books

MATHEMATICS
Count streets crossed
Measure things observed

LOCATION
Follow/notice street signs and addresses

WRITING
Dictate, write invitations
Write thank you notes

THE ARTS
Visual
Draw, paint
construct impressions
of the trip

Music
Sing, dance,
move to express
the experiences

One class took a walk to a nearby field. The children ran through tall grass, found insects under rocks, picked seed pods, and collected stones. Returning to their room, they read *In the Tall, Tall Grass* (Fleming, 1993) and wrote their own poem entitled *In the Busy, Busy, Field*. This teacher, when questioned why the children were not spending the allocated twenty minutes a day in writing activities, articulated how the trip to "explore the Earth" integrated the curriculum. She listed the reading and writing concepts, and because the children had seriated seed pods and counted legs on insects and spiders, she listed the mathematics and science concepts the children had experienced as well. The principal, so impressed, later used the books children had written in a show and tell about the curriculum at a parents' meeting.

Direction and Location

Concepts of direction develop gradually throughout the period of childhood. Studies suggest that even 8- and 9-year-olds still have difficulty with accurately identifying left and right, and it is not until after age 12 that an adequate understanding of cardinal directions develops (Lord, 1941). Relative directions develop slowly as well. Second and 3rd graders are still confused about relative directions, and they do not understand that a person facing them will raise the opposite hand when asked to raise their right hand.

Concepts of location are believed to begin at birth. From birth through about 14 months of age, infants explore and attend to the qualities of things in their environment. By age 3, children can distinguish between objects that are near and far away, and can identify the boundaries of their immediate environment, such as their classroom and play yard. If concepts of direction and location are to be constructed by children, it is not enough to simply take children on trips into the community. Sensory intake is an important part of the process of learning, but not the only process. Back in the classroom materials are necessary through which children can reflect on their excursions into the community as well as express their thinking about it.

The perfect tool for this expression and reflection is blocks. Especially in the primary grades, blocks give children the opportunity to recreate the world they have physically explored, construct images of this world, and develop concepts of how they can locate self in space. Paints, drawing tools, and things to construct with such as paper boxes, rolls, and pieces of fabric and wood offer children other ways to express and reflect on their trips through their personal spaces and into the wider community.

Despite the opportunities children's explorations of their immediate neighborhood and community offer in enabling them to construct concepts of direction and location, any formal teaching of directions will not be profitable until the period of middle childhood. Through the period of early and middle childhood, it will be necessary for children to experience their world firsthand in order to build the knowledge necessary for them to gain concepts of direction and to benefit from direct instruction when in high school.

Relationships within Places

Through play, children develop a sense of personal geography (Hinitz, 1987). By the preschool years there is an understanding of the spatial relationships between objects, and children express these as they build with blocks, play in sand and water, or construct with other materials. "Place" is important to children. Blades (1993) believes children are attached to their personal places such as home, school, and neighborhood. Beginning with trips to explore these personal spaces, trips throughout the neighborhood are taken to expand children's idea of place and help them develop and refine their concepts of location and direction. While on excursions through the community, teachers can point out street signs, refer to the location of the school in relation to where they are and where they are going, and use direction vocabulary. Children can follow a simple map, perhaps one made by the teacher.

It is not expected that children understand mapping concepts such as perspective or scale, but only that they gain awareness of maps and their use. According to Piaget and Inhelder (1969), children must achieve formal thinking before they can fully understand the complexity of mapping. Spencer, Harrison, and Darvizeh (1980) reported that 3-year-olds interpreted aerial photographs and maps in geographical terms, indicating that even young children have concepts of maps. Stages of mapping skills were outlined by Copeland (1974).

Children in stage 1 could locate objects using the concepts of proximity and enclosure. In stage 2, children between the ages of 4 and 7 could locate and develop reference points and locate items in terms of left, right, in front of, and behind. After the age of about 7, children in stage 3 could locate or place items on another map without difficulty (Hinitz, 1987). Because young children enjoy using and making maps and researchers have demonstrated their ability to use maps, mapping activities should be included as one way to enhance geographical concepts. Maps are a great way to integrate other curricula areas. Not only will social studies concepts be emphasized, but the language arts and mathematics will also be supported. In using mapping activities, teachers should keep in mind that mapping should stem from children's own experiences and should be on a continuum from the concrete to the abstract.

Economics

It would be impossible for the preschool or primary child not to experience or be aware of concepts from the field of economics. In today's world, nearly everyone, regardless of how old or young, comes in contact with the processes of economics. Daily children observe their parents exchanging money for goods, or they make purchases themselves. Some receive money as gifts and open bank accounts, and others begin saving for some special toy or activity.

Observing children's play reveals that children do come in contact with economic concepts and have developed an initial awareness of the field. They play store, pretending to purchase goods, count pretend money, and argue over not having enough money when they play as if they were a parent.

Nevertheless, children's economic concepts, as those of geography and history, are embryonic. They are beginning to be developed and will require years of experiences before conventional economic concepts are formed. In fact, it will not be until after age 9 or so that children will be able to understand the concept of money, be able to compare coins, and comprehend the idea of credit or profit (Berti & Bombi, 1988). According to Piagetian theory, children's economic concepts are first unreflective and preoperational, exemplified by a highly literal reasoning based on the physical characteristics of objects or processes. Next, transitional or emerging concepts develop, similar to those at the concrete operational stage. Finally, by adolescence, children gain the ability to reason abstractly and develop conventional economic concepts (Kourilsky, 1985; Schug & Birkey, 1985). Children will view each of the concepts key to the study of economics, scarcity and wants, producing and consuming, and the use of money and barter, from the perspective of their preoperational or concrete operational thinking.

Scarcity and Decision Making

When you spend time with young children you think there will never be enough of anything—toys, cookies, friends, or time. Children's "I wanna's" are constant. In part, learning concepts of scarcity is closely tied to learning about decision making. Children will need to learn to differentiate between those things they "wanna now" and the things they need in order to learn to make wise decisions.

But children are too young to make decisions concerning many aspects of their lives. They are too young, without the cognitive maturity or knowledge necessary, to make decisions affecting their health, education, and welfare. Children must depend on others to think and make these decisions for them.

At the same time, however, children must *not* learn the habit of being dependent on others to think and decide for them. Thus, teachers must carefully plan for children to make real decisions. Daily children decide which centers they will work in and what they will do in the center. They are the ones who will decide how much time they will spend in the center, and when to leave and move to another center. Other decisions children can make safely are who they will play with and work with, what songs to sing, where to plant seeds, and which books they will read. And even though children do not often decide on the menu, they must decide what and how much they will eat of a given meal.

Helping children make decisions concerning their wants and needs is important. Diverting the materialism that surrounds Christmas, a teacher capitalized on children's increasing demands for toys and other things they wanted to receive. Bringing in a number of toy and other catalogs, she asked children to make charts of all the things they wanted, categorizing these into toys, clothes, foods, and trips. Next she asked children to think of the things they really needed. Discussing their needs, children then drew pictures and made books of the few things they really wanted and those things they believed they really needed.

Dewey (1944) reminds us that the power of decision making lies in experiencing the consequences of the decision. There is no way to learn other than to experience the consequences of an action, yet children must have the right to make mistakes without the loss of self-esteem. As children experience the initial frustration of having made a wrong decision, they can learn how to live with the consequences of that decision and ways to decide more wisely the next time.

Consuming, Producing, Money, and Barter

You only need to observe children in a grocery, toy, or department store to realize they are consumers that have definite ideas about what they will purchase. Children's understanding of consuming increases with age, but it is also influenced by personal experiences and socioeconomic factors (Caruso, 1989). As children have more opportunities to experience being consumers, they show more awareness of the process. According to McNeal (1987), children between the ages of 4 and 12 spend over $4 billion annually on purchases that they choose. While preschoolers express interest in purchases of goods such as clothing and influence the purchases made by their parents, kindergartners are even more involved in the process (Haynes, et al., 1993). By the time children are at the concrete operational stage of development, they indicate strong brand preferences (Moschis & Moore, 1982).

Children's ideas of what to purchase are heavily influenced by advertisement (Notar, 1989). It's not surprising that they have ideas about specific items to purchase because children are believed to watch three to five hours of television daily. To help children make decisions about what they will, and will not purchase, they can be asked to weigh their purchases in terms of their goals and values, make selections from the alternatives, and then accept the consequences and responsibilities arising from their decisions.

As consumers, children are aware that money is necessary. As young as 3, children can distinguish between money and things that are not money, but are not able to differentiate between coins (Berti & Bombi,

1988). By 4 and 5 years of age, children are aware that they need money to buy things, but they think the clerks or shopkeepers give money to customers and that any type of coin is suitable to make a purchase. Nor do children under 6 or 7 understand that people go to work to get money, and they do not understand the relationship between money and pay. To them, one works *and* gets money, rather than one gets money because one works (Berti & Bombi, 1988). Around the time concrete operations appear, children develop the concept that they do need enough money to make a specific purchase, and are moving toward some clarity in understanding the employer–employee relationship. Yet they are still far from a clear understanding of customer and producer concepts.

Interwoven with concepts of consumer are those of producer. The best way for a young child to develop concepts of producer is to become one (Waite, Smith, & Schug, 1991). Children can produce many types of goods at school, and even work to provide services to others. Children might produce gifts for parents, for children in a sister school in another country, or for themselves. Some things primary children can produce are greeting cards, wrapping paper, plants contained in decorated containers, and cookies or other baked goods (see table 7.5).

During the process of producing enough "stone soup" to feed all four 2nd grade classes, children in one school found that their work was more efficient when jobs were divided among them. Some

TABLE 7.5
Economics Concept Development

Sensorimotor 0–2	*Preoperational* 2–6/7	*Concrete* 6/7–10
Observes and attends to shape and size of coins	Plays store—demonstrating initial concepts of consuming and purchasing	After 9+ can compare coins, knows relative value of coins
Observes shopping, consuming, and purchasing	Counts more or less	Understands that people work because they get money
	Recognizes coins/money	Shows some clarity in understanding employer–employee relationship
	Knows money is necessary to make purchases	

children cut carrots; others, potatoes. Still others made invitations and placemats, while another group was in charge of setting the tables. Following the eating of the stone soup, children reflected on their experiences by drawing and writing their stories of how they made stone soup.

Field trips into the community are useful in fostering children's awareness of concepts of consumer and producer (Cox, 1993). Taking children to a nearby ice cream parlor, for instance, opened up opportunities for lively discussion of the role of producers and consumers inside one classroom. Back in the classroom, the group set up a pretend ice cream store, complete with the making and selling of ice cream. The fact that the social studies serves to integrate the curriculum was clear from this experience. Not only were concepts of producer and consumer discussed, but before, during, and after the trip, children also discussed and researched topics such as health, hygiene, diet, and the history of ice cream making (Cox, 1993).

Summary

What are the social studies? Are they only those studies revolving around the social world of children? Or are they mathematics, language arts, science, music, or art? The answer is that the social studies, an integrated collection of social science disciplines and processes that are integral to the total curriculum, are in fact, integrated with every other subject and content area of the total curriculum.

Stemming from children's social and physical world, and not activity sheets or "hundreds of activities" found in purchased teaching kits, experiences and content from the social studies give children something to think, talk, find out, read, and write about. "The centrality of the *social* in social studies repeatedly brings questions and ideas back to children" (Cuffaro, 1995, p. 84).

Experiences push children to ask why. "Why didn't Auntie mail me my gift?" "How does the mail carrier find my house?" "What happens if I write a letter to my aunt?" When children experience, they feel, think, and imagine. These feelings and ideas push children to expression. By writing, talking, playing, drawing, painting, singing, dancing, or constructing, children give form to their feelings and thoughts—forms that others now can take meaning from.

Seeking to express their experiences through language or find an answer to a question using mathematics, children practice emerging skills. Because the skills of reading, writing, and computing are of immediate use to children, they have meaning. With meaning, children have the opportunity to gain skills, that if taught through isolated skill and practice, could never be mastered.

No child has ever done much thinking when completing "over 700 pages of seasonal activity sheets, make-and-do projects, and reproducible patterns" (IBC, 1994). But a great deal of thinking is required when children are asked to keep a record of their work and discuss it with their parents during a conference revolving around their own portfolio. Nor can children take a trip into the community and then recreate their experiences by building with blocks without recalling their experiences and thinking about them.

Perhaps more important, however, content from the social studies makes us human. The social processes of interacting and negotiating, and the social skills of our society, are practiced, honed, and built through the social studies. As children explore concepts of consumers and producers, they plan and work together, gaining knowledge and practicing the skills of negotiating, cooperating, and sharing. Listening to the stories of others, those close to them, or perhaps those far away in place and time or from their here-and-now world, children share in the lives of others. They recognize others share the same feelings, joys, disappointments, fears, and hopes they have, and begin to feel at one with others.

Social studies educators would say there is no doubt that the social studies are the true integrator of the curriculum. Nevertheless, those who are experts of mathematics, the sciences, language, visual, or musical arts, or any other discipline, would say the same thing, for there really is no way to separate curriculum for young children into separate subjects. Life is whole, children are whole, learning is whole.

Thus, regardless of which subject matter discipline is chosen as an integrator, the early childhood curriculum is based in children's experiences. These experiences cannot be separated into different subjects or disciplines. Experiences, as children and their learning, are whole.

References

Acredo, C., & Schmid, J. (1981). The understanding of relative speeds, distances, and durations of movement. *Developmental Psychology, 17*, 490–93.

Berti, A.E., & Bombi, A.S. (1988). *The child's construction of economics*. Cambridge: Cambridge University Press.

Blades, M. (1993). Children's understanding of places. *Geography, 78*, 367–80.

Brainerd, C.J., Reyna, V.F., Howe, M.L., & Longman, J. (1990). The development of forgetting and reminiscence: With commentary by Robert E. Guttentag and a reply by C.J.H. Brainerd. *Monographs of the Society for Research in Child Development, 55*.

Bredekamp, S. (Ed.). (1987). *Developmentally appropriate practice in early childhood programs serving children from birth through age 8*. Washington, DC: National Association for the Education of Young Children.

Bredekamp, S., & Copple, C. (Eds.). (1997). *Developmentally appropriate practice in early childhood programs: Revised*. Washington, DC: National Association for the Education of Young Children.

Bredekamp, S., & Rosegrant, T. (1992). Reaching potentials through appropriate curriculum: Conceptual frameworks for applying the guidelines. In S. Bredekamp & T. Rosegrant (Eds.), *Reaching potentials: Appropriate curriculum and assessment for young children*: Vol. 1 (pp. 28–42). Washington, DC: National Association for the Education of Young Children.

Brown, M. (1947). *Stone soup*. New York: Scribners & Sons.

Bruner, J. (1960). *The process of education*. Cambridge, MA: Harvard University Press.

California State Board of Education (CSBE). (1989). *History social science framework*. Sacramento, CA: Author.

Caruso, P.L. (1989). *Consumer socialization of preschool children*. Unpublished master's thesis, Louisiana State University, Baton Rouge.

Clifton, L. (1973). *All us come across the water*. New York: Harper & Row.

Cobb, P. (1994). Constructivism in mathematics and science education. *Educational Researcher, 22* (7), 4–5.

Copeland, R. (1974). *How children learn mathematics: Teaching implications of Piaget's research.* New York: Macmillan.

Cox, C. C. (1993). The field trip as a positive experience for the learning disabled. *Social Education, 92* (3), 92–95.

Cuffaro, H. (1995). *Experimenting with the world.* New York: Teachers College Press.

Dewey, J. (1944). *Democracy and education.* New York: The Free Press.

Dunfee, M. (1970). *Elementary social studies: A guide to current research.* Washington, DC: Association for Supervision and Curriculum Development.

Elkind, D. (1981). Child development and the social studies curriculum of the elementary school. *Social Education, 45,* 435–37.

Fleming, D. (1993). *In the tall, tall grass.* New York: Holt.

French, L. A. (1989). Temporal knowledge expressed in preschoolers' descriptions of familiar activities. *Papers and Reports in Child Language Development, 20,* 61–69.

Friedman, W.J. (1990). Children's representations of the pattern of daily activities. *Child Development, 61,* 1399–1413.

Galper, A., Jantz, R.K., Seefeldt, C., & Serock, K. (1980). Children's concepts of age. *International Journal of Aging and Human Development, 12,* 129–57.

Grace, F. & Shores, E.F. (1992). *The portfolio and its use: Developmentally appropriate assessment for young children.* Little Rock, AR: Southern Association for the Education of Young Children.

Greeley, V. (1990). *White is the moon.* New York: Macmillan.

Haynes, J.L., Burts, D.C., Dukes, A., & Cloud, R.M. (1993). Consumer socialization of preschoolers and kindergartners as related to clothing consumption. *Psychology and Marketing, 10* (2), 151–66.

Hinitz, B.F. (1987). Social studies in early childhood education. In C. Seefeldt (Ed.), *The early childhood curriculum: A review of current research* (pp. 237–55). New York: Teachers College Press.

Instructor's Pre-School Book Club (IBC). (1994). *Seasonal patterns, projects, & plans.* Delran, NJ: Newbridge Book Club.

Jarolmek, J., & Parker, W.C. (1993). *Social studies in elementary education* (9th ed.). New York: Macmillan.

Kourilsky, M. (1985). *Children's use of cost benefit analysis: Developmental or nonexistent?* Paper presented at the annual meeting of the American Educational Research Association.

Levinson, R. (1985). *Watch the stars come out.* New York: Dutton.

Lord, F. (1941). A study of orientation of children. *Journal of Educational Research, 34,* 481–505.

Martin, B. (1968a). *Good morning, good night.* New York: Holt.

Martin, B. (1968b). *Knots on a counting rope.* New York: Holt.

McNeal, J.U. (1987). *Children as consumers: Insights and implications.* Lexington: Heath.

Mead, M. (1970). *Culture and commitment.* New York: The American Museum of Natural History.

Milne, A.A. (1924). The end. In A.A. Milne (Ed.), *Now we are six.* New York: Dutton.

Mitchell, L.S. (1934). *Young geographers.* New York: Bank Street College.

Moschis, G.P., & Moore, R.L. (1982). Decision making among the young: A socialization perspective. *Journal of Consumer Research, 6,* 101–11.

National Council for the Social Studies (NCSS). (1989). *Social studies for early childhood and elementary school children: Preparing for the 21st century.* Washington, DC: Author.

National Council for the Social Studies in the Schools. (NCSSS). (1989). *Charting a course: Social studies for the 21st century.* New York: Author.

Notar, E. (1989). Children and TV commercials: Wave after wave of exploitation. *Childhood Education, 66,* 66–68.

Patrirarca, L.A., & Alleman, J. (1987). Journey in time: A foster grandparent program. *Young Children, 34,* 30–39.

Piaget, J. (1965). *The child's conception of the world.* Totowa, NJ: Littlefield Adams.

Piaget, J. (1971). *The child's concept of time.* New York: Ballantine.

Piaget, J., & Inhelder, B. (1969). *Psychology of the child.* New York: Basic Books.

Pintrich, P.R., Marx, R.W., & Boyle, R.A. (1993). Beyond cold conceptual change: The role of motivational beliefs and classroom contextual factors in the process of conceptual change. *Review of Educational Research, 63,* 167–201.

Schug, M.C., & Birkey, C.J. (1985). *The development of children's economic reasoning.* Paper presented at the annual meeting of the American Educational Research Association, Chicago, IL.

Seefeldt, C. (1975). Is today tomorrow? History for young children. *Young Children, 30* (2), 99–105.

Seefeldt, C. (1993a). History for young children. *Theory and Research in Social Education, 21,* 143–46.

Seefeldt, C. (1993b). *Social studies for the preschool/primary child.* (4th ed.). Columbus, OH: Macmillan.

Slaby, R.G., & Frey, J.W. (1975). Development of gender constancy and selective attention to same-sex models. *Child Development, 49,* 1264–65.

Spencer, C., Harrison, M., & Darvizeh, Z. (1980). The development of iconic mapping ability in young children. *International Journal of Early Childhood, 21* (2), 57–64.

Spodek, B. (1977). What constitutes worthwhile educational experiences for young children? In B. Spodek (Ed.), *Teaching practices? Re-examining assumptions* (pp. 332–77). New York: Macmillan.

Waite, P., Smith, S., & Schug, M.C. (1991). Integrating economics into the curriculum: Teaching ideas from England. *The Social Studies, 82,* 67–71.

Vukelich, R., & Thornton, S.J. (1990). Children's understanding of historical time: Implications for instruction. *Childhood Education, 66,* 22–25.

Vygotsky, L. (1986). *Thought and language.* Cambridge, MA: MIT.

CHAPTER EIGHT

Visual Arts in the Developmentally Appropriate Integrated Curriculum

CYNTHIA COLBERT

Art experiences are important to young children. Children are intrinsically motivated to create art and become fully engaged in the artistic process. Children also demonstrate a strong sense of purpose when they create art. When given choices of media and activities, some children may experiment with media, while others may stay with a material with which they are comfortable and know they can control. Children are consciously working to express their ideas through symbols and images. Through their art, children reveal their individual thoughts, feelings, and moods and through symbols they describe their very existence with sophistication and simplicity, often leaving adults in awe of their powerful and authentic voice. Those who study children's art have long believed that adult artists such as Picasso, Kandinsky, Klee, Miro, Dubuffet, and others studied children's artwork and liberally borrowed from it in their own adult work. For the past ten years, Jonathan Fineberg (1995) has been documenting his discoveries that many internationally renowned artists had original collections of children's works that bear a striking resemblance to their own work.

Making art is something children do naturally, without adult instruction or intervention. There are those who believe that children would be better off if they were left alone to create art without interference from adults. Franz Cizek's feelings on adult intervention in child art are that teaching technique or "method poisons art," believing that children should be allowed to develop from within and the role of the teacher is to encourage (Efland, 1976, p. 71). Similarly, Viktor Lowenfeld believed in children's natural creativity. Lowenfeld's important text, *Creative and Mental Growth*, first appeared in 1947, and has influenced generations of teachers who prefer to allow a more natural unfolding of artistic development. Those holding the noninterventionist philosophical view of children's education and development in art champion beliefs that range from offering children stimulating experiences about which they make art (Lowenfeld, 1947) to fear that adults have a vexing, negative impact on children and their work and should be essentially banned from the experience (Kellogg, 1970).

Yet there are others who seek adult intervention in art experiences with young children, believing that children need to be instructed or assisted in creating work or discussing the work they have created. Research by Eisner (1976), Wilson and Wilson (1982), and others suggest that teachers intervene in early childhood instruction. Colbert and Taunton (1990), among others, suggest providing appropriate experiences for children that promote growth, gently moving children toward their potential in making art, looking at art, and talking about art.

In teaching art to young children, most teachers find that some children need little help or encouragement, while others require prodding and discussion about their ideas before they take on a big, empty sheet of paper or a lump of unformed clay. When teachers teach art badly, children would certainly be better off without their intrusions. When teachers nurture the visual arts in their classrooms well, building on children's interests and abilities, encouraging individual expressions, and praising children's work, a magical enthusiasm for learning grows within the children and adults involved. One has only to look at the environment and the children's artwork from Reggio Emilia to see that moving art to the center of the curriculum has a strong impact on children's self-expression and learning (Spaggiari, 1987).

The visual arts are about self-expression. Good teachers enable children to express themselves by setting up interesting problems to be solved and by offering children quality materials that facilitate their expression in an environment that supports their efforts. The content in the visual arts is not just in the making of paintings and drawings. Talking about works of art made by children and reproductions of works of art made by adults and chosen for their interest to children is equally important. Instruction in the visual arts combines creating art with looking and talking about art and connecting art with other, global concepts. Art teachers try to offer children a balance of two- and three-dimensional experiences using a variety of appropriate media and focusing on various themes or artistic elements.

When art is taught to young children, good teaching resembles a collaboration of young artists with an adult guide. Teachers set the conditions that facilitate the growth of children's artistic development by creating the atmosphere of trust, comfort, and acceptance for children and their work. Teachers decide on the amount of time to be spent in creating art and in looking and talking about works of art, remembering that children work at different rates and have different interest levels. They choose art materials children can use and place them where either the children can readily use them, or where they have control of them. Teachers either encourage or discourage the use of imaginative self-discovery, depending on their responses to children's efforts. Teachers of art must be willing to give their time and attention to each child's work, offer specific praise worthy of the work and the child. Teachers also choose the reproductions of work by adult artists that will be shared with children. The decisions about how children will experience adult works of art are often ruled by the teacher when group discussions of the work occur. Teachers may guide discussions by asking appropriate and open-ended questions to invite discussion. Changing displays of interesting works of art in the early childhood setting allows children to look and think about the works on their own, and to come up with their own ideas and narratives about specific images that interest them.

Children's Artistic Development

The drawings, paintings, and sculptures children produce offer tangible evidence of their thoughtful planning, their perceptual and conceptual development, their individuality, and their interests. From developmental research studies, much is known about children's artistic and aesthetic development. Children all over the globe go through the same sequences of development, but individual children go through these sequences at individual rates and have unique outcomes. In looking at children's artistic developments there are parallels between the stages or sequences described by Lowenfeld and those described by Piaget. Usually we find children from one to almost four years are scribbling, although some 4-year-olds are drawing representational images, as do some 3-year-olds. By the age of 5 years, many children are making representational drawings, although it may take a very sensitive audience to discern the intentions of the young artists. Researchers who study the artistic development of young children are convinced of the value of the visual and kinesthetic pleasure that occurs in relation to scribbling of young children and of the importance of this early mark making to later representational skills (Taunton and Colbert, 1984, p. 58). In these early attempts, children's scribbles can be

FIGURE 8.1
Fingerpainting by a 3-year-old girl. The child was reluctant to put her hands in the paint, so the teacher made the circular lines. The child made the fingerprints in the center. Photo: Cynthia Colbert.

divided into three subsets: random scribbling, controlled scribbling, and named scribbles.

Random scribbling is characterized by the child's lack of control of the drawing instrument and the short attention span. Controlled scribbling occurs when the child realizes she can think about making a particular line or shape and approximate the line or shape on the page. With control, the child often spends more time with mark making than before. In naming scribbles, children place labels or tell stories about the marks on the page. These marks are not recognizable to adults, but the child has reached the important point of using mark making as a means of communication (see figures 8.1–8.3).

The named scribbles are usually quickly followed by the child's first early representational drawings. Usually the first drawings are of the child who makes them. These drawings progress in their approximations to reality in proportion and detail very quickly. Soon children

FIGURE 8.2
Well-controlled fingerpainting by a 3-year 4-month-old girl. Notice the bold lines that cross in the center of the page that show her control of the media and her confidence. Photo: Cynthia Colbert.

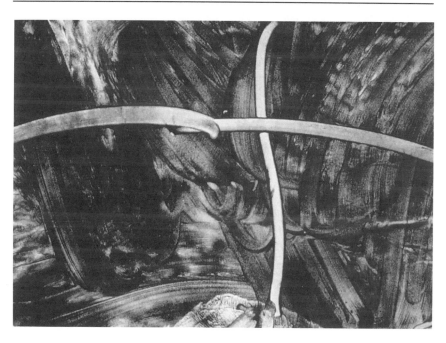

draw the figures within the context of a house or landscape. This
generally happens at about the time the child begins to read. With the
use of a baseline, the child is well on the way to making representational art that includes a sense of gravity that anchors the figures and
objects to one plane. After spending an extended period of time
working within the plane of the baseline, children will begin to show
depth in the picture plane by overlapping figures and objects and by
moving the baseline to become the horizon line (see figures 8.4–8.6).

Integrating the Visual Arts within the Early Childhood Curriculum

In the 1920s and 1930s the integrated curriculum was very much in
vogue in American schools. When the arts were integrated into the
curriculum, our content, concepts, and skills became disintegrated.

FIGURE 8.4
Titled, "Our Vacation," by a 3-year 9-month-old girl. Notice the mountain, sailboat, lake, horses, and dotted lines creating roads for travel. The girl is the tall, blue figure with the ponytail (line with colored circular shape at its end). The drawing is a jumble of symbols that have a rich verbal narrative. The symbols are recognizable, but their orientation shows evidence of the preschematic time of artistic development.
Artist: Gillian Siple. Photo: Cynthia Colbert.

Our media and techniques were used to support the other subject areas, while our own curriculum was lost. Today, when visual arts educators hear talk of integrating the curriculum, they may not jump into the conversation with as much enthusiasm as other teachers might expect. The visual arts are an excellent vehicle for integrating the curriculum. Through the proper use of the visual arts, literature, writing, social studies, mathematics, and science can be brought to life for children and made concrete and meaningful for them (Bredekamp & Copple, 1997). To do so while maintaining the integrity of the visual arts takes masterful teachers who are knowledgeable, flexible, and willing to collaborate.

What has often happened in the integration of subjects in the elementary and early childhood setting is that the visual arts become the

FIGURE 8.5
Titled, "My family at dinner at a restuarant, and it's my mom's birthday," this drawing was completed by a 4-year 1-month-old girl while her family waited to be served at a restaurant. Notice the increasing detail when compared to the work in figure 8.4, done by the same child. Artist: Gillian Siple. Photo: Cynthia Colbert.

glue that holds the other subjects together without regard for the teaching of art as a discipline. In these settings, art too often becomes making salt maps to satisfy the needs of a geography lesson or arranging precut teddy bears in graphs, while adding bow ties or buttons with glitter pens to satisfy the needs of a math lesson. Neither of these lessons would work in satisfying the goals of art instruction. But both could be improved to utilize art concepts with conscientious planning. Integration of subjects requires the development of important, broad themes. Literature, language, math, social studies, music, and art can be taught thematically when important, broad themes are chosen. Too often

FIGURE 8.6
Titled "My Bad Dream," by a 4-year 3-month-old girl. This is an unusual drawing by the same girl who completed the drawings in figures 8.4 and 8.5. She went back to this piece on three different days to work on it, bringing a different media to it on two occasions. The time spent on this drawing exceeds two hours. Done in graphite, colored marker, and ball point pen, this drawing is a fine example of the unusual work children create when they have a very personal connection to the content of their work. Artist: Gillian Siple. Photo: Cynthia Colbert.

teachers choose trivial themes that don't work well for integration. For example, when teachers choose to focus on themes such as teddy bears or the seasons of the year, the visual arts are often trivialized. Children are left to make pictures of teddy bears or texture rubbings of autumn leaves. In such thematic units, children may look at art reproductions of landscapes that show the changes of seasons as illustrations of the theme, but without responding to these images as works of art.

Integrating disciplines for the sake of integration is a meaningless practice. Observing such instruction leaves us asking, "Why are these things being taught together?" Integrating disciplines under the umbrella of important, meaningful themes through which the subjects can be studied and that have connections to the lives of children and their previous knowledge is a good practice. We know that young children learn more easily when subjects are taught in real, concrete, hands-on, interrelated ways. Making art and looking and talking about art use concrete, hands-on instruction that is easily interrelated to good literature, social studies, science, language arts, and mathematics. Identifying important themes through which these can be taught is a challenge to educators of young children.

There are also aspects of children's art making that lend themselves to integration with other kinds of learning. Although Lowenfeld (1947) is most well known for the delineation of stages of development in children's art, some of the most profound ideas in his early and widely used text are in his "view of children's development in the visual arts as a reflection of their emotional, intellectual, physical, perceptual, social, aesthetic and creative development" (Colbert, 1990, p. 102). Gardner's work on multiple intelligences also supports the notion that some children learn best in ways other than the verbal, mathematical, or logical approach, including bodily kinesthetic, interpersonal, and spatial ways of learning (Gardner, 1983). Implications for the applications of Gardner's work in relation to curriculum development and the visual arts education of young children has been positive (Kantner, 1990). These multifaceted views of children's art and art making and the connections to the development of the whole child offer one of the most compelling arguments for integrating the arts in the early childhood classroom.

In the integration of subjects in the early childhood curriculum, the visual arts naturally lend themselves to explorations in the other subject areas, but a visual arts specialist is needed in the planning and implementation of the curriculum to assure that the content of the visual arts is adequately addressed. Most states have curriculum frameworks for the visual arts with goals and objectives for the instruction of children in the early childhood years that will help teachers see the broad view of what children need to know in the visual arts and approximately when experts recommend the information be taught.

The National Art Education Association (NAEA) has developed a policy statement, *Developmentally Appropriate Practices for the Visual Arts Education of Young Children* (Colbert & Taunton, 1992), which addresses the integration of the visual arts with other areas of the curriculum as follows:

Appropriate Practice. The visual arts utilize concepts and skills that are taught in other areas of the curriculum. Many of the goals and objectives of a quality visual arts program designed for young children are the goals of early childhood education programs. Learning about art can be a catalyst for the development of language and vocabulary skills; increased visual and tactile perception; knowledge about shapes, colors, and patterns; and classification of concepts.

Sometimes the visual arts are used to enhance other areas of the curriculum and at other times the other areas are used to enhance the visual arts. Art is taught as an integrated part of the curriculum.

Inappropriate Practice. Art is taught as a separate area of the curriculum. It is approached as a "make and take" activity, one that warrants little discussion or attention. Art concepts and skills are not used to enhance learning in other areas of the curriculum, nor are other curricular goals applied to learning about art.

What Art Is Not

Sometimes well-meaning teachers of children get confused about what art is. Not every time children use art materials are they engaged in creating art. Coloring five birds blue, for example, is not an art activity, nor is it an especially good math activity. What follows are some ideas about what art is not:

- Coloring in predrawn sheets, using water and paint brushes on embedded paint sheets, or cutting out preprinted shapes and pasting them onto a predetermined pattern
- Assembling projects such as using precut construction paper to make a figure like the teacher's example, or gluing a magnet to a vinyl leaf to use on a refrigerator door
- Copying projects, such as the teacher's instructions on how to draw a tree or dog, when all the work looks like the teacher's model
- Tactile experiences, such as shaving cream paintings, pudding paintings, or similar activities
- Working in craft materials to create products that are all alike and often so difficult that the teachers end up doing the work

What these experiences have in common, besides being very easy to find in most elementary schools and early childhood learning centers, is that they fail to meet the criteria for self-expression. Art is equal to more than the sum of its parts—materials, techniques, and methods. Real art is when children can put some of themselves into the work, to make the work as unique as they are (see figures 8.7–8.10). Most of the activities listed above could be changed slightly to become art experiences. Art is:

- Encouraging children to draw their own images and color or paint them, or to cut shapes from paper and arrange them into their own designs.
- Helping children create their own designs from shapes they cut themselves (children, not teachers, need to learn to use scissors). They can also create from torn paper. Brainstorm what objects might be used to create refrigerator magnets. Children can use

FIGURE 8.7
Children looking at themselves and discussing the details of their appearance.
Photo: Cynthia Colbert.

FIGURE 8.8
Children measuring the faces of children's portraits in art reproductions and
comparing the sizes to their own faces. Photo: Cynthia Colbert.

clusters of buttons they choose, arrange, and glue to a paper
shape, colored rice that can be arranged into patterns, bundles
of sticks made from colored string and sticks found on the
playground or during a nature walk, or small, special pebbles,
or stones.

- Teaching how to look and see, rather than teaching a "how to
  draw" lesson. Go outside and look at trees. Point out the relationships of the branches to the trunk. Look closely at the
  shapes of the leaves. Take paper outside to draw what you see.
  Look closely and discuss the visual characteristics of animals.
  Use art reproductions to see how artists have used animals in
  their own work. Draw classroom animals from observation or
  bring in a dog or cat and let children draw, paint, or model the
  animal from observation.
- Encouraging tactile experiences such as crayon rubbings,
  fingerpainting, or monoprinting from painting with the hands

FIGURE 8.10
Putting her finishing touches on the collage. Photo: Cynthia Colbert.

to create beautiful papers. The child's need for self-expression has not yet been fully met, however. Using these papers as an important element in a collage is a way of developing a rich art lesson from tactile experiences.

- Choosing materials that children can easily manipulate and choosing appropriate goals for the use of materials. If, for example, you use scraps of wood to let children create their own stacking sculptures or enclosures, encouraging them to make their work unique, you will likely be successful. When the teacher's goals are inappropriate for the materials and the developmental level of the children, the teacher often ends up doing the work for the children. The message the child receives is "I can't do this," or "I can't do this well enough to please my teacher." These messages often stay with children for a lifetime.

The NAEA policy statement, *Developmentally Appropriate Practices for the Visual Arts Education of Young Children* (Colbert &

Taunton, 1992), offers the following advice on involving young children in creating art:

Appropriate Practice. Children are given appropriate materials in a playful, supportive setting and receive encouragement from the teacher as they work. They are given adequate time to involve themselves in their creation, including time to go back to the work and complete it later in the day or the next day, if needed.

Children are encouraged by the teacher to create their own images and to use their own ideas.

Children are given help when they indicate they need it. Children are given opportunities to create based on their imaginations, their life experiences, events, and objects of importance to them in their world.

Children are given opportunities to work individually and in groups.

Inappropriate Practice. Children work in a tense, intimidating atmosphere. They are not allowed to use materials in experimental ways. The teacher does not circulate to view their work, nor does he or she respond to the work in progress. Children are repeatedly told to hurry. Children are not allowed to continue their work after the art period has ended.

Children are told to follow examples shown by the teacher. They are not encouraged to deviate from examples.

Children's progress is not monitored, nor is help offered.

Examples of Integrating Art in the Classroom

Three-year-olds are working with experimental painting techniques this week. On the first day, children paint with their hands on cookie sheets. Using two colors of tempera mixed with detergent, children learn that when two colors are mixed together, another color can be made. Children paint with their fingers to the sounds of classical music. The teacher encourages them to listen to the music and let their fingers create movements to match what they hear. During a staccato portion of the musical piece, some children make stabbing motions, creating a dotted image on the cookie sheets. At the end of the music a teacher demonstrates how to place a piece of thirsty manila paper over the cookie sheet to make a print of the expressionistic work. Children help each other in placing the paper on their work and peeling it away.

In this same 3-year-old class on the next day, students are discussing the different feathers found on a single bird and what the functions of those feathers might be in keeping the bird dry and in helping the bird fly. *Hey, Al* (Yorinks & Egielski, 1986) is read at story time and the teacher takes care to point out the differences in the birds shown in the illustrations and the differences in large, strong feathers and more fragile, downy ones. The children pretend to be birds, flapping their bent or extended arms and stretching their necks like flamingos. Children experiment in the art center by painting with feathers. Using one color, the students choose a large feather or a group of smaller feathers that have been attached to a stick with rubber bands, dip the feathers into paint-filled Styrofoam trays, and brush the paint onto construction paper. Later that day, after the paint has dried, the children choose a different feather and paint more feathery strokes with another color over their morning's work. One child exclaims that her work looks like "what the air would look like if birds left tracks in it." The experimental paintings from these two days are displayed on a classroom wall and children sit on the floor and talk about the paintings. They recall what they thought and felt as they painted and they talk about how the paintings are different and alike. The children hum and move to the music their paintings help them recall. They move like small sparrows, large hawks, and timid doves. A teacher plays a portion of the music the children listened to while doing their first paintings and a tape of bird calls as the children make their movements match what they hear.

Four- and 5-year-old children are using colored cards, arranging them in a/b; a/b patterns. They look for patterns in the environment. They have found leaves on a tree that look the same. Someone noticed the bricks on the outside wall of the school were laid in patterns. Some children had on clothing that had repeated shapes and colors. The teacher keeps a list of the patterns found, writing and drawing sketches of the patterns. Another teacher and students create a graph of the different kinds of patterns found in the classroom. There were three students wearing stripes and stripes on the curtains over the sinks, so four examples of stripes were found. During story time, the teacher reads poetry from *Ride a Purple Pelican* and the children clap with the rhythm of the poems (Prelutsky, 1986). Students are invited to stand in a circle and march to music. Soon they are creating patterns with their arms, marching with both arms up and then both arms extended to the sides. At one art center, children can draw representations of the patterns they created in their march with music. At another art center, they can make stamp prints, choosing from many shapes carved into potatoes and colors of tempera paint. The paint has been poured onto sponges in pie tins. Children press their potatoes onto the sponges and stamp print them onto large, green pieces of construction paper, creating repeating patterns. The teachers put away the stamp-printed patterns for a future activity.

The next week, students and teachers are working with ideas about self-awareness. Students have brought photographs of themselves to school and they are tacked to a display, placed beside drawn self-portraits of the children and their families. Biographies and stories about families are read during story time during this week. Children tell stories about their own families. Children are weighed and measured by a nurse. These statistics are graphed by students and teachers to get a picture of the overall size of children in the class and differences in sizes and weights. In the art center, children study themselves by looking in a mirror. They describe themselves using many adjectives and discuss their observations with classmates. Children are invited to discuss similarities and differences between two artists' portraits of young children. They speculate about where artists get their ideas. They measure the sizes of the faces of the children in the portraits and compare them with the sizes of their own faces. Children then select a sheet of construction paper from an array of many colors and draw their faces using pencils, markers, and oil pastels. Some children take time to mix colors, using the oil pastels, to reflect the colors they saw in their eyes or hair when observing themselves in the mirror. Children cut out the heads of their self-portraits and paste them onto a large sheet of construction paper.

The stamp-printed paper from a previous lesson is used to create patterned clothing. Children are invited to cut or tear shapes for clothing and paste them onto the page to complete the body. Skin-tone papers are used to complete the figures' feet, arms, hands, and necks and are pasted to the page. The self-portrait collages are displayed in the hallway outside of the classroom. The children take pride in seeing their work in their daily comings and goings and the images provoke much discussion among children and adults from outside the class, who recognize students from the images in their artwork. Teachers

FIGURE 8.11
Exploring Visual Arts Concepts

Social Studies—Artworks by artists from different countries and ethnic backgrounds, artworks representing people from around the world engaged in different activities, illustrating folktales, cooperation between and among children in sharing materials, cleaning up, and discussing their work.

Science—Drawing from observation, collection of data through drawing, metamorphosis (clay, firing in sawdust, pit, or kiln), resist and emulsion (oil and water resist in crayon and water-color resist; adhere in emulision when soap is added to paint for crayon etching).

Mathematics—Creating repeating patterns, building graphs and grids, weaving using numbered warp, concentrating on even and odd numbers (tabby weave, ababab; basket weave, aabbaabb), geometry of shapes, balance, symmetry, proportion.

EXPLORING VISUAL ARTS CONCEPTS: MAKING ART, LOOKING AT ART, AND TALKING ABOUT ART

Music—Translating sound into symbol and music into symbol, movement to music translated into two- and three-dimensional works of art, use of pattern and texture in music and in visual art.

Language—Describing works of art, comparing and contrasting, learning new vocabulary—names of tools and art processes, translating verbal descriptions into drawings or symbols, illustrating their own stories.

Reading—Reading images in adult works or art or in children's work, creating narratives from works of art, creating narratives through drawing stories, creating patterns, writing what a child says on drawings or paintings, children illustrate stories read to them.

take children out into the hallway to sit and discuss the self-portraits they created.

Planning the Art Curriculum

Just as there are essential elements and global themes that come from subject areas such as language arts or mathematics, the visual arts have four distinct components that are considered in planning instruction: aesthetic perception, creative expression, cultural heritage, and aesthetic valuing. Teachers of young children use their knowledge of children's artistic and aesthetic development, recognizing children's interests, abilities, and needs when planning art instruction. The four components of art are integrated within the instruction that includes making art, looking at art, and talking about art. When planning units of instruction, teachers select from a variety of art materials and resources to support students as they learn about art. Teachers attempt to balance the study of works of art to include different historical periods, styles of art, and work by male and female artists from many cultural and ethnic backgrounds.

Teachers set goals for students based on the essential elements of the art curriculum, interdisciplinary themes, and with a clear vision of how art links students to the larger, human activities of communication and discovery. In the area of aesthetic perception, young children may be asked to identify the visual characteristics of design elements (line, color, value, shape, texture, and space) in forms that are natural or made by humans. Later, children might build on those skills by discriminating among those design elements, or comparing and contrasting them. In the area of self-expression, children may be exploring design principles by organizing paintings or collages that demonstrate balance, repetition, and dominance. As these concepts are mastered, children may be asked to design work using overlapping shapes or variation in lines, colors, sizes, and textures to further work with design principles such as balance, repetition, and dominance.

Children may look at an array of art reproductions by adult artists and connect one or more of them with their own work, describing themes found in these works and using art vocabulary to describe them. They may begin to explore how artists make art. Children can analyze how images are organized, what media were used in the creation of art works, and talk about design elements used in works of art or in natural forms (South Carolina Visual and Performing Arts Framework, 1993).

Assessment

There are may ways of looking at assessment in the visual arts. The main goal of assessment is to improve instruction. Teachers assess their instruction to learn if their goals were reached. Teachers must constantly reflect on their performance and assess their curriculum content to insure that the essential elements of the visual arts curriculum are included. Usually teachers use a variety of assessment techniques to get a more comprehensive view of their program's effectiveness. If the artwork is very similar, the instruction was perhaps too controlling, offering little room for self-expression. If the children did not master the concept studied, perhaps it could be broken down into smaller parts and taught in increments.

Student work is generally collected in a portfolio and each child's progress is assessed. Comparisons are made between a student's early work and recent work, looking for signs of growth in concepts and skills. In early childhood arts there is no need to compare the work between students for rankings. Teachers often record observations, conduct individual interviews, and collect narrative summaries and self-evaluations of work. Students may keep a journal where they draw and write ideas for work and these journals may be included in portfolios.

Conclusion/Summary

The teacher is the most important catalyst in integrating the visual arts in the early childhood classroom. It is the teacher who sets the goals for student learning and facilitates art instruction by supplying appropriate materials and an environment where children's self-expressions in art are held in high regard. Teachers create environments of psychological safety and freedom where students feels free to take risks and where they can actively learn and create. Teachers who are good listeners learn what children have to say about their own work and the work of adult artists. With simple questions, teachers can encourage children to verbalize their descriptions and analyses of works of art that may be surprisingly sophisticated and honest. Teachers who care about the visual arts give children adequate time to immerse themselves in these experiences.

Since studies of young children indicate they learn best when they are involved in active, hands-on, concrete, and integrated study, children should be offered many experiences where subjects are integrated. Teachers who plan units of integrated study must be vigilant in their efforts to insure that the visual arts curriculum is not diminished in its content and substance by its integration with other subjects.

References

Bredekamp, S., & Copple, C. (Eds.). (1997). *Developmentally appropriate practice in early childhood programs: Revised*. Washington, DC: National Association for the Education of Young Children.

Colbert, C. (1990). The visual arts: Multiple ways of knowing. In W.H. Moody (Ed.), *Artistic intelligences, implications for education* (pp. 102–8). New York: Teachers College Press.

Colbert, C., & Taunton, M. (1990). *Discover art: Kindergarten*. Worcester, MA: Davis.

Colbert, C., & Taunton, M. (1992). *Developmentally appropriate practices for the visual arts education of young children*. Reston, VA: The National Art Education Association.

Efland, A. (1976). Changing views on children's artistic development: Their impact on curriculum and instruction. In E. Eisner (Ed.), *The arts, human development and education* (pp. 65–86). Berkeley, CA: McCutchan.

Eisner, E. (1976). What we know about children's art—and what we need to know. In E. Eisner (Ed.), *The arts, human development and education* (pp. 5–18). Berkeley, CA: McCutchan.

Fineberg, J. (1995, April). The innocent eye. *ARTnews*, pp. 118–25.

Gardner, H. (1983). *Frames of mind: The theory of multiple intelligence*. New York: Basic Books.

Kantner, L. (1990). Visual arts education and multiple intelligences: Before implementation. In W.J. Moody (Ed.), *Artistic intelli-*

gences, implications for education. New York: Teachers College Press.

Kellogg, R. (1970). *Analyzing children's art.* Palo Alto, CA: Mayfield.

Lowenfeld, V. (1947). *Creative and mental growth.* New York: Macmillan.

Prelutsky, J. (1986). *Ride a purple pelican.* New York: Greenwillow.

South Carolina Visual and Performing Arts Framework. (1993). Columbia, SC: South Carolina State Department of Education.

Spaggiari, S. (1987). *The hundred languages of children.* Reggio Emilia, Italy: Department of Education.

Taunton, M., & Colbert, C. (1984). Artistic and aesthetic development: Considerations for early childhood educators. *Childhood Education, 61* (1), 55–63.

Wilson, M., & Wilson, B. (1982). *Teaching children to draw: A guide for parents and teachers.* Englewood Cliffs, NJ: Prentice-Hall.

Yorinks, A., & Egielski, R. (1986). *Hey, Al.* Toronto: Collins.

CHAPTER NINE

Integrating Literacy Learning for Young Children

A Balanced Literacy Perspective

D. RAY REUTZEL

Children construct meaning differently from their experiences with language than do adults. From the first time they utter the pledge of allegiance to the flag saying, "one nation under God, *invisible*, with *liverty* and justice for all," to the time they write a string of letters and ask somewhat bewildered teachers or parents, "What did I write?" they evidence this very fact (Whitmore & Goodman, 1995). All participants in a child's education must concern themselves with the developmental appropriateness of the language concepts to be taught and the practices employed to convey these concepts. Developmental appropriateness is a concept anchored in the imperative that educators match educational practices to the ways children think and learn (Gullo, 1992; Bredekamp, 1987; Bredekamp & Copple, 1997; Bredekamp & Rosegrant, 1992; Bredekamp & Rosegrant, 1995). In order to accomplish this aim, all who assist children in the acquisition of literacy skills must understand the whole child and the nature of the language learning process (Auerbach, 1989; Taylor, 1983). F. Smith (1985, p. 5) once declared, "I would make sure I knew enough about reading [and writing] in general and about those children in particular" to provide competent instruction. For school-based literacy programs to meet the needs of young children, Bredekamp (1987) and Bredekamp and Copple (1997) suggests that such programs of instruction be carefully matched to children's development. For this match to occur, it is necessary to come to understand children's growth and development in relation to the acquisition of reading and writing.

Understanding the Development of Reading and Writing among Young Children

Research over the past two decades has gradually led to a profound change in the understanding of early literacy acquisition as represented in the terminology of emergent literacy (Ferreiro & Teberosky, 1982; Kantor, Miller, & Fernie, 1992). N. Hall (1987) describes several assumptions associated with the emergent literacy perspective:

1. Reading and writing are closely related processes and should not be artificially isolated for instruction.
2. Learning to read and write is essentially a social process and is influenced by a search for meaning.
3. Most preschool children already know a great deal about printed language without exposure to formal instruction.
4. Becoming literate is a continuous, developmental process.
5. Children need to act like readers and writers to become readers and writers.
6. Children need to read authentic and natural texts.
7. Children need to write for personal reasons.

From the early studies in language learning begun around 1956, researchers in language acquisition have carefully studied and observed young children to determine how they solved the puzzle of printed language. Chief among these are recent investigations into solving the puzzle of how children learn to read and write.

Reading Development

Sulzby (Sulzby and Teale, 1991; Sulzby, 1985) researched and tested a classification scheme for describing children's emergent reading of storybooks (see figure 9.1). In the earliest stages of storybook reading,

FIGURE 9.1
Development of Story-Reading Behaviors in Young Children

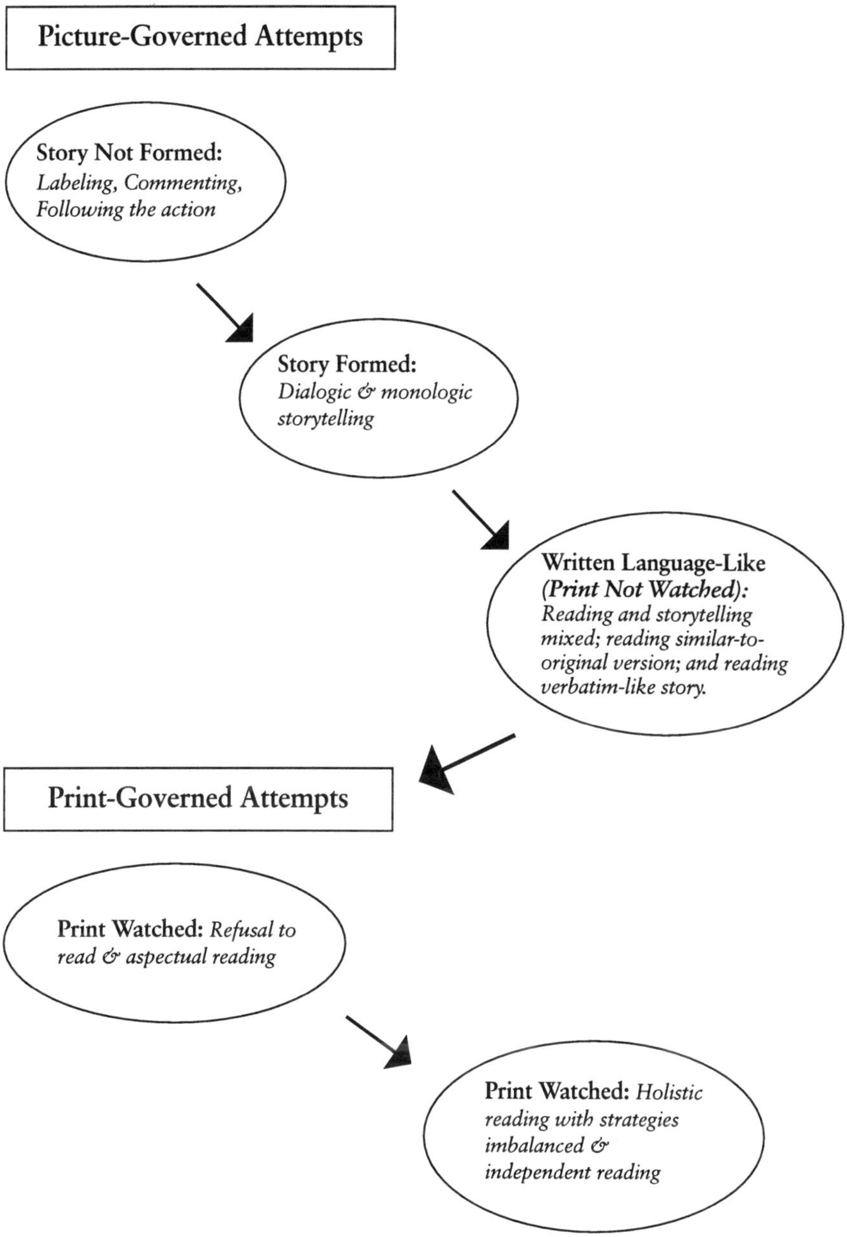

| Picture-Governed Attempts |

Story Not Formed:
*Labeling, Commenting,
Following the action*

Story Formed:
*Dialogic & monologic
storytelling*

**Written Language-Like
(Print Not Watched):**
*Reading and storytelling
mixed; reading similar-to-
original version; and reading
verbatim-like story.*

| Print-Governed Attempts |

Print Watched: *Refusal to
read & aspectual reading*

Print Watched: *Holistic
reading with strategies
imbalanced &
independent reading*

reading behaviors seem to be largely governed by pictures. Children's earliest picture-governed but not-well-formed storybook reading behaviors often included labeling, commenting, pointing, or even slapping at the pictures. At later stages in picture-governed storybook reading, children's storybook readings become more well formed to the story in the book. Children engage in dialogic and monologic storybook reading.

In dialogic storybook reading, children either create a "voice" for the characters in the story or they tell the story by making comments directed to a listener of the story. Hence characters are lived as if the child is in the story or the child tells the story for the benefit of the listener. In any case, these story readings are often disjointed and difficult to follow. When children shift to monologic storytelling, a complete story is told and understood. The story is also told with a storytelling intonation rather than a reading intonation (Sulzby, 1985, p. 468).

After children reach the monologic storybook reading stage, they begin to tell well-formed stories that approximate written language. Children's written language-like reading attempts fall into three subcategories: (1) reading and storytelling mixed; (2) reading similar-to-original story; and (3) reading verbatim-like. Once children enter into these storybook reading behaviors, they tend to focus their attention partially on the print as a means for governing their reading. Consequently, the move into Sulzby's (1985) second supercategory of storybook reading behaviors, print-governed attempts.

Within this second supercategory of storybook reading behaviors, children often engage in three initial responses to storybook print: refusal, aspectual reading, and holistic. In the first response, refusal, children refuse to try to read as they learn that print carries the story rather than the pictures. For example, a child might remark, "I don't know the words. I can't read yet. I can't really read—I was just pretending." In the aspectual stage, children focus on one or two aspect of the print to the exclusion of others. Some children focus on memory for certain words, while others focus more intently on specific letter-sound combinations for sounding out.

The final category, holistic, is divided into two subcategories: (1) reading with strategies imbalanced, and (2) reading independently. In the strategies imbalanced stage, children might read a storybook by overdepending on certain strategies such as substituting known words for unknown words or sounding out every unknown word. In this stage children have not yet learned to become strategic about their reading strategy selections and use during reading. In the independent stage, children have learned to self-regulate their strategy selection and balance the use of these strategies during reading. These youngsters should like "word perfect" readers sometimes and at other times make deviations from the printed page but continue to demonstrate an awareness and control of the process of reading. Sulzby (1985, p. 479) remarks in summary: "Finally, and most important, the development that was observed in these studies appears to make sense in light of theoretical ideas about general and language development and the findings of other current research. . . . These discoveries about literacy development appear to challenge traditional assumptions about the nature of young children—assumptions built upon a conventional model."

Writing Development

Many children attempt to solve the written language puzzle through drawing and scribbling. Just as with reading, teachers and parents may be tempted to dismiss these early attempts as unreal writing. This may be just as dangerous as rooting out a flower in the early stages of growth because the roots do not look much like the flower. Through careful study over a period of decades, researchers have discovered that young children pass through developmental stages similar to those discussed with respect to reading development in their writing and spelling development (Dyson, 1993). An understanding of these stages of writing help those who work with children to recognize the "roots" of writing and spelling development and, as such, enable them to help nurture the roots of scribbling and drawing into the flower of writing.

Scribbling and Drawing Stage. When young children first take a pencil or crayon in hand, they use this instrument to explore the vast empty space on a blank sheet of paper. In the earliest stages, children's writing is often referred to as scribbling by adult observers (Clay, 1987; Harste, Woodward, & Burke, 1984; Temple et al., 1994). These random marks are the wellsprings of writing discovery. Scribbles often appear to be the result of acting on the paper just to see what happens without any particular intent. Hence, these scribbles do not evidence much of what adults normally consider to be conventional or even purposeful writing.

Next, children's scribbles begin to take on the characteristics of adult cursive writing, becoming linear and moving from left to right and top to bottom. When questioned, children at this stage of writing development can often tell what they meant by each of their scribbles. Clay (1987) calls the tendency to reuse and repeat certain scribblings and drawings recursive writing. The purpose behind recursive writing seems to be to fulfill a need for comfort and familiarity as children prepare to move into the next levels of writing development.

Later, drawings with scribbles or symbols convey a message. When children use symbols and drawings together, they demonstrate a knowledge that drawing and writing are not the same processes (Whitmore & Goodman, 1995), that meaning can be captured and conveyed by alternate representational forms.

Prephonemic Stage. The next stage of writing and spelling development is the prephonemic stage (Temple et al., 1994). At this stage, children use real letters, usually capital letters, to represent their meaning. Letters do not represent their phonemic or sound values. Rather, children use letters as place holders for meaning, representing anything from a syllable to an entire thought. But only by asking the child to explain the meaning can one readily discern the fact that the child used letters as meaning place holders and not to represent their phonemic values. Clay (1975) points out that children in the prephonemic stage of writing development will usually produce a string of letters and proudly display them to a parent while asking, "What does this say?" or "What did I write?"

Early Phonemic Stage. During the early phonemic stage of writing development (Temple et al., 1988), children typically use capital consonant letters to represent words. At this stage of writing development, children discover the fact that letters represent sound values. Words are represented by one or two consonant letters, usually the beginning or ending sounds of the word (Schickendanz, 1990).

Letter-Naming Stage. The letter-naming stage of writing development is a small but important jump from the early phonemic stage.

This stage is recognized by the addition of more than one or two consonant letters used by young writers to represent the spelling of words (Temple et al., 1988).

Transitional Stage. Writing produced by youngsters in the transitional stage looks like English, but the words are a mix of phonic and conventional spellings. Typically these writers neglect or overgeneralize certain spelling generalizations. For example, the final silent e is often omitted by these writers; familiar phonic elements are substituted for less familiar phonic elements; and double consonants are typically neglected. Table 9.1 shows how reading ability and writing ability develop along roughly similar paths.

Implications

By carefully reflecting on and analyzing the previous information, several clear implications for publishers, curriculum designers, teachers,

TABLE 9.1
Development across the Language Modes of Reading and Writing

Reading *Development Stages*	*Writing* *Development Stages*
Picture-Governed Attempts: Story Not Formed	Scribbling & Drawing
Picture-Governed Attempts: Story Formed	Prephonemic
Picture-Governed Attempts: Written Language-Like Print Not Watched	Early Phonemic
Print-Governed Attempts: Print Watched	Letter Naming
Print-Governed Attempts: Strategies Imbalances	Transitional
Print-Governed Attempts: Independent Reading	Conventional

and parents become readily apparent in relation to providing developmentally appropriate instruction in literacy learning. These implications, for the convenience of presentation and discussion, are divided into three categories: (1) designing developmentally appropriate reading and writing curriculum; (2) creating developmentally appropriate literacy learning classrooms; and (3) developmentally appropriate language instructional practices: balanced literacy programs.

Designing Developmentally Appropriate Reading and Writing Curriculum

Developmentally appropriate reading and writing curriculum focuses on developing the whole child (i.e., cognitive, social, physical, and emotional experience) both as an individual being and as a member of a larger society. One way to shape and inform curriculum choices is to engage in what has come to be known as kid watching (Goodman, 1986). Teachers observe what students are trying to do in their daily reading and writing experiences and record observations on checklists that allow them to keep track of the connections children make between printed and spoken language. From these observations, language learning experiences can be adjusted as necessary.

Another practice called language watching can be used to inform and direct instructional decisions (Reutzel, 1992). Like kid watching, language watching implies that teachers also carefully observe and analyze the texts they select to read for opportunities to teach, point out patterns, or emphasize language functions. For example, after having observed children's reactions to Shel Silverstein's (1976) poems, a teacher may select the poem entitled, *How Not to Have to Dry the Dishes*. This poem could be used for multiple instructional purposes. Through language watching, the teacher may determine that during the initial reading(s) the /h/ sound could be highlighted for discussion and attention. And on a second or subsequent readings, the /d/ sound could be the focus of attention. Thus, the poem was selected based on student observations or kid watching, but potential instructional uses were determined by the teacher through language watching.

Reading and writing curriculum for young children should be integrated, connected, whole, and meaningful and should focus on developing thematic and interdisciplinary studies. Young children learn best when they engage in topics, concepts, and events that move from self, near, and the familiar outward toward the social, distant, and the unfamiliar. Because language learning is a social enterprise, socially situated learning arrangements that encourage collaboration rather than competition (workshops, teams, etc.) tend to help younger learners excel. To capture and maintain children's engagement in reading and writing, they must experience a steady diet of recognized literature of enduring quality. Teachers and parents must not underestimate their importance as role models for young children learning to read and write. Emphasizing this point, Smith (1985) indicated that children have the right to learn to read and write from people, not from programs. Finally, reading and writing outcomes and expectations must be reasonable and attainable for young students to progress with confidence while instilling a sense of success.

Creating Developmentally Appropriate Literacy Learning Classrooms

A supportive and inviting literacy classroom is integral to achieving a balanced and successful reading instructional program for young children. The way teachers design the classroom environment will in large measure affect the value attached to literacy and literacy instruction. "Schools too have atmosphere. . . . For a young child the school can have the feel of an alien and threatening place, or it can create an atmosphere which shelters the child and inspires him or her with security and confidence" (Van Manen, 1986, p. 32).

When teachers evidence sensitivity for young children and enthusiasm for reading and writing, the classroom becomes a supportive and productive worklike atmosphere in which children are treated with respect and affection. As a result, the risks commonly associated with learning to read and write are minimized and the benefits maximized.

Research by Neuman and Roskos (1990, 1992) and Wasserman (1992) demonstrates a clear relationship between classroom environments and literacy learning. Based on recent literacy environmental research, I developed a model entitled, *Balanced Literacy Classrooms: Understanding Environment Behavior Relationships* (shown in figure 9.2). To help teachers understand how classroom environments shape literacy learning, I discuss in some detail each aspect of the model: provisioning, arranging, prompting interactions, and literacy places.

FIGURE 9.2
The Environment–Behavior Relationship Model

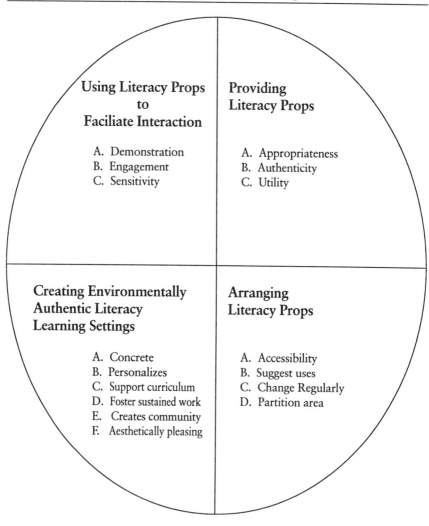

Using Literacy Props
to
Faciliate Interaction

A. Demonstration
B. Engagement
C. Sensitivity

Providing
Literacy Props

A. Appropriateness
B. Authenticity
C. Utility

Creating Environmentally
Authentic Literacy
Learning Settings

A. Concrete
B. Personalizes
C. Support curriculum
D. Foster sustained work
E. Creates community
F. Aesthetically pleasing

Arranging
Literacy Props

A. Accessibility
B. Suggest uses
C. Change Regularly
D. Partition area

Provisioning

Enriching play centers for young children with a variety of literacy props leads to dramatic increases in child literacy learning (Neuman &

TABLE 9.2
Selected Props for Literacy

Telephone books	Calendars	Business forms
Real telephone	Note pads	Typewriter
Cookbook	Writing instruments	Computer
Recipe cards	Appointment books	Clipboards
Magnetic letters	Signs	Post-it notes
Stationery	Magazines	Envelopes
Message board	Books	Posters
Food coupons	Index cards	Stamps
Newspapers	Business cards	Paper of assorted sizes

Roskos, 1990, 1992; Wasserman, 1992). In table 9.2, a partial listing of possible props for literacy classrooms is shown. When provisioning classrooms with literacy props, it is important that teachers consider the reasons for including specific literacy props. Teachers should consider whether the props are appropriate and authentic and have general utility for young children.

Arranging

Research by Morrow and Rand (1991) has shown that the arrangement of literacy props in classroom play centers significantly increased children's literacy learning. Issues specifically related to arranging classroom literacy props for optimal effectiveness focused on three major points: (1) Clearly mark or label containers so that each can be easily accessed and easily put away; (2) suggest possible uses for literacy props; used in a kitchen play center, a message board may be used to post a grocery list, take telephone messages, and so on; (3) literacy props should be added to, deleted from, and rotated on a regular basis.

Prompting Interactions

F. Smith (1988) and Cambourne and Turbill (1987) described three environmental conditions that must be present for literacy learning to successfully take place: demonstrations, engagement, and sensitivity. When people have access to literacy props, they demonstrate what it means to be literate and how reading and writing are done. When children engage in the literacy demonstrations of others or on their own using available literacy props, they "learn by doing," as described by John Dewey. It is important to understand that children do not choose to engage in literate behaviors spontaneously without a degree of personal sensitivity to the literate demonstrations of others. Consequently, children and teachers must understand and assess the sensitivity of self and others to the available demonstrations in literacy environment

When teachers share their favorite books such as *Poems for Laughing Out Loud* (Prelutsky, 1991) and chuckle or laugh or read the *Bridge to Terabithia* (Paterson, 1977) and tears stream down their cheeks, children learn that books, one type of literacy prop, mediate an emotional response that teachers and children share, discuss, and ponder. When a child brings the teacher some cookies from home and finds a thank you card on her desk the following morning, she learns that cards, a writing prop, facilitate the mutual sharing of gratitude between teacher and child. In each of these examples, demonstrations using various literacy props help children see the value, utility, and purposes for becoming literal—for learning to read and write.

Having seen, experienced, and understood the value and power of reading and writing through demonstrations, children choose to engage in literacy themselves or with others. It is no longer enough to allow teachers the singular privilege of using literacy props. Drawing on the demonstrations provided in the classroom environment and the available literacy props, children engage in reading books, writing notes, telling stories, and listening to poems. In short, they come to explore, experiment with, and use literacy props in ways that approximate the demonstrations they have experienced. This decision does not occur without sensitivity to previous literacy demonstrations.

Children do not engage in literate acts without a belief or confidence that learning to read and write is possible. Literacy props, particularly a variety of these, provide for a broad spectrum of attitudes and interests that spark desire and press children into engaging in literacy learning. A computer in the corner of the room may be just what the child whose handwriting is difficult to read needs to move ahead with literacy. A telephone for talking and a notepad for taking down messages may be just the set of tools needed to influence a reluctant student to write. Literacy props influence the motivations or sensitivity of children to engage in literate behaviors in the first place. And, conversely, children's engagement in literacy in the classroom affects the tone, feel, and available demonstrations of literate behavior for the other children in the classroom as well.

Literacy Places

Recommendations regarding the way in which literacy places are designed for classrooms fall into several broad categories according to Loughlin and Martin (1987) and Neuman and Roskos (1993): creating spatial boundaries, aggregating literacy props, and using personal touches. At the core of each of these recommendations is the concept of organization—organizing the classroom to inform children in concrete and personal ways.

Classrooms, as research suggests, should be broken up into smaller specific literacy places such as offices, libraries, kitchens, hospitals, and television stations (Reutzel & Wolfersberger, 1996). Doing so encourages busy classrooms, sustained engagement in literacy learning, more cooperative behaviors, and a sense of privacy to pursue personal projects. The arrangement of furnishings is one way of cardoning off specific activity areas in the classroom. Another way of designating activity areas is through the use of displays, labels, and signs. Each of these objects should attract attention, teach, and inform children as they roam around the room.

The key to displays and storing literacy props is the concept of *aggregation*. This means that props are collected into a related network of materials or objects for a particular purpose. For example, when designing a classroom library area teachers would aggregate or collect literacy props such as library books, cards, due date stamps, book marks, posters of favorite children's books, pictures of authors, advertisements of new books, and so on for display and use in this area. There might be a card catalogue, a librarian's desk, a rotating wire book display rack, and a checkout. Bookshelves could be labeled with section headers such as biographies, fiction, fables, folk tales, fairy tales, and so on. Each of these areas should enjoy a personal touch from home. Here again furnishings and objects provide the key to this concept. Plants, bean bag chairs, pillows, children's portraits, mailboxes, message boards, galleries for artwork, and mobiles for displaying the main characters in books enhance the "personal" nature of the classroom. All combined, these elements of classroom design create a press for children to engage in literacy as an ongoing and enjoyable source of learning, creating, and growing.

Developmentally Appropriate Language Instructional Practices: Balanced Literacy Programs

The elements of balanced literacy programs have been well defined for over two decades by literacy scholars and practitioners working in New Zealand and Australia (Holdaway, 1979; Mooney, 1990). These elements insure, when included in the design of classroom experiences, that children will receive a well-rounded, developmentally appropriate, balanced exposure to and experiences with reading and writing (Reutzel, in press; Morrow & Gambrell, in press). In the next sections of this chapter, I describe the elements of balanced literacy programs in connection with selected developmentally appropriate instructional practices.

Reading TO Children (Infancy to Adulthood)

There are several good reasons to read aloud to children at least daily, if not more often. Trelease (1989) states: "The reasons are the same reasons you talk to a child: to reassure, to entertain, to inform or explain, to arouse curiosity, and to inspire—and to do it all personally, not impersonally with a machine. All those experiences create or strengthen a positive attitude about reading" (p. 2)

When reading is careful and deliberate, children's conceptual understandings can be expanded. In short, children can learn about their world from hearing about ideas, concepts, and events that are within their ability to comprehend through listening but beyond their ability to access through the act of reading. Hence, teachers ought to read books to children that challenge their intellectual development but do not exceed their emotional levels of experience. Consequently, books written at children's reading levels that can be read on their own or with support should be reserved for reading *with* and *by* young children. Based on Trelease's (1989) *The New Read-Aloud Handbook*, several other "dos" and "don'ts" of read-aloud for teachers are listed in table 9.3.

TABLE 9.3
Read-Aloud Dos and Don'ts

Dos

- Begin reading to children as soon as possible. The younger you start them, the better.
- Use Mother Goose rhymes and songs to stimulate children's language and listening.
- Read as often as you and the child (or class) have time for.
- Try to set aside at least one traditional time each day for a story.
- Picture books can be read easily to a family of children widely separated in age.
- Start with picture books, and build to storybooks and novels.
- Vary the length and subject matter of your readings.
- Follow through with your reading.
- Occasionally read above the children's intellectual level and challenge their minds.
- Remember that even 6th-grade students love a good picture book now and then.
- Allow time for class discussion after reading a story.
- Use plenty of expression when reading.
- The most common mistake in reading aloud is reading too fast. Read slowly enough for the child to build mental pictures.
- Bring the author to life, as well as his or her book.
- Add a third dimension to the book whenever possible.
- Reluctant readers or unusually active children frequently find it difficult to just sit and listen.
- Follow the suggestion of Dr. Caroline Bauer and post a reminder sign by your door: "Don't Forget Your Flood Book."
- Fathers should make an extra effort to read to their children.
- Lead by example.

Don'ts

- Don't read stories that you don't enjoy yourself.
- Don't continue reading a book once it is obvious that it was a poor choice. Admit the mistake and choose another.
- If you are a teacher, don't feel you have to tie every book to classwork.
- Don't read above a child's emotional level.
- Don't impose interpretations of a story on your audience.
- Don't confuse quantity or quality.
- Don't use the book as a threat—"If you don't pick up your room, no story tonight!"
- Don't try to compete with television.

Adapted from *The New Read-Aloud Handbook*, by Jim Trelease © 1989.

Small-Group or One-to-One Reading (*Ages 4–9*).   Although most reading aloud takes place with an entire group of children, Morrow (1988) reminds teachers not to overlook the benefits and importance of reading aloud to smaller groups and individuals. One of the benefits associated with reading to children at home is the interaction between parent and child. This same benefit can be replicated in the school setting. Children whose reading development is lagging behind that of their peers can be helped a great deal by teachers who take time to read to them in small-group or individual settings. Children can stop the teacher to ask questions, make comments, or respond to the story. This seldom happens in whole groups.

Reading WITH Children

Shared Book Experiences (*Ages 3–12*).   Many children have learned to read from having books read to them. These books were usually shared by parents or siblings during bedtime reading or lap reading. The shared book experience is an effective way to simulate the bedtime or lap reading event in school classrooms (Holdaway, 1979, 1981).

The shared book experience is begun by introducing the book. The teacher discusses the front and back of the book and may demonstrate certain features of the book, such as author and illustrator names, publisher, copyright, and table of contents. Next, the teacher may ask, "What do you think this story may be about?" After looking at the cover and reading the title aloud, children may want to relate personal anecdotes or make predictions about the contents of the book. The sensitive teacher will not only tolerate these contributions to the discussion but will encourage and praise children.

Next, the teacher reads the story with "full dramatic punch, perhaps overdoing a little some of the best parts" (Barrett, 1982, p. 16). Soon after the teacher begins reading, the children will begin chiming in on the repetitive and predictable parts with little more than an invitation. In the story, *The Gingerbread Man* (1985), the children may join in on the phrase, "Run, run as fast as you can. You can't catch me; I'm the Gingerbread man!" At key points, the teacher may pause during reading to encourage predictions about what is coming next in the book.

After reading, a discussion usually ensues. Children want to talk about their favorite parts, share their feelings and experiences, and discuss how well they were able to predict. The story can be reread on subsequent days and will eventually become a part of the stock of favorite stories to be requested for rereading. One means for increasing involvement on a second reading is to use hand movements or rhythm instruments along with sounds of animals or objects. In a recent study, Reutzel, Hollingsworth, and Eldredge (1994) and Eldredge, Reutzel, and Hollingsworth (1996) showed that the shared book experience resulted in substantial reading progress for 2nd grade children across measures of word recognition, vocabulary, comprehension, and fluency.

Shared Song, Chant, and Poetry (*Ages 3-12*). Music is a great motivator for reading and a natural integration of the fine arts with the language curriculum. Music broadens reading into a multisensory experience, heightens interest and involvement, brings variety and pleasure to reading, and reduces the tedium of repetition and drill (O'Bruba, 1987). Lundberg, Frost, and Peterson (1988) found that the use of patterned, rhymed text in oral story reading as well as singing from chart stories and big books fosters phonemic awareness in preschool children. For example, to emphasize the letter /s/ for a day or so, teachers might select and enlarge onto chart paper the text of the chants *Sally go round the sun* or *Squid Sauce* to be read aloud by the group. Songs such as *See Saw, Margery Draw* or *Sandy Land* may be selected and the lyrics enlarged onto charts for practice and group singing. Shel Silverstein's (1974) *Sister for Sale* or Jack Prelutsky's (1984) *Sneaky Sue* poems could be likewise enlarged and used to emphasize the name and sound of the letter "S" through repeated group readings.

Language Experience (*Ages 4-9*). The *language experience approach* (LEA) is an approach for developing and supporting children's reading and writing ability through the use of firsthand and/or vicarious experiences. The essence of this approach is to use children's oral language and personal experiences as the basis for creating personalized reading materials. These reading materials typically take the form of group experience charts (Allen & Allen, 1963).

A group experience chart is a means for recording young children's firsthand or vicarious experiences. An entire group of children shares an experience in common such as a field trip, a new book read aloud, or the visit of an outside expert. Although entire groups of children are often involved in the creation of group experience charts, it is also advisable to involve smaller groups of children periodically rather than the entire class to maximize the involvement of individual children. The typical course of events associated with the creation of a group experience chart follows:

1. The children participate in a shared experience.
2. The teacher and children discuss the shared experience.
3. Children dictate the chart, while the teacher transcribes the dictation.
4. The teacher and children share in reading the chart.
5. The chart is used to teach about words and other important language concepts.

Imagine a teacher who has read aloud to her class the book *The Polar Express* by Chris Van Allsburg (1985) as a part of a holiday social studies unit. After inviting children to respond to the book, the teacher asks, "If you had been chosen by Santa to receive the first gift of Christmas, what would you have said?" The teacher calls on individual children to give their responses to the book. After plenty of discussion, she calls on children to respond to the book by dictating aloud their best ideas for responding to this question. The teacher records each child's dictation on the chart. With emergent readers, the teacher may take each child's dictation down with different colored markers. The colors help children identify their own dictation more easily in the future. Later, the teacher may write the child's name by his or her dictation. When the chart is complete, the teacher typically reads the chart aloud to the children while pointing to each word as she reads. After the teacher has read the chart aloud, she invites the children to read along with her a second time. Next, she may ask individual children to read their own responses aloud or invite volunteers to read aloud the responses of other children.

The teacher may read aloud a certain line from the chart and ask for a child to come up to the chart and point to the line the teacher just read aloud. She may copy the lines of the chart on sentence strips and have children pick a sentence strip and match it to the line in the chart. Favorite words in the chart story can be copied onto word cards for matching activities. Thus, the text generated by the children for the chart story can be used in subsequent large- and small-group meetings to build the students' sight vocabulary of words in the chart, demonstrate word-recognition strategies, and even help children learn about letter sounds for decoding purposes. The chart also can be copied on a duplicating master and sent home with each child for individual practice.

Reading BY Children

Drop Everything and Read (DEAR) (*Ages 5–Adult*).   An important part of a balanced reading program is the inclusion of reading *by* children. Children must be given opportunities to enjoy reading self-selected materials on a regular basis. Drop Everything and Read (DEAR) is a structured approach that provides needed regular reading events for young children. Experts believe that the more children read, or even pretend to read, the more they become successful readers. R. Allington (1977) once raised the question, "If they don't read much, how they ever gonna get good?" Implementing a DEAR program is a relatively straightforward process:

1. Designate a specific daily time for reading. Teachers have found that three time slots work well for DEAR: first thing in the morning; following lunch or recess; right before children go home for the day. For younger children, a ten-minute session is usually optimal.

2. Hold a procedural mini-lesson to describe the rules of DEAR. Successful experiences with DEAR begin with a brief lesson on the rules and expectations associated with this time. Teachers state the purposes of DEAR. Second, they review the rules for participation in DEAR. It is helpful to enlarge the rules and illustrate each. Then the illustrated rules can be placed on a chart to help students take responsibility for their own behavior. Finally, teachers explain how students can ready themselves for this time each day. The rules for DEAR are shown in table 9.4.

3. Extend the experience through sharing. Children can be asked to share their books with other students at the conclusion of DEAR through a "say something" or "turn to your neighbor" activity. In addition to these informal share sessions, groups of children may respond to a book through art, drama, writing, or musical performances to be shared with others. In any case, beginning a DEAR

TABLE 9.4
Rules for Implementing DEAR

- Children must select their own books or reading materials.
- Changing books during DEAR is discouraged to avoid interruptions.
- Each individual in the classroom is expected to read silently without interruption during the fixed period of time for DEAR.
- The teacher and other visitors in the classroom are expected to read materials of their own choosing silently as well.
- Children are not expected to make reports or answer teacher questions about the books they have been reading during DEAR.

program with young children, even in kindergarten, convinces them of the value of reading and gives them important practice time.

Writing TO Children

Message Board (*Ages 5–12*).   Children like to receive notes from their teachers. One way to communicate with a classroom of children is to display a message board that is set aside for writing notes to children. The notes left on the message center are compliments, comments, directions, and the like. These notes are often brief, and many children consult these notes at the beginning or throughout the school day. Our students enjoyed writing and reading responses to books posted in the book message center.

Using Environmental Print (*Ages 3–7*).   Hiebert and Ham (1981) documented that children who were taught to read and write with environmental print learned significantly more letter names and sounds than did children who learned alphabet letters without using environmental print. Old cereal boxes, signs, bumper stickers, and candy wrappers can be used in interesting ways to give children confidence in reading and to help them understand how print works. A display area, bulletin board, or wall can be designated as an environmental print wall. Children may be asked to bring environmental print or product logos from home to put on this display wall. Environmental print can then be used to make messages on the message board by teachers and children. Other possibilities for using environmental print include producing classroom signs using product logos to substitute for written word(s), cutting up environmental print to compose notes between teachers and children, or making word collages for an art activity.

Writing WITH Children

Innovations and Reproductions—Alphabet Books (*Ages 4–7*).
Teachers ought to acquire collections of quality alphabet trade books
(Reutzel, 1992). Books such as *On Market Street* (Lobel, 1981),
Animalia (Base, 1986), and *The Z was Zapped* (Van Allsburg, 1987)
are just a few of the many delightful alphabet books that may be used
to teach children the alphabet as a whole rather than a letter a week.
In addition to repeated readings of commercially produced alphabet
books, teachers and children can compose their own highly predictable alphabet books using commercial books as patterns. In an established writing center, young students can create both reproductions
and innovations of any commercial alphabet books shared in class. A
reproduction is a student-made copy of a commercially produced
alphabet book. Children copy the text of each page exactly and draw
their own illustrations for a reproduction. Innovations borrow the
basic pattern of commercially produced alphabet books, but change
the selected words. For instance, one group of kindergarten students
made innovations on the book *The Z Was Zapped* (Van Allsburg,
1987). Each child chose a letter and made a new illustration as an
innovation. One child, Kevin, picked the letter "D" and drew a picture
of the letter in the shape of a doughnut being dunked into a cup of hot
chocolate. The caption underneath the picture read, THE "D" WAS
DUNKED. Reproductions and innovations of alphabet books help
students take ownership of familiar text while encouraging them to
experiment with the writer's craft.

Writing BY Children

Daily Journal Writing (*Ages 5–12*).   Children write to record things,
to manage their lives, and to share their feelings and truths for much
the same reasons adults do. In fact, it is often in the modeling of
writing that adults help stimulate the desire to write in young children.
Children learn that there are two writing forums, public and private.
Journals are largely private but may be shared selectively. Journals are
places where we share the story of our lives. Young children all have
stories as well. Opportunities to draw, write, or scribble in a journal is
a means for encouraging the writing habit. Even young children enjoy
having their own writing place and tools.

Several tips for engaging young children in journal writing are listed in table 9.5. Teachers of young children need to model daily journal writing during the time young children are writing. Telling young children to draw and caption drawings with help from the teacher and other children is an easy, effective way to introduce children to writing independently for their own purposes. Calkins (1986) tells of a young lad who said that he didn't know yet what he was going to write about because he "hadn't drawed it yet."

Integrating the Language Arts: Themed Literature Units

Krogh's chapter in this book addresses various issues related to designing developmentally appropriate practice and culminates in a recommendation for early childhood educators to integrate subject matter across content boundaries to support "mindful rather than mindless" activities. Reutzel and Cooter (1996) as well as others (Raines, 1995) recommend that topic or theme centered literature units provide one means for integrating other subject or content matter around the core purposes society holds for early schooling—young children learning to read and write.

Designing thematic literature units for young children requires considerable advanced planning. The process often begins with selecting an appropriate topic or theme. For example, a teacher might focus on "Independence Day" for a kindergarten themed literature unit. Next,

TABLE 9.5
Using Dialogue Journals

1. Each day set aside about ten minutes for children to write or draw something about an interest, concern, or experience.

2. Use a bound composition book or other similarly bound writing book as the journal.

3. To start children writing, tell them that writing is a way of saving what you think and say. Some people use pictures; others make marks on paper to save their thoughts. Drawing is a good way to get started. Then try to label or caption the drawing with writing.

4. If children have a difficult time getting started, you may want to suggest some topics such as favorite foods, afterschool activities, and so on. You may also want to provide stimulus sentence "leads" such as "My favorite thing to do after school is . . ."

potentially available resources to support the "Independence Day" theme are assessed and selected. For example, the following resources might be considered for creating themed literature units:

Trade books (story, hot-to, non-fiction)
Basals (current and past adoptions)
Media (films, slides, videotapes, etc.)
Reference materials (picture encyclopedia, picture atlas)
Specialized books (cookbooks, how-to books)
Technology (computer CD books, encyclopedias, atlas, America Online)

Next, a curriculum web (Paradis, 1984; Whitmore & Goodman, 1995) is created that includes all of the subject areas of the curriculum. This web is used to brainstorm potential questions students may ask or specific curriculum objectives that may be potentially supported with the selection of the "Independence Day" theme. An example of a completed "Independence Day" theme curriculum is shown in figure 9.3. Next children contribute to the curriculum web. By using a KWL chart as described by D. Ogle (1986) children can be asked, What do you KNOW, What do you WANT to know, and What did you LEARN. The students' brainstorming ideas are placed on a three-column chart with one of the three questions mentioned above used as the column headings. Once the first two columns of the KWL chart are completed (What do you know, What do you want to know), activities are suggested to accomplish those "things they want to learn" by children and the teacher. Potential activities, projects, or inquiry topics are added to each curriculum area represented in the "Independence Day Theme" curriculum web shown in figure 9.3.

Once advanced planning is completed, instructional projects, activities, demonstrations, and lessons, will need to be created. Begin by deciding which of the many approaches to literature-based instruction will be used. With young children (P–1), teachers would typically choose to use a "big book" or "shared book" approach, where all the children in the class read the same enlarged book or multiple copies of the same book as a whole group. For children in grades 2–3, teachers may decide to use "literature circles," where multiple small groups of children meet with the teacher to discuss their responses to different titles related to the theme. After deciding which instructional approach to use with the "Independence Day" literature theme, independent and

FIGURE 9.3
Thematic Unit: Independence Day

P.E.
- Colonial Games
- Colonial chores
- Parade and Drill
- Reenact Valley Forge

Reading
- Predictable books
- Read Aloud - Ben and Me
- Color Words
  (Red, White, Blue
- Statue Books
- Martha Washington
- Betsy Ross
- The story of the flag
- Declaration of Independence
- CD Rom Encyclopedia
- The history of fireworks

Music
- Singing Patriotic Music
- Rhythm Band
  Marching
- Creative Dance to Patriotic Music

Language Arts
- Language
= Experience Stories
- Word Banks
- Word Wall
- Puppetry
- Dramatize the Boston Tea Party
- Choral Readings of Revolutionary War Poetry
- Bill of Rights ... "We the students..."
- Pictures...Then and Now

Independence Day

Social Studies
Video
- Johnny Tremain
- George Washington
- Statue of Liberty
- 1776
- Ben and Me

Resource
- People/guests
- Role play historical events
- Costume rental from D.C. & Willamsburg

Activities
- raising and lowering the flag
- folding the flag
- food experiences butter churn
- smash fruit to make jam
- clothing: paper dolls
- map of U.S.
- read aloud of journal entries of famous historical figures
- make a colonial cookbook

Art
- watermelon seeds collage
- historical look at US flags
- swirl painting of fireworks
- colonial newspaper hats
- mural of fireworks

Math
- watermelon - count seeds
- flag(s) stars and stripes count and graph
- geographical patterns in early colonial art
- number twister game
- map and counting out steps in a treasure hunt

Science
- how fireworks are made
- safety in using fireworks
- black powder rifles
- candle making
- soap making
- oxidizing metals
- pulleys, levers

teacher-directed learning centers are designed to support all or some of the several curriculum areas represented in the curriculum web shown in figure 9.3.

Teachers can also use the "Independence Day Theme" curriculum web to look for ways to connect various subject fields to one another. Creative movement and dramatics could be linked to learning and performing "early patriotic" songs in music such as "Yankee Doodle" or "When Johnny Comes Marching Home." Reading color words could be integrated with graphing the number of stars, and stripes in the U.S. flag in a math activity. Reading aloud diaries, newspaper articles, memoirs such as those found in *The American Revolutionaries: A History in Their Own Words, 1975–1800* (Meltzer, 1987) could also be linked to role playing various colonial events in Social Studies. Science activities related to fireworks could be linked to art activities such as swirl painting and mural making. Writing or dictating a class colonial recipe book could be integrated with children's food experiences in Social Studies. Mathematics watermelon seed counting could be integrated with art to make collages. Resource people could be invited to teach children how to perform various colonial tasks such as marching, butter churning, candlemaking, and soap making. Reading "color" words that are phonically regular such as red, green, pink, tan, and white as well as words that should be learned by sight such as orange, blue, purple, and yellow could be used to make word walls thus integrating reading, science, and art activities. In this way, the curriculum web around "Independence Day" helps teachers see and make curriculum connections for students in the design of activities. To track progress during an integrated or themed unit, an approximate timeline for completion of the themed unit is decided upon and displayed in the classroom with benchmark dates associated with project/lesson/activity completion.

Lastly, an assessment rubric or criteria for the "Independence Day" themed literature unit needs to be decided on. A project and activity completion record may be designed to keep records for children's projects throughout the literature unit. Student knowledge acquisition may also be assessed by recording children's learnings on the KWL chart. Observational checklists may be designed to assess children's participation, skill acquisition, and knowledge gain as a part of determining the overall effectiveness of the themed literature unit as well as the quantity and quality of learning that occurred in the classroom.

Summary

In summary, teachers need to provide opportunities (writing topics, books for personal reading, projects, etc.) for making personal choices for young children to understand that language is a tool for exploring, discovering, discussing, and learning across the curriculum. Every encounter with language is an experience, and daily experiences are opportunities for language learning and development. Teachers must establish print-rich environments to stimulate and support literacy learning. They should provide opportunities to read and write in a balanced literacy program where reading and writing to, with, and by children is the daily routine. And, finally, teachers can help children find meaning in learning to read and write by integrating this learning process with other curriculum content, using themed literature units centered on an appropriately chosen topic or theme.

In view of these recommendations, parents and teachers provide ongoing and numerous demonstrations of, support and encouragement for, and gentle guidance toward the development of independent reading and conventional writing abilities. This is best accomplished when parents and teachers remember that young children can perform many tasks successfully with help they cannot yet accomplish alone. Hence, parents and teachers must never underestimate the important role they play in shaping their young children's future reading and writing abilities.

References

Allen, R.V., & Allen, C. (1963). *Language experience activities* (2nd ed.). Boston, MA: Houghton Mifflin.

Allington, R.L. (1977). If they don't read much, how they ever gonna get good? *Journal of Reading, 21,* 57–61.

Auerbach, E.R. (1989). Towards a social-contextual approach to family literacy. *Harvard Educational Review 59* (2), 159–81.

Barrett, F.L. (1982). *A teacher's guide to shared reading.* Richmond Hill, Ontario, Canada: Scholastic-TAB.

Base. G. (1986). *Animalia.* New York: Harry N. Abrams.

Bredekamp, S. (1987). *Developmentally appropriate practice in early childhood programs serving children from birth through age 8.* Washington, DC: National Association for the Education of Young Children.

Bredekamp, S. (Ed.). (1986). *Developmentally appropriate practice.* Washington, DC: National Association for the Education of Young Children.

Bredekamp, S., & Copple, C. (Eds.). (1997). *Developmentally appropriate practice in early childhood programs: Revised.* Washington, DC: National Association for the Education of Young Children.

Bredekamp, S., & Rosegrant, T. (1992). *Reaching potentials: Transforming early childhood curriculum and assessment* (Vol. 1). Washington, DC: National Association for the Education of Young Children.

Bredekamp, S., & Rosegrant, T. (1995). *Reaching potentials: Transforming early childhood curriculum and assessment* (Vol. 2). Washington, DC: National Association for the Education of Young Children.

Calkins, L. (1986). *The art of teaching writing.* Portsmouth, NH: Heinemann.

Cambourne, B., & Turbill, J. (1987). *Coping with chaos.* Rozelle, NSW, Australia, Primary English Teaching Association (PETA).

Clay, M.M. (1975). *What did I write? Beginning writing behaviour.* Portsmouth, NH: Heinemann.

Clay, M.M. (1987). *Writing begins at home: Preparing children for writing before they go to school.* New York: Richard C. Owens.

Department of Education (1985). *Reading in junior classes.* Wellington, New Zealand.

Dyson, A.H. (1993). *Social worlds of children learning to write in an urban primary school.* New York: Teachers College Press.

Eldredge, J.L., Reutzel, D.R., and Hollingsworth, P.M. (1996). Comparing the effectiveness of two oral reading practices: Round-robin reading and the Shared Book Experience. *Journal of Literacy Research, 28* (2), 201–25.

Ferreiro, E., & Teberosky, A. (1982). *Literacy before schooling.* Portsmouth, NH: Heinemann.

Goodman, K.S. (1986). *What's whole in whole language?* Ontario, Canada: Scholastic.

Goodman, Y.M. (1978). Kidwatching: An alternative to testing. *National Elementary Principal 57* (4), 41–45.

Goodman, Y.M. (1986). Children coming to know literacy. In W.H. Teale, E. Sulzby *Emergent literacy: Writing and reading* (pp. 1–14). Norwood, NJ: Ablex Publishing Corporation.

Gullo, D.F. (1992). *Developmentally appropriate teaching in early childhood.* Washington, DC: National Education Association.

Hall, Nigel. (1987). *The emergence of literacy.* Portsmouth, NH: Heinemann.

Harste, J., Woodward, V., & Burke, C. (1984). *Language stories and literacy lessons.* Portsmouth, NH: Heinemann.

Hiebert, E., & Ham, D. (1981). *Young children and environmental print.* Paper presented at the annual meeting of the National Reading Conference, Dallas, TX.

Holdaway, D. (1979). *The foundations of literacy.* New York: Ashton Scholastic.

Holdaway, D. (1981). Shared book experience: Teaching reading using favorite books. *Theory into Practice, 21,* 293–300.

Kantor, R., Miller, S., & Fernie, D. (1992). Diverse paths to literacy in a preschool classroom: A sociocultural perspective. *Reading Research Quarterly, 27* (3), 185–201.

Lobel, A. (1981). *On market street.* New York: Scholastic.

Loughlin, C.E., & Martin, M.D. (1987). *Supporting literacy: Developing effective learning environments.* New York: Teachers College Press.

Lundberg, I., Frost, J., & Peterson, O. (1988). Effects of an extensive program for stimulating phonemic awareness in preschool children. *Reading Research Quarterly, 23,* 263–84.

Meltzer, M. (1987). *The American revolutionaries: A history in their own words, 1750–1800.* New York: Crowell.

Mooney, M. (1990). *Reading to, with, and by children.* New York: Richard C. Owens.

Morrow, L.M. (1988). Young children's responses to one-to-one story reading in school settings. *The Reading Teacher., 23* (1), 89–107.

Morrow, L.M. (1989). *Literacy development in the early years: Helping children read and write.* Englewood Cliffs, NJ: Prentice Hall.

Morrow, L.M., & Rand, M.K. (1991). Promoting literacy during play by designing early childhood classroom environments. *The Reading Teacher, 44* (6), 396–402.

Morrow, L.M., & Gambrell, L. (in press). *The radical middle: Creating a balanced literacy program.* Newark, DE: International Reading Association.

Neuman, S.B., & Roskos, K. (1990). Play, print, and purpose: Enriching play environments for literacy development. *The Reading Teacher, 44* (3), 214–21.

Neuman, S.B., & Roskos, K. (1992). Literacy objects as cultural tools: Effects on children literacy behaviors in play. *Reading Research Quarterly, 27* (3), 202–25.

Neuman, S.B., & Roskos, K. (1993). *Language and literacy learning in the early years: An integrated approach.* New York: Harcourt, Brace, Jovanovich.

O'Bruba, W.S. (1987). Reading through the creative arts. *Reading Horizons, 27* (3), 170–77.

Ogle, D.M. (1986). K-W-L: A teaching model that develops active reading of expository text. *The Reading Teacher, 39* (6), 564–70.

Paradis, E.E. (1984). *Comprehension and thematic units.* Laramie, WY: University of Wyoming TV Productions.

Paterson, K. (1977). *Bridge to Terabithia.* New York: Greenwillow.

Prelutsky, J. (1984). *A new kid on the block.* New York: Greenwillow.

Prelutsky, J. (1991). *Poems for laughing out loud.* New York: Knopf.

Raines, S.C. (1995). *Whole language across the curriculum: Grades 1, 2, 3.* Newark, DE: International Reading Association.

Reutzel, D.R. (1992). Breaking the letter a week tradition: Conveying the alphabetic principle to young children. *Childhood Education, 69* (1), 20–23.

Reutzel, D.R. (1996). A balanced reading approach. In J. Baltas and S. Shafer (Eds.), *A staff development guide to balanced reading: K–2.* New York, Scholastic Inc.

Reutzel D.R., & Cooter, R.B., Jr. (1996). *Teaching children to read: from basals to books* (2nd ed). Columbus, OH: Merrill-Prentice Hall.

Reutzel, D.R., Hollingsworth, P.M., & Eldredge, J.L. (1994). Oral reading instruction: The impact on student reading development. *Reading Research Quarterly, 23* (1), 40–62.

Reutzel, D.R., & Wolfersburger, M. (1996). An environmental impact statement: Designing supportive literacy classrooms for young children. *Reading Horizons, 36* (3), 266–82.

Schickendanz, J. (1990). *Adam's righting revolution: One child's literacy development from infancy to grade 1.* Portsmouth, NH: Heinemann.

Silverstein, S. (1974). *Where the sidewalk ends.* New York: Harper & Row.

Silverstein, S. (1976). *A light in the attic.* New York: Harper & Row.

Smith, F. (1977). The uses of language. *Language Arts, 54* (6), 638–44.

Smith, F. (1985). *Reading without nonsense* (2nd ed.). New York: Teachers College Press.

Smith, F. (1988). *Understanding reading* (4th ed.). Hillsdale, NJ: Erlbaum.

Sulzby, E. (1985). Children's emergent reading of favorite storybooks: A developmental study. *Reading Research Quarterly, 20* (4), 458–81.

Sulzby, E., & Teale, W. (1991). Emergent literacy. In R. Barr, ML. Kamil, P.B. Mosenthal, & P.D. Pearson (Eds.), *Handbook of reading research* (Vol. 2, pp. 727–57). New York: Longman.

Taylor, D. (1983). *Family literacy: Young children learning to read and write.* Exeter, NH: Heinemann.

Taylor, D., & Dorsey-Gaines, C. (1988). *Growing up literate: Learning from inner-city families.* Portsmouth, NH: Heinemann.

Teale, W.H. (1987). Emergent literacy: Reading and writing development in early childhood. In J.E. Readence, R.S. Baldwin, J.P. Konopak, & H. Newton (Eds.), *Research in literacy: Merging perspectives* (pp. 45–74). Rochester, NY: National Reading Conference.

Temple, C., Nathan, R., Burris, N. & Temple, F. (1994). *The beginnings of writing* (2nd ed.). Newton, MA: Allyn & Bacon.

Trelease, J.(1989). *The new read-aloud handbook.* New York: Penguin.

Van Allsburg, C. (1986). *The polar express.* Boston: Houghton-Mifflin.

Van Allsburg, C. (1987). *The Z was zapped.* Boston: Houghton-Mifflin.

Van Manen, M. (1986). *The tone of teaching.* Ontario, Canada: Scholastic.

Wasserman, S. (1992). Serious play in the classroom. *Childhood Education 68* (3), 133–39.

Whitmore, K.F., & Goodman, Y.M. (1995). Transforming curriculum in language and literacy. In S. Bredekamp and T. Rosegrant (Eds.), *Reading potentials: Transforming early childhood curriculum and assessment* (Vol. 2). Washington, DC: National Association for the Education of Young Children.

PART TWO

Selected Topics and Special Issues

CHAPTER TEN

Social Development and Behavior in the Integrated Curriculum

MICHELE DEWOLF
JOAN BENEDICT

An observer enters a kindergarten classroom during the time the children are involved in centers. She notices an interaction between two boys at the mathematics center. Both boys shake film cans and roll out beans as though they are dice. They are recording the number of beans by looking at what appears on each side of the bean. Chris confidently says to Tony, "What did you find? Okay. You got three raindrops. Two suns. Put two [meaning the numeral 2 on his paper]. Put two right there. No, Tony, like that. Just put two like that." They continue writing equations each time they shake out the beans.

In the book center, Vera is turning the pages of a book that was made by the class. Several other children are gathered around looking at the book and listening to Vera read. Vera says, "I read this book and I love it. Oh, I just love a book like this. Aaron likes pizza. Me, too. Angella likes spaghetti. Me, too. Anthony likes Pop Tarts. Me, too. I don't know the name of this. I just call it. Dorothy likes white. Me, too." Reading continues until the book is completed. In the dramatic play center, three girls are involved. Danitta says, "Yea, I see you, baby. Now, you sit up. It's our toaster. I'm the daddy. Get out the street, baby. Now! [angrily] She suppose to get out. Better not get out the street again, baby."

In each episode, children are using social skills. These did not "just happen" upon entering school. Many factors went into the development of each child's ability to function as a social human being. Cooperative learning was taking place in this classroom. Notice that the teacher was not actively involved in any of the examples. Children were coaching, directing, and sharing with their peers. Such social interactions have a profound influence on children's overall development. Unfortunately, the potential for both formal and informal learning that can occur in these social contexts is often overlooked in the early childhood curriculum.

Role of Social Development
in the Integrated Curriculum

Socialization plays an integral role in children's normal growth and development (Rubin & Rose-Krasnor, 1992). It is a process that directs the development of children's personalities and guides their learning of how to interact with other children and adults (Salkind & Ambron, 1987). Ramsey (1991) emphasizes that the main goal of socialization should be to assist children in discovering their own ways of interacting with peers and to ensure that they feel good about themselves during those interactions. Hopefully, the result of this socialization will be the development of social competence. According to Rubin and Rose-Krasnor (1992), social competence is the "ability to achieve personal goals in social interaction while simultaneously maintaining positive relationships with others over time and across situations" (p. 285).

Socialization also serves as a mechanism through which children learn skills necessary to become participating citizens in a democracy. According to Hendrick (1992), affording young children opportunities to have "the power to choose," "the power to try," and "the power to do" provides an important introduction to democratic values. During social interactions young children acquire and utilize skills essential to decision making, problem solving, working together, and handling conflicts. This gives them a context for "choosing, trying, and doing."

As described by Suzanne Krogh (chapter 2, this volume) an integrated curriculum provides meaningfulness to children's learning by combining various curricula areas into a unified whole. What role does social development play in the integrated curriculum? Socialization is the common thread that ties the entire curriculum together. The skills and/or behaviors acquired through social development are important for successful functioning in a learning environment such as the classroom (Bredekamp & Copple, 1997). According to Birch and Ladd (in press), the quality of classroom relationships (i.e., teacher–child, child–child) may determine the extent to which children are motivated to engage in actively exploring the school environment. It may also inhibit this type of exploration. Indeed, one of the best predictors of academic failure and school dropout is social rejection by the peer group (Kupersmidt, Coie, & Dodge, 1990; Parker & Asher, 1987; Rubin, Bukowski, & Parker, in press). The following sections will hopefully serve as a guide for understanding the social world of the young child in ways that will facilitate overall school adjustment. We begin by reviewing theoretical perspectives on social development. We then discuss ways that social development can be facilitated across the early childhood years in home, school, and peer contexts.

Learning about the Social World

According to Charlesworth (1992), a theory is "a plan or set of rules that explains, describes, or predicts what happens and what will happen when children grow and learn" (p. 1). Taken together with recent advances in the understanding of genetic contributions (Plomin, 1994), each theory provides insight into how nature and nurture may interact to influence children's social development. Acceptance of one or more of these theories influences the way we view children and the way we interact with them (Salkind & Ambron, 1987). Of the many theories that are relevant to children's social development (see Rubin, Bukowski, & Parker, in press, for a review) we chose to narrow our discussion to Bandura's social cognitive theory, Piaget's cognitive developmental theory, Dodge and Rubin's social information processing models, and Erikson's psychosocial theory. Each is helpful in explaining how children develop social skills in the context of environmental factors discussed later. An eclectic approach was chosen so that various aspects of each theory could be applied as a means of encompassing the many complexities of social development.

Social Cognitive Theory

Social cognitive theory is primarily concerned with socialization, which in this case is defined as "the process by which society attempts to teach children to behave like the ideal adults of that society" (Miller, 1989, p. 191). Bandura felt that children acquire behavior as an outcome of learning through direct or indirect reinforcement (see table 10.1), or through observing and imitating models (see table 10.2). While the environment is central to this theory, children take an active role in their learning by interacting with their environment (Bandura, 1977).

Attention to models is affected by the perceived attractiveness or power of the model as well as the situation in which the behavior is viewed. Therefore, models are usually persons whom children respect

TABLE 10.1
Reinforcement

Direct Reinforcement: Positive or negative consequences determine if a behavior will be repeated.
Indirect Reinforcement: Child imitates a behavior for which another person was reinforced.
Functions of Reinforcement:
　　1. Provides child with information on appropriateness of behavior for a certain situation.
　　2. Influences behavior based on the anticipatoin of particular outcomes.

(Bandura, 1977; Grusec & Lytton, 1988; Miller, 1989)

TABLE 10.2
Modeling

Modeling: Mechanism for gaining competence or knowledge or changing behavior by observing others.
Modeling Processes:
　　1. Attention: Child must attend to model's behavior.
　　2. Retention: Behaviors attended to must be symbolically represented in child's memory.
　　3. Transformation: Symbolic representations must be transformed into actions similar to model's behavior.
　　4. Motivation: Child must be motivated to perform the modeled bahaviors.

(Bandura, 1977; Grusec & Lytton, 1988)

and who are similar to themselves. Typically, parents are the most important models in early childhood, while peers and teachers become more important as children grow older. Also, the kinds of behavior imitated by children depend on the kinds of behavior that exist and are valued in the culture (Grusec & Lytton, 1988).

Cognitive Developmental Theory

Cognitive functioning plays an important role in children's social development (DeVries, 1997; Musatti, 1986). According to Piaget's cognitive developmental theory, children learn by actively constructing knowledge through interaction with their environment. Experiences provide the basis for developing mental structures called schemes (i.e., organized patterns of behavior that are used to interact with the environment in certain ways). For example, an infant has a scheme for sucking, one for seeing, one for grasping, and so on. Over time, these schemes become differentiated. For example, the infant has distinct ways to suck on a bottle as opposed to a pacifier. Schemes also become coordinated. For example, the infant becomes able to grasp what is seen (Miller, 1989; Overton & Reese, 1973; Piaget, 1970).

Piaget utilized three principles to explain the development of mental structures from basic behavioral sequences in infancy to formal operations in adolescence. These principles include maintaining equilibrium, organization, and adaptation (see table 10.3). Piaget also believed that children's learning is different from that of adults. He asserted that this learning progresses through invariant stages. Within each stage, children have a qualitatively different way of viewing reality (see Krogh, chapter 2, this volume, for a review).

TABLE 10.3
Piaget's Principles of Cognitive Development

Maintaining Equilibrium: bringing ideas into balance with reality.

Organization: arranging information or mental structures in an orderly fashion.

Adaptation: changing knowledge or behavior to meet the demands of the environment. This results from assimilation (incorporating new information into existing structures) and accommodation (altering existing structures to take in new information).

(Miller, 1989; Piaget, 1970)

During the sensorimotor stage, children's socialization relies on their activities or interactions with others. During this stage children acquire representational abilities that enable them to recall persons and objects in their absence (i.e., object permanence). Children also accumulate a system of mental symbols about relations between persons that are then used during social interactions. Children's symbolic play, deferred imitation, and language use are the first indications that children possess representational abilities (Musatti, 1986).

During the preoperational stage, a characteristic of thinking that is important for understanding social development is the difficulty children have understanding any perspective but their own. This is known as egocentrism. To preschoolers, reality is seen only from their own point of view, and they expect everyone else to see it that way also. This egocentrism makes social interactions difficult for small children because they have trouble understanding the feelings and thoughts of others (Grusec & Lytton, 1988).

When adults offer children reasons for changing a particular behavior, these reasons often contain information about other people's viewpoints and feelings. This helps children internalize this information by incorporating it into existing schemas (Brody & Shaffer, 1982) which can then be used for negotiating the social world. Additionally, the social negotiation, discussion, and conflict found in peer relations help children learn to understand others' thoughts, emotions, motives, and intentions. This understanding then enables children to think about the consequences of their behavior both for themselves and for others, which in turn leads to appropriate and effective social behavior (Rubin & Rose-Krasnor, 1992).

Social Information Processing Model

Dodge (1986) has proposed a model that describes the mental processes involved in evaluating social information and provides a model of social exchange between children (see also Crick & Dodge, 1994). Social information processing consists of five sequential steps that help children make sense of social information and then choose an appropriate social response (see table 10.4). Rubin and Rose-Krasner (1986) have described similar processes by focusing on less interactive behavioral domains (see also Rubin & Rose-Krasnor, 1992).

TABLE 10.4
Steps in Social Information Processing

1. **Encoding:** requires attending to and perceiving a social signal (e.g., a smile, a push) that must be processed.
2. **Interpreting:** involves determining the meaning of social information by comparing it to existing knowledge.
3. **Response search:** requires generating a variety of response alternatives.
4. **Response evaluation:** involves anticipating consequences of behavior and choosing the most appropriate alternative for the current situation.
5. **Enactment:** involves performing the chosen response.

(Dodge, 1986)

Psychosocial Theory

Erik Erikson's psychosocial theory specifically focuses on personality development and tracks this development across the life span. The influences of family and society on the process of achieving ego identity are emphasized. Ego identity has two features: (1) knowing and accepting oneself, and (2) recognizing and identifying with the ideals and basic patterns of the culture. As part of this process, the individual passes through eight psychosocial stages. Each stage builds on the preceding one and is concerned with a turning point or crisis in the personality related to a specific major conflict (Crain, 1992; Thomas, 1992).

Each crisis emerges according to a predetermined timetable due to maturation. Healthy development of the self relies on making adjustments to the demands of the crisis. If an unsatisfactory resolution of the conflict occurs, the struggle continues and obstructs healthy development of the self (Crain, 1992; Thomas, 1992).

A successful resolution of the conflict for each stage involves balancing the positive trait with the negative trait. Although the positive quality should be prevalent, some aspect of the negative quality is needed also. For example, healthy trust of the world must be accompanied by some mistrust in order to be prepared to handle a dangerous situation (Crain, 1992; Thomas, 1992). The stages of Erikson's theory that apply to childhood are summarized in table 10.5.

TABLE 10.5
Erikson's Stages of Psychosocial Adjustment

Basic trust versus mistrust (birth to 12–18 months)
    Infants learn if they can rely on people and things in the environment. Development of a healthy self occurs if an appropriate balance is reached between trust (which allows intimacy) and mistrust (which allows self-protection).

Autonomy versus shame & doubt (12–18 months to 3 years)
    Toddlers want to do everything themselves and are developing autonomy. Successful resolution of this stage will lead to the development of self-control and self-regulation.

Initiative versus guilt (3 to 6 years)
    Preschoolers exhibit more daring and curiosity due to increased language and cognitive skills. Successful resolution of this stage will give children the ability to pursue goals and a sense of responsibility.

Industry versus inferiority (6 years to adolescence)
    School-age children learn the skills (e.g., reading, writing, etc.) required by their culture and compare their own abilities to those of their peers to construct a sense of who they are. The successful resolution of this stage leads to competence, which involves the completion of tasks without feelings of inadequacy or inferiority.

(Crain 1992; Thomas, 1992).

Encouraging Social Development Appropriately

Theoretical and empirical knowledge about children's developing social skills can serve as a basis for creating environments that encourage positive social interactions. Caregivers with realistic expectations of children's abilities are effective facilitators of young children's learning about the social world.

Social Relationships in Infancy through Early Childhood

An infant immediately becomes a member of the familial social group at birth. The family is part of a community contained in a culture. Newborns are not social but their physical behaviors (i.e., posture and reflexes) result in parents changing their own responses due to their interpretation of the newborn as a social being (Brazelton, Koslowski, & Maen, 1974). By the age of 2, children are interacting both within and outside the family as social participants.

    The caregivers' relationship with newborns is the foundation for further developmental accomplishments as children grow (Isabella &

Belsky, 1991). Both parents and professionals, along with friends and other family members, are involved in the social development of infants. Understanding behavior and acquiring skills to facilitate social development in infants is an important accomplishment (see tables 10.6–10.7). The value of the caregiver understanding the competencies of infants cannot be underestimated during this equally important growth period. The toddler years are usually considered to be between the ages one and 3 years. Social development during these years focuses on gaining independence or autonomy, self-awareness, and

TABLE 10.6
Activities Related to Social Development
(Birth–2 Months)

During quiet alert states caregivers should:
- talk to the infant
- show the infant bright objects (toys)
- touch the infant
- read "infant" storybooks to the infant

During crying periods caregivers should:
- pick up the infant
- rock the infant
- wrap the infant while holding him or her upright
- sing to the infant

TABLE 10.7
Activities Related to Social Development
(3–12 Months)

Caregiver should:
- recognize the infant's preference for certain objects such as blankets, stuffed animals, or other items
- comfort the infant during reactions to unpleasant noises
- listen for the infant to imitate the pitch used during singing by the caregiver
- introduce new persons slowly (due to stranger anxiety) beginning around 6 months
- respond with information as the infant gains mobility and begins to explore the world
- initiate interactions with infants who have easy-going temperaments and who may not demand attention.
- allow time for the infant to separate from parent when leaving becomes difficult
- allow the infant control over body movement (i.e., not confining him or her to swings, cribs, walkers)

TABLE 10.8
Activities Related to Social Development
(1–3 Years)

Caregivers should:
- encourage the parent to form a routine for leaving the room (i.e., share a book or toy, say good-bye, leave room promptly)
- verbalize child's feelings honestly when the parent leaves (i.e., "You want your daddy.")
- encourage child to bring a special toy or blanket from home
- read books to child about saying good-bye to loved ones
- play hide and seek
- display pictures of child's home and family
- actively coach child on approved and disapproved behaviors (i.e., hurting others, taking others' possessions)
- be aware that negative behavior is normal
- know that egocentric behavior for toddlers is not "misbehaving"

knowing right from wrong. Caregiver suggestions for this age span are presented in table 10.8.

As children grow and mature during the preschool, kindergarten, and early elementary school years, play provides many opportunities for them to interact socially through informal means. The stages of play viewed by Rubin and Coplan (1992) as social participation were identified by Parten (1932) and have been observed through the years. Parten (1932) viewed play as evolving from nonsocial behavior to social participation during the preschool and middle childhood period. Six increasingly sophisticated, sequential categories were noted: unoccupied behavior, solitary play, onlooker behavior, parallel play, associative play (plays and shares with others but may take the same roles), and cooperative play (social play where each individual's role is defined and different from that of others).

As children develop, they become better able to understand the perspectives of their peers. This lends itself to more successful and sophisticated social interactions (Bjorklund, 1995). Selman proposed the idea of different levels of perspective taking in children. Ages 3 to 6 years is the earliest, known as the egocentric, role-taking stage. Children are aware of the differences existing between themselves and others, including the existence of others' thoughts and feelings. However, these children believe that others' thoughts and feelings are the same as their own. Children ages 6 to 8 are in the social informational role-taking stage and are better able to coordinate mental processes described earlier in table 10.4. Children understand that different people can have separate perspectives on things and can take different actions. These children have difficulty keeping both viewpoints in mind, and are likely to concentrate on one perspective eliminating the other choices (cited in Bjorklund, 1995).

Social skills proceed through developmental stages just as other areas of growth in children that follow developmental sequences (see Rubin, Bukowski, & Parker, in press, for an extensive review). Observing these changes is an important part of caring for and about children. Preschoolers' "sense of self" is seen as they describe themselves in terms of external physical qualities such as who members of their own families are, their actions, and where they live. Six- or 7-year-olds describe themselves by psychological traits, such as relationships with others, feelings, and personality characteristics (Brooks, 1991).

Positive and negative peer interactions also increase during the preschool and early grade school years in ways that are linked to acceptance or rejection by peers (e.g., Howes, 1988). While nonsocial/ withdrawn behavior typically decreases, aggressive exchanges, rough-and-tumble play, as well as cooperative and sociable behaviors, increase over the preschool years (see Hart, DeWolf, & Burts, 1993). As children progress through the early grades they become more mature in their relationships with peers. More effective communication strategies aid in the development of friendships among and acceptance by peers across this older age span (Santrock & Yussen, 1987; Rubin, Bukowski, & Parker, in press). Ideas for facilitating social development across this age span are summarized in table 10.9.

Contexts for Social Development

Children develop socially in a variety of contexts. Families play an important role in children's socialization, especially during early childhood. Additionally, the context of "school" becomes increasingly significant to this process as more children are being enrolled in some type of school or child care setting at earlier ages. The following provides information about how family and school influence children's social development.

TABLE 10.9
Activities Related to Social Development
(3–8 Years)

Caregivers should:
- plan schedules that are flexible
- allow for free-play time in accordance with successful social interactions of the children
- emphasize names or other attributes of preschool children, helping them become more aware of their peers
- suggest ways peers may interact in classroom or outdoor activities
- provide opportunities for children to work in small groups on special projects in the curricula areas
- arrange spaces to allow elementary children to see one another's faces in group discussions, encouraging the sharing of ideas and information

Family

Parents and other caregivers are the earliest socializing agents and provide interaction contexts that can enhance or diminish social competencies in young children (Salkind & Ambron, 1987). These contexts can assist in the development of social skills as well as provide emotional and cognitive resources useful to the child as he or she investigates the social world (Rubin & Rose-Krasnor, 1992). Familial interaction contexts work in combination with a host of personal (e.g., genetic/temperamental factors) and extrafamilial variables (e.g., sources of stress and support) in ways that are linked to child competence with peers (Hart, Olsen, Robinson, & Mandleco, 1997).

The influence of parents on children's peer relations occurs in either an indirect or direct way. Attachment relationships and discipline are two ways parents indirectly influence children's peer relationships (Ladd & LeSieur, 1995). As suggested by Ladd (1992), an indirect influence "implies that the family's effect on children's peer relations is mediated through some intervening child outcome" (p. 4) (e.g., discipline influences children's problem-solving skills or social behavior, which in turn influences children's peer relations).

Attachment refers to an affectional tie that one person forms to another specific person or other persons (Ainsworth, 1973). Infants form attachments to their mothers as well as to their fathers and other significant caregivers (Lamb, 1977). Attachments develop within the context of, and are influenced by, infant–caregiver interactions. These attachments are unique to individual pairs, in that they are based on the patterns of behavioral exchange that the pair has established. Through interactions with a significant caregiver, the infant acquires certain expectations regarding availability and responsiveness. Once the attachment relationship has developed, the infant's behaviors will be organized around the caregiver in a manner that is consistent with his or her interaction-based model of the relationship. These models are then incorporated into the personality of the individual infant (Ainsworth, 1973; Ladd, 1992; Sroufe, 1988).

A child with secure attachments has a representational model of the caregiver as responsive, sensitive, and helpful, and therefore a model of himself or herself as a lovable and valuable person. In accordance with psychosocial theory, these positive feelings about and confidence in oneself and others enables the child to develop a sense of trust and to feel comfortable in establishing social relationships with others. On the other hand, insecure attachments resulting from less sensitive parenting and inconsistent responsiveness do not provide children with the resources required for later peer relationships (Ainsworth, 1973; Ladd, 1992; Sroufe, 1988).

Two forms of discipline have been associated with ways children construct social cognitions and behavior in peer group situations (Brody & Shaffer, 1982; Ladd, 1991; Maccoby & Martin, 1983; Putallaz & Heflin, 1990). Inductive discipline involves reasoning, explaining, establishing limits, and setting up logical consequences. In accordance with the cognitive developmental perspective, these types of practices provide cues on which children can act to construct more adaptive and positive views of the social world (see Hart, DeWolf, & Burts, 1993). Conversely, power-assertive discipline is characterized by the use of physical punishment, threats, and stating directives with little or no justification as ways to regulate behavior (Burleson, 1983; Hart et al., 1992). From a social cognitive theoretical standpoint, such tactics model aggression as an efficacious means of resolving interpersonal conflict.

Not surprisingly, inductive discipline is linked to more adaptive social cognitions, prosocial behaviors, and acceptance by peers. Power-assertive discipline, on the other hand, is associated with less adaptive social cognitions, antisocial behaviors, and rejection by peers (Hart, DeWolf, & Burts, 1993; Hart, Ladd, & Burleson, 1990). Additional areas of indirect influences include marital relationships, parental cognitions (e.g., beliefs, perceptions), parenting styles, parent-child inter-actions, sibling relationships, and features of the overall familial and extrafamilial environment (see Hart et al., 1997, for a review).

Parents also directly influence their children's peer relations when they engage in activities that purposefully foster children's skills and relationships with peers. This direct influence is evident when parents design children's social environments by living in neighborhoods where opportunities for peer interaction abound or by enrolling children in activities involving peers. Parents serve as "mediators" when they organize informal peer contacts or control their children's choice of play partners. As parents monitor children's peer interactions and provide support, instruction, or guidance, they act as "super-visors" or "teachers" (Ladd & Hart, 1992; Ladd & LeSieur, 1995; Profilet & Ladd, 1994). Table 10.10 summarizes some practical ways parents can facilitate positive social development across these years.

School

It is important to develop curriculum that provides various learning experiences to ensure the development of competence for each of a

TABLE 10.10
Ways Parents Can Facilitate Children's Social Development

Parents should:
- form strong attachments with their child (i.e., by expressing affection, being dependable, and responding to needs of the child)
- use authoritative, inductive discipline (i.e., reasoning, explaining, setting limits, and allowing logical consequences for behavior to occur)
- live in neighborhoods where many opportunities for peer interaction occur
- enroll children in activities involving peers (i.e., sports teams, scouts, church)
- organize informal peer contacts (i.e., arrange play dates, supervise children during peer contacts)
- control children's choice of play partners when appropriate or necessary (i.e., other children home without adult supervision, when child is easily influenced by other children to do wrong or dangerous activities)
- support social autonomy (i.e., encourage child to initiate play dates and create own activities)
- instruct children about play activities (i.e., explain games, suggest alternatives to agressive behavior)

child's selves (i.e., physical, emotional, social, creative, cognitive). The major focus of this chapter is the child's social self. Development of the child's social self depends on interactions between the child and others, both adults and peers. According to Hartup (as cited by Birch & Ladd, in press), adult–child relationships are vertical in nature (i.e., the adult has greater knowledge and social power) whereas peer relationships are horizontal in nature (i.e., characterized by reciprocity and equality). Whereas vertical relationships provide protection, security, and modeling of basic social skills, horizontal relationships provide opportunities for elaboration of social skills and the emergence of themes of cooperation and competition.

Curriculum designed to enhance social development fosters competent social behaviors (e.g., getting along in a group, playing with other children, helping others, etc.) as well as the ability to control antisocial impulses (see Hyson, this volume). Additionally, children should be encouraged to value their own and others' ethnic and sexual identities (Hendrick, 1986). When planning curriculum teachers should give thought to the role of play, peer relationships, and teacher–child relationships in the development of children's social competence.

Play.   It is necessary to integrate learning so as to educate the whole child in a life-oriented approach. Play provides a context in which all the selves are utilized simultaneously (Hendrick, 1986). Additionally, whether in the classroom or on the playground, play serves as an integrating element of the curriculum (Blatchford & Sharp, 1994; Hart, 1993). It affords children a chance to define who they are and who they are not, and helps children differentiate reality from fantasy (Hendrick, 1986). Sociodramatic or fantasy play, in particular, serves a variety of important developmental functions across a variety of home, neighborhood, and school settings during the early childhood years (see Goelman & Jacobs, 1994; Haight & Miller, 1993; Howes, 1992; MacDonald, 1993; Pellegrini, 1995).

Play has a key role in social development (Bredekamp & Copple, 1997) by providing a context in which children can obtain many social skills related to social competence, such as cooperation, sharing, social problem solving, or putting themselves in another's place thus helping them develop an understanding of the intents and feelings of others (Hart, 1993; Johnson, Christie, & Yawkey, 1987). Sociodramatic play with peers is particularly important across this age span. With a little imagination, teachers can easily incorporate features of dramatic play across the integrated curriculum (e.g., language and math areas in figure 10.1; see also Davidson, 1996 for practical application ideas), particularly when orchestrated carefully in center experiences (Howe, Moller, & Chambers, 1994). Recent research suggests that such play varies by center type (Petrakos & Howe 1996), and enhances children's creativity, social competence, language and literacy development, and the understanding of others' feelings and beliefs (see Christie, 1991; Daiute, 1993; Halliday-Scher, Urberg, & Kaplan-Estrin, 1995; Rubin, Bukowski, & Parker, in press; Youngblade & Dunn, 1995). It should be noted, however, that immature, solitary-dramatic forms of play are reflective of problematic peer relations and other psychosocial difficulties across these early years (Coplan et al., 1994).

Recently in *National Geographic*, Brown (1994) reported that play occurs in humans and animals in similar forms such as playfully fighting and chasing. Children who play more seem to be happier and therefore are preferred as playmates by other children (Chance, 1979). Play encourages children to form attachments with other children. Children who initiate ideas for play with other children, directing them into play themes, are preferred as playmates. These children give reasons for their ideas or may give reasons for rejecting other playmates' ideas (Hazen & Black, 1989). These successful interactions require understanding of others' perspectives, which typically increases as children develop.

Peer Relationships.   There is value in children playing alone or side by side. However, the social self profits most when children play together in associative or cooperative play. As argued by Hendrick (1986) it is during these kinds of play that the best opportunities for social learning occur (e.g., getting along together, entering a group, etc.).

Peer relationships in the form of friendships (voluntary, reciprocal relationship between two children) and peer group acceptance (how well children fit into the social network of the classroom) serve as supports for children within the classroom setting (Birch & Ladd, in press). On the other hand, children who are rejected by peers due to the enactment of varying forms of aggression or withdrawal (Crick, Casas, & Mosher, in press; Coplan et al., 1994; McNeilly-Choque et al., 1996) tend to have later psychosocial adjustment problems. More specifically, social rejection is a predictor of academic failure, school

FIGURE 10.1
Content Web—Social Development

Literacy
Books
Will I Have a Friend?
Peter's Chair,
    Ezra Jack Keats
The Giving Tree
We Are Best Friends,
    Aliki
The Lion and the Rat,
    Wildsmith
Friends, Helme Heine

Language
Dramatize:
    Three Little Pigs
    Billy Goats Gruff
    Goldilocks
Use written names of
    children in classroom—
    birthdates, helpers,
    "Look who's here"
    board
Have a writing center:
    Display a book with
        children's names
        and snapshots
    Provide stationery for
        writing family or
        friends
Place "home" props in
    dramatic play center

Social Studies
Cultures in our class
    Children bring pictures,
    artifacts, foods, etc.
Helpers in our
    community
at work (occupations)

Mathematics
Graph number of
    family members
Graph number of
    boys
Graph number of
    girls
Count body parts—
    fingers, toes, etc.
Measure height/weight
    of children
Block center, build
    houses with friends
Props, family figures,
    cars, etc.

All about Me

Music
"What Is Your
    Name?", Hap
    Palmer
"What a Miracle Am
    I!"
"Hey Daddy, There's a
    Hippo in the
    Bathtub"
Use rhythm
    instruments, swap
    with a friend
Sing: "Paw Paw Patch"
    using children's
    names
"Catelina, Matelina"
    body parts

Science
Smelly cans—
    Like/Dislike
Taste foods—
    Like/Dislike
Changes related to
    growth
    (baby, seeds,
    animals)

Movement
Outdoor play with
    friends
Climb, slide, swing,
    sandplay, tricycles
Chase a friend
Play games with rules
    Duck, Duck, Goose
    Hide and Seek
    Drop the
        Handkerchief

Art
Draw yourself
Collage of faces cut
    from magazines
Weave a doormat
    (small-group families
    use diaper pins with
    strips of cloth to
    weave)
Draw outline of a
    friend on large sheet
    of paper, fill in
    features and clothes

dropout, and adolescent delinquency and psychological difficulties such as anxiety or depression (Parker et al., 1995).

Normal peer relationships represent contexts within which a significant amount of social development (e.g., perspective-taking skills and a sense of self) occurs (Rubin & Coplan, 1992). The social negotiation, discussion, and conflict found in peer relations help children learn to understand others' thoughts, emotions, motives, and intentions. This understanding then enables children to think about the consequences of their behavior both for themselves and for others, which in turn leads to appropriate and effective social behavior (Rubin & Rose-Krasnor, 1992). Additionally, the child receives feedback about his or her abilities from the peer group and evaluates the appropriateness of his or her behavior accordingly (Santrock & Yussen, 1987).

According to Rubin and Coplan (1992), the factors most significantly associated with children's status in the peer group include their social behavior and social cognition (i.e., way of thinking about social phenomena). The processes children employ to interpret and process information about the social world determine the social behaviors they enact (Dodge, 1986; Rubin & Rose-Krasnor, 1986). Consequently, the behaviors children exhibit in interactions with their peers influence their acceptance by the peer group. Higher levels of cooperative play and social conversation are positively related to peer status. However, arguing, aggression, and rough play are negatively related to peer status during early childhood (Hart et al., 1992; Ladd, 1983; Ladd & Price, 1987; Ladd, Price, & Hart, 1988; 1990; Rubin & Daniels-Beirness, 1983).

In addition to issues raised concerning developmentally appropriate and inappropriate curricula on young children's overall development (see Hart, Burts, & Charlesworth, chapter 1, this volume), teachers should be aware of effects the peer environment has on children's school adjustment. For example, peer victimization, lack of friendship, and less acceptance by peers can have negative ramifications for overall school adjustment (Ladd & Kochenderfer, 1996) whereas positive features of the social environment (including nurturing teacher–child interactions) can facilitate overall adjustment (Birch & Ladd, 1996; Kontos & Wilcox-Herzog, 1997; Taylor & Machida, 1996).

Teacher-Facilitated Contexts. Teachers play a crucial role in promoting children's social development in the classroom through direct instruction, modeling, planning the environment, and discipline (Kontos & Wilcox-Herzog, 1997; Ladd, 1984; Ramsey, 1991). Through direct instruction, teachers can suggest specific prosocial skills (e.g., sharing, taking turns, initiating and joining play) as strategies for achieving a social goal such as making a friend (Ladd, 1984).

Teachers can serve as powerful prosocial models by exhibiting caring and respect for all people in their interactions with others. They can also arrange for children to learn positive skills (e.g., being considerate, cooperating, taking responsibility, helping, and sharing) by observing peers (Howes & Clements, 1994; Ladd, 1984; Ramsey, 1991).

Teachers can plan the environment (i.e., schedule, physical space, materials and activities, group structure) to support and facilitate peer interactions (Phyfe-Perkins, 1980). The daily schedule influences the social dynamics of the classroom. Therefore, teachers should provide time for diverse social interactions (e.g., small groups, partners, class discussions, independent projects). Blocks of time should be sufficient so as to facilitate social interactions in both indoor and outdoor playground settings (Hartle & Johnson, 1993). Also, children acquire social responsibility when working cooperatively in caring for the classroom (Ramsey, 1991).

When planning the physical space of the classroom, teachers should provide a variety of areas, with obvious boundaries, that encourage different types of social interactions (e.g., working alone, in pairs, and/or in groups) and play (e.g., sedentary to highly active). The indoor and outdoor space should be adequate so as to discourage aggression, but not so large that children do not interact (Hartle & Johnson, 1993; Phyfe- Perkins, 1980; Ramsey, 1991).

Teachers also plan for the type, content, quantity, and availability of materials and activities. Developmentally appropriate materials should be provided in an accessible manner so as to encourage a wide range of social and independent play (Ramsey, 1991). Unstructured, open-ended play materials, such as blocks, puppets, and play costumes, enhance fantasy and sociodramatic play. This, in turn, increases the potential for more advanced social interactions. Books enable teachers to facilitate children's learning about how to make and keep friends, and skills to get along with one another. Cooperative activities and games provide children with experience working in groups, while role-playing activities enhance children's understanding of others' intentions and perspectives. Children also should be given the opportunity to regularly participate in helping and sharing activities (Ladd, 1984). Finally, materials and activities representing and respecting diverse racial, cultural, and class backgrounds and abilities are desired (Ramsey, 1991).

Teachers as planners can orchestrate chances for children to interact with peers who are more skilled in positive social interactions (Ladd, 1984). It is important to create groups that are of various sizes (i.e., pairs vs. three or four children) and that enable all members to participate equally. These groups should be provided with activities (e.g., cooperative games rather than competitive games) that encourage group "cohesiveness" (p. 119) (Ramsey, 1991).

Social development can be enhanced by teachers when they employ positive discipline. This type of discipline involves firm, fair, consistent guidance, establishing and setting limits. According to Ramsey (1991), "teachers should maintain an authoritative role by establishing and enforcing clear expectations, yet involving children in discussions about rules and consequences" (p. 126). Children also should be encouraged to think about the possible effects of their behavior on others (Ramsey, 1991). (See table 10.11 for a summary.)

Many variables affect the lives of children socially. Knowledgeable adults encourage social development as they interact with children in various settings and as part of an integrated curriculum (see figure 10.1). Children who are socially well adjusted are ready for the many challenges that they will meet in their world.

Summary

Few classroom curriculum activities occur in the absence of social interaction with peers and/or adults. Theoretical tenets help our understanding of the different mechanisms involved in the acquisition and enactment of different social behaviors. Foundation stones covered here included modeling, the development of social-interaction structures, social information processing, and ego identity. Armed with an understanding of how these processes work (e.g., perspective taking, stage sequences), parents, teachers, and caregivers should be in a better position to facilitate optimal social development during early childhood across family, play, peer, and teacher–child interaction

TABLE 10.11
Ways Teachers Can Facilitate Children's Social Development

Teachers should:
- use direct instruction for promoting prosocial skills (e.g., sharing, taking turns, initiating and joining play)
- model care and respect for all people (e.g., being considerate, cooperating, taking responsibility, helping, sharing
- plan environment to support and facilitate peer interactions (i.e., schedule, physical space, materials, activities, group structure)
- provide time for diverse social interactions (e.g., small groups, partners, whole-class discussions, independent projects)
- provide unstructured, open-ended play materials (i.e., blocks, puppets, play costumes, dramatic play props)
- provide materials and activities representing and respecting diverse racial, cultural, and class background and abilities
- employ positive discipline (i.e., firm, fair, consistent guidance, establish and set limits, involve children in discussions about rules and consequences)
- look for reasons children may be isolated socially (e.g., short attention spans, inability to see another's point of view or to follow elaborate play themes, emotionally disturbed behavior)

contexts using strategies considered here. If social development is considered a vital component of all activities in which children are engaged, development will be optimized in all areas of children's lives.

References

Ainsworth, M. (1973). The development of infant–mother attachment. In B. Caldwell & H.N. Ricciue (Eds.), *Review of child development research*. (Vol. 3, pp. 1–94). Chicago: University of Chicago Press.

Bandura, A. (1977). *Social learning theory*. Englewood Cliffs, NJ: Prentice Hall.

Birch, S.H., & Ladd, G.W. (1996, April). *Continuity and change in the quality of teacher–child relationships: Links with children's early school adjustment*. Paper presented at the American Educational Research Association meetings, New York.

Birch, S.H., & Ladd, G.W. (in press). Interpersonal relationships in the school environment and children's early school adjustment: The role of teachers and peers. To appear in K.W. Wentzel & J.H.

Juvonen (Eds.), *Social motivation: Understanding children's school adjustment.* New York: Cambridge University Press.

Bjorklund, D.F. (1995). *Children's thinking: Developmental function and individual differences* (2nd ed.). New York: Brooks/Cole.

Blatchford, P., & Sharp, S. (1994). *Breaktime and the school.* London: Routledge.

Brazelton, T.B., Koslowski, B., & Maen, M. (1974). The origins of reciprocity: The early mother–infant interactions. In M. Lewes & J. Rosenblum (Eds.), *The origins of behavior.* New York: Wiley.

Bredekamp, S., & Copple, C. (Eds.). (1997). *Developmentally appropriate practice in early childhood programs: Revised.* Washington, DC: National Association for the Education of Young Children.

Brody, G.H., & Shaffer, D.R. (1982). Contributions of parents and peers to children's moral socialization. *Developmental Review, 2,* 31–75.

Brooks, J. (1991). *The process of parenting* (3rd ed.). Mountain View: Mayfield.

Brown, S.L. (1994). Animals at play. *National Geographic, 186,* 2–35.

Burleson, B.R. (1983). Interactional antecedents of social reasoning development: Interpreting the effects of parent discipline on children. In D. Zarefsky, M.O. Sillars, & J.R. Rhodes (Eds.), *Argument in transition: Proceedings of the third summer conference on argumentation* (pp. 597–610). Annandale, VA: Speech Communication Association.

Chance, P. (1979). *Learning through play.* New York: Gardner.

Charlesworth, R. (1992). *Understanding child development* (3rd ed.). Albany, NY: Delmar.

Christie, J.F. (1991). *Play and early literacy development.* Albany, NY: State University of New York Press.

Coplan, R.J., Rubin, K.H., Fox, H.A., Calkins, S.D., & Stewart, S.L. (1994). Being alone, playing alone, and acting alone: Distinguishing among reticence and passive and active solitude in young children. *Child Development, 65,* 129–37.

Crain, S. (1992). *Theories of development: Concepts and applications* (3rd ed.). Englewood Cliffs, NJ: Prentice Hall.

Crick, N.R., Casas, J.F., & Mosher, M. (in press). Relational and overt aggression in preschool. *Developmental Psychology.*

Crick, N.R., & Dodge, K.A. (1994). A review and reformulation of social- information-processing mechanisms in children's social adjustment. *Psychological Bulletin, 115*, 74–101.

Daiute, C. (Ed.). (1993). The development of literacy through social interaction. *New Directions for Child Development, 61.*

Davidson, J. (1996). *Emergent literacy and dramatic play in early education.* Albany, NY: Delmar.

DeVries, R. (1997). Piaget's social theory. *Educational Researcher, 26*, 4–17.

Dodge, K.A. (1986). A social information processing model of social competence in children. In M. Perlmutter (Ed.), *Cognitive perspectives on children's social and behavioral development. The Minnesota Symposia on Child Psychology* (Vol. 18, pp. 77–126). Hillsdale, NJ: Erlbaum.

Goelman, H., & Jacobs, E.V. (1994). *Children's play in child care settings.* Albany, NY: State University of New York Press.

Grusec, J.E., & Lytton, H. (1988). *Social development: History, theory, and research.* New York: Springer-Verlag.

Haight, W.L., & Miller, P.J. (1993). *Pretending at home: Early development in a sociocultural context.* Albany, NY: State University of New York Press.

Halliday-Scher, K., Urberg, K.A., & Kaplan-Estrin, M. (1995). Learning to pretend: Preschoolers' use of metacommunication in sociodramatic play. *International Journal of Behavioral Development, 18* (3), 451–61.

Hart, C.H. (Ed.). (1993). *Children on playgrounds: Research perspectives and applications.* Albany, NY: State University of New York Press.

Hart, C.H., DeWolf, D.M., & Burts, D.C. (1992). Linkages among preschoolers playground behavior, outcome expectations, and parental disciplinary strategies. *Early Education and Development, 3*, 265–83.

Hart, C.H., DeWolf, D.M., & Burts, D.C. (1993). Parental disciplinary strategies and preschoolers play behavior in playground settings. In C.H. Hart (Ed.), *Children on playgrounds: Research perspectives and applications* (pp. 271–313). Albany, NY: State University of New York Press.

Hart, C.H., DeWolf, D.M., Wozniak, P., & Burts, D.C. (1992). Maternal and paternal disciplinary styles: Relations with preschoolers' playground behavioral orientations and peer status. *Child Development, 63,* 879–92.

Hart, C.H., Ladd, G.W., & Burleson, B.R. (1990). Children's expectations of the outcomes of social strategies: Relations with sociometric status and maternal disciplinary styles. *Child Development, 61,* 127–37.

Hart, C.H., Olsen, S.F., Robinson, C.C., & Mandleco, B.L. (1997). The development of social and communicative competence in childhood: Review and a model of personal, familial, and extrafamilial processes. *Communication Yearbook* (Vol. 20, pp. 304–73). Thousand Oaks, CA: SAGE.

Hartle, L., & Johnson, J.E. (1993). Historical and contemporary influences of outdoor play environments. In C.H. Hart (Ed.), *Children on playgrounds: Research perspectives and applications* (pp. 14–42). Albany, NY: State University of New York Press.

Hazen, N.L., & Black, B. (1989). Preschool peer communication skills: The role of social status and interaction content. *Child Development, 60,* 867–76.

Hendrick, J. (1986). *Total learning: Curriculum for the young child* (2nd ed.). Columbus, OH: Merrill.

Hendrick, J. (1992). Where does it all begin? Teaching the principles of democracy in the early years. *Young Children, 47* (3), 51–53.

Howe, N., Moller, L., & Chambers, B. (1994). Dramatic play in day care: What happens when doctors, cooks, bakers, pirates and pharmacists invade the classroom? In H. Goelman & E.V. Jacobs (Eds.), *Children's play in child care settings* (pp. 102–18). Albany, NY: State University of New York Press.

Howes, C. (1988). Peer interaction of young children. *Monographs of the Society for Research in Child Development, 53* (1).

Howes, C. (1992). *The collaborative construction of pretend: Social pretend play functions.* Albany, NY: State University of New York Press.

Howes, C., & Clements, D. (1994). Adult socialization of children's play in child care. In H. Goelman & E.V. Jacobs (Eds.), *Children's play in child care settings* (pp. 20–68). Albany, NY: State University of New York Press.

Isabella, R., & Belsky, J. (1991). Interactional synchrony and the origins of infant-mother attachment: A replication study. *Child Development,* 373–84.

Johnson, J.E., Christie, J.F., & Yawkey, T.D. (1987). *Play and early childhood development.* Glenview, IL: Scott, Foresman.

Kontos, S. & Wilcox-Herzog, A. (1997). Teachers' interactions with children: Why are they so important? *Young Children, 52,* 4–12.

Kupersmidt, J.B., Coie, J.D., & Dodge, K.A. (1990). The role of poor peer relationships in the development of disorder. In S.R. Asher & J.D. Coie (Eds.), *Peer rejection in childhood* (pp. 273–305). New York: Cambridge University Press.

Ladd, G.W. (1983). Social networks of popular, average, and rejected children in school settings. *Merrill-Palmer Quarterly, 29,* 283–307.

Ladd, G.W. (1984). Promoting children's prosocial behavior and peer relations in early childhood classrooms. A look at four teacher roles. *Dimensions, 12* (4), 6–11.

Ladd, G.W. (1991). Family–peer relations during childhood: Pathways to competence and pathology? *Journal of Social and Personal Relationships, 8,* 307–14.

Ladd, G.W. (1992). Themes and theories: Perspectives on processes in family–peer relationships. In R.D. Parke & G.W. Ladd (Eds.), *Family–peer relationships: Modes of linkage* (pp. 3–34). Hillsdale, NJ: Erlbaum.

Ladd, G.W. & Hart, C.H. (1992). Creating informal play opportunities: Are parents and preschoolers initiations related to children's competence with peers? *Developmental Psychology, 28,* 1179–87.

Ladd, G.W., & Kochenderfer, B.J. (1996, April). *Classroom peer acceptance, friendship, and victimization: Distinct relational systems that contribute uniquely to children's school adjustment.* Paper presented at the American Educational Research Association meetings, New York.

Ladd, G.W., & Le Sieur, K.D. (1995). Parents' and children's peer relationships. In M. Bornstein (Ed.), *Handbook of parenting,* vol. 4, *Applied and practical parenting* (pp. 377–410). Hillsdale, NJ: Erlbaum.

Ladd, G.W., & Price, J.M. (1987). Predicting children's social and school adjustment following the transition from preschool to kindergarten. *Child Development, 58,* 1168–89.

Ladd, G.W., Price, J.M., & Hart, C.H. (1988). Predicting preschoolers' peer status from their playground behaviors. *Child Development, 59,* 971–91.

Ladd, G.W., Price, J.M., & Hart, C.H. (1990). Preschoolers' behavioral orientations and patterns of peer contact: Predictive of peer status? In S.R. Asher & J.D. Coie (Eds.), *Peer rejection in childhood* (pp. 90–118). New York: Cambridge University Press.

Lamb, M.E. (1977). The development of mother-infant and father-infant attachments in the second year of life. *Developmental Psychology, 13*, 637–48.

Maccoby, E.E., & Martin, J.A. (1983). Socialization in the context of the family: Parent–child interaction. In E.M. Hetherington (Ed.) & P.H. Mussen (Series Ed.), *Handbook of child psychology*, vol. 4, *Socialization, personality, and social development* (pp. 1–102). New York: Wiley.

MacDonald, K. (1993). *Parent–child play.* Albany, NY: State University of New York Press.

McNeilly-Choque, M.K., Hart, C.H., Robinson, C.C. ,Nelson, L.J., & Olsen, S. (1996). Overt and relational aggression on the playground: Correspondence among different informants. *Journal of Research in Childhood Education, 11*, 47–67.

Miller, P.H. (1989). *Theories of developmental psychology.* New York: Freeman.

Musatti, T. (1986). Early peer relations: The perspectives of Piaget and Vygotsky. In E. Mueller & C.R. Cooper (Eds.), *Process and outcome in peer relationships* (pp. 25–53). New York: Academic.

Overton, W.F., & Reese, H.W. (1973). Models of development: Methodological implications. In J.R. Nesselroade & H.W. Reese (Eds.), *Life-span developmental psychology* (pp. 65–86). New York: Academic Press.

Parker, J.G., & Asher, S.R. (1987). Peer relations and later personal adjustment: Are low-accepted children at risk? *Psychological Bulletin, 102*, 357–89.

Parker, J.G., Rubin, K.H., Price, J.M., & DeRosier, M.E. (1995). Peer relationships, child development and adjustment: A developmental psychopathological perspective. In D. Cicchetti & E. Cohen (Eds.), *Developmental psychopathology*, vol. 2, *Risk, disorder and adaptation* (pp. 96–161). New York: Wiley.

Parten, M.B. (1932). Social participation among preschool children. *Journal of Abnormal and Social Psychology, 27*, 243–69.

Pellegrini, A.D. (1995). *School recess and playground behavior: Educational and developmental roles.* Albany, NY: State University of New York Press.

Petrakos, H., & Howe, N. (1996). The influence of the physical design of the dramatic play center on children's play. *Early Childhood Research Quarterly, 11,* 63–77.

Phyfe-Perkins, E. (1980). Children's behavior in preschool settings: A review of research concerning the influence of the physical environment. In L.G. Katz (Ed.), *Current topics in early childhood education* (Vol. 3, pp. 91–126). Norwood, NJ: Ablex.

Piaget, J. (1970). Piaget's theory. In P.H. Mussen (Ed.), *Carmichael's manual of child psychology* (pp. 703–32). New York: Wiley.

Plomin, R. (1994). Nature, nurture, and social development. *Social Development, 3,* 37–53.

Profilet, S.M., & Ladd, G.W. (1994). Do mothers' perceptions and concerns about preschoolers' peer competence predict their peer-management practices? *Social Development, 3,* 205–21.

Putallaz, M., & Heflin, A.H. (1990). Parent-child interaction. In S.R. Asher & J.D. Coie (Eds.), *Peer rejection in childhood* (pp. 189–216). New York: Cambridge University Press.

Ramsey, P.G. (1991). *Making friends in school: Promoting peer relationships in early childhood.* New York: Teachers College Press.

Rubin, K.H., Bukowski, W., & Parker, J.G. (in press). Peer interactions, relationships, and groups. In W. Damon (Series Ed.) & N. Eisenberg (Vol. Ed.), *Handbook of child psychology,* vol. 4, *Social, emotional, and personality development.* New York: Wiley.

Rubin, K.H., & Coplan, R.J. (1992). Peer relationships in childhood. In M. Bornstein & M. Lamb (Eds.), *Developmental psychology: An advanced textbook.* Hillsdale, NJ: Erlbaum.

Rubin K.H., & Daniels-Beirness, T. (1983). Concurrent and predictive correlates of sociometric status in kindergarten and grade 1 children. *Merrill-Palmer Quarterly, 29,* 337–51.

Rubin, K.H., & Rose-Krasnor, L.R. (1986). Social-cognitive and social behavioral perspectives on problem solving. In M. Perlmutter (Ed.), *Cognitive perspectives on children's social and behavioral development. The Minnesota Symposia on Child Psychology* (Vol. 18, pp. 1–68). Hillsdale, NJ: Erlbaum.

Rubin, K.H., & Rose-Krasnor, L. (1992). Interpersonal problem solving and social competence in children. In V.B. Hasselt and M.

Hersen (Eds.), *Handbook of social development: A lifespan perspective* (pp. 283–323). New York: Plenum.

Salkind, N.J., & Ambron, S.R. (1987). *Child development* (5th ed.). New York: Holt, Rinehart, & Winston.

Santrock, J.W., & Yussen, S.R. (1987). *Child development: An introduction* (3rd ed.). Dubuque, IA: W.C. Brown.

Sroufe, L.A. (1988). The role of infant–caregiver attachment in development. In J. Belsky & T. Nezworski (Eds.), *Clinical implications of attachment* (pp. 18–40). Hillsdale, NJ: Erlbaum.

Taylor, A.R., & Machida, S. (1996, April). *Student–teacher relationships of Head Start children.* Paper presented at the American Educational Research Association meetings, New York.

Thomas, R.M. (1992). *Comparing theories of child development* (3rd ed.). Belmont, CA: Wadsworth.

Youngblade, L.M., & Dunn, J. (1995). Individual differences in young children's pretend play with mother and sibling: Links to relationships and understanding of other people's feelings and beliefs. *Child Development, 66,* 1472–92.

CHAPTER ELEVEN

Developmentally Appropriate Guidance and the Integrated Curriculum

MARION C. HYSON
SHAWN L. CHRISTIANSEN

It's work time in the kindergarten room. Sarah, Azra, and Maurice are sitting around a table in the corner, looking at a collection of stones from the playground. Boxes, paper, and markers have been set out for children to use in sorting, drawing, or writing about their discoveries. Sarah picks up two stones and examines them thoughtfully. "I like this one better," she declares. "No way!" says Azra. "That stone is a yucky color." "Well, so what?" Sarah retorts. "You are a yucky color, too, Azra—and you can't come to my birthday. Maurice can!" Maurice smiles smugly. From the next table, Randolph looks up from his book about stones. He glares at Sarah. "Don't talk to my friend like that, Sarah," he says, reaching for a large stone and holding it threateningly above his head.

This chapter adds another layer of complexity to the ideas presented in previous chapters. Besides its implications for classroom activities, adoption of a developmentally appropriate, integrated curriculum requires early childhood practitioners to reconsider the ways in which they guide, direct, manage, control, and influence children's behavior.

The National Association for the Education of Young Children (NAEYC) guidelines for developmentally appropriate practices (Bredekamp, 1987; Bredekamp & Copple, 1997) contain explicit guidance goals, emphasizing self-esteem, self-control, and concern for others. To further these goals, NAEYC defines the teacher's role as one of acceptance, support, and promotion of desirable behavior through prevention, redirection, and collaboration.

Project-based, thematic learning presents special guidance challenges to teachers of young children. As children investigate the properties of stones, study birds' nesting habits, or explore their neighborhood environment, they often have more freedom than in traditionally organized classrooms. Like Sarah, Azra, and Maurice, they have blocks of time when they may choose their own activities and select those with whom they work and play. This freedom may foster intrinsic motivation, responsibility, and cooperation, but it may also bring conflict and chaos. Project-related materials and topics may arouse strong, unexpected feelings in some children. Working in groups may strain young children's self-control. Children may make inappropriate or even dangerous choices.

What should be the teacher's role in all of this? Is she or he to be a benevolent bystander? Or should the adult be a master puppeteer, pulling the strings behind the curtain, subtly but powerfully controlling children's behavior? Or is there yet another way?

These are the kinds of questions this chapter discusses. We begin by reminding ourselves that the subject of guiding young children has a long history in early childhood education. Not everyone has agreed about what the goals of guidance (or management, or discipline) should be, and little agreement has emerged about the "best" ways to implement those goals. Those who favor different curriculum models have generally tended to use different approaches to guidance or discipline, and the effects of curriculum on children's development may often be entangled with the effects of the kinds of discipline, guidance, or management strategies employed in the classroom. As practitioners look for a knowledge base to help them create appropriate guidance strategies, they may find three areas of research particularly relevant: the study of early emotional development, the study of motivation, and the study of children's sociomoral understanding and prosocial behavior.

This knowledge base, combined with the NAEYC standards for developmentally appropriate practices, makes it possible to agree on some important guidance goals—goals that go beyond the day-to-day discipline issues that practitioners must address. After outlining these goals, we note some of the ways in which an integrated curriculum can help practitioners to influence young children's emotional, motivational, and sociomoral development in positive ways. But we also take a realistic look at some of the unique "guidance challenges" that the integrated curriculum may present to the early childhood practitioner.

Finally, to illustrate these concepts in action, we describe some "best practices" used by a teacher of 4-year-olds, as she guides her children within a developmentally appropriate, integrated curriculum.

"Guidance" in Early Childhood Programs: Tradition and Diversity

Examining the history of early childhood education and the history of teacher education for early childhood programs, one is struck by the different ways in which this topic has been treated (Braun & Edwards, 1972; Spodek, 1993; Weber, 1984). As compared with materials on elementary and secondary education, early childhood has actually had relatively little discussion of "discipline" or "guidance" as a separate topic. Perhaps because of the developmental basis for much early childhood programming, discussions of these issues have frequently been embedded within broader child development themes. When the topic is discussed, it is given diverse names; at various times, textbooks and textbook chapters on this general topic have had titles such as *Discipline without Tears* (Dreikurs & Cassel, 1972), "Principles of Reinforcement: Behavior and Its Consequences" (Vance, 1973), *Assertive Discipline: A Take-Charge Approach for Today's Educator* (Canter & Canter, 1976), *Guiding Young Children* (Hildebrand, 1985), and *Constructive Guidance and Discipline* (Fields & Boesser, 1994). These variations in terminology represent more than minor semantic differences; rather, the words that are used reflect deeply held beliefs about the nature of childhood and the appropriate relationship between adults and children.

What has sometimes been called the core tradition of early childhood education (Hyson & Cone, 1989) has generally held the view that children are to be "guided" toward personally satisfying, socially desirable patterns of behavior. Influenced by psychoanalytic (Freud,

1964; Erikson, 1950), humanistic (Rogers, 1961), and maturationist (Gesell, 1940) theories, guidance goals within this perspective tended to emphasize catharsis (the "draining off" of negative feelings through vigorous play and fantasy) and mastery of pressing emotional issues through dramatic play, art, and supportive relationships with adults and other children. The use of the term "guidance" reflected a belief that children's impulses were naturally healthy, and that the adults' role was gently to direct or "guide" those impulses into socially acceptable, developmentally healthy outlets.

Other writers have used phrases such as "classroom management" and "behavior management" to describe this aspect of early childhood teaching (Vance, 1973). These phrases suggest a more directive approach to the task, with more focus on adult-selected goals. Although not necessarily advocating punishment or harsh discipline, this viewpoint has emphasized the importance of specific techniques of environmental management, modeling, and systematic reinforcement.

Still others, primarily influenced by Piagetian theory, have regarded "guidance" as one part of a process in which children actively construct understandings about appropriate, productive ways of behaving in classroom settings (DeVries & Zan, 1994; Fields & Boesser, 1994). According to these writers, stage-specific cognitive developmental characteristics influence young children's ability to understand social situations and to respond appropriately to others' needs and wishes. Like those whose perspective is influenced by psychoanalytic theory, cognitively influenced writers have tended to label this aspect of early childhood programs as "guidance" rather than "discipline" or "management," with the teacher being viewed as a facilitator and support for children's gradual development of prosocial, moral behavior.

Guidance Strategies and Curriculum Models

Most people would agree that, whether the domain is called "guidance," "discipline," or "classroom management," the goals and strategies used in guiding young children's behavior should be consistent with the goals of the curriculum or program model that has been adopted by the practitioner.

Links between Curriculum and Guidance

These kinds of guidance/curriculum consistencies do exist. One study (Hyson, Hirsh-Pasek, & Rescorla, 1990) found that programs that used more formally academic, adult-directed curriculum approaches were more likely to use discipline strategies such as criticism or comparison; in addition, those teachers were less likely than more "developmentally appropriate" teachers to discuss children's feelings or to be physically affectionate (cf. Kontos & Wilcox-Herzog, 1997). Similar results were found in a study by Stipek (1991), in which teachers in more formally academic classrooms were apt to be less warm and more punitive when children misbehaved. Likewise, in classrooms influenced by Piaget's constructivist theory, teachers have been observed to employ guidance or discipline practices that support children's construction of social understanding and that encourage children's collaboration in setting up classroom rules (DeVries & Zan, 1994).

Curriculum/Guidance Inconsistencies

Ideally, every aspect of the early childhood program—including guidance and discipline—should support the program's goals and overall philosophy of care and education. However, inconsistencies between curriculum and guidance practices are sometimes observed. For example, some self-proclaimed "Montessori" programs use stars as rewards, contradicting Montessori's belief that children's self-chosen work provides its own rewards. Another example of inconsistency might be the frequent use of "time-outs" in a classroom whose learning activities encourage children's independence and critical thinking.

What is the reason for these kinds of inconsistencies? Frequently, they result from teachers' incomplete understanding of a curriculum's theoretical framework and goals. Careful preparation and training of early childhood practitioners is a key to consistent, effective curriculum implementation. Sometimes teachers' beliefs about guidance may be consistent with the program's curriculum emphasis, but the teachers' actual behavior or guidance practices may be quite different than their beliefs. These belief/behavior inconsistencies often happen because administrators require teachers to adopt discipline models with which they do not agree.

At times, however, what may look like inconsistency may actually be a positive effort to meet individual children's needs. Even within a curriculum that stresses child-chosen activities and spontaneous learning of academic skills, individual children may need more focused, directive guidance. For example, a child who has a specific learning disability may benefit from some external rewards or brief time-outs. A chaotic class of 1st graders that has had a parade of ineffective substitute teachers may need a great deal of adult-imposed order as a transition to more subtle management strategies. Children whose families and cultures place a high value on conformity to adult behavioral expectations may gain comfort, not anxiety, if their teachers' expectations are equally explicit (Hyson & DeCsipkes, 1993; McAdoo, 1992).

These practices are not really inconsistent. Rather, they underscore NAEYC's insistence on a broad, inclusive concept of "developmental appropriateness." The individual needs and styles of children, including children with disabilities, have a legitimate claim on teachers' decisions about guidance or discipline strategies—at least as strong a claim as the theoretical basis of the program's particular curriculum.

Influences of Guidance Practices on Development

In family settings, a great deal of evidence indicates that "authoritative" child rearing helps children become self-directed in guiding their own behavior (Baumrind, 1967, 1989). Parents who set clear limits and also explain their reasoning (induction) are apt to rear children who can control their own behavior without external sanctions, and who develop more positive relationships with other children (Hart et al., 1992). In contrast, harsh discipline and physical punishment generally fail to produce long-term compliance and may lead to an escalating, coercive cycle of misbehavior and aggression (Patterson, 1982).

Two cautions should be kept in mind about this research, however. First, in recent years researchers have taken a closer look at families' cultural values as "filters" through which children interpret their parents' discipline strategies. For example, in some cultural contexts "Do it because I say so" may seem harsh and abrupt, but in other sociocultural contexts children may view these kinds of commands in a more positive light (Lynch & Hansen, 1992). Second, studies of parents' discipline patterns at home may not be directly applicable in considering the effects of teachers' guidance strategies in classroom settings.

As compared with family research, we know less about the effects of specific discipline practices in early childhood programs. Work by DeVries (DeVries, Reese-Learned, & Morgan, 1991) and by Schmidt and colleagues (1995) suggests that children's sociomoral understanding and interpersonal competence may be strengthened by teacher strategies that emphasize inductive reasoning, active listening, and natural consequences in a developmentally appropriate, "constructivist" environment.

Few studies of this kind have been done. However, guidance-related influences on children's development may also be seen indirectly. When researchers have tried to trace the long-term effects of different kinds of early childhood curricula, the differences tend to appear more in the motivational or socioemotional aspects of children's behavior than in the narrowly academic area. For example, Schweinhart, Weikart, and Larner (1986) found that low-income children who had participated in a direct-instruction preschool program were, as adolescents and young adults, significantly more likely to report engaging in antisocial behavior than children who had attended constructivist or Piagetian preschools. The validity and meaning of this finding have been debated, but one possible reason for the difference may lie in the guidance or disciplinary practices that these two program models employed (with the behavioral program emphasizing compliance with adult-enforced rules and the constructivist program stressing autonomy and compliance based on reasoning).

Knowledge Bases for Developmentally Appropriate Guidance

When searching for approaches to classroom guidance that support and are consistent with a developmentally appropriate, integrated curriculum, practitioners may find three areas of research especially useful. First, recent research on early emotional development provides a solid foundation for early childhood professionals to use in devising guidance strategies to use in an integrated curriculum setting. "Emotion-centered guidance" provides a framework that fits well with a general emphasis on developmentally appropriate practices as well as with a thematically integrated or project-focused curriculum. Second, recent research on the development of young children's motivation (including some cautions about the use of rewards) can be very useful as practitioners make decisions about guiding young children's behavior and creating positive dispositions toward learning. And, third, theory and research on the development of young children's sociomoral understanding and prosocial behavior will help practitioners construct developmentally appropriate ways of guiding young children.

Emotional Development: Theory and Research

Early childhood educators have always been concerned with children's feelings, but until recently little research was available to support practitioners' interest in this aspect of development. Today the field of early emotional development is one of the most active and fascinating areas of developmental psychology (Campos et al., 1983; Wieder & Greenspan, 1993). Much of this work is very relevant for early childhood practitioners.

Emotions and Human Adaptation. As young children work on projects together or attempt to solve difficult problems independently, strong feelings surface. Joseph may slump in despair when his papier-mâché dragon falls apart; Andrea and Dana may come to blows over who gets the first turn in the math game about turtles. Rather than ignoring or dismissing these feelings, many researchers emphasize that children's feelings—including negative ones—have important functions in children's development (Izard, 1991). In a developmentally appropriate program, emotions must be taken seriously.

Emotions, Motivation, and Learning. According to many child development theorists and researchers, the "emotion system" is the basic force behind learning. Even Piaget, whose work emphasized cognitive development, asserted that cognition only provides the structures for development, while emotions provide the motivation (Piaget, 1951). Children's memory and learning can be enhanced when their interest and happiness are heightened (Renninger & Wozniak, 1985). When children are in a positive emotional state, they are more likely to tolerate frustration, they can wait to receive a reward, and they are more inclined to be generous to others (Chapman et al., 1987; Denham, 1986).

The Development of Emotional Expression, Understanding, and Regulation. Children's ability to express, understand, and control or regulate emotions comes about gradually. From birth to age 8, typically developing children progress through a series of milestones in their emotional development. Erikson's developmental theory (Erikson, 1950) presents one description of these milestones, and Greenspan's more recent work (Weider & Greenspan, 1993) presents another, complementary perspective (table 11.1).

Recent research provides an impressive picture of early emotional development. Even babies are attuned to others' emotional expressions, and 3-year-olds have definite ideas about the causes of fear, anger, and sadness (Stein & Jewett, 1986). Toddlers try to comfort others when they are distressed (Radke-Yarrow & Zahn-Waxler, 1984), although they also enjoy provoking others to display anger or distress (Dunn & Munn, 1985). Despite these early accomplishments, young children still have difficulty understanding complex or multiple emotions ("I like you, but I'm really angry with you right now"). They also are better at noticing feelings than at labeling their own or others' emotions. And their egocentrism sometimes causes them to think others must feel exactly the same way that they do.

Young children are also working on ways of regulating, managing, or controlling their expressions of anger, sadness, fear, and excitement. Even young babies are able to soothe themselves and to turn away—or even fall asleep—when things get too stimulating. As children develop language and other cognitive competencies, they become better at deliberately directing their feelings into appropriate channels (Eisenberg & Fabes, 1992; Fox, 1994; Izard & Kobak, 1991).

Cultural and Individual Differences in Emotional Development. Beyond these general developmental tendencies, there are many individual and cultural variations in how children express their feelings and in how they come to control or regulate these emotions. Some children will appear exuberant and uninhibited as they explore the stones that the teacher has brought to class; others (whether because of cultural norms or individual temperament characteristics) will inhibit their expressions of feeling. Every culture has different ideas

TABLE 11.1

Milestones of Emotional Development from Birth to Age 8

	Erikson	Greenspan
Birth	Basic trust versus mistrust (Favorable outcome: Hope and trust in environment. Unfavorable outcome: Suspicion and fear)	Self-regulation and interest in the world (0–3 months)
3 months		"Falling in love" (2–7 months)
6 months		Developing intentional communications (3–10 months)
9 months		
1 year	Autonomy versus shame and doubt (Favorable outcome: Ability to exercise choice and self-restraint; sense of self-esteem and pride. Unfavorable outcome: Propensity for shame and doubt about ability to control one's actions.)	Emergence of an organized sense of self (9–18 months)
18 months		Creating emotional ideas (18–36 months)
2 years		Emotional thinking—the basis for fantasy, reality, and self-esteem (30–48 months)
3 years	Initiative versus guilt (Favorable outcome: Ability to initiate actions, enjoy accomplishments. Unfavorable outcome: Fear of punishment.)	
4 years		
5 years		
6 years	Industry versus inferiority (Favorable outcome: Feeling of competence, ability to use skills to make things well. Unfavorable outcome: Feelings of inadequacy and inferiority.)	
7 years		
8 years		

about which emotions are appropriate for children to express at different ages, and about which emotions should be targeted for socialization (Gordon, 1989). In Japan, for example, preschool programs typically encourage children to express anger and physical aggression (Lewis, 1988), believing that this helps children in their social development.

In addition to these cultural differences, children differ in their basic patterns of emotional response. The "exciting" new activities offered in an integrated curriculum may be greeted quite differently by Amy and Andy—partly because of their earlier experiences with these activities, but also because Amy and Andy may have innate differences in how sensitive they are to novel events (Kagan et al., 1984). Children, even those from similar cultural environments, differ greatly in how intensely they express feelings, how well they can regulate or control their emotions, and how they respond in stressful situations (Izard, Hembree, & Huebner, 1987).

Positive Influences on Children's Emotional Development.   Many so-called discipline problems are really signs of difficulties in young children's understanding of their own and others' feelings, or difficulties in children's ability to exercise self-control. Some children have difficulties understanding and regulating emotions because of cognitive immaturity or a specific learning disability; more often, the difficulty seems to be in a lack of support from adults. Secure attachments to adult caregivers help children manage their feelings in positive ways (Fox, 1994). Many children in today's early childhood programs come from families in which conflict and violence prevail; frequently these experiences impair children's expression and understanding of basic human emotions (Camras, Grow, & Ribordy, 1983).

Teachers in developmentally appropriate programs can do much to enhance positive emotional development in young children. As Vygotsky (1978) has emphasized, children develop within a sociocultural context, and they are often capable of higher levels of functioning with close adult support than they would be able to achieve on their own. Adult scaffolding or explicit support for children's positive behavior seems to help preschoolers react in helpful, constructive ways when others express sadness, anger, or pain (Denham, Mason, & Couchoud, 1993). Adults who talk with children about feelings, especially during conflicts, have children who later develop better understanding of emotions (Dunn & Brown, 1991). When adults take children's feelings seriously, and do not punish them for feeling angry or sad, children have been found to develop better abilities to regulate or control their displays of emotion (Eisenberg & Fabes, 1992). Research on early emotional development suggests that the following strategies will promote positive emotional development in young children and will build the foundation for a developmentally appropriate, emotion-centered approach to guidance (see table 11.2).

Motivating Appropriate Behavior in Young Children

In the preceding section, we saw that many psychologists now emphasize that children's own emotions serve to motivate their behavior. But how can teachers best channel those emotions into appropriate patterns of learning and socially acceptable behavior?

Problems with Reward and Punishment Systems. Until the past decade or so, many educational psychologists believed that external systems of rewards and punishments were the most effective way to guide children into desirable patterns of behavior. In many early childhood programs, children receive stars, stickers, or tokens for completing activities or for exhibiting acceptable behaviors. Even if learning centers are used, children may be required to complete a certain number of activities, receiving rewards for doing a certain number by the end of the day. Sometimes children "earn" opportunities to play in certain areas, such as dramatic play or art, by successfully completing other activities, such as work sheets or writing assignments. Children often seem to love these tokens and eagerly race to get as many as possible.

In encouraging positive social behavior, teachers have also been attracted to systems of rewards and punishments. Structured behavior management systems such as "Assertive Discipline" (Canter & Canter, 1976) set up clear rules for children and set equally clear consequences. For example, if the teacher has stated a rule such as "Children must put away a game after they finish using it," infractions of the rule have clear consequences (for example, for the first infraction a child's name will be listed on the board; the second violation will cause a brief time-out, and the next one will cause the child to lose a desired privilege).

TABLE 11.2
Promotion of Emotional Development

1. **Create a secure emotional enviornment**
    Set up predictable routines and limits; offer reliable comfort and support; engage in warm, personal interactions; convey sincere acceptance of children as individuals and as members of a culture and community.

2. **Help children to understand feelings**
    Make time for unhurried, emotion-rich pretend play; respond to and label (but don't overlabel) children's feelings; talk with children about the causes of feelings.

3. **Model genuine, appropriate emotional responses**
    Use your own expressions of emotion to show children what natural, mature emotional responses really are; use books, puppets, and skits to model emotional responses; offer praise and attention when children display appropriate responses.

4. **Support children's regulation of emotions**
    Create open emotional exchanges with children; actively help children work on emotion issues; encourage friendships and peer interactions; offer pretend play and creative activities as avenues for emotion regulation; support cultural and community standards for self-control and regulation.

5. **Identify and honor children's "emotional styles"**
    Observe and record children's behavior; offer activities that allow unique approaches; practice respect and tolerance for differences related to temperament, culture, and family environment.

6 **Unite children's lerning with positive emotions**
    Stimulate positive dispositions about learning through activities that offer control, mastery, and novelty; honor children's preferences; provide time for exploration and engagement; support children's efforts through challenges and active adult scaffolding (Hyson, 1994).

These beliefs in the motivational power of reward and punishment systems have been called into question by recent research (Stipek, 1988). Not all children are equally susceptible to external rewards such as grades, stickers, and stars. If children's family or cultural environments do not value these rewards, the rewards are unlikely to be effective in changing children's behavior. Interestingly, children who come to school with the least motivation to learn are actually the least responsive to external rewards and punishments (Stipek, 1988).

In addition, the use of extrinsic rewards has been found to decrease children's interest in trying challenging tasks (Harter, 1978; Kohn, 1993). Even activities that children tend to enjoy, such as drawing, become less appealing if children are rewarded for doing them. Thus, rewards may backfire, undermining children's motivation to learn and behave appropriately. Like external rewards, the use of punishment in managing children's behavior also has a tendency to backfire. Certainly the fear of punishment can cause children to keep "in line." But anxiety about being punished also inhibits children's learning (cf. Gartrell, 1987).

The Value of Intrinsic Motivation.   More and more, educational psychologists are coming to value the power of intrinsic motivation. Observations of human behavior—and even the behavior of other animals—shows that rewards are usually unnecessary to motivate exploration and learning. Human beings seem to value learning and achievement for its own sake. Even in the absence of rewards, children and adults actively seek out opportunities to develop competencies. Children and adults like to engage in novel activities for their own sake. Furthermore, human beings seem to value autonomy or independence. We prefer to set our own challenges and do tasks that we have selected. "Me do it!" is the cry not only of toddlers, but of human beings in general. Humans are social beings, but they are also beings who resist control and domination by others (Stipek, 1988).

Learning that takes place through intrinsic motivation has some real advantages over learning that is motivated by extrinsic rewards. When children are intrinsically motivated (by novel, interesting activities freely chosen), they actually develop a better understanding of concepts than if they are learning the material in order to obtain a reward. Furthermore, children stay more focused on learning tasks if they have chosen the tasks for their intrinsic interest. At times, a little praise or other incentive may help "prime the pump" if children have trouble getting started with an activity. But the best learning will take place if these external supports are quickly removed, allowing children to experience the developmental benefits of intrinsic motivation (Kohn, 1993; Stipek, 1988; Stipek, Feiler, Daniels, & Milburn, 1995).

Encouraging Intrinsic Motivation.   Although intrinsic motivation does seem to be innate, children differ in how enthusiastically they approach new and challenging tasks. Adults play an important part in building these dispositions. By offering activities that are appropriately challenging but not overwhelming, adults build children's sense of competence and create even more eagerness to move on to the next level of complexity. A developmentally appropriate, integrated curriculum is ideally suited to this task, since children are able to select from a rich array of choices those learning tasks that are optimally challenging, and to move on to a fresh challenge when they have exhausted the possibilities of one activity. By giving children choices, teachers increase children's interest in activities and enhance their intrinsic motivation (Morgan, 1984).

Finally, teachers who give children control over their own learning (with appropriate guidance) are helping children build patterns of autonomy and responsibility (Stipek, 1988). When children are intrinsically motivated, the classroom becomes a self-generating community of independent learners who do not need external threats or prods.

Sociomoral Development and Prosocial Behavior

A third area of research that is helpful to teachers working in a developmentally appropriate, integrated curriculum has to do with the development of young children's sociomoral understanding and prosocial behavior (DeVries & Zan, 1994).

Consistent with studies of motivation, an important point in this work is that young children are actively engaged in the process of building an understanding of their social and moral worlds. As we have seen, even at a very early age children are aware of others' feelings, and they spontaneously express empathy (Zahn-Waxler & Radke-Yarrow, 1982) and offer assistance to others. Just because children are cognitively egocentric does not mean that they are uncaring or selfish. Especially if they spend time in child care programs from an early age, children develop close ties with their classmates (Howes, 1988). Friendships bring conflicts—in fact, children have more quarrels with friends than with nonfriends (Hartup & Laursen, 1993)—but they also bring out children's helpful, loving behavior. Thus, a program that offers opportunities for collaboration and cooperation through group projects and shared activities will help children develop prosocial behavior and social competence.

Influenced by Piagetian theory, researchers emphasize that young children's view of right and wrong, fair and unfair is influenced by their level of cognitive development (Lickona, 1991; Turiel, 1983). In early childhood programs, teachers need to keep children's limited cognitive perspectives in mind. However, recent work on this aspect of development emphasizes adults' responsibility in setting the stage for children to move forward in their understanding and application of higher levels of sociomoral reasoning. Adults can help children "decenter" from their own narrow perspective by encouraging children to think of alternative solutions to social problems (Shure, 1992) and to consider ideas that conflict with or are on a slightly higher level than their own.

A developmentally appropriate, integrated curriculum affords many such opportunities. Children have repeated daily encounters with others' points of view. They may disagree on how to build the block tower, what the title of the class book should be, and how the guinea pig should be cared for. Teachers can lead children to reflect on these issues together. Like emotional development researchers, those who study children's sociomoral development value children's conflicts as important learning opportunities. Conflicts between children force them to confront different points of view and to work toward mutually acceptable resolutions. Constructivist teachers do not impose solutions on children but encourage children to suggest their own solutions; if teachers present ways of dealing with conflicts, they do so only as suggestions with which children may agree or disagree. Like the emphasis on intrinsic motivation discussed earlier, this approach builds autonomy and self-efficacy in young children.

Developmentally Appropriate Guidance Goals

Guidance is such a pressing issue, especially for novice teachers, that it is easy to get bogged down in coping with daily challenges. Fortunately, a wealth of practical resources is available to assist with guidance and management tasks such as room arrangement, scheduling, classroom routines, and specific problems like biting, whining, and aggressive play (Carlsson-Paige & Levin, 1990; Fields & Boesser, 1994; Hildebrand, 1985; Marion, 1991). Keeping the "big picture" in mind is more difficult. The three areas of theory and research that have just been discussed, together with the NAEYC standards for the guidance of children's socioemotional development (Bredekamp, 1987; Bredekamp & Copple, 1997), suggest four key guidance goals (see table 11.3).

TABLE 11.3
Research-Based Guidance Goals

1. Self-regulation

Teachers in developmentally appropriate programs want to help children become able to control or regulate their impulses in ways that are consistent with their age, abilities, and individual characteristics. Children who are guided toward self-regulation have the tools that they need to reach their goals and to become a welcome part of their social and cultural world.

2. Self-efficacy and self-respect

Teachers in developmentally appropriate programs want to help children view themselves as capable, worthy human beings. Children who are guided toward self-efficacy and self-respect will tackle difficult learning problems with zest and persistence. They will build a realistic but generally positive sense of their abilities, and they will take responsibility for their own efforts and the outcomes of those efforts.

3. Emotional Understanding

Teachers in developmentally appropriate programs want to help children to become sensitive to their own and others' feelings. Children who are guided toward emotional understanding are not afraid of feelings, but they also know that they and others have many alternatives in dealing with emotional issues. They respond to the human qualities that unite us all, and they honor differences in culture, values, and individual preferences.

4. Sociocultural competence

Teachers in developmentally appropriate programs want to help children become skilled in living and working within a just community. Children who are guided toward sociocultural competence can use their individual talents in the service of a common goal. They can worl collaboratively, gaining satisfaction from the joint efforts of diverse people. While not avoiding conflict, they can make productive use of disagreements and apply effective strategies to solve social problems.

Guidance and Curriculum Integration

A developmentally appropriate, integrated curriculum, such as that presented in this book, has some real advantages in helping teachers achieve these goals. Yet the integrated curriculum also presents some guidance challenges to teachers who may be used to more adult-directed approaches.

How Curriculum Integration Supports Positive Guidance

Throughout this book, the practices that are recommended for curriculum content also support positive, developmentally appropriate guidance. An integrated, appropriate curriculum offers much to stimulate children's feelings of interest, curiosity, and pleasure. In turn, these feelings motivate children to continue to explore the materials and activities in their classroom and to work cooperatively with others on projects they value. Positive learning dispositions, focused engagement, and intrinsic motivation are enhanced in programs where children routinely get to select their own activities and pursue individual interests with friendly adult support. Sociodramatic play not only creates contexts for literacy and math activities (such as in a "whale" project, where children are recording the type and number of whales they observe on their pretend whale-watching trip), but this kind of play also supports the expression, understanding, and regulation of emotions. The wide range of choices that children are given in a developmentally appropriate, integrated curriculum supports the development of children's self-efficacy and self-worth, as does the kind of rich documentation of children's project work seen in the schools of Reggio Emilia and other project-based classrooms. A project-based curriculum can sometimes be organized around emotion-rich "developmental themes" (Carter & Curtis, 1994) that teachers have observed to be especially meaningful for the children in their care. For example, a class of 4-year-olds might explore the theme of "power," and 2-year-olds may investigate activities around the developmental theme of "hiding and finding."

Even the inevitable conflicts that occur when young children work on joint activities and try to make joint decisions are positive guidance opportunities; as we have seen, children's emotional and moral understanding is heightened by constructive involvement in disputes. Who should make the signs for the art exhibit? How many children should be able to work at the workbench? How can Luis, who has not learned English, contribute to the class scrapbook? These questions are the raw materials of positive guidance. Finally, in each chapter of this book the teacher's role is one of active engagement in children's learning. This activist role also supports the guidance of children's behavior.

Guidance Challenges in the Integrated Curriculum

The developmentally appropriate, integrated curriculum also presents some guidance challenges. Whenever young children get together, their cognitive and emotional limitations will create conflicts and, often, inappropriate behavior. For some children, the relative freedom of a child-initiated program may encourage impulsive, out-of-control behavior, especially at transition times. The noise and movement of the classroom may strain the tolerance of some children, because of temperament or disability. Even among children of the same age, some may have especially great difficulties doing group work or working on projects that do not provide instant gratification. In supporting children's emotional and social development, it may be easy to overlook the quiet child in the bustle of group projects, documentation, and "Let's all learn about bees."

Best Practices in Action: Jane Guides the Fours

To see how one teacher meets these challenges and opportunities, we will visit Jane's classroom of 4-year-olds. As she works with the group during a free-choice period, Jane makes use of many of the "best practices" suggested by theory and research on developmentally appropriate guidance in early childhood programs.

For the past week or so, much of the curriculum has been organized around a library theme. Even before the children arrive, a secure emotional environment is created. Children's stories and artwork cover the walls; covers from favorite storybooks decorate one corner. A comfortable chair awaits the solitary reader. Each area of the room invites exploration within a secure, orderly framework. As children arrive, Jane greets parents and children by name, smiling warmly and making personal connections. All of these features of Jane's program create the foundation for positive guidance by forging secure emotional bonds among Jane, the children, and the program.

The library theme contains rich opportunities to encourage self-efficacy and sociocultural competence. Individual choice is an essential part of going to the library. Everyone has favorite books, and no one choice is best. Books themselves are powerful stimuli for experiencing and expressing emotions. Many of the ideas and activities that emerge from the library theme support Jane's guidance goals and lead to exploration of important "developmental themes." At group time, for example, Jane is discussing the idea of a library. She asks the children about the difference between a bookstore and a library, and they agree that in a bookstore you buy books, while at a library you borrow books. Alex interjects that taking a book from a bookstore would be stealing; this leads to an energetic discussion. Other aspects of the theme also stimulate the children's thinking about sociomoral issues. In preparing for play in the "library" dramatic play, Jane shows the children the card on which they may stamp the due date. The children discuss how to stamp the books and agree that the card should be taken out of the book so that the book itself does not get ink on it. Jane talks with them about how other people may want to read the books in the library, so it is important to keep the books clean and easy to find.

Jane allows many choices, but she makes sure that children know what the choices are. Every day, she begins by describing what free-choice activities will be available. She stimulates children's interest in the activities by her intriguing descriptions and demonstrations. The children's eyes widen as she shows how they can use colored dots to shelve books in the pretend "library." Her descriptions acknowledge children's individual interests and preferences: "I know some of you love to play with clay, and today we will have the clay out on that table"; "Some of you like dinosaurs [shouts of "Yes!"], and we have dinosaur books in the library for you to borrow." Choice does not become chaos, because Jane reminds children of rules before problems develop: "The indoor climber is set up in the hall. Remember the rules for the climber: You need to wait in line and then go in the little climber door and wait until the person ahead of you is all the way through the climber" (the children had developed these rules with Jane earlier in the year). At the end of the group meeting, Jane asks children to choose the area in which they would like to begin playing and dismisses them by ones and twos, again respecting their preferences while also avoiding a frantic rush. Children know that they can choose what to do, and that there will be lots of time to investigate all of the activities in the room (and even to make up new ones).

During free-choice time, each child busily works at self-chosen tasks. Because the classroom environment has been set up in clearly established interest areas, children can see what there is to do. Luis, Frieda, and Manny create paper puppets of their favorite book characters, using Popsicle sticks. Melanie, Jane's assistant, sits with them, keeping the activity flowing through her interest and involvement. Celia and Kara work by themselves, using library stamps to create designs. In the dramatic play area, Ethan, Raphael, Susan, and others play "library," checking out and shelving books, browsing, and reading. Children freely move in and out of each activity. As children are invested in each activity, self-regulation takes over the need for external "discipline."

But self-regulation does not mean adult passivity in Jane's program. Jane and her assistant Melanie work closely with the children. Melanie sits with the puppet-making group, keeping the activity flowing with conversation, provision of some new materials, and a helping hand. If children cannot find an activity, Jane or Melanie will invite them to engage in new activities. Tim has been wandering around absently for some time. Looking up from her seat in the library area, Jane asks Tim if he could help in the library by putting the returned books back on the shelf. Tim goes to the "returned" bin and gathers the books, busily placing them on the shelf according to their category. Because Tim has a developmental disability, Jane is especially active in channeling him into activities that will focus his attention and build physical and cognitive skills. As with other children in the class, Jane's guidance of Tim is individually appropriate.

As children move through the day, Jane encourages children's self-regulation while remaining actively involved in scaffolding children's appropriate behavior. Jeremy wanders over to the bookshelf and finds the "Waldo" book. Just as he takes it, Alex rushes toward Jeremy and tries to grab the book out of Jeremy's hands. Stepping in to what seems to be an impasse, Jane asks if it would be okay for Jeremy to hold the book on his lap, since he had the book first, and if Alex could perhaps turn the pages since he is such a good helper. Alex and Jeremy sit in the beanbag chair to read the book together. They both eagerly try to find Waldo and point out interesting things in the picture to each other. Jeremy puts his arm around Alex as they continue looking through the book.

When conflicts occur, Jane's actions emphasize emotional under-standing. Feelings are respected, and children are encouraged to work out solutions to social problems in ways that are fair and satisfying. Jane knows that 4-year-olds need a lot of support in this process. Alex (in his typically boisterous style) bounces around the room announcing that it is time to clean up. He bumps into Brendan and continues on his way. Brendan stares at Alex with a hurt and troubled face and wanders over to Jane to tell her of the trouble. Jane asks how it made Brendan feel when he got bumped, and Brendan says that it hurt. Jane suggests that maybe Brendan could go over to Alex and tell him that it hurts when you get bumped, and that you don't like being bumped. Brendan agrees, but asks Jane to go with him (many of the children are a little afraid of Alex). Jane asks Alex if he will listen to something that Brendan wants to say. Alex nods and listens. "I'm sorry, Brendan," Alex says sincerely. Jane asks if everything is okay now; both children agree and go their separate ways.

Summary

This chapter encourages practitioners who use a developmentally appropriate, integrated curriculum to consider how their guidance strategies meet children's emotional, motivational, and sociomoral development. To meet these needs of children, coherent links between guidance strategies and curriculum should be fostered. Links between guidance strategies and curriculum should focus on the individual needs and styles of children and meet the needs of children in a developmentally sensitive manner.

Research and theory on children's emotional development, children's motivation as it relates to learning, and children's sociomoral development offer important guidance strategies for teachers.

Teachers can promote emotional development through six strategies:

1. Create a secure emotional environment.
2. Help children understand feelings.
3. Model genuine, appropriate emotional responses.
4. Support children's regulation of emotions.
5. Identify and honor children's emotional styles.
6. Unite children's learning with positive emotions.

Practitioners must also be sensitive to how particular guidance strategies relate to children's motivation to learn. Extrinsic rewards are not effective with all children, and their use can also decrease children's interest in learning. When classrooms offer developmentally appropriate and challenging activities from which children can choose, children's learning and intrinsic motivation are enhanced.

Teachers working in a developmentally appropriate, integrated curriculum must also consider how guidance strategies influence children's sociomoral development and prosocial behavior. In developmentally appropriate classrooms, conflict is seen as an opportunity for children to develop social skills as they work toward compromise and confront opposing viewpoints. Constructivist teachers do not impose solutions, but encourage children to find solutions to their conflict. This approach can build autonomy and self-efficacy in young children.

In conclusion, four key guidance goals are offered that encourage developmentally appropriate guidance strategies. Guidance strategies should foster self-regulation, self-efficacy and self-respect, emotional understanding, and sociocultural competence. Keeping these goals in mind can help teachers guide children's behavior in a developmentally appropriate, integrated curriculum.

References

Baumrind, D. (1967). Child care practices anteceding three patterns of preschool behavior. *Genetic Psychology Monographs, 75,* 43–88.

Baumrind, D. (1989). Rearing competent children. In W. Damon (Ed.), *New directions for child development: Adolescent health and human behavior.* San Francisco: Jossey-Bass.

Braun, S., & Edwards, E. (1972). *History and theory of early childhood education.* Worthington, OH: Charles A. Jones.

Bredekamp, S. (Ed.). (1987). *Developmentally appropriate practice in early childhood programs serving children from birth to age 8.* Washington, DC: National Association for the Education of Young Children.

Bredekamp, S., & Copple, C. (Eds.). (1997). *Developmentally appropriate practice in early childhood programs: Revised.* Washington, DC: National Association for the Education of Young Children.

Campos, J.J., Barrett, K.C., Lamb, M.E., Goldsmith, H.H., & Sternberg, C. (1983). Socioemotional development. In M. Haith & J.J. Campos (Eds.) & P.H. Mussen (Series Ed.), *Handbook of child psychology,* vol. 2, *Infancy and developmental psychobiology* (pp. 783–915). New York: Wiley.

Camras, L., Grow, G., & Ribordy, S. (1983). Recognition of emotional expressions by abused children. *Journal of Clinical and Child Psychology, 12,* 325–28.

Canter, L., & Canter, M. (1976). *Assertive discipline: A take-charge approach for today's educator*. Santa Monica, CA: Lee Canter & Associates.

Carlsson-Paige, N., & Levin, D.E. (1990). *Who's calling the shots? How to respond effectively to children's fascination with war toys*. Philadelphia: New Society.

Carter, M., & Curtis, D. (1994). *Training teachers: A harvest of theory and practice*. St. Paul, MN: Redleaf

Chapman, M., Zahn-Waxler, C., Cooperman, G., & Iannotti, R. (1987). Empathy and responsibility in the motivation of children's helping. *Developmental Psychology, 23,* 140–45.

Denham, S.A. (1986). Social cognition, prosocial behavior, and emotion in preschoolers: Contextual validation. *Child Development, 57,* 194–201.

Denham, S.A., Mason, T., & Couchoud, E. (1993). *Scaffolding young children's prosocial responsiveness: Preschoolers' responses to adult sadness, anger, and pain*. Manuscript submitted for publication.

DeVries, R., Reese-Learned, H., & Morgan, P. (1991). Sociomoral development in direct-instruction, eclectic, and constructivist kindergartens: A study of children's enacted interpersonal understanding. *Early Childhood Research Quarterly, 6,* 473–517.

DeVries, R., & Zan, B. (1994). *Moral classrooms, moral children: Creating a constructivist atmosphere in early education*. New York: Teachers College Press.

Dreikurs, R., & Cassel, P. (1972). *Discipline without tears* (2nd ed.). New York: Hawthorne.

Dunn, J., & Brown, J. (1991). Relationships, talk about feelings, and the development of affect regulation in early childhood. In J. Garber & K.A. Dodge (Eds.), *The development of emotion regulation and dysregulation* (pp. 89–108). New York: Cambridge University Press.

Dunn, J., & Munn, P. (1985). Becoming a family member: Family conflict and development of social understanding. *Child Development, 56,* 480–92.

Eisenberg, N., & Fabes, R.A. (Eds.). (1992). *Emotion and its regulation in early development*. San Francisco: Jossey-Bass.

Erikson, E. (1950). *Childhood and society*. New York: Norton.

Fields, M.V., & Boesser, C. (1994). *Constructive guidance and discipline: Preschool and primary education*. New York: Merrill.

Fox, N.A. (Ed.). (1994). The development of emotion regulation: Biological and behavioral considerations. *Monographs of the Society for Research in Child Development, 59.*

Freud, S. (1964). New introductory lectures on psycho-analysis. In J. Strachey (Ed. & Trans.), *The standard edition of the complete psychological works of Sigmund Freud* (Vol. 22). London: Hogarth. (Original work published 1933)

Gartrell, D. (1987). Assertive discipline: Unhealthy for children and other living things. *Young Children, 42,* 10–11.

Gesell, A. (1940). *The first five years of life: A guide to the study of the preschool child.* New York: Harper.

Gordon, S.L. (1989). The socialization of children's emotions: Emotional culture, competence, and exposure. In C. Saarni & P.L. Harris (Eds.), *Children's understanding of emotion* (pp. 319–40). New York: Cambridge University Press.

Hart, C., DeWolf, D., Wozniak, P., & Burts, D. (1992). Maternal and paternal disciplinary styles: Relations with preschoolers' playground behavioral orientations and peer status. *Child Development, 63,* 879–92.

Harter, S. (1978). Pleasure derived from challenge and the effects of receiving grades on children's difficulty level choices. *Child Development, 49,* 788–99.

Hartup, W., & Laursen, B. (1993). Conflict and context in peer relations. In C.H. Hart (Ed.), *Children on playgrounds: Research perspectives and applications* (pp. 44–84). Albany, NY: State University of New York Press.

Hildebrand, V. (1985). *Guiding young children* (3rd ed.). New York: Macmillan.

Howes, C. (1988). Peer interaction of young children. *Monographs of the Society for Research in Child Development, 53.*

Hyson, M.C. (1994). *The emotional development of young children: Building an emotion-centered curriculum.* New York: Teachers College Press.

Hyson, M.C., & Cone, J. (1989). Giving form to feeling: Emotions research and early childhood education. *Journal of Applied Developmental Psychology, 10,* 375–99.

Hyson, M.C., & DeCsipkes, C. (1993, March). *Educational and developmental belief systems among African-American parents of kindergarten children.* Paper presented at the biennial meeting of the Society for Research in Child Development, New Orleans, LA.

Hyson, M.C., Hirsh-Pasek, K., & Rescorla, L. (1990). The Classroom Practices Inventory: An observation instrument based on NAEYC's Guidelines for Developmentally Appropriate Practices for 4- and 5-year-old Children. *Early Childhood Research Quarterly, 5,* 475–94.

Izard, C.E. (1991). *The psychology of emotions.* New York: Plenum.

Izard, C.E., Hembree, E.A., & Huebner, R.R. (1987). Infants' emotion expressions to acute pain. *Developmental Psychology, 23,* 105–13.

Izard, C.E., & Kobak, R.R. (1991). Emotions system functioning and emotion regulation. In J. Garber & K.A. Dodge (Eds.), *The development of emotion regulation and dysregulation* (pp. 303–21). New York: Cambridge University Press.

Kagan, J., Reznick, J.S., Clarke, C., Snidman, N., & Garcia-Coll, C. (1984). Behavioral inhibition to the unfamiliar. *Child Development, 55,* 2212–25.

Kohn, A. (1993). *Punished by rewards: The trouble with gold stars, incentive plans, A's, praise, and other bribes.* Boston: Houghton Mifflin.

Kontos, S., & Wilcox-Herzog, A. (1997). Teachers' interactions with children: Why are they important? *Young Children, 52,* 4–12.

Lewis, C.C. (1988). Cooperation and control in Japanese nursery schools. In G. Handel (Ed.), *Childhood socialization* (pp. 125–42). New York: Aldine deGruyter.

Lickona, T. (1991). *Educating for character: How our schools can teach respect and responsibility.* New York: Bantam.

Lynch, E.W., & Hansen, M.J. (1992). *Developing cross-cultural competence: A guide for working with young children and their families.* Baltimore: Brookes.

Marion, M. (1991). *Guidance of young children* (3rd ed.). New York: Macmillan.

McAdoo, H.P. (Ed.).(1992). *Black families* (2nd ed.). Newbury Park, CA: Sage.

Morgan, M. (1984). Reward-induced decrements and increments in intrinsic motivation. *Review of Educational Research, 54,* 5–30.

Patterson, G.R. (1982). *Coercive family process.* Eugene, OR: Castalia.

Piaget, J. (1951). *Play, dreams, and imitation in childhood.* New York: Norton.

Radke-Yarrow, M., & Zahn-Waxler, C. (1984). Roots, motives, and patterns in children's prosocial behavior. In E. Staub, D. Bar-Tal, J. Karylowski, & J. Reykowski (Eds.), *Development and maintenance of prosocial behavior: International perspectives on positive behavior* (pp. 81–98). New York: Plenum.

Renninger, K.A., & Wozniak, R. (1985). Effect of interest on attentional shift, recognition, and recall in young children. *Developmental Psychology, 21,* 624–32.

Rogers, C.R. (1961). *On becoming a person.* Boston: Houghton Mifflin.

Schmidt, H.M., Charlesworth, R., Burts, D., Rice, G., & Hart, C. (1996). *The impact of teacher guidance strategies on children's interpersonal relations.* Manuscript submitted for publication.

Schweinhart, L.J., Weikart, D.P., & Larner, M.B. (1986). Consequences of three preschool curriculum models through age 15. *Early Childhood Research Quarterly, 1,* 15–45.

Shure, M. (1992). *I can problem solve. (ICPS): An interpersonal problem-solving program.* Champaign, IL: Research Press.

Spodek, B. (Ed.). (1993). *Handbook of research on the education of young children.* New York: Macmillan.

Stein, N.L., & Jewett, J.L. (1986). A conceptual analysis of the meaning of negative emotions: Implications for a theory of development. In C.E. Izard & P.B. Read (Eds.), *Measuring emotions in infants and children* (Vol. 2, pp. 238–67). New York: Cambridge University Press.

Stipek, D. (1988). *Motivation to learn: From theory to practice.* Englewood Cliffs, NJ: Prentice Hall.

Stipek, D. (1991). Characterizing early childhood education programs. In L. Rescorla, M.C. Hyson, & K. Hirsh-Pasek (Eds.), *Academic instruction in early childhood: Challenge or pressure? New directions for child development* (pp. 47–55). San Francisco: Jossey-Bass.

Stipek, D., Feiler, R., Daniels, D., & Milburn, S. (1995). Effects of different instructional approaches on young children's achievement and motivation. *Child Development, 66,* 209–23.

Turiel, E. (1983). *The development of social knowledge: Morality and convention.* Cambridge: Cambridge University Press.

Vance, B. (1973). *Teaching the prekindergarten child: Instructional design and curriculum.* Belmont, CA: Wadsworth.

Vygotsky, L.S. (1978). *Mind in society: The development of higher mental processes.* Cambridge, MA: Harvard University Press.

Weber, E. (1984). *Ideas influencing early childhood education: A theoretical analysis.* New York: Teachers College Press.

Wieder, S., & Greenspan, S.I. (1993). The emotional basis of learning. In B. Spodek (Ed.), *Handbook of research on the education of young children* (pp. 77–87). New York: Macmillan.

Zahn-Waxler, C., & Radke-Yarrow, M. (1982). The development of altruism: Alternative research strategies. In N. Eisenberg-Berg (Ed.), *The development of prosocial behavior.* New York: Academic.

CHAPTER TWELVE

Assessment in an Integrated Curriculum

PAMELA O. FLEEGE

During the 1960s and 1970s, due in part to an influx of federal and state resources for schools, standardized tests were used increasingly to measure the achievement of school age children (Perrone, 1991). By the end of the 1980s the use of these tests had become widespread and prevalent even in many early childhood classrooms. As the use of standardized tests has escalated, so has criticism of their use. According to Charlesworth, Fleege, and Weitman (1994) these tests have been criticized for many reasons, including the following:

- Test items do not match what is taught.
- Test items do not match the content or procedural guidelines set forth by professional organizations.
- Tests exert direct influence on curriculum.
- Tests do not accurately reflect children's knowledge or abilities.
- Tests undermine teachers' feelings of competency.
- Tests directly influence teaching strategies.

Standardized tests have also been shown to have negative effects on young children. When observed, kindergarten children showed increased levels of stress-related behaviors during the administration of standardized achievement tests (Fleege et al., 1992). The level of stress-related behaviors, such as nail biting, crying, and refusal to complete

313

tasks, increased during testing as compared to the levels before and after testing.

Because of growing dissatisfaction with standardized tests, many educators sought to develop alternative means for assessing children. Numerous terms have been used to refer to these alternatives, the most frequently used being alternative assessment, authentic assessment, performance assessment, direct assessment, and portfolio assessment. Regardless of the term used, these assessments are all grounded in the following assumptions:

- Assessments are more valid when children are directly assessed through their products.
- Assessments are a natural part of children's day-to-day classroom experiences.
- The teacher is the primary director of children's learning rather than a test designer.
- Children actively construct their own knowledge. (Grady, 1992; Neuman, 1993; Perrone, 1991; Wiggins, 1989; Wolf et al., 1991)

Another impetus for the growing importance of alternative assessment in early childhood classrooms is its congruence with the constructivist perspective on child development. The term "constructivism" implies that children construct their knowledge of the world through interactions with objects and people in their environment, as demonstrated in the theory of Piaget (Wadsworth, 1989). More recently, constructivist viewpoints have also encompassed the research of Vygotksy (1962), which emphasizes the importance of social interaction in knowledge construction, and Howard Gardner (1983), whose work has expanded our definition of intelligence to encompass multiple facets. (For a more complete discussion of constructivist theory, see chapter 2 of this volume.)

According to Hipps (1993), alternative forms of assessment are more appropriate in a constructivist approach because the assumptions underlying both are compatible. If, as constructivists argue, learning is multidimensional, then assessment techniques and strategies must also be multidimensional. Because interaction is an integral part of knowledge construction, then it must also be a part of appropriate assessment. In a constructivist view, where reality is a multiple construction rather than a fixed, objective entity, multiple means of assessment are required to record or capture those multiple realities. To quote Hipps, the assessor's job then "becomes one of adequately portraying and understanding the constructions (the realities) of the informants from whom information is collected" (p. 6).

Although research on alternative assessment in the classroom has been limited, recent studies do support its effectiveness. Teachers using alternative assessment have reported a better understanding of children's abilities and a greater ability to use that understanding in short- and long-term planning (Joyner, 1994). Implementing alternative assessment can also lead to changes in the classroom environment and organization as well as changes in teachers' interaction patterns with children. Changes have also been reported in children's decision making and involvement in their own assessment (Gooding, 1994).

Alternative assessment strategies have begun to be implemented in programs serving young children. One such program is the North Carolina Assessment Program (Joyner, 1994). The North Carolina Program developed and implemented a statewide, mandated alternative assessment program for grades 1 and 2. Evaluations of the program indicate that children had more positive images of themselves as learners. Parents were enthusiastic about the depth of information available as a result of alternative assessment methods. Teachers reported that the amount and quality of information they gained about children far outweighed the extra time alternative assessment requires.

Founded on Howard Gardner's theory of multiple intelligences, Project Spectrum (Krechevsky & Gardner, 1990) was designed as an alternative means of assessing preschool children's cognitive abilities. Results suggest that alternative forms of assessment, in contrast to standardized testing, provide children with a sense of ownership and active involvement in the assessment process. Unlike standardized instruments, alternative methods furnish richer and more complex portraits of children in context-sensitive ways. Parents and teachers reported greater understanding of children's individual differences, strengths, and potentials. It is especially important to note that Project Spectrum results emphasize the integration of alternative assessment with integrated instructional practices.

Despite the limited amount of research, especially with young children, results thus far support the developmental appropriateness of alternative assessment. To ensure that curriculum and assessment are both appropriate and integrated, teachers must understand what assessment is, how it operates in the classroom, and the steps involved in its planning and implementation.

Defining Assessment

What is assessment? Assessment is a process by which we record what children know and do and how they do it. We use assessment as a basis for making decisions about what experiences to offer children in the classroom and if intervention is needed. It is also used to communicate with parents.

In Bredekamp's (1987) publication on developmentally appropriate practices, she recommends that assessment of young children be accomplished through informal means rather than through standardized tests. She defines informal means as observation. The goal of this type of assessment is to give children the opportunity to express through language and actions their knowledge using activities that closely match the ones they experience every day in the classroom.

Guidelines for conducting assessment of young children have been expanded with the publication of Bredekamp and Rosegrant's (1992) *Reaching Potentials: Appropriate Curriculum and Assessment of Young Children*. In this volume Tynette Hill discusses what should be assessed and how this assessment should be accomplished. These guidelines define assessment as "the process of observing, recording and otherwise documenting the work children do and how they do it, as a basis for a variety of educational decisions that affect the child" (Bredekamp & Rosegrant, 1992, p. 43). Appropriate assessment methods now include both observation and interview. According to Hill, the primary use of assessment is for planning instruction and communicating with parents. It is not used to keep students out of programs or to retain them. Assessment is an integral part of a teacher's curriculum and uses processes that reflect the activities that normally take place in the classroom. Authentic assessment, as it's been called, should be performed in a systematic way at regular intervals.

Assessment Techniques

Using NAEYC's definition of assessment, a teacher would rely primarily on observation and interview to monitor the progress of children in the classroom. Observation is considered to be the least intrusive method of assessment available to educators. It allows the observer to see what a child can do in a familiar environment. Observation can be an effective way to learn about children. We can gain information about children's progress in all developmental domains. It links our knowledge of child development with teaching strategies. Observation also provides useful information for parents, teachers, and other professionals. Using information gained from observations we make decisions about what is an appropriate next experience for a particular child.

What do we observe? We observe what children are doing and how they are doing it—what behaviors they are exhibiting and how well established they seem to be. We also observe under what conditions the children exhibit these behaviors. We ask ourselves such questions as, Are they able to complete the task independently or do they need help?

Teachers also compare what they see children doing with what is considered age-appropriate or inappropriate. For example, if a teacher observes a 5-year-old and ascertains that the child engages predominantly in parallel play, the teacher would then ask: Do 5-year-olds engage in cooperative play most of the time? If the answer is yes, then observation of this child's play behavior is looked at from the individually appropriate aspect. The teacher draws on what she knows about this individual child. She may ask herself several questions. Can this behavior be attributed to the child's socioeconomic status, gender, or ethnic background? Are there occasions when the child chooses to engage in cooperative play? If so, with whom? Is this parallel play a choice the child makes—in other words, does the child simply prefer to play alone? These questions should be answered before making a decision to intervene or to refer for screening to see if specialized services are needed.

Teachers engage in observation every day. This type of informal observation is called "kid watching" (Goodman, 1985). Through kid watching teachers learn that Keshia can count to ten or that Bobby has learned a new word. Kid watching is not systematic or ongoing. Primarily, it lacks the purposefulness and the documentation needed to be considered thorough and valid for making important decisions about children. Kid watching has its place in the classroom, but to document the growth of children, a more systematic and formal means of observing is needed. These more formal or planned observations focus on observing children for particular behaviors and recording those seen.

Interviews consist of teachers asking children either preplanned or spontaneous questions. Interviews can be both informal and formal. Informal interviews are those where teachers ask children questions suggested by something they have heard the child say or seen the child do. The questions are not preplanned but develop based on observations made in the classroom. An example of this would be when the teacher observes a child in the block center and joins him or her. The teacher then might ask questions such as: "Tell me about what you're building. How many long blocks are you using? Is there another way you could build your tower?"

More formal interviews consist of preplanned questions that may be asked of one child or all children in the classroom. Some teachers want to know how children view themselves in literacy and may ask each child in the class individually, "Are you a writer?" or "What do you write?" Another example would be assessing a child's rational counting. The teacher might ask a child to give each child in the class a certain number of raisins for snack time. Regardless of whether a teacher uses observation or interview, the tasks that children are asked to perform should be congruent with the everyday activities in the classroom.

Documentation Strategies

There are several documentation strategies that are appropriate for recording the observations and interviews completed with children. These strategies include checklists, rating scales, photographs, audiotapes, videotapes, and work samples. Narrative recording systems include anecdotal records, running records, time sampling, and event sampling.

Checklists are a list of behaviors or traits the teacher is observing for in a particular domain. A checklist records the presence or absence of a behavior. An example of a checklist can be seen in figure 12.1. The presence of a behavior should not be recorded the first time the teacher sees the child demonstrate it. The teacher should wait until the child exhibits the behavior consistently and in more than one setting.

There are several advantages to using checklists. Checklists are easy to use and require little training. Another advantage is that they can be

FIGURE 12.1
Checklist

Child's Name _____

SMALL MOTOR DEVELOPMENT CHECKLIST

PRE   POST

____ Shows hand preference (which is _____)   ____

____ Turns with hands easily (knobs, lids, eggbeaters)   ____

____ Pours liquid into glass without spilling   ____

____ Unfastens and fastens zippers, buttons, velcro   ____

____ Picks up and inserts objects with ease   ____

____ Uses drawing/writing tools with control   ____

____ Uses scissors with control   ____

____ Pounds in nails with control   ____

Adapted from Beaty, J.J. (1986). *Observing development of the young child.* Columbus, OH: Merrill.

developed by the teacher to record the behaviors exhibited during actual classroom activities. Some of the disadvantages associated with checklists are: (1) teachers may not feel secure enough in their knowledge to develop checklists that reflect the actual activities going on in their classroom; (2) checklists do not tell the observer how well established a behavior is; (3) checklists do not indicate the context in which the behavior is exhibited.

Rating scales, on the other hand, do tell the reader something about the degree of mastery or the frequency of the behavior. They require the teacher to make a qualitative judgment about the extent to which a behavior is present. Rating scales can use either numerical or graphic categories to indicate the degree to which a behavior is present (see figure 12.2 for an example).

Some of the advantages of rating scales are that they take a minimum of time to complete, are easy to develop, and require little training to use. However, there are some disadvantages. Descriptors can be ambiguous, like checklists, and rating scales tell little about the context under which behaviors are exhibited.

One narrative documentation system is anecdotal records. Anecdotal records are used to record specific events that demonstrate a

FIGURE 12.2
Literacy Rating Scale

Child's Name _____

M = Most of the Time				
S = Some of the Time				
NY = Not Yet				

	DATE	DATE	DATE	DATE
1. Chooses books for personal enjoyment				
2. Asks to be read to				
3. Knows print/picture difference				
4. Knows print is read from left to right				
5. "Reads" familiar books to self/others				
6. Can read personal words				
7. Can read logos				
8. Willing to "write"				
9. Willing to dictate				
10. Writes some words conventionally				

particular behavior in nonjudgmental language. They tell what happened, where, and when. Usually there is a separate column for teacher comments or interpretation (see figure 12.3 for an example).

Another narrative method is the running record. The running record is a detailed description that records everything that happens over a specified period of time. Again, objective language is used to describe what is observed and the child's language is recorded verbatim. Running records also use a separate column for comments. Running records can be used to record behaviors that are exhibited for a few minutes or even for a few weeks (see figure 12.4). Anecdotal and running records both provide the teacher with a rich description of the context in which behaviors occur, but the disadvantage to these is that they are both time-consuming. Many teachers find it hard to sit down and write for more than a few minutes.

Time sampling is used to record what happens within a specified period of time. Unlike running records, time sampling is done for a specified period of time that is short in duration. During this time period specific behaviors are looked for. A tally is kept to record the

FIGURE 12.3
Anecdotal Record

Child's Name(s): _____ Keshia _____ Date: _Thurs., 9/14/95 9:30 a.m._

Location: _Dramatic Play Center_____

Type of Development Observed: _____Cognitive—Rational Counting_____

Incident	Comments
During center time Keshia had the dolls seated in the two highchairs and proceeded to place crackers on each tray in front of each doll. She seated herself at the table and began to talk to the dolls. "Eat the three crackers I gave you and and I'll see if there's any more." "You want some more?" "Okay, here's five." "One, two, three, four, five."	Today is the first time Keshia counted to five aloud. Typically, she gets to three and then says, eight, nine, ten.

FIGURE 12.4
Running Record

Date__2/9_____ Child's Name ___Katy_____

Time __9:00_____ Place___S. Nursery_____

Observation	Comments
Katy is playing by herself with plastic blocks, making guns; she walks into the other room: "Lisa, would you play with me? I'm tired of playing by myself." They walk into the other room to the slide & climbing area.	Clips blocks together to make gun, then copies it to make one for Lisa. Cleverly done. Intricate. Shows creativity. (Does teacher allow guns?)
K: "I am Wonder Woman."	
L: "So am I."	
K: "No, there is only one Wonder Woman. You are Robin."	Seems to be the leader here as in other activities I have observed. Lisa is the friend she most often plays with.
L: "Robin needs a Batman because Batman & Robin are friends.	

Adapted from: Beaty, J.J. (1990). *Observing development of the young child.* Columbus, OH: Merrill.

frequency of the behavior. Time sampling is frequently used when a problem is suspected. If a child has a problem with hitting others, the teacher might record the number of times the child uses this behavior to obtain what he or she wants. For an example, see figure 12.5.

Event sampling differs from time sampling in that it is used when a specific behavior tends to occur in one setting or at odd times. With event sampling the teacher tries to determine what causes or precedes a behavior. For an example, see figure 12.6. The real advantage of event sampling is that it allows a teacher to look closely at the context in which the behavior occurs. The disadvantage is that the behavior may not occur when the teacher expects it to, and therefore observation time can be wasted.

Another way to record children's progress is through photography. Photographs can be used to document development in all areas. They can be used to show the increased complexity of block structures as

FIGURE 12.5
Time Sampling

Child's Name: ___Sara___
Age: ___2 yrs. 3 mo.___
Location: ___Red room___
Date: ___Oct. 17, 1995___
Time: ___9:45–10:00___
Observer: ___Joan___
Type of Development Observed: <u>Social/Emotional Uses hitting to achieve wants.</u>

Event	Time	Comments
Art Center—Sara stands near Jeff as he paints, watching intently.	9:45	She seems to want to paint.
Sara tries to take the paintbrush from Jeff. When he resists she hits him. Jeff begins to cry and looks for Ms. Smith. When he leaves Sara takes the paintbrush and begins to paint on Jeff's paper.	9:50	Sara uses no sound to indicate she wants to paint. She seems startled when Jeff begins to cry but quickly begins to paint once he leaves.

FIGURE 12.6
Event Sampling

Child's Name: _____Sara_____

Age: _____2yrs. 3mo._____

Location:___Red room_____

Date: _____Oct. 17, 1995_____

Time: _____9:00 - 11:30_____

Observer: ____Joan_____

Type of Development Observed: ___Social/Emotional___

Time	Antecedent Event	Behavior	Resulting Event
9:15	Sara wants to paint	Sara hits Jeff	Sara takes the paintbrush and Jeff goes to Ms. Smith
10:00	Jane is looking at a book. Sara holds out her hand. Jane ignores her.	Sara grabs the book and hits Jane.	Jane cries but gets another book.

they develop throughout the year. Items that have been sorted can be photographed to show evidence of classification. Social development can also be documented through the use of photographs. Pictures taken during cooperative group work can be used to show a child's ability to work well with others.

Audiotapes are an excellent way to document a child's oral language development. They can also be used to record interviews. While audiotapes provide a rich example of a child's development, there are two major disadvantages. The first is that audiotapes can be expensive; the second disadvantage is that transcribing tapes is time-consuming and costly if a teacher must pay someone to do it.

Videotapes can be used in much the same way. They provide both audio and visual proof of a child's development. Videotapes are an excellent way to show a child's gross motor development. Because videotapes are also costly and many teachers do not have access to a videorecorder, they may not be a practical method of assessment for all teachers.

Work samples are another method used to document children's progress. The work samples produced by children over a period of time can tell a great deal about how a child is developing. Examples of work samples would be drawings, paintings, handwritten stories, and products that demonstrate a child's problem-solving capabilities.

Teachers use some or all of these recording methods to document a child's progress. Often this collection of information is put into a portfolio to create a profile of a child's development. Because individual children's interests and needs differ, not all portfolios in a given classroom will look alike. All portfolios in a given classroom may have some of the same items, such as checklists and rating scales, but they would differ in work samples, audio- and videotapes, and photographs. However, portfolios are more than just a collection of information. The next step in the portfolio process involves interpreting what this collection of information tells us and making decisions based on these interpretations. Interpretations are used to make decisions about what experiences to offer in the classroom and whether special services may be needed, as well as to communicate with parents and others about a child's progress.

When interpreting assessment information, teachers should look for patterns in the collection of information and materials. They look to see what concepts and behaviors are exhibited multiple times, and they also look to see what concepts and behaviors are not exhibited. Teachers then compare this to what concept development and behaviors are considered typical for the child's chronological age.

Assessment Snapshots: Integrating with Curriculum

The previous section discussed how appropriate assessment may be accomplished. This section focuses on how assessment might look in classrooms with different age children.

Infants/Toddlers

Because infants and toddlers learn through their senses, experiences such as opportunities to manipulate objects are provided. Time is set aside for toddlers to explore their environment, and caregivers provide mobility if necessary. Social interaction is also encouraged and supported so that socioemotional skills and language develop.

Assessment in an infant/toddler classroom would probably consist of a checklist that recorded developmental milestones in all domains, such as rolling over, crawling, laughing or smiling, and babbling. Anecdotal records would also be used to provide the context within which the developmental milestone was reached.

Preschoolers

During the preschool years a teacher would continue to assess developmental milestones in the areas of gross and fine motor, language and literacy, and socioemotional development. With preschoolers, assessment begins to include factual knowledge or content knowledge. Content knowledge is not assessed at the exclusion of other areas, but is now added to the areas previously being assessed.

Checklists and rating scales might still be used to assess gross and fine motor skills such as running, jumping, balancing, cutting, and painting. They could also be used to demonstrate socioemotional development. Items that might be found on a socioemotional checklist or rating scale might include self-control, cooperating, or helping. Dictated stories as well as beginning writing efforts could be collected to assess literacy development. Audiotapes could document oral language development.

Appropriate math concepts that might be assessed include one-to-one correspondence, rational counting, and classification. All these concepts could be assessed through observation or interview, and documented using checklists, audiotapes, and photographs. Science processes that one would expect to see demonstrated in the preschool classroom include making observations, communicating observations to others, and acquiring data through the senses. These processes could be assessed through interviews or work samples such as drawings.

Primary Grades

In the primary grades content-specific knowledge takes on a more important role than ever before. However, a teacher does not focus on it to the exclusion of the other areas of development. Physical motor and socioemotional development should be given the same importance as content-specific development. It is the duty of the teacher to create an assessment profile of the whole child.

Because children in the primary grades are refining gross motor skills such as batting a ball, skipping rope, and balancing on a beam, daily opportunities to engage in these activities should be offered. As children play individually and in small groups the teacher might use rating scales or videotapes to document the child's growing skills.

Socioemotional development is still an important part of the primary school curriculum. It is during this time that children continue to learn about perseverance, industry, and independence. They also continue to refine skills such as negotiating and working cooperatively together. Checklists and rating scales would be appropriate strategies to document this progress. Anecdotal records would also provide rich snapshots of how refinement of these skills takes place.

Curriculum in the primary grades is integrated so that learning occurs mainly through learning centers, projects, and play incorporated into thematic units. An example of a thematic unit web that could be used in a 2nd or 3rd grade classroom can be seen in figure 12.7.

This unit web would be used by a group of children studying about estuaries. Some of the activities shown above would be completed by individuals or small groups, and some would be completed as a whole group. There would also be time within this unit for projects that the children wanted to pursue that are not on the unit web.

Using the above unit web as an example, content area knowledge might be assessed in a number of different ways. Creative writing as well as the mechanics of writing could be assessed through work samples taken from the stories written by children about their trip to an estuary, their interviews of people having occupations connected with estuaries, or through creative drama. Oral language could be assessed through audio or video accounts of occupational interviews.

The mathematics concepts of classification and graphing could be assessed after data have been collected about plants and animals found in estuaries. Samples could be collected during the field trip and sorted and graphed upon the children's return. Another approach would be for the children to keep notes about what plants and animals they have seen; then the teacher could provide pictures to be sorted and graphed after their return. Upon completion of these activities

FIGURE 12.7
Thematic Unit Web

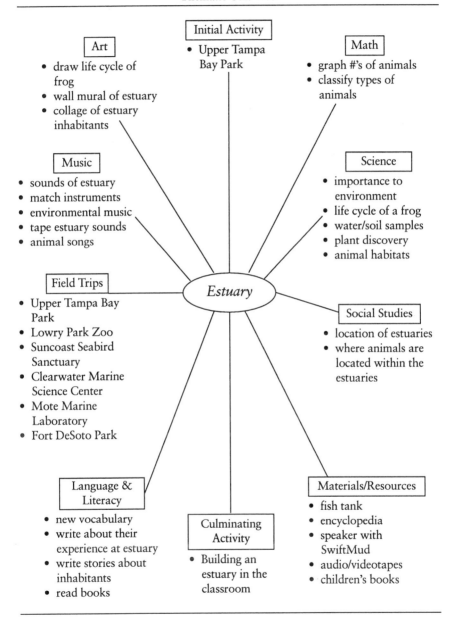

Curran, L., Hensley, M., Pingley, L., & Fowler, A. (1995). *Estuary thematic web.* Unpublished course project, University of South Florida, Tampa.

328 *Pamela O. Fleege*

photographs could be taken or the children could draw or write about what they have done.

The estuary unit would include social science concepts in the areas of both geography and economics. Geography concepts of location and land forms could be assessed through pictures and stories about what estuaries look like. The economics concept of services could be assessed through written, audio, or video accounts of occupational interviews.

Science content could also be assessed through life cycle drawings, written descriptions of animal habitats, and reflection journals that children have kept that include their understandings, conclusions, and questions about the projects. This content lends itself to checklists, rating scales, anecdotal records, and work samples.

In the area of art the teacher might assess the children's representational drawing or ability to use new materials. Using the sounds recorded in the estuary the children could select and demonstrate instruments that approximate the sounds found in the environment. The instruments could also be used to creatively express the "mood" the children associated with the estuary. Locomotion activities such as imitating the movement of the animals studied could be added to the music. All of these could be documented through the use of audio- and videotape as well as photographs.

In an integrated curriculum, the opportunities to assess children are endless. The only limitations are the teacher's imagination and the supplies available such as film and audio- and videotapes. In any case, appropriate assessment can be implemented in *every* classroom and does not require elaborate or expensive materials.

Developing an Assessment Plan

This section focuses on developing an assessment plan beyond the individual classroom, for a grade level, center, or school. The key process involved in developing an assessment plan is decision making. Whether an individual teacher or a group of professionals is beginning an assessment plan, the process is still the same. Although both individuals and groups will go through the same steps, negotiation is required when developing the project as a group.

At the beginning, group members should hold discussions to answer the following questions:

1. What is considered typical development for the age level we teach?
2. What do we want the children to know and be able to do when they leave our program or grade level?
3. What will be assessed in each of the developmental domains? content areas?
4. What methods will we use to assess and document progress?

Each person will have personal ideas about what is considered typical development for the age level he or she teaches. As an important part of the assessment plan, the group needs to reach a consensus about what is typical for children across all developmental domains so that all group members hold the same level of expectations. Child development books as well as publications such as *Curriculum and Evaluation Standards for School Mathematics* (National Council of Teachers of Mathematics, 1989) can be used to help spark and clarify the content of these discussions.

Next, what the group wants children to know and be able to do when they leave the program should be discussed and decided. This helps the individual teacher select which experiences he or she wants to offer, and enhances the integration of these experiences across the entire program. However, the teacher must never lose sight of the fact that each child has a unique rate of knowledge and skill development. Children are rarely at the same point at the same time, and individual children will also vary in their rates of development from one domain to another. Rather than worrying about children acquiring specific knowledge or skills at a given time, teachers should focus instead on whether the children's rate of progression in any given content area is within an acceptable range as outlined in the group's assessment plan.

This means that the group will have to make decisions about what will be assessed in each domain and content area. A framework for assessment should be developed, but room should be left for learning that occurs as the "teachable moment" arises. No teacher can know ahead of time all things that can and will be assessed; teachers who feel that they can make all their assessment decisions ahead of time probably have a very rigid curriculum that is not based on children's needs or interests.

Deciding what specific methods will be used to assess and document children's progress should be determined by each individual teacher.

This decision should be made based on the needs and abilities of the children, the content to be assessed, and the teacher's level of comfort with a particular method. For example, a teacher's assessment plan is doomed if it relies on audiotapes as a large portion of the assessment package and the children being assessed are preverbal.

Resources that might be helpful when planning what to assess and how to assess would include Charlesworth and Lind's (1995) *Math and Science for Young Children*, Genishi and Dyson's (1984) *Language Assessment in the Early Years*, Ostlund's (1992) *Science Process Skills: Assessing Hands-on Student Performance*, Gullo's (1994) *Understanding Assessment and Evaluation in Early Childhood Education*, Grace and Shores' (1990) *The Portfolio and Its Use*, MacDonald's *Portfolio and its use, Book II* (1996), Wortham's (1996) *The Integrated Classroom*, and Bredekamp and Rosegrant's (1995) *Reaching Potentials: Transforming Early Childhood Curriculum and Assessment*.

The Charlesworth and Lind (1995) text has chapters on mathematics and science concepts at both the preschool and primary levels. All chapters include activities and assessment tasks. The text also has a math assessment appendix.

Literacy development is discussed in-depth in the Genishi and Dyson (1984) book. This text is filled with numerous oral and written language samples. The authors also discuss and give illustrations of appropriate assessment techniques.

In early childhood classrooms science process skills are a large part of the curriculum. They are taught but not to the exclusion of content. Assessing science process skills is easy when using Ostlund's (1992) book. The book covers assessment of the process skills through the intermediate grades. Early childhood educators would be interested in the level one and some of the level two assessments.

Gullo's (1994) book discusses formal and informal assessment and the role it plays in an early childhood classroom. Both the Gullo and Grace and Shores (1990) books give an overview of standardized instruments currently available. In addition, the Grace and Shores and MacDonald texts center on portfolio assessment at the preschool and kindergarten levels (Grace and Shores) and primary (MacDonald).

Volume 2 of Bredekamp and Rosegrant's *Reaching Potentials* looks closely at individual content areas and provides detailed information about appropriate content. Wortham's (1996) book takes an encompassing look at integrating assessment and curriculum with diverse populations. This book is a good resource for a more expanded discussion of integration. These are only a few of the many resources that are available to those beginning an assessment project.

Summary

Alternative methods of assessment have come into greater use as a reaction to the influence of standardized testing, as an outgrowth of the constructivist perspective in early childhood education, as a means of implementing developmentally appropriate practices in classrooms, and as an avenue for integrating assessment with curriculum. Based on these reactions, the field of early childhood education advocates assessing young children through observation and interview. These methods can be formal or informal, but must be systematic and ongoing.

Documentation strategies that are appropriate for recording the observations and interviews conducted with children would include checklists, rating scales, photographs, audiotapes, videotapes, work samples, anecdotal records, running records, time sampling, and event sampling. Choosing a documentation method appropriate for an individual child depends on several factors. One would need to think about the characteristics of the child, the developmental domain to be assessed, and the teacher's level of comfort and expertise with a particular method. An assessment plan should be individually tailored to each child.

As the assessment snapshots demonstrate, the effective use of alternative assessment with young children requires educators to be knowledgeable about child development, assessment techniques and strategies, and the steps needed in the planning and implementation process. Regardless of whether one teacher or a group engages in the assessment process, the steps are the same. One needs to answer the following questions: (1) What is considered typical development for the age level I teach? (2) What do I want the children to know and be able to do when they leave my classroom(program)? (3) What will be assessed in each developmental domain and content area? (4) What methods will I use to assess and document the progress of each child? Although alternative assessment may demand a greater time investment, it provides rich benefits for teachers, families, and children.

References

Beaty, J.J. (1986). *Observing development of the young child.* Columbus, OH: Merrill.

Bredekamp, S. (1987). *Developmentally appropriate practice in early childhood programs serving children from birth through age 8.* Washington, DC: National Association for the Education of Young Children.

Bredekamp, S., & Rosegrant, T. (1992). *Reaching potentials: Appropriate curriculum and assessment for young children* (Vol. 1). Washington, DC: National Association for the Education of Young Children.

Bredekamp S., & Rosegrant, T. (1995). *Reaching potentials: Transforming early childhood curriculum and assessment* (Vol. 2). Washington, DC: National Association for the Education of Young Children.

Charlesworth, R., Fleege, P.O., & Weitman, C. (1994). Research on the effects of group standardized testing on instruction, pupils, and teachers: New directions for policy. *Early Education and Development, 5* (3), 195–212.

Charlesworth, R., & Lind, K.K. (1995). *Math and science for young children* (2nd ed.). Albany, NY: Delmar.

Fleege, P.O., Charlesworth, R., Burts, D.C., & Hart, C.H. (1992). Stress begins in kindergarten: A look at behavior during standardized testing. *Journal of Research in Childhood Education, 7* (1), 20–26.

Gardner, H. (1983). *Frames of mind.* New York: Basic Books.

Genishi, C., & Dyson, A.H. (1984). *Language assessment in the early years.* Norwood, NJ: Ablex.

Gooding, K. (1994, April). *Teaching to the test: The influence of alternative modes of assessment on teachers' instructional strategies.* Paper presented at the meeting of the American Educational Research Association, New Orleans, LA.

Goodman, Y.M. (1985). Kidwatching: Observing children in the classroom. In A. Jaggar & M.T. Smith-Burke (Eds.), *Observing the language learner.* Newark, DE: International Reading Association & National Council of Teachers of English.

Grace, C., & Shores, E.F. (1990). *The portfolio and its use.* Little Rock, AR: Southern Early Childhood Association.

Grady, E. (1992). *The portfolio approach to assessment.* Bloomington, IL: Phi Delta Kappa.

Gullo, D.F. (1994). *Understanding assessment and evaluation in early childhood education.* New York: Teachers College Press.

Hipps, J. (1993, April). *Trustworthiness and authenticity: Alternate ways to judge authentic assessments.* Paper presented at the meeting of the American Educational Research Association, Atlanta, GA.

Joyner, J.M. (1994). Implementing the professional standards for teaching mathematics: Linking teaching, learning, and assessment. *Arithmetic Teacher*, 41, 550–52.

Krechevsky, M., & Gardner, H. (1990). The emergence and nurturance of multiple intelligences: The Project Spectrum approach. In M.J.A. Howe (Ed.), *Encouraging the development of exceptional skills and talents.* Leicester, Eng.: British Psychological Society.

MacDonald, S. (1996). *Portfolio and its use: Book II.* Little Rock, AR: Southern Early Childhood Association.

National Council of Teachers of Mathematics. (1989). *Curriculum and evaluation standards for school mathematics.* Reston, VA: Author.

Neuman, D. (1993). Alternative assessment: Promises and pitfalls. In C.C. Kuhlthau, M.E. Goodin, & M.J. McNally (Eds.), *School library media annual* (pp. 13–21). Littleton, CO: Libraries Unlimited.

Ostlund, K.L. (1992). *Science process skills: Assessing hands-on student performance.* Menlo Park, CA: Addison-Wesley.

Perrone, V. (1991). On standardized testing: A position paper for the Association for Childhood Educational International (ACEI). *Childhood Education, 67* (3), 131–42

Vygotsky, L. (1962). *Thought and language.* Cambridge, MA: MIT.

Wadsworth, B.J. (1989). *Piaget's theory of cognitive and affective development* (4th ed.). New York: Longman.

Wiggins, G. (1989, May). A true test: Toward more authentic and equitable assessment. *Phi Delta Kappan*, 703–13.

Wolf, D.J., Bixby, J., Glenn, J., III, & Gardner, H. (1991). To use their minds well: Investigating new forms of student assessment. In G. Grant (Ed.), *Review of educational research* (pp. 31–74). Washington, DC: American Educational Research Association.

Wortham, S.C. (1996). *The integrated classroom: The assessment-curriculum link in early childhood education.* Englewood Cliffs, NJ: Merrill.

CHAPTER THIRTEEN

The Integrated Curriculum and Students with Disabilities

DONNA E. DUGGER-WADSWORTH

As regular early childhood education (ECE) programs reexamine their theoretical basis and program models, early childhood special education (ECSE) is exploring how children's needs can be met within full inclusion experiences and integrated environments. Full inclusion is defined as placing a student with special needs in a child's natural educational setting and providing the necessary support for this child to benefit from this placement. At the root of these explorations are questions of whether the two fields can coexist in the same classroom, and how the needs of all children can be appropriately met. Bredekamp (1993b) points out that quite possibly as much diversity exists within the individual fields of ECE and ECSE as differences that might be attributed to two fields separately. A continuum of philosophical or pedagogical perspectives could be constructed for both fields. Brede-kamp (1993b) suggests that differences within each field and similarities between fields should be used to encourage the formation of partner-ships and collaborative efforts in implementation of developmentally appropriate practices through an integrated curriculum for all children.

The developmentally appropriate practices as suggested in the position statement of National Association for the Education of Young

Children (NAEYC) (Bredekamp, 1987) were based on two major dimensions: age appropriate and individually appropriate. This position was predicated on the principle that learning environments, teaching practices, and other aspects of the early childhood program should reflect the typical developmental expectations of children at various ages and stages. At the same time, in or to be developmentally appropriate the early childhood program must also make modifications and accommodations for the diversity that might exist within individual children. As suggested in Krogh's chapter in this volume, developmentally appropriate practices reflect a constructivist, interactive approach to learning and teaching, along with emphasis on play and active, child-initiated learning.

The Division for Early Childhood of the Council for Exceptional Children (DEC) outlined its support of developmentally appropriate practices (DAP) and their basic philosophical assumptions for an effective early education and early intervention for young children with special needs in its position paper on personnel standards for early education (1993). The assumptions recognized the uniqueness of early childhood development, the significant role of families, the importance of developmentally and individually appropriate practices, the preference for inclusion settings, the importance of cross-cultural competence, and collaborative planning and implementation. These were later endorsed by NAEYC and the Association of Teacher Educators.

Despite this apparent unification among fields some controversy remains (Bredekamp, 1993b). The issues seem to arise primarily from misunderstanding. For example, some of the issues center on whether DAP is a rigid set of curriculum standards, emphasizes only child-initiated learning experiences, and prohibits formal instruction and whether individualized goals and objectives are compatible with the practices (Carta et al., 1991). Recent research efforts have eliminated the validity of these areas of disagreement (Carta et al., 1991; Burton et al., 1992). While the early childhood environment that reflects developmentally appropriate practices will encourage children to explore their interests through play some children may require more purposeful, carefully structured activities and materials along with systematic monitoring to effectively progress. These issues have received more detailed attention in the revised DAP guidelines (Bredekamp & Copple, 1997).

The Conceptual and Empirical Basis for DAP in ECSE

With the prominence given full inclusion and integration of children with disabilities into regular early childhood programs, it would seem only natural that an emphasis would be placed on understanding the differing points of view (i.e., DAP versus ECSE).

DAP	*ECSE*
Individualization	Individualization
Constructivist developmental philosophy	Behavioral and education psychology theories of learning as philosophical base
Developmentally appropriate	Developmentally appropriate
Encourages family involvement	Emphasis on more family involvement
Encourages assessment	Emphasis on more intense, precise, and frequent assessment
Uses more child-initiated learning	Uses more direct instruction when needed

The conceptual bases for DAP curriculum guidelines and ECSE are quite similar. For example, both support a broad-based curriculum to include children's varying interests and skills. According to DAP, children are motivated to learn by their interests and curiosity. DAP and ECSE each recognizes the importance of individualization. Children are individual and vary in their development and learning. The definition and guidelines of full inclusion for each student must be individualized within the child's individualized education plan (IEP) or individualized family service plan (IFSP).

Children with or without disabilities learn best when their physical and psychological needs are satisfied. The recent emphasis on "people first" language and accompanying attitudes and behavior provide additional support to the concept that children with disabilities are children first with needs common to all children.

The theoretical framework of DAP is based on developmental and constructivist approaches to learning along with the interactive process between teaching and learning (discussed with greater detail in the chapter by Krogh in this volume). While the theoretical framework of

ECSE has been primarily based on behavioral and educational psychology theories of learning with the emphasis on remediation of deficit areas and prevention of future difficulties (Fox et al., 1994), there is a trend away from this to building from strengths.

The focus on the interactive process within DAP contributes to and facilitates the integration of children with special needs into an inclusive program (Carlson & Udell, 1992). This interactive process is further enhanced by children's experiences and interactions with people and their environment. Children learn through their social relationships with peers and adults. The opportunity to observe and interact with age-appropriate peers can provide significant benefits to children with disabilities (Odom & McEvoy, 1990). The value of this increased social competence with peers is also shown in the studies of Guralnick (1989, 1990). Direct benefits of these implementations of DAP were noted in development of communication, prosocial behavior, and social/cognitive skills. This is congruent with Vygotsky's view of scaffolding by more advanced peers.

In a developmentally appropriate classroom children are said to learn through a process of awareness, exploration, inquiry, and utilization that is recurrent. As Krogh states in her chapter, children benefit the most from learning experiences that are concrete and relevant in nature. Young children with and without disabilities benefit from the emphasis on active engagement and participation in DAP early childhood programs (Mahoney, Robinson, & Powell, 1992). The DAP curriculum emphasis on more nondirective instructional techniques may not meet the needs of children lacking the requisite skills to participate in the activity. Often disabilities prevent the child from spontaneously engaging and learning from his or her environment (Carta et al., 1991). Some children with disabilities may require varying degrees of teacher support to learn and benefit from these types of play/learning experiences.

Applying the Principles of Developmentally Appropriate Assessment to ECSE for an Inclusive Curriculum

In the previous chapter Fleege describes assessment as an ongoing process for the teacher to follow in order to learn what children know and do, and how they do it. Assessment is used to make decisions about children's learning and should be an integral part of the curriculum. It should be authentic or reflective of normal activities of young children. For ECSE teachers' assessment must also guide them in planning for students' next learning experiences, based on their individual developmental needs.

The principles of DAP Assessment for ECSE are as follows:

1. Assessment should be continuous.
2. Assessment should include learning in all domains.
3. Assessment should emphasize a child's strengths.
4. Assessment should acknowledge individual diversities.
5. Assessment should include families.
6. Assessment is conducted in natural situations and environments.

While these principles are easily applied to ECSE programs, the analysis and assessment of a child's strengths and weaknesses and determination of skills needed within many DAP programs seem to lack the intensity, precision, and frequency needed for a child with disabilities (Carta et al., 1991) under the mandates of the Individuals with Disabilities Education Act legislation. Children with disabilities often need specialized team members, such as occupational, physical, or speech therapists to assist with the assessment process (Cavallaro, Haney & Cabello, 1993). This transdisciplinary approach to assessment is necessary for the development of an integrated program for children with special needs.

The assessment process within the classroom should acknowledge individual diversities due to culture, gender, linguistics, socioeconomic status, learning styles, and rates of learning. Bredekamp (1993b) states that too often in the past, early childhood programs in the United States have placed children in groups according to their chronological ages. Due to this type of grouping teachers have tended to use normative data to determine a child's desired outcomes and learning needs. Bredekamp suggests this perspective and approach to teaching is particularly limited now with the increasingly diverse population. The age-appropriate skill may not be functionally significant for the child with disabilities.

Families and school personnel need to be actively involved from the beginning in the assessment process and designing the IEP or IFSP. Early childhood special education best practices call for the inclusion of parents in forming the assessment plan, identifying areas of concern, and sharing observations and information (Wadsworth, Knight, & Balser, 1993).

Assessment is collected in natural situations and environments for the child and uses a variety of methodologies and materials. Both informal and formal assessment procedures such as observations, interviews, time sampling, event sampling, checklists, and portfolios of children's work as also suggested in Fleege's chapter are appropriate within ECSE. Early childhood special educators must continue to look at their assessment practices to make them more comprehensive, versatile, focused, and precise. They must include more detailed descriptions of children's development, observe their needs in various environments, be aware of their interests, recognize influences in their social and physical environment, and identify interaction patterns (Wolery, Strain, & Bailey, (1992).

Integrating and Modifying DAP
for an ECSE Inclusive Curriculum

The major tasks of early childhood regular education teachers and those of early childhood special education teachers are both similar and different. According to Wolery (1991) *major tasks of all early childhood teachers* are to determine the curriculum content, match individual needs and abilities to curriculum content, manipulate the environment to facilitate learning, and ensure the skills learned are generalized. The process of implementing these major tasks and resolving the related issues is complicated by the introduction of personnel from disciplines other than education with completely different knowledge bases and theoretical perspectives. In order to better perform the four instructional tasks outlined by Wolery (1991) professionals will need a collaborative spirit that calls for a desire to learn about new fields, role release, and provision of in-service time. This collaboration also calls for reference to the databases of interdisciplinary fields, early childhood education, and early childhood special education in order to effectively expand the developmental appropriate practice guidelines to meet the needs of all children.

Specific Tasks

Specific tasks of early childhood special education teachers, according to Bailey and Wolery (1992), are based on legislative mandates, parental preferences, theoretical perspectives, research, and practical needs of the child and family. The goals are:

1. to support families in achieving their own goals
2. to promote child engagement, independence, and mastery
3. to promote development in key domains
4. to build and support children's social competence
5. to promote the generalized use of skills
6. to provide and prepare for normalized life experiences
7. to prevent the emergence of future problems or disabilities (Bailey & Wolery, 1992, p. 35)

In the development of both individual and family goals in ECSE, Bailey and Wolery (1992) emphasize the importance of developing concrete and relevant goals and objectives that are functional for young children and prepare them for future environments. Wolery, Strain, and Bailey (1992) state the process of setting goals and using goal-driven instruction for children with disabilities should be viewed as within the DAP guidelines continuum and critical to the progress of these children.

For example, McDonnell and Hardman (1988) suggested ECSE best practices should include integration with nonhandicapped peers and be comprehensive from assessment to programming and service coordination. Services should be outcome-based and plan for both present and future needs.

Wolery, Strain, and Bailey (1992) point out the similarities in ECE and ECSE. They suggest that DAP can be applied to children with disabilities, but the children will not receive maximum benefits unless modifications and expansions are made. The DAP guidelines call for a focus on the whole child—all developmental domains as required by ECSE. However, a program based on the guidelines alone would be inadequate in meeting the needs of many children with disabilities. For example, simply placing children with and without disabilities in the same setting will not ensure a successful, socially integrated, inclusive program where all children's socioemotional skills are enhanced (Cavallaro, Haney, & Cabello, 1993).

When Finger (1992) interviewed parents and teachers as to what they felt the intervention outcomes should be for children with disabilities, the suggestions were very similar to what DAP guidelines recommend for moral and intellectual autonomy. Specifically, they said children should be able to:

> develop as "normally" as possible by working toward their functional potentials; move into the least restrictive environment—possibly an integrated or mainstreamed class setting—to enable them to have a "regular" education along with whatever special education would be necessary; make choices (decisions) independently; regulate their own behavior within their environments; and solve some of their own problems (Finger, 1992, p. 171).

Individualization

Individualizing a child's educational program has long been a tenet of quality education and is a commonality between DAP and ECSE. This individualization should be broad-based to encourage the child's interests and skills. For the child with disabilities the teacher may need to break down tasks into smaller steps, pair progression with reinforcers, provide flexible pacing in the presentation of materials, adjust daily schedules, increase structure for an activity, or prepare for transitions (Dodge, 1993).

Cavallaro, Haney, and Cabello (1993) suggest additional strategies for individualization within an integrated inclusive classroom setting. The strategies seem to meet the criteria of both DAP and ECSE. They describe most of these strategies as building on developmental opportunities and facilitating independence. Suggestions for individualizing for various disabilities are included in table 13.1. These recommendations should not be construed as an intervention recipe for every child with these disabilities.

The construct of age-appropriate practice has often been ignored in ECSE programming. The normative data have been used primarily to provide benchmarks for a child's delay and to target goals and objectives. Children with disabilities need to be placed in environments that are age-appropriate. Research has shown that both age-appropriate placement and selection of age-appropriate materials are beneficial to the social/cognitive development of children (Guralnick, 1990).

TABLE 13.1
Guidelines for Assisting Children with Specific Disabilities

Children with language delays
- provide good language models
- use simple, concrete language and limit direction to one and two steps
- when a child speaks, expand on what the child says (for example, when the child says, "Blue ball," the teacher could respond "You have a blue ball")
- provide experiences that give input from more than one sense
- encourage children to initiate communication, ask for assistance, request objects
- avoid anticipating what a child is attempting to say
- have hearing evaluated

Children with physical disabilities
- provide adequate physical space in the classroom to accommodate a child using wheelchair, crutches, and/or walker
- consult with parents and medical personnel about child's limitations in strength and stamina
- provide orientation for all children regarding adaptive equipment safety issues, such as the handling of a wheelchair
- ask parents about adaptive equipment the child may need to function more independently
- plan activities that encourage use of all parts of the body
- place toys and equipment in accessible locations
- consult with parents and appropriate health care personnel regarding medical treatments that may need to be incorporated into daily schedule (such as breathing treatments)
- develop an emergency care plan file for medically fragile children
- consult with physical therapist and occupational therapist regarding appropriate positioning and transporting

Children with developmental/cognitive delays
- plan shorter activities, vary pace, or change tasks frequently for children with limited attention span
- be prepared to provide level of prompts needed to succeed
- present limited number of choices in an activity
- allow children adequate time to respond
- present directions simply and sequentially
- simplify or break down tasks as needed
- provide frequent, meaningful, positive reinforcement
- structure and prepare students for transitions
- provide appropriate seating arrangements to facilitate a child's listening and/or watching

Children with sensory impairments (hearing and visual)
- provide appropriate seating arrangement to facilitate a child's listening and/or watching

TABLE 13.1 *(continued)*
Guidelines for Assisting Children with Specific Disabilities

- provide prompts as necessary
- interact with hearing impaired children face to face in areas that are well lighted and at eye level
- be willing to repeat words, phrases, and sentences as needed
- demonstrate/model activities or tasks for the hearing impaired
- include more hands-on physical guidance with the visually impaired
- provide both hearing and visually impaired with a hearing and/or sighted peer as a partner in the classroom
- provide visually and hearing impaired students with orientation and mobility training in safely moving around the classroom and school environment

---

Ways of integrating

Some ways of integrating learning experiences, assuring age-appropriate materials and instruction, have been pointed out by Krogh in her chapter; specifically, immersion and embedding instruction can easily be modified to include the common practices of thematic teaching, activity-based instruction, generalization, cooperative learning, and peer tutoring already used in ECSE. Children with disabilities also need to be engaged in learning experiences that are meaningful to them, make sense, and facilitate conceptual development. Fox and Hanline (1993) explored the technique of embedding systematic skill instruction for children with disabilities within the ongoing activities of a DAP early childhood program. The children in the study learned the skills targeted for intervention through naturalistic teaching procedures and generalized them to another setting and person. While the research was limited, there seems to be considerable relevance to embedding instruction in naturalistic settings. Another principle of developmentally appropriate early childhood education is the involvement of all stakeholders in sharing information and responsibility.

The principle of involving the family through sharing of information and responsibility is supported and encouraged in both DAP and ECSE. As with the assessment process, the provision for family inclusion in ECSE is both more involved and intense (Bredekamp, 1993b). ECSE programs focus on enabling and empowering families as their needs dictate. DAP calls for ongoing communication and sharing of information between teachers and families. Families' rights and responsibilities in participating in decisions regarding child care and education are recognized by both.

With ECSE the involvement of families via sharing information and responsibilities are not recommendations but rather legal mandates. They also reflect the prevailing view of best practice in ECSE (DEC Task Force on Recommended Practices, 1993; McDonnell & Hardman, 1988; Wolery, Strain, & Bailey, 1992). Families with children from infancy through age 2 participating in ECSE are the driving force of the individualized family service plan (Dunst, Trivette, & Deal, 1988). Parents and families of children with disabilities above the age of 2 years are required to be included in their child's individualized education plan (IDEA, 1990).

Beginning with the initial contact, educators need to be cognizant of the family's concerns and interests. An ongoing, sensitive, and positive communication effort will help establish a harmonious balance and minimize differences on selection of content and practices for the IEP (Knight & Wadsworth, 1993).

There are times when planned lessons may not be as effective as taking advantage of natural opportunities for incidental instruction. This view is supported by both DAP and ECSE. Bailey and McWilliam (1990) cite several studies where naturalistic teaching resulted in greater skill generalization and was equally effective in teaching skills to children with and without disabilities. Fox and Hanline (1993) describe naturalistic teaching as an approach that occurs in the natural environment, is brief and recurrent over a period of hours and days, is child-initiated, and uses natural consequences. The research of Fox and Hanline (1993) discussed in the embedded instruction section also supported the use of naturalistic teaching procedures for a variety of skills with children who are disabled. Brown, Ragland, & Bishop (1989) suggests the use of incidental teaching episodes throughout the school day to provide additional opportunities for children to interact with peers and facilitate language development. Problems with children's lack of attention and motivation can be circumvented by using the brief teaching episodes that occur when children are interested in a material, activity, or other children, as the following vignette illustrates.

Bobby, a child without special needs, is playing at the sand table during choice time. Becky, another child with special needs, approaches and watches Bobby play. He decides to bury the truck under the sand and declares that the truck has disappeared. At this point the teacher, who has been observing from a close distance, can use this opportunity to emphasize object permanence by first having Bobby find the truck and then repeat the hiding process. At this point in time the teacher may want to invite Becky to look for the truck. When she finds the truck the teacher will want to reinforce her efforts with the appropriate language. For example, "That's great Becky! You found the truck. Can you hide it from Bobby?" This activity not only encourages the development of the concept of object permanence, but also social turn taking.

Cultural, socioeconomic, gender, ability, and linguistic diversity are factors that influence the way young children are taught and learn. Children do not enter early childhood programs without an awareness of diversity. Their beliefs are often constructed from personal experiences, exposure to adults' behaviors and attitudes, and self-constructed theories (Derman-Sparks, 1992). The diversity issue is also addressed through the emphasis on individualism in both fields. Teachers should use the principles of DAP and modify them to be individually appropriate for their situations.

Derman-Sparks (1992) suggests goals of constructing a competent self-identity, fostering appropriate interactions among children with diversities, encouraging critical thinking about biases, and developing feelings of pride and advocacy for diversity as a basis for DAP early childhood multicultural curriculum. Children may also need individualized teaching to address their differences in learning styles and behaviors. Teachers in both ECE and ECSE programs need to understand their own cultures and promote a positive understanding of the diversities represented in their classrooms (Morrison, 1995). The total curriculum should reflect an antibias, multicultural approach and include individualized variations for each new group of children in a program. Dodge & Colker (1992) and Dodge (1993) interprets the DAP guidelines as calling for respect and value for differences among children, whether cultural, economic, ethnic, ability, or gender-related.

Child-Initiated Learning

While child-initiated learning may be of preference within DAP and certainly fosters independence it should not be viewed as the only approach to implementation of DAP (Bredekamp, 1993a). Interactive teaching is described "as a continuum of possible teaching behaviors from non-directive (withholding attention, acknowledging) to directive (more intrusive), with the mediating behaviors of facilitating, supporting and scaffolding in the middle" (Bredekamp, 1993b, p. 267). All of these behaviors, from ignoring to actively intruding, may be appropriate given the individual child's needs and the situation. The danger of the continuum lies in the possibility of ECE teachers missing the opportunity to use direct intervention and ECSE teachers intervening too quickly.

DAP does not call for the teacher to simply stand back and let children construct knowledge without providing guidance or support for building that knowledge (Johnson & Johnson, 1992). Charlesworth, Hart, Burts, and Dewolf (1993) suggest that Vygotsky's theory provides a foundation for adults to guide the provisions of support for children's knowledge search through scaffolding within his construct of the zone of proximal development. This construct also seems to tie the DAP guidelines and the needs of ECSE students together. The teacher is there as needed to lend support and provide appropriate scaffolding to facilitate learning.

Further, Bailey and McWilliam (1990) state that instructional strategies for teaching young children with disabilities should be effective, efficient, functional, and normalized. Effectiveness in teaching strategies facilitates skill acquisition while efficiency in strategies makes the best use of instructional time. Functional teaching strategies refer to efforts to foster generalization of skills learned across people, settings, and materials. Normalization strategies use the least intrusive and most natural techniques. All four of these characteristics can be fit within the interactive teaching continuum suggested by Bredekamp (1993a). Carta et al. (1991) suggest that teachers of children with disabilities frequently have to teach their students how to participate in free-choice activities.

Effectiveness may involve using modeling of adults and children without disabilities within the natural environment to teach children (e.g., teaching appropriate table manners during pretend play in the housekeeping center). When children learn skills in a natural setting they are more likely to generalize them. Efficiency may be accomplished through the use of naturalistic teaching opportunities or including skill instruction and practice across domains (e.g., using counting in completing therapy exercises). Normalization describes strategies planned to include children with disabilities in a general education setting. It might be accomplished by taking a child out of wheelchair during a large-group activity and having a peer/buddy provide the necessary physical support for sitting. Functional instructional strategies involve selecting goals and objectives that children can use in their natural environment across people, settings, and materials. For example, children with special needs can be provided opportunities to make choices in centers, the cafeteria, the home, and the community.

ECSE programs must include more opportunities for children to develop independent work skills, make choices, problem solve, participate in large-group activities, and be less teacher-directed (Fowler, Schwartz, & Atwater, 1991). The study of Mahoney, O'Sullivan, and Fors (1989) seems to indicate an overdependence in ECSE on the use of structured activities instead of play and premature focus on academics. Developmentally appropriate decisions must be made not only about curriculum content, but about teaching strategies (Finger, 1992). The child-initiated learning issue is best addressed when teachers of inclusive classrooms following an integrative curriculum are able to determine and implement the best instructional format for a child (Sainato & Lyon, 1989).

Learning experiences may be horizontal or vertical in nature. Balancing types of experiences becomes a challenge for the teacher of children with disabilities in a DAP inclusive classroom. A conflict would seem to exist between ECSE's goal of encouraging children to acquire basic skills as early as possible to prevent additional delay in achieving more complex skills and DAP's admonition to avoid artificial acceleration. The DAP intent seems to be allowing children to develop normally, and expanding learning through horizontal enrichment and connections of experiences to concepts on a day-to-day basis (Johnson & Johnson, 1992).

The emphasis on horizontal learning experiences also seems to be in conflict with ECSE's effort to assess and prepare children for their next learning environment. The justification for inclusion of vertical learning experiences in ECSE seems to come from the focus on selection of outcomes that are concrete and relevant to the child along with the legal mandate to do transition planning. The curriculum could then include prerequisite and transition objectives as social skills, basic academic skills, and support skills for the child to succeed in his or her next environment (Sainato & Lyon, 1989). Children with disabilities frequently need both the opportunities to generalize, offered through horizontal learning experiences, and the direction and intervention of vertical experiences to accelerate their developmental progress beyond that which would occur naturally (Odom & McEvoy, 1990). The responsibility for deciding whether to provide horizontal and/or vertical learning experiences for the child with disabilities lies with the teacher and the family. The ECSE and the family must also decide to what degree process orientation will be emphasized.

Process Orientation

The implementing of process orientation within DAP lends support to the emphasis within ECSE on function rather than form. Special education curriculum best practices focus on the importance of children understanding the process and being able to perform the function rather than dwelling on the mastery of a specific form. For example, young children can master the concept of stacking without ever building a tower of ten one-inch blocks or duplicating a bridge pattern.

Learning experiences occur within all types of environments. Providing an inclusive, supportive environment for students with special needs that is also developmentally appropriate requires considerable planning. Dodge (1993) suggests the teacher must build an environment that promotes a sense of trust and belonging, facilitates cooperative learning experiences, enhances children's independence, and encourages engagement and perseverance. The teacher also must consider the issues of accessibility, availability, and variability of activities and materials along with safety of the environment (Winter, Bell, & Dempsy, 1994).

Accessibility refers to the child's ability to physically enter all desired parts of the learning environment. The teacher will need to consider a child's developmental level, mobility, range of vision, and reach potential when organizing the learning environment. Accommodations for accessibility may include having ramps to the playground or other areas of the school, wider doors, and larger entrances into classroom centers. The lowering of shelves, cabinets, and sinks in the classroom and restroom will specifically foster independence. For example, toys placed at floor level or table level are more easily viewed and removed. This easy access will also minimize safety problems and encourage the possibility of integrative play. Some examples of accessibility include ramps to playgrounds; hand-holds and safety belts on equipment for support; wide doors; lowered shelving, cabinets, sinks, and water fountains; selection of toys varying in size and weight; selection of toys that respond to minimal tactile pressure; and wider entrances to center areas.

Activities in the inclusive classroom must provide equal opportunities for all students to participate according to their individual interests. This does not mean that all potential special needs must be addressed in advance. Rather, the teacher will want to survey the types of experiences and activities available to the majority of the children in the program. Next, the teacher must ensure that these experiences are also available to the children with disabilities in his or her classroom. These activities, whether in dramatic play, construction, games with rules, or sensorimotor manipulation, should provide children a balance of successful and challenging experiences (Winter, Bell, & Dempsey, 1994).

Variability within the inclusive classroom environment refers to providing opportunities for choices. Children with and without disabilities need to increase their skills in making independent decisions and the accompanying responsive actions. For example, the decision to paint in the art center might require the responses of putting on a smock, acquiring a brush, selecting a color, and manipulating the brush for painting. While children with disabilities may require a more gradual introduction to variables and changes in their environment, they should not be deprived of the opportunities to deal with these typical experiences. Duplication of the rigid structure characteristic of a self-contained special education classroom in an inclusive setting would limit the child's opportunity to learn about both accommodation and assimilation. Each child's developmental level, chronological age, and individual needs should be considered in order to create a safe environment.

Additional strategies to consider in structuring the environment for children with disabilities include selecting materials to facilitate engagement and interaction. These materials should be attractive, appropriate to a wide range of abilities, and require some child engagement. They might include the following:

- Battery operated toys that require a switch to activate, such as animals, vehicles, radios
- Construction toys, such as wooden, lego, or bristle blocks, dominoes, or nesting objects
- Books that make noises when pages are pressed or turned, have pull tabs to move objects, or are textured
- Stuffed animals and dolls that make sounds or have moving parts
- Musical instruments
- Gross motor equipment, such as tunnel, box, ball, wagon, rocking boat, tricycle
- Fine motor equipment, such as paint and brushes, clay, puzzles, beads
- Dramatic play articles, such as clothes, hats, purses, suitcases, puppets

Structuring activities to promote interaction, provide choices, maintain appropriate adult proximity, and facilitate peer proximity are also beneficial (Cavallaro, Haney & Cabello, 1993). Appropriate adult proximity does not require constant "shadowing" of the child, but an ongoing awareness of the activity and when to intervene. Environmental modifications for an activity and intervention procedures should be the least intrusive and most natural (Bailey & McWilliam, 1990). Effective environmental planning that addresses the constructs of accessibility, availability of activities, variety, and safety will also likely increase the generalization of skills, enhance ability to problem solve, and create a more functional curriculum.

Adapting Traditional ECSE Techniques to an Inclusive DAP Early Childhood Program

Behavioral Approaches

Behaviorism or behavioral analysis, a frequently used ECSE classroom management technique, and DAP must be evaluated as to their compatibility in the classroom. The use of behaviorism in ECSE has been unfairly criticized (Strain et al., 1992). The operant behavior model does not have to be deterministic. Behaviorism allows for choices and variations in individual behavior. While initially there may be more emphasis on external control, the ultimate goal is the child's responding to natural reinforcers and intrinsic motivation. Carefully and appropriately selected positive reinforcers should reflect the child's preferred interests, likes, and activities (Alberto & Troutman, 1990). The scope of behaviorism is not limited to behavior problems, but can be applied to developmental problems, decision-making skills, academic competence, social interaction and school survival skills, as well as facilitate increased independence, self-management, and peer monitoring. Some behavioral strategies are observing what happens before an event or behavior; determining the targeted behavior; analyzing the child's needs to learn the task (task analysis, prompts, cues, special materials); selecting meaningful reinforcers for the child; planning a system of fading reinforcers; and monitoring behavior maintenance, self-motivation, and self-monitoring.

Children with disabilities often require prompting strategies such as visual, verbal, modeling, or physical guidance to master a developmentally appropriate task. These prompts can be presented in ways consistent with Vygotsky's bridging as suggested earlier by Charlesworth et al. (1993). This stage would be followed by a fading of the prompts and a transition to independent performance of a task.

Landes and Caccamo (1992) suggest that prompts should provide support in varying degrees, from one-on-one interaction with an adult to minimal involvement, but at all times encouraging the child to control events. Within a "best practices" behavior model children have the opportunity to acquire, become fluent, maintain, and generalize skills to many situations. The developmentally appropriate cycle of learning, as explained in chapter 2 in this volume, can easily fit within these four steps of learning in behaviorism and special education. The opportunity to move from teacher-directed to child-initiated, self-instruction and self-management is also present within this understanding of behaviorism.

Accountability and Monitoring

Accountability and monitoring of intervention efforts and their outcomes is not only professionally desirable but mandated by the ECSE legislation. The monitoring and data collection systems of both behaviorism and the techniques of assessment presented earlier in this chapter and in Fleege's chapter can be effectively used to provide the needed information for including meaningful challenges to children and changing the criteria of their outcomes, goals, or objectives. The same information can provide the teacher with guidelines for selection of appropriate materials, preferred learning style, and methodology for children with disabilities. The use of prompting, positive reinforcement, fading, and data collection for children with disabilities has contributed to the assessment, planning, and monitoring of individualized interventions. Strain et al. (1992) cite numerous examples where the behavioral perspective and other theoretical perspectives such as Piagetian and DAP have been used in conjunction with one another successfully. Cavallaro, Haney, and Cabello (1993) incorporate behaviorism and DAP in their strategies of adult mediation and peer mediation. Adult mediation would include the teacher using questions to expand language or encouraging comments to fine tune responses and provide feedback to the child with disabilities. Behaviorism as viewed from a broader perspective can be included within the DAP continuum of individualization, child- and teacher-directed instruction, and classroom management techniques. It would seem shortsighted to exclude the contributions of behaviorism to special education as DAP and ECSE concepts are integrated into an inclusive curriculum.

The ECSE curriculum does not function in isolation. Related services must be integrated to assure an effective DAP curriculum for each student with special needs. The involvement of more than one discipline in teaching children with disabilities is unavoidable. The integrated curriculum that emphasizes the total child cannot be complete or appropriate until it addresses the unique individual needs of a child with disabilities. A broader concept of the team approach will need to include not only teachers and families as members, but physical, occupational, and speech therapists and other related service personnel. Best practices in ECSE also call for the integration of these related services as much as possible into the daily routine.

Putting DAP in Practice within the Inclusive Classroom

The inclusive early childhood classroom should be arranged so independence is encouraged. For example, children should be provided opportunities to select their preferred play center or preferred activity within the center; materials need to be readily accessible for removal and replacement. Play in each of the centers can be an opportunity for development of cognitive, language, social, motor, and self-help skills. In each center, the teacher should provide only the amount of assistance required for the child with disabilities to succeed. If a child has a severe cognitive impairment it may be necessary for the teacher to provide more adult proximity in order to discern subtle communication cues. The skills targeted for children with disabilities to learn must be useful. Intervention strategies in the DAP inclusive classroom should be embedded into the natural routines and child-selected activities. Implementation of incidental and naturalistic teaching procedures will present learning opportunities throughout the day. This repetition within varying situations will be of significant value to the child with disabilities.

Examples of learning opportunities within four centers are described below. In each the teacher will need to be prepared to assist children with disabilities through the modification of materials or by the level of support provided. The four centers could also be designed to reflect themes, such as "Things We Eat," as illustrated in figure 13.1.

In the block/truck center children can construct buildings, roads, and bridges; drive and park cars/trucks; and play with toy people. The play

FIGURE 13.1
Web: Things We Eat

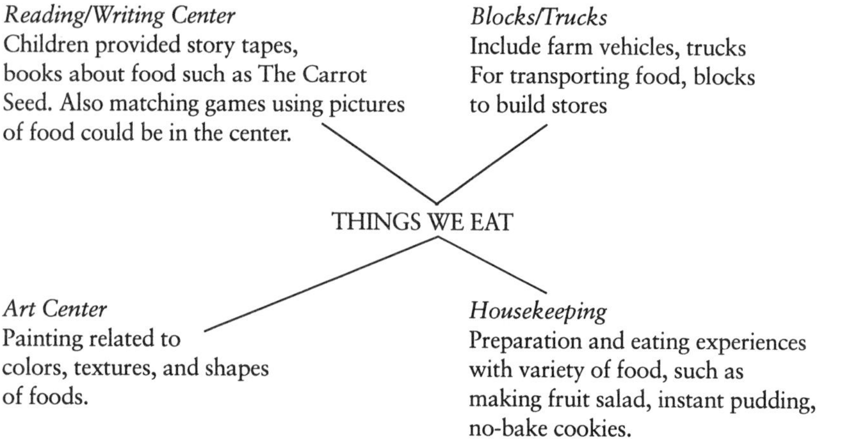

Reading/Writing Center	*Blocks/Trucks*
Children provided story tapes, books about food such as The Carrot Seed. Also matching games using pictures of food could be in the center.	Include farm vehicles, trucks For transporting food, blocks to build stores

THINGS WE EAT

Art Center	*Housekeeping*
Painting related to colors, textures, and shapes of foods.	Preparation and eating experiences with variety of food, such as making fruit salad, instant pudding, no-bake cookies.

activities with these toys can be used to facilitate cognitive/language learning of shapes, names of objects, sizes, directionality, problem solving, sorting, cause and effect, sequencing, and counting. The actual playing activities can encourage independent or group work. The interactions during the play will encourage the expression of needs, requesting, turn taking, and sharing. Potential motor skill development in the block center includes learning to use large and small muscles in grasping, lifting, pushing, and balancing, along with improvement in eye–hand coordination skills. Self-help skills are mastered through participation in the cleanup process.

Block/Truck Center
Sarah is a child with cognitive and motor disabilities. She is watching Bill build a road and service station with the blocks. He invites her to join him and to bring more blocks to his work area from the shelf. Sarah will benefit from following simple directions along with grasping and carrying the blocks to develop fine motor skills and eye–hand coordination. This will also provide the teacher with an opportunity to encourage appropriate creeping.

In the housekeeping center children might play house, feed and care for dolls, or dress up for dramatic play. Cognitively children can learn object names, child care, order, colors, and sizes; problem solve; use symbolic representation; and identify and plan play scenarios. Socioemotional development might be fostered through interaction with other children, role playing, cooperative play, turn taking, sharing materials, and reenacting life experiences through dramatic play. Motor development will be enhanced as small muscles are used in dress up, cooking activities, and play with dolls. The same dress up skills and role playing would foster the development of self-help skills.

Housekeeping Center
Edward has cerebral palsy. While playing with the dress up clothes Diane suggests they pretend to be mail carriers and deliver mail to each other. Edward volunteers to deliver the letters first. The activity will provide Edward the opportunity to put on the mail carrier's coat and hat, pick up the letters, and pack them in his bag. This play activity can be used by the teacher to reinforce Edward's mastering self-help skills of dressing.

The art center could include painting, coloring, drawing, cutting, and clay activities. Again, children will cognitively have the opportunity to learn the names of objects, colors, and shapes; represent concepts and thoughts through art; make choices; solve problems; and experience a variety of art materials. Socioemotional skills developed in the art center might include expressing emotion, turn taking, and self-esteem. Cutting with scissors, molding clay, painting with a brush, and using other art materials will also enhance small motor skills and eye–hand coordination.

Art Center
Ellen suggests to Jennifer that they paint today. Jennifer is developmentally delayed in all areas but greatly admires Ellen. The easel, paint brush, primary color paints, and presence of a peer model will encourage Jennifer to experiment with colors, brush strokes, and social interaction as they converse about their pictures. The teacher can enhance this activity by encouraging both girls to talk about their pictures and the colors they used.

Activities in the reading/writing center might include looking at books, writing stories, listening to story tapes or music, or playing quiet games. In the reading/writing center children might increase these cognitive/language skills: expressive vocabulary, making choices, receptive language, visual and auditory discrimination, problem solving, and creative storytelling. Socioemotional skills of cooperation, turn taking, independence, perseverance, and self-discipline might be enhanced in the reading/writing center. Fine motor skills can be used in page turning and operation of recorders and record players.

Reading/Writing Center
Michael is very shy during almost every activity of the preschool day, but in the reading center he is very comfortable and confident. His favorite activity is to find colorful picture storybooks to share with John, who has cerebral palsy. Michael points to the pictures and asks John, "What is this?" When John does not respond with any type of sound he tells him the name and tells John to try to say the word. The speech therapist has observed that John seems to be improving in his sound production and the classroom teacher has found that Michael is starting to participate more in daily activities.

Summary

Early childhood special education programs that have embraced the synthesis of best practices suggested by McDonnell and Hardman (1988) prior to or since their publication should find themselves comfortable with DAP. Many of the practices suggested by McDonnell and Hardman were already being implemented in ECSE prior to the publication of DAP by NAEYC. As stated earlier, both fields agree that the curricula must be diverse enough to meet children's varying needs and interests. The concept of individualization and identifying naturalistic opportunities for learning are stressed by both. Child initiation, active engagement, and parent involvement were also supported by both fields. Unfortunately, not all in the ECSE profession have made the guidelines of McDonnell and Hardman part of their philosophical continuum and daily practice. Similar rigidity has been cited within the ECE profession (Bredekamp, 1993a). In the inclusive classroom, developmentally appropriate practices guidelines, constructivism, and behaviorism should not be viewed as incompatible entities. The early childhood special educator and early childhood educator should add those guidelines recommended by their respective and complementary fields to the continuum of their traditional practices and philosophical base. The areas of emphasis in developmentally appropriate practices, in many cases, could be transformed into the long-term goals for children with disabilities. These expansions will greatly enhance the individualization process. A new level of creativity and compromise between early childhood educators and early childhood special educators is needed. Flexibility in attitudes will be required by all parties involved to ensure the development of effective, integrated, and inclusive early childhood programs. Neither DAP guidelines nor legislative mandates should be viewed by either field as a limitation or threat but rather as an opportunity to expand the potential development of all children.

References

Alberto, P.A., & Troutman, A.C. (1990). *Applied behavior analysis for teachers*. New York: Merrill.

Bailey, D.B., Jr., & McWilliam, R.A. (1990). Normalizing early intervention. *Topics in Early Childhood Special Education, 10* (2), 33–47.

Bailey, D.B., Jr., & Wolery, M. (1992). *Teaching infants and pre-schoolers with disabilities.* New York: Macmillan.

Bredekamp, S. (1993a). Myths about developmentally appropriate practice: A response to Fowell and Lawton. *Early Childhood Research Quarterly, 8* (1), 117–20.

Bredekamp, S. (1993b). The relationship between early childhood education and early childhood special education: Healthy marriage or family feud? *Topics in Early Childhood Special Education, 13* (3), 258–73.

Bredekamp, S. (Ed.). (1987). *Developmentally appropriate practice in early childhood programs serving children from birth through age 8.* Washington, DC: National Association for the Education of Young Children.

Bredekamp, S., & Copple, C. (Eds.). (1997). *Developmentally appropriate practice in early childhood programs: Revised.* Washington, DC: National Association for the Education of Young Children.

Bredekamp, S., & Rosegrant, T., (1992). Guidelines for appropriate curriculum content and assessment in programs serving children ages 3 through 8. In S. Bredekamp & T. Rosegrant (Eds.), *Reaching potentials: Appropriate curriculum and assessment for young children* (pp. 9–27). Washington, DC: National Association for the Education of Young Children.

Brown, W.H., Ragland, E.U., & Bishop, N. (1989). *A socialization curriculum for preschool programs that integrate children with handicaps.* Nashville, TN: John F. Kennedy Center for Research on Education and Human Development, Peabody College, Vanderbilt University.

Burton, C., Hains, A.H., Hanline, M.F., McLean, M., & McCormick, K. (1992). Early childhood intervention and education: The urgency of professional unification. *Topics in Early Childhood Special Education, 11* (4), 53–69.

Carlson, L., & Udell, T. (1992). *Integrating children with special needs into a developmentally appropriate program: A model that works.* Monmouth, OR: Teaching Research Models.

Carta, J.J., Schwartz, I.S., Atwater, J.B., & McConnell, S.R. (1991). Developmentally appropriate practice: Appraising usefulness for young children with disabilities. *Topics in Early Childhood Special Education, 11* (1), 1–20.

Cavallaro, C.C., Haney, M., & Cabello, B. (1993). Developmentally appropriate strategies for promoting full participation in early childhood settings. *Topics in Early Childhood Special Education, 13* (3), 293–307.

Charlesworth, R., Hart, C.H., Burts, D.C., & DeWolf, M. (1993). The LSU studies: Building a research base for developmentally appropriate practice. In S. Reifel (Ed.), *Advances in early education and day care* (pp. 3–28). Greenwich, CT: JAI.

DEC Advocacy Statements and Positions. (1994). Reston, VA: Division for Early Childhood, The Council for Exceptional Children.

DEC Task Force on Recommended Practices. (1993). *DEC recommended practices: Indicators of quality in programs for infants and young children with special needs and their families.* Reston, VA: Council for Exceptional Children.

Derman-Sparks, L. (1992). Reaching potentials through antibias, multicultural curriculum. In S. Bredekamp & T. Rosegrant (Eds.), *Reaching potentials: Appropriate curriculum and assessment for young children* (pp. 114–27). Washington, DC: National Association for the Education of Young Children.

Dodge, D.T. (1993). Places for all children: Building environments for differing needs. *Beginnings Workshop-Exchange,* 41–43.

Dodge, D.T., & Colker, L.J. (1992). *The creative curriculum for early childhood* (3rd ed.). Washington, DC: Teaching Strategies.

Dunst, C., Trivette, C., & Deal, A. (1988). *Enabling and empowering families: Principles and guidelines for practice.* Cambridge, MA: Brookline Books.

Finger, W. (1992). Can I use a constructivist approach with children with special needs? In D.G. Murphy & S.G. Goffin (Eds.), *Project Construct: A curriculum guide.* Jefferson City, MO: Missouri Department of Education.

Fowler, S.A., Schwartz, I., & Atwater, J. (1991). Perspectives on the transition from preschool to kindergarten for children with disabilities and their families. *Exceptional Children, 58* (2), 136–45.

Fox, L., & Hanline, M.F. (1993). A preliminary evaluation of learning within developmentally appropriate early childhood settings. *Topics in Early Childhood Special Education, 13* (3), 308–27.

Fox, L., Hanline, M.F., Vail, C.O., & Galant, C.O. (1994). Developmentally appropriate practice: Applications for young children with disabilities. *Journal of Early Intervention,* 18 (3), 243–57.

Guralnick, M.J. (1989). Social competence as a future direction for early intervention programs. *Journal of Mental Deficiency Research, 33*, 275–81.

Guralnick, M.J. (1990). Major accomplishments and future directions in early childhood mainstreaming. *Topics in Early Childhood Special Education, 10* (2), 1–17.

IDEA (Individuals with Disabilities Education Act). (1990). Washington DC: U.S. Government Printing Office.

Johnson, J.E., & Johnson, K.M. (1992). Clarifying the developmental perspective in response to Carta, Schwartz, Atwater, and McConnell. *Topics in Early Childhood Special Education, 12* (4), 439–57.

Knight, D., & Wadsworth, D. (1993). Physically challenged students: Inclusion classroom. *Childhood Education, 69* (4), 211–15.

Landes, J., & Caccamo, N. (1992). How do I use a constructivist approach with special needs children? In D.G. Murphy & S.G. Goffin (Eds.), *Project Construct: A curriculum guide* (pp. 188–96). Jefferson City, MO: Missouri Department of Education.

McDonnell, A., & Hardman, M. (1988). A synthesis of "best practices" guidelines for early childhood services. *Journal of the Division for Early Childhood, 12* (4), 328–41.

Mahoney, G., O'Sullivan, P., & Fors, S. (1989). Special education practices with young handicapped children. *Journal of Early Intervention, 13* (3), 261–68.

Mahoney, G., Robinson, C., & Powell, A. (1992). Focusing on parent-child interaction: The bridge to developmentally appropriate practices. *Topics in Early Childhood Special Education, 12* (1), 105–20.

Morrison, G.S. (1995). *Early childhood education today* (6th ed.). Englewood Cliffs, NJ: Merrill.

Odom, S.L., & McEvoy, M.A. (1990). Mainstreaming at the preschool level: Potential barriers and tasks for the field. *Topics in Early Childhood Special Education, 10* (2), 48–61.

Sainato, D.M., & Lyon, S.R. (1989). Promoting successful mainstreaming transitions for handicapped preschool children. *Journal of Early Intervention, 13* (4), 305–14.

Strain, P.S., McConnell, S.R., Carta, J.J., Fowler, S.A., Neisworth, J.T., & Wolery, M. (1992). Behaviorism in early intervention. *Topics in Early Childhood Special Education, 12* (1), 121–41.

Wadsworth, D., Knight, D., & Balser, V. (1993). Children who are medically fragile or technology dependent: Guidelines. *Intervention in School and Clinic, 29* (2), 102–4.

Winter, S.M., Bell, M.J., & Dempsey, J.D. (1994). Creating play environments for children with special needs. *Childhood Education, 71* (1), 28–32.

Wolery, M. (1991). Instruction in early childhood special education: "Seeing through a glass darkly . . . knowing in part." *Exceptional Children, 58* (2), 127–35.

Wolery, M., Strain, P.S., & Bailey, D.B., Jr. (1992). Reaching potentials of children with special needs. In S. Bredekamp & T. Rosegrant (Eds.), *Reaching potentials: Appropriate curriculum and assessment for young children* (pp. 92–111). Washington, DC: National Association for the Education of Young Children.

CHAPTER FOURTEEN

Diversity and the Multicultural Perspective

ANDREW J. STREMMEL

We live in a diverse human society. It is a fact that all of human existence is inherently and universally multicultural, even though throughout most of history, human beings have resisted recognizing this (Wurzel, 1988). Rogoff and Morelli (1989) have acknowledged that most of us are blind to our own cultural heritage. And yet each of us is a member of a variety of cultures defined by race, ethnicity, gender, socioeconomic status, religion, family background, functional status, value orientation, and other characteristics that differentiate us and make us human. By virtue of this membership, we think and behave in ways that are greatly influenced by culturally prescribed beliefs, values, perceptions, and ways of interacting. As Fu (1993) suggests, we are most likely to notice the role of culture when we attempt to comprehend the realities of others by comparing the practices of different groups, particularly minority groups.

The understanding that we are a pluralistic society composed of people from many diverse backgrounds and traditions carries important implications for both the professional development of teachers and the planning and implementation of curriculum for young children in early education settings. First, teachers of young children need to develop an awareness of the many cultural and historical experiences that shape their own cultural realities before they can begin to appropriately incorporate a multicultural perspective in their classrooms. Second, teachers must understand that child development occurs within a sociocultural context. Third, they need to view multiculturalism, like development itself, as a lifelong, dynamic process of moving beyond individual experience and one point of reference, in order to benefit from and contribute to the experiences of others (Maxey, 1989; Wurzel, 1988). All have an important bearing on the way teachers approach and implement a multicultural curriculum.

While most early childhood educators in this country would agree that teaching practices must be developmentally appropriate, taking into account the developmental characteristics, needs, and interests of children, there is still uncertainty regarding the extent to which the values, goals, and teaching methods of other cultures should determine educational aims and developmentally appropriate practices. Considerable debate about what should be taught, to whom, by which methods, and under what circumstances continues as early childhood educators struggle with how to prepare teachers and children for living in a diverse world. This chapter builds on the foundation of developmentally appropriate integrated curriculum previously established in this book, and asserts that underlying a multicultural perspective are "values and beliefs inherent to a democracy: the promotion of human rights and privileges, the sharing of power, and equal participation in all social contexts" (Fu, 1993, p. 40). Critical to this assumption is the need for a negotiated curriculum and teaching practices that recognize, respect, and support different cultural groups and their knowledge and experiences (Bartolome, 1994; Connell, 1994; Fu, 1993).

Further, I argue that unless early childhood teachers thoughtfully and carefully examine their own system of values, attitudes, and beliefs, they cannot begin to understand and be responsive to the perspectives and needs of diverse children. Self-reflection is advocated as an ongoing and deliberate means to help teachers develop cultural self-awareness and to critically examine how their cultural realities may influence their teaching practices.

The aim of this chapter, then, is to focus on what I believe to be two essential and intextricably related components of developmentally appropriate and culturally sensitive practice: (1) culturally responsive interaction in mutually directed activity, and (2) a pedagogy of caring. Mutually directed activity is intrinsic to culturally responsive interactions in which adults negotiate and share power with children by viewing them as equal participants in learning and by building on their culturally different ways of learning (e.g., see Stremmel, 1993, 1996; Stremmel & Fu, 1993; Tharp & Gallimore, 1988). A pedagogy of caring extends the need to value and accept children's knowledge, culture, and life experiences by being caring and thoughtful in our relationships with them (e.g., Fu & Stremmel, 1996; Van Manen, 1991). Both elements should be part of a developmentally appropriate integrated curriculum in which activities that are meaningful and relevant to children abound. By framing the curriculum as mutually constructed activity settings that maximize opportunities for constructive intercultural communication and connectedness, emphasis is placed on the interactive processes that emerge in the context of teaching–learning, while fostering respect for individual and cultural diversity (Stremmel & Fu, 1993).

A developmental framework is offered here that draws on the constructivist perspectives of both Piaget and Vygotsky. Both theorists acknowledged that children construct knowledge and understanding and that development is facilitated in the spontaneous and contrived interactions that occur among children and other members of their communities. Thus, what children learn is a cultural curriculum, structured and orchestrated by the sociocultural activities and members of the communities in which they live and develop (Rogoff, 1990; Wood, 1988). I also draw on feminist epistemology, which acknowledges and values personal experience as a means for allowing more flexible interactions with others.

Before addressing issues of how to provide developmentally appropriate and culturally sensitive curriculum, and how best to prepare teachers who can do so, it is necessary to examine accounts of children's developing awareness of diversity (e.g., racial, ethnic, gender, and other categories of difference), and the current diversity of perspective on the substance of multicultural education. For more thorough and cogent analyses of these issues, I refer the reader to the writings of Goodman (1970), Katz (1983), and Ramsey (1987) on the acquisition of cultural differences, and Sleeter and Grant (1987) and Sleeter (1991) on various approaches to multicultural education in the United States.

When Do Children Become Aware of Diversity?

The question of when an awareness of cultural differences begins is important to early childhood educators as they plan for the provision of developmentally appropriate multicultural experiences. There is general agreement among cultural anthropologists (Goodman, 1970; Hirschfeld, 1988), social psychologists (Katz, 1982, 1983; Porter, 1971), and educators (Ramsey, 1987) that young children, by the age of 3 or 4 years, readily see differences and begin to acquire negative assumptions and stereotypes related to racial, ethnic, gender, and class distinctions. Thus, attitudes toward others are already being formed when children are very young.

Most researchers seem to agree that the emergence of this early sensitivity to different types of social categories is based on observations of external and immediately discernible attributes, such as skin color and language (see Hirschfeld, 1993, for a review). The cognitive developmental theories of Piaget and Vygotsky support this view that young children use easily perceptible surface cues to categorize social and nonsocial phenomena. However, a number of researchers have found that perceptual criteria alone are insufficient to account for young children's knowledge of cultural difference (e.g., Gelman, 1990; Hirschfeld, 1993). In fact, Hirschfeld (1993) claims that young children's early representations of racial and other social categories appear to be guided by expectations about the relations between perceptually and ontologically oriented categories and the kinds of information relevant to these relations. For example, Hirschfeld's study revealed that when preschool children were asked to recall social descriptions (e.g., a tall black postman, an overweight Chinese grocer) embedded in a social context (i.e., a verbal narrative) paralleling the complexity of daily interaction, occupational and behavioral categories were more salient social descriptors for preschool children than race or gender, presumably because they are more meaningful to the interpretation of events. Hirschfeld concluded that young children readily differentiate people on the basis of racially relevant perceptual information because of their proclivity to categorize aspects of their social world, not because membership in a particular race means sharing intrinsic, physical properties.

If, as the above research suggests, children's representations of racial categories are not based primarily on perceptual cues, then how do we interpret the numerous studies that suggest young children do evaluate categories of difference? While young children prefer to classify individuals on the basis of race and gender in experimental sorting tasks, race has been shown to be a poor predictor of preschool children's interactions, especially choosing play partners (Katz, 1982; Porter, 1971). Thus, in more natural and meaningful activities, children's preferences appear to be determined by the circumstances of social context, comprising language and other dimensions of difference. For example, racial differences may predict children's interactions when accompanied by language differences (e.g., Finkelstein & Haskins, 1983). The development of cultural attitudes and prejudices, then, is a function of the sociocultural context in which development occurs. Children reconstruct the values, views, and practices of their culture.

Though children may lack the cognitive sophistication needed to deal with the complexity of issues related to diversity, early childhood educators can build on the evidence that children are aware of cultural differences and the notion that knowledge and attitudes are socially constructed, reflecting the values, beliefs, and behaviors of a particular culture. How can we find developmentally appropriate ways of incorporating curriculum and teaching practices that prepare children to live in a diverse democratic society, and that recognize potential differences in the values, perceptions, and practices of parents, teachers, and communities?

Moving beyond the "Alike and Different" Approach

Sleeter and Grant (1987) have delineated five applications of multicultural education in the United States, ranging from approaches designed to teach human relations skills to those designed to help students acquire basic academic skills and develop both an understanding of their and others' cultural backgrounds. In schools, one goal of multicultural education has been to improve the academic performance of lower class and minority children so that they can more effectively participate and benefit from educational experiences (Maxey, 1989). A common element of most approaches is the goal of teaching children to recognize and appreciate cultural differences, while celebrating our common humanity.

Too often, however, early childhood multicultural education is conceived in oversimplified terms as the teaching of likenesses and differences through the celebration of "foods, fashions, and festivals" (Kagan, 1991; Ramsey, 1987; Wurzel, 1988). According to this view, children are provided opportunities to experience culinary diversity or to examine the art and artifacts of a variety of countries. Similarly, some educators view multicultural education as the presentation of separate units on different countries or ethnic groups represented in the classroom or larger society. While these approaches may have potential to promote an awareness and appreciation of diversity, they risk promoting negative stereotypes and may be counterproductive to the goals of multicultural education. In respecting cultural differences, it is important to also recognize and appreciate natural variations within cultural groups. This helps guard against the construction of misunderstandings that all people from a particular culture share the same views and practices.

The antibias curriculum (Derman-Sparks & ABC Task Force, 1989) extends the likeness and difference approach by incorporating ideals of democracy into the classroom and encouraging children to develop skills for recognizing injustices and counteracting the impact of bias. Among other aspects, this approach emphasizes the formation of positive attitudes and the creation of an inclusive classroom environment, wherein all forms of diversity are fairly and consistently represented, and children are encouraged to think critically, confront bias, peacefully resolve conflicts, and exhibit empathic interactions with others. In this curriculum, the teacher's role in mediating knowledge, attitudes, and behaviors is important.

Some educators (e.g., Kagan, 1991; Williams, 1991) have indicated that the implementation of inclusionary practices in early childhood classrooms is an inadequate vision for multicultural education. While it is important to promote acceptance of cultural differences through the incorporation of activities and materials that reflect different cultures, abilities, and ways of being, a multicultural perspective should impel us toward understanding ourselves as we attempt to understand the experiences of others. Because the teacher is the key to creating environments and teaching practices that promote positive and constructive interpersonal and intercultural relations, the teacher's self-reflection and self-understanding are prerequisite to implementing any multicultural approach (Fu, 1993; Ramsey, 1987; Williams, 1991; Wurzel, 1988).

Accordingly, multicultural education can be viewed as an effort "to help children understand and appreciate their own experience and to extend that experience in broader contexts" (Maxey, 1989, p. 280).

Developing Cultural Self-Awareness

Systematically exploring one's attitudes and practices is essential to moving toward cultural self-awareness and multiculturalism. Jaime Wurzel (1988) has proposed a developmental model that systematically illustrates the process by which individuals move toward heightened cultural self-awareness. Elsewhere, Kendall (1996) presents a thorough analysis of this model. Here I draw on Wurzel's conceptual framework for purposes of discussing a means of assisting teachers to recognize and challenge the arbitrary nature of their cultural realities; in so doing, teachers are better able to incorporate different perspectives and values into their own system of cultural knowledge. Accepting the notion that we are continuously exposed to different cultural realities, I suggest that the development of cultural self-awareness is a dynamic and evolving process involving self-reflection, guided questioning, and the willingness to examine one's perspective in face of new challenges and insights.

Self-reflection is a dialectical mental process that allows one to challenge, reinterpret, reframe, and reconstruct assumptions, attitudes, beliefs, and values. Through reflection, individuals subject their action and belief systems to critical assessment. Because reflection invites self-examination, it may lead to greater self-awareness, open-mindedness, introspection, and an enlightened attitude toward diversity.

For teachers, thoughtful and careful examination of their cultural and historical experiences (e.g., as both teacher and learner) can help them identify and confront assumptions that underlie their teaching beliefs and practices. Smyth (1992) claims that teachers can be assisted to examine these assumptions through a series of guiding questions, which might consist of the following:

- What do I believe?
- How have I come to believe this? Where do these beliefs come from?
- What do my daily actions say about what I believe and value?

- What contributes to the tenacity of my beliefs? (What has influenced me to maintain certain beliefs?)
- How do my beliefs constrain what is possible (i.e., restrict my freedom to make choices and take actions that would move me toward greater multicultural understanding)?

This kind of self-examination enables teachers to become aware of the degree to which their beliefs, actions, and patterns of communication are based on cultural learning rooted deep in early childhood experiences (Smyth, 1992; Wurzel, 1988). In sum, the process of self-reflection can stimulate the development of cultural self-awareness necessary to establishing more meaningful understanding of and communication with others. As will become increasingly apparent in the pages that follow, a teacher's willingness and ability to locate and create caring and empathetic spaces to reflect on competing value systems are critical to teaching in settings where diverse perspectives are common.

What Is Developmentally Appropriate Multicultural Curriculum?

Seefeldt (1990) reminds us that the content of early childhood curriculum has long been an issue of debate. In response to this debate, the National Association for the Education of Young Children (NAEYC) published a position statement on developmentally appropriate practice in early childhood programs serving children from birth through age 8 (Bredekamp, 1987; Bredekamp & Copple, 1997). This statement emphasizes the need to consider individual child background, experience, and learning style as well as age in planning learning activities. As has been suggested throughout this text, the early childhood curriculum should provide opportunities for children to interact with others and to engage in active exploration and discovery, rather than passive activities. Moreover, the child should be the primary source of the curriculum, in that activities and experiences focus on the "here and now" and take into consideration what is truly worth knowing (e.g., Duckworth, 1987; Katz & Chard, 1989). Taken together, this philosophy suggests that teachers of young children must be continually responsive to the spontaneously expressed interests and intentions of children as they pursue informal learning activities (Elkind, 1976; Katz, 1987; Katz & Chard, 1989; Lay-Dopyera & Dopyera, 1990).

There has been much discussion recently as to whether developmentally appropriate practice guidelines, by virtue of specifying what constitutes "best practice" in early childhood education, really meet the needs of culturally diverse children (e.g., see Kessler & Swadener, 1992; Lubeck, 1994). Among the criticisms are those suggesting that developmentally appropriate practices represent the reasoned consensus, based on child development theory and research, of the dominant cultural group. Some argue (cf. Delpit, 1993; Holloway and Fuller, 1992; Lubeck, 1994) that, in our efforts to provide best practice, we actually may be promoting a "one size fits all" approach that downplays the deeply set values and beliefs of families from differing cultural groups. While most early childhood educators would agree that we should guard against promoting generic instructional recipes by adjusting teaching methods to the cues and learning styles of children (e.g., Bredekamp & Rosegrant, 1992), it is important to understand that schools and child care centers are seldom the fair and democratic educational settings where all children are provided with similar opportunities and conditions for meeting their needs for optimal learning and quality care (Bartolome, 1994; Helburn et al., 1995).

Should we then abandon developmentally appropriate practices in an attempt to better meet the needs of children with diverse backgrounds and learning styles? The answer to this question is a resounding "No!" As Bowman and Stott (1994) have aptly pointed out, "Making child development a linchpin for practice is a major contribution to early childhood pedagogy" (p. 119). Furthermore, research has shown that children from diverse backgrounds benefit from participation in developmentally appropriate classrooms (see Charlesworth et al., 1993 for a review). Child-centered classrooms, in which developmentally appropriate practices occur, provide time and opportunities for children to actively participate in and choose from among a variety of activity options, few of which are designed to be used in prescribed or correct ways, thus allowing them to choose when and how to learn (Lay-Dopyera & Dopyera, 1990). Perhaps, then, the question should be, "Is multicultural education for young children any different from a developmentally appropriate curriculum?" The answer to this question is "Yes."

If early childhood teachers are going to sufficiently meet the needs of children from diverse cultural backgrounds, their teaching strategies must be appropriate for all children within their classrooms. This is not easily accomplished in any classroom. Teachers generally are not aware of their own learning styles, let alone the learning styles of the children they teach. Furthermore, the curriculum is only as good as the teachers who implement it. Beyond the need for self-reflection and examination of their own views of multiculturalism and tolerance for diversity, teachers' instructional practices should relate to the personally meaningful experiences of children and utilize "culturally important" activities and contexts. This implies the need to move toward developmentally appropriate teaching practices that are derived from a variety of sources, including

- knowledge of child development within a sociocultural context
- the learning patterns, culture, and life experiences of individual children
- the value systems of differing cultures
- knowledge of other disciplines (e.g., education, history, cultural anthropology, and philosophy)
- pedagogical reflection on what is in the best interests of children's development (Fu, 1993; Garbarino, 1992; Van Manen, 1991; Williams, 1994)

Such a vision of multicultural pedagogy integrates the best of what developmentally appropriate practice offers with ideas crucial to educating for democracy. It also suggests focusing more broadly on the sociocultural context in which children learn and develop (Vygotsky, 1978; Rogoff & Morelli, 1989).

In the remaining pages, I discuss culturally responsive teaching in mutually directed activity and a pedagogy of caring as ways to help children having various backgrounds and experiences establish their own voices and develop the skills necessary to interact with others in establishing and maintaining a democratic community. I suggest that a multicultural perspective requires a pedagogical shift toward a more negotiated curriculum and more participatory classroom practice (Connell, 1994). Further, I provide examples of mutually directed activities within an integrated, developmentally appropriate curriculum.

Culturally Responsive Teaching

Culturally responsive teaching involves the sensitive, often moment-to-moment gauging of a child's current level of understanding in order to make decisions about the nature and type of assistance that will be most beneficial (see Stremmel, 1993, 1996). The underlying responsive teaching is the assumption that knowledge and understanding are products of shared constructions by teachers and children in mutually directed activity (Rogoff, 1990; Vygotsky, 1978; Wood, 1988). In order for teachers to be responsive to individual and cultural differences, they must create contexts wherein teachers use strategies that recognize, appreciate, and build on preschool children's diverse perspectives, learning patterns, and ways of communicating.

Responsive teaching is predicated on the interactive patterns observed between adults and children in many cultures and in joint activity settings where participants have different skills and skill levels (Tharp & Gallimore, 1988). There are at least three essential features of responsive teaching practice that differentiate it from more traditionally defined (i.e., teacher-directed) means of instruction:

- Collaboration in structuring learning situations
- Construction of shared meaning (intersubjectivity)
- Utilization of various teaching methods, ranging from non-directive to directive

First, in responsive teaching, both adults and children collaborate in structuring the situations that provide the latter with opportunities to observe and participate in culturally valued activities, thereby enabling them to extend their current skills and knowledge to a higher level of competence (Moll, 1990). Unlike traditional instructive practices, responsive teaching does not assist children in developing skills they do not already possess; rather, it "rouses to life" those functions and skills that are in the process of maturing (Vygotsky, 1978). Second, the construction of shared meaning and understanding (intersubjectivity) between teachers and children is essential in developing sensitivity to the problems that children are attempting to solve; in fact, it is this ability to achieve a shared meaning, with social guidance building on the child's perspective, that is most significantly associated with children's successful learning and performance (Rogoff, 1990). The attainment of shared meaning and understanding in collaborative activity has far-reaching implications for the way we view early educational activity. It suggests that the child's development of knowledge and understanding can only be described *in relation to* a partner (or partners) who, with the child, achieve shared meaning in activities that are mutually constructed in a culturally defined context (Uzgiris, 1992). Because activity emerges out of an interactive context, it is impossible to say "whose" an object of joint understanding or focus is, or "to whom" a collaborative idea belongs (Rogoff, 1990).

Third, responsive teaching requires the planned utilization of a variety of teaching strategies and techniques that must be continually constructed and reconstructed, through action and reflection, in order to sensitively consider and build on children's previously constructed knowledge and skills. This requires that the teacher possess some understanding of children's ways of learning and using language, as well as a sense of how and when to intervene and when to hold back that is based on a reading of children's cues. The responsive teacher allows children to make self-discoveries when they are able, but he or she also provides the necessary assistance when children are in need. Children meanwhile must be intrinsically motivated and engaged in culturally meaningful activity.

Responsive interactions empower children to succeed, because they involve the systematic use of a variety of strategies and techniques that are likely to be suitable to children having diverse needs and learning styles. Because children actively participate in the construction of knowledge and understanding in meaningful activity, interactions between teachers and children proceed in egalitarian and purposeful ways. Conversely, traditional or teacher-directed instruction typically involves the implementation of generic teaching methods without careful consideration of how they may constrain the learning styles and needs of culturally diverse children.

Though proponents of developmentally appropriate practice recognize the complex and interactive nature of teaching young children (e.g., Bredekamp & Rosegrant, 1992), responsive interactions are not routinely observed in early childhood classrooms. Even in developmentally appropriate classrooms, where individualized learning is encouraged daily through the provision of activity centers (e.g., art, dramatic play, blocks, manipulatives, etc.) that provide multiple options and challenges for child involvement, children having diverse backgrounds do not necessarily interact equally with adults in classroom activities. In reality all children, but primarily those outside of the majority culture, are routinely confronted with discontinuities in their cognitive, social, and linguistic experiences (e.g., see Brown, Palinscar, & Purcell, 1986; Heath, 1982). Despite what we know to be true about the disparities in teacher–child interactions that occur in children's earliest group experiences, children on the margins of society continue to be taught in ways that limit their opportunities to help create meaningful learning experiences (Gomez, 1992).

Reconceptualizing an understanding of informal learning activities in early childhood classrooms as mutually directed activity settings extends any discussion of developmentally appropriate practice, especially involving children from diverse backgrounds. With this in mind, it would seem that the best way to ensure sensitivity to the diverse learning patterns of children is through responsive teaching in a variety of mutually constructed contexts that are consistent with children's developmental and sociocultural needs (Linney & Seidman, 1989; Tharp, 1989).

Mutually Directed Activity

Mutually directed activity, in which adults negotiate and share power with children by viewing them as equal partners in learning, should be common in early childhood classrooms. And yet the emphasis on child-directed activity, particularly self-exploration and discovery through play, has long been considered the hallmark of child-centered approaches to early childhood education. Certainly play is an essential feature of any developmentally appropriate classroom, but the almost exclusive focus on play ignores a wealth of research demonstrating the potential of collaborative activity in children's development (see Henry, 1990; Tizard & Hughes, 1984; Rogoff, 1990).

Tizard and Hughes (1984), in contrasting home and nursery school as learning environments, have pointed out that nursery schools are often deficient in opportunities for children to observe and participate with adults in challenging collaborative pursuits. Conversely, there is convincing evidence of collaborative activity, particularly joint constructions and elaborations of conversation, in adult–child activity in home settings (Henry, 1990; Wells, 1985).

If early childhood classrooms are to provide educational settings that are compatible with diverse backgrounds, cultures, and communities, then teachers must provide children with demands and challenges that are continuous with those encountered in everyday experiences (e.g., in homes and communities). Continuity between home and classroom is not only desirable; it is essential if learning and development are viewed as social enterprises. Early childhood programs should attempt to incorporate to a greater degree the values, beliefs, and learning patterns of the children and families they serve. This means more actively encouraging children to share their ideas and experiences in curricular activities involving language expression as well as involving parents in meaningful and authentic ways in the classroom. Both strategies legitimize and value cultural differences that may otherwise be ignored in addition to creating activity settings where power can be shared by teachers and children.

At the same time, while it is important to be sensitive to the learning patterns of various cultures, child care centers or preschool classrooms must be seen as having a culture of their own, with demands that are unique to that "culture" (Wood, 1988). Although early educational settings for children may impose demands that are not regular or frequent features of their everyday experiences outside the classroom (Wood, 1988), many outcomes with respect to knowledge, skills, and dispositions should be the same for all children. For example, Katz (1987) argues that it is reasonable to expect all children to develop competence in self-expression and in understanding others, the ability to form and maintain satisfying relationships, and the disposition of interest or intrinsic motivation. All of these are promoted and strengthened in developmentally appropriate, responsive interactions that lead to shared understanding and reciprocal interchange.

Some Examples of Mutually Directed Activity

Mutually directed activities—collaborative conversation, story sharing, art activities, cooking activities, and project work—provide contexts in which adults and children can negotiate and share power as equal participants in meaningful learning.

Conversation is the quintessential mutually constructed activity. Conversational interaction is integral to establishing and maintaining democratic community. Activity settings that encourage extended conversations with adults enable children to socially construct language skills that are critical for success in school. Teacher-child collaborative exchanges are most frequent in classroom activities designed to promote literacy, such as large- and small-group experiences, sharing time (also known as "show and tell"), storytelling and sharing, and reading to children. Meal and snack times also routinely include conversations with adults and peers. In all of these activity settings, it is important for teachers to encourage all children to share their experiences using their culturally preferred styles, while assisting children in the development of more conventional ways of using language in conversation. For example, teachers can ask questions that assist, support, and extend children's ideas and utterances, and thereby help them to be more articulate and coherent.

More specific ways to infuse the experiences and perspectives of diverse children through language experiences include reading and telling stories that are inclusive of all cultural groups on a regular basis. When children can share their stories as well as read and hear stories depicting their and others' backgrounds, a sense of interdependence and community is created. Teachers who incorporate children's life experiences and knowledge into the curriculum in this way demonstrate a genuine valuing of diversity, promote democratic learning environments where all children can be viewed as competent individuals, and foster a shared responsibility for learning within the classroom culture.

Like storytelling, art is an activity engaged in by people all over the world to symbolically express historical and cultural events and daily life experiences (Ramsey, 1987). And, like adults in their society, children use various tools and materials to express their ideas, thoughts, and feelings through art activities. Though art activities are very common in early childhood classrooms, an understanding of how they can be viewed as mutually directed is not. Thus, an example is helpful.

Prior to interacting with children who choose to participate in art, responsive teachers select and arrange the tools and materials that are likely to afford a creative and successful experience for the children in their classroom. As children approach and begin the art activity, teachers quickly learn that children's ideas and intentions in attempting the activity may not be the same as theirs, and indeed, they may be ever changing. The responsive teacher must accurately tailor his or her assistance to each child by being sensitive to the child's understanding of the activity. If the child has a limited understanding of what to do, the teacher may offer a suggestion or ask a question to help the child get started. As the interaction continues, different ideas about how to use the materials may evolve as the teacher and child work together toward achieving increasing intersubjectivity. When some mutual conception of an appropriate way to use the materials has been constructed through dialogue, the child is allowed to work creatively and unassisted within acceptable and mutually defined parameters.

The art activity described above may require less initial adult responsibility or control than activities that are likely to need careful adult supervision, such as a cooking activity. Nevertheless, it requires the attainment of shared meaning and understanding and involves both child and adult in joint performance of the activity. Like art, cooking or preparing food is an activity observable in many cultures and home settings. Children take part in the preparation of food through the process of guided participation, in which opportunities to observe through modeling are common in everyday experience (Rogoff, 1986, 1990). This kind of collaborative activity typically requires the adult to take greater responsibility. However, children can actively and meaningfully participate at points where their skill level is congruent with the demands of the task. Children may take part in stirring, cutting, and serving, while the teacher demonstrates certain procedures or describes what is happening as ingredients are mixed, measured, and cooked.

The opportunities described above for mutual involvement in culturally meaningful activity allow teachers to share with children the responsibility of decision making and task performance. The value of mutually directed activity is also evident in the project approach as advocated by Katz and Chard (1989). A project is a group undertaking that enables children with different abilities and backgrounds to collaborate on a theme or topic that may extend over a period of days or weeks, depending on the children's interests. In project work, the teacher assists and supports children's undertakings that evolve from ideas, discussions, and matters that are interesting and meaningful to them.

As has been suggested here, it is important to think about curriculum development and implementation from the point of view of those who are least likely to have a voice. From this multicultural perspective, teachers and children negotiate the curriculum based on the perceived interests, ideas, and experiences of the children and the considered knowledge and experiences of the teacher, who has identified activities that will assist children in developing the knowledge, skills, and dispositions thought to be important for children to function competently in the larger society. Further, efforts should be made to help parents teach their children to respond appropriately and successfully to classroom activities, while teachers attempt to incorporate to a greater degree the values, beliefs, and learning patterns of the families they serve. At times this may include negotiating values and beliefs about learning that are in conflict with standards of appropriate practice articulated by early childhood professionals. If knowledge and understanding are indeed products of shared constructions, then teachers must treasure opportunities to learn from the beliefs and practices of others.

Parents might become more readily involved in early childhood classrooms if they saw teachers and children engaged in mutually directed, family-like activities (e.g., cooking, woodworking, caring for pets and plants, washing and folding clothes, and helping maintain the classroom) on a daily basis, in addition to mutually directed play, where teachers are participant conversers as well as observers (Henry, 1990). The rationale for this assumption centers on the opportunity for more open and meaningful information exchange between parents and teachers about ways that teachers can support parent–child home activities. Such exchange would empower all participants in the development of children.

Moreover, the inclusion of more mutually directed or collaborative activity in early childhood classrooms would provide a context where both parents and teachers are viewed as acceptable partners in the learning process. Opportunities for parents and children from various ethnic and racial groups to participate in joint activity would provide children with a strong sense of cultural identity, frequent sharing of authentic cultural activity, and a merging of cultural and "classroom-specific" skills (Swadener, 1988).

A Pedagogy of Caring

A pedagogy of caring extends the need to value and accept children's knowledge, culture, and life experiences by acknowledging the importance of educating and caring for children as a rich and cultural human activity. Teachers are charged with a responsibility of supporting parents in fulfilling their primary pedagogical role in teaching young children to live in a diverse society, "to take responsibility for themselves, for others, and for the continuance and welfare of the world" (Van Manen, 1991, p. 7). It is a pedagogy that demands that teachers be caring and thoughtful in their relationships with children (Fu & Stremmel, 1996).

As children spend more time outside the home, in schools and in child care programs, the importance of building linkages between parents and children in childhood socialization is becoming more crucial in our society. Most parents hope that their children will grow up to be adults who are educated, responsible, productive, healthy, happy, caring, loved and able to love others. Multicultural education that is developmentally appropriate should focus on helping children develop care and concern for the well-being of themselves and others, and to live and work in a democracy.

Noddings (1993) believes that teachers must create caring relationships with children in order to expect children to develop the capacity to care. Children first learn ideas about caring and compassion at a concrete, meaningful level, in their own immediate environments and through their shared experiences in these contexts. On one level children can learn how to care for themselves and others in adult–child interactions that encourage understandings and skills needed for living in a diverse, democratic society. These include understandings of fairness, cooperation, and compromise, and skills like listening to others' views, making and being a friend, decision making, and problem solving, all of which contribute to the well-being of the classroom culture. On a second level, children construct an understanding of caring through listening, conversing, and sharing their ideas, feelings, and intentions in a variety of stories that have meaning to their lives. Through "storying," children construct understandings of caring, justice, fairness, and responsibility that influence their developing sense of self and others (Paley, 1981, 1993). Concepts of caring become understandable when children apply these principles in their own homes, classrooms, and communities.

Caring teachers listen and are responsive to the varying needs of children, by reflecting on their interactions in ways that accommodate children's interests and perspectives. Orienting differentially to each child using caring and thoughtful guidance contributes positively to a child's developing sense of self. It is this capacity to feel good about oneself and to care for others that may provide the most reasonable and meaningful starting point in developing multicultural awareness in young children.

Preparing Early Childhood Teachers to Be Caring and Responsive
to the Needs of Diverse Children

In order to optimally meet the needs, interests, and abilities of culturally diverse children teachers must engage in caring, responsive teaching. Responsive teaching presumes the notion of intersubjectivity, in which perspectives are coordinated in mutually directed activity. Further, it is recognized that developmentally appropriate teaching practices must relate to personally meaningful experience and utilize culturally important materials and contexts (e.g., mutually directed activity and the meaningful involvement of parents). But before teachers can effectively implement curriculum and teaching practices that recognize, respect, and support the knowledge and experiences of diverse children, teachers themselves need considerable education and training to develop understanding of the historical experience of diverse groups and reflective dispositions. Both are essential to avoid promoting counterproductive ways of thinking about and dealing with children from diverse backgrounds.

Comer (1989) suggests that all teachers need to be educated on how structural forces, policies, and practices influence families, communities, and child development. More positive home–school relationships, better understanding and facilitation of child development, and positive self-identity and a sense of community all begin with an enhanced understanding of the social, political, and historical conditions that have shaped the experiences of various groups in our society.

Further, teachers must be given time and opportunities to develop reflective dispositions. Earlier, reflection was discussed as a means of developing increased self-awareness. Teacher educators can assist novice and prospective teachers to develop reflective attitudes by helping them consider critically their own teaching–learning experiences as children, and how these experiences contribute to their current teaching beliefs and practices as well as their daily interactions with children and parents. These interactions should be examined against the experiences, values, and beliefs of families from diverse backgrounds. Teachers also need time to reflect on and share stories of pedagogy with each other. Through these experiences, early childhood teachers can develop reflective dispositions that will allow them to critically examine their own cultural identities, which lead to beliefs and practices that influence their interactions with young children.

As Gomez (1992) points out, cultural identity provides the lens through which teachers view others; left unexamined, cultural lenses become restraints, narrowing the possibilities of our understandings of and interactions with those who hold different perspectives. Thus, the thoughtful and careful examination of teachers' own prior experiences is necessary for achieving intersubjectivity in responsive teaching. A teacher cannot begin to understand the perspective of the learner without first considering his or her own system of values and attitudes about teaching and children's learning. Van Manen (1991) reminds us that teachers who reflect on their interactions with children may be able to increase their own ability to be thoughtful and caring in subsequent teaching.

Conclusion

In this chapter I have articulated an approach that emphasizes responsive and caring interactions in collaborative activities in which teacher and child work together to achieve mutual understanding of purpose and perspective. A negotiated curriculum that incorporates the principles of developmentally appropriate practice with ideals of democracy allows for the valuing of diverse ways of knowing and experiencing and opportunities for teachers, children, and parents to participate fully in the conversation on what curriculum and teaching practices are best for children.

Multicultural education is a highly complex and political issue. It must be more than something teachers add to their curriculum during the celebration of seasonal and religious holidays. It must go beyond the understanding and appreciation of real cultural differences. It should represent a perspective that permeates all of the curriculum, every day of the year, and is reflected in culturally responsive interaction in mutually directed activity. Responsive teachers engage children in egalitarian and meaningful ways in culturally relevant activities like sharing stories, doing art, preparing foods, and other experiences and projects that build on diverse ways of learning, perceiving, and using language. Such activities provide opportunities for connectedness and a sense of belonging that should prevail over the idea of differences. Finally, a pedagogy of caring, which promotes in children feelings of self-worth, love, and care of others, must be at the heart of any developmentally and culturally appropriate curriculum. A pedagogy of caring requires teachers to be reflective and to not lose sight of social, historical, and political conditions that have shaped the life experiences of people from different cultural groups.

However, no early childhood curriculum infusion can be a panacea for eliminating social inequities and other deeply rooted problems that confront our society (Delpit, 1993; Lubeck, 1994). A vision to bring diversity and democracy more in harmony must transcend pedagogy and serve as a foundation for future research and practice (Kagan, 1991). Should we continue to search for a best approach? Does the curriculum matter or the approach of the teacher? Perhaps it is time to let children's knowledge, culture, and life experiences (and the meanings they attach to their experiences) more seriously guide our practices.

References

Bartolome, L.I. (1994). Beyond the methods fetish: Toward a humanizing pedagogy. *Harvard Educational Review, 64*, 173–94.

Bowman, B.T., & Stott, F.M. (1994). Understanding development in a cultural context: The challenge for teachers. In B.L. Mallory & R.S. New (Eds.), *Diversity and developmentally appropriate practices* (pp. 119–33). New York: Teachers College Press.

Bredekamp, S. (1987). *Developmentally appropriate practice in early childhood programs serving children from birth through age 8.* Washington, DC: National Association for the Education of Young Children.

Bredekamp, S., & Copple, C. (Eds.). (1997). *Developmentally appropriate practice in early childhood programs: Revised.* Washington, DC: National Association for the Education of Young Children.

Bredekamp, S., & Rosegrant, T. (Eds.). (1992). *Reaching potentials: Appropriate curriculum and assessment for young children.* Washington, DC: National Association for the Education of Young Children.

Brown, A.L., Palinscar, A.S., & Purcell, L. (1986). Poor readers: Teach, don't label. In U. Neisser (Ed.), *The school achievement of minority children: New perspectives* (pp. 105–43). Hillsdale, NJ: LEA.

Charlesworth, R., Hart, C.H., Burts, D.C., & DeWolf, M. (1993). The LSU Studies: Building a research base for developmentally appropriate practice. In S. Reifel (Ed.), *Perspectives on developmentally appropriate practice: Advances in early education and day care* (Vol. 5, pp. 3–28). Greenwich, CT: JAI.

Comer, J.P. (1989). Racism and the education of young children. *Teachers College Record, 90,* 352–61.

Connell, R.W. (1994). Poverty and education. *Harvard Educational Review, 64,* 125–49.

Delpit, L.D. (1993). The silenced dialogue: Power and pedagogy in educating other people's children. In L. Weis & M. Fine (Eds.), *Beyond silenced voices: Class, race, and gender in United States Schools* (pp. 119–39). Albany, NY: State University of New York Press.

Derman-Sparks, L., & the A.B.C. Task Force. (1989). *Anti-bias curriculum: Tools for empowering young children.* Washington, DC: National Association for the Education of Young Children.

Duckworth, E. (1987). *The having of wonderful ideas and other essays on teaching and learning.* New York: Teachers College Press.

Elkind, D. (1976). *Child development and education.* New York: Oxford University Press.

Finkelstein, N., & Haskins, R. (1983). Kindergarten children prefer same-color peers. *Child Development, 54,* 502–8.

Fu, V.R. (1993). Culture, schooling, and education in a democracy. In *Multiculturalism in early childhood programs, Perspectives from ERIC/EECE: A Monograph Series, No. 3* (pp. 38–51). Urbana, IL: ERIC Clearinghouse on Elementary and Early Childhood Education.

Fu, V.R., & Stremmel, A.J. (1996). A pedagogy of caring and thoughtfulness: Living and sharing our lives with our and other people's children. In V.R. Fu & A.J. Stremmel (Eds.), *Affirming diversity through democratic conversations.* Manuscript submitted for publication.

Garbarino, J. (1992). *Children and families in the social environment* (2nd ed.). New York: Aldine de Gruyter.

Gelman, R. (1990). First principles organize attention to and learning about relevant data. *Cognitive Science, 14,* 79–106.

Gomez, M.L. (1992). Breaking silences: Building new stories of classroom life through teacher transformation. In S. Kessler & B.B.

Swadener (Eds.), *Reconceptualizing the early childhood curriculum: Beginning the dialogue* (pp. 165–88). New York: Teachers College Press.

Goodman, M.E. (1970). *The culture of childhood: Child's-eye views of society and culture.* New York: Teachers College Press.

Heath, S.B. (1982). What no bedtime story means: Narrative skills at home and school. *Language in Society, 11,* 49–76.

Helburn, S., Culkin, M.L., Howes, C., Bryant, D., Clifford, R., Cryer, D., Peisner-Feinberg, E., & Kagan, S.L. (1995). *Cost, quality, and child outcomes in child care centers* (Executive Summary). University of Colorado–Denver.

Henry, M. (1990). More than just play: The significance of mutually directed adult-child activity. *Early Child Development and Care, 60,* 35–51.

Hirschfeld, L.A. (1988). On acquiring social categories: Cognitive development and anthropological wisdom. *Man, 23,* 611–38.

Hirschfeld, L.A. (1993). Discovering social difference: The role of appearance in the development of racial awareness. *Cognitive Psychology, 25,* 317–50.

Holloway, S.D., & Fuller, B. (1992). The great child-care experiment: What are the lessons for school improvement? *Educational Researcher, 21* (7), 12–19.

Kagan, S.L. (1991, October). *Exploring multicultural education in a culturally diverse society: A sociocultural perspective.* Discussant paper presented at the annual meeting of the National Association for the Education of Young Children, Denver, CO.

Katz, L.G. (1987). Early childhood education: What should young children be doing? In S.L. Kagan & E.F. Zigler (Eds.), *Early schooling: The national debate* (pp. 151–67). New Haven: Yale University Press.

Katz, L.G., & Chard, S.C. (1989). *Engaging children's minds: The project approach.* Norwood, NJ: Ablex.

Katz, P.A. (1982). Development of children's racial awareness and intergroup attitudes. In L.G. Katz (Ed.), *Current topics in early childhood education* (Vol. 4, pp. 16–54). Norwood, NJ: Ablex.

Katz, P.A. (1983). Developmental foundations of gender and racial attitudes. In R. L. Leahy (Ed.), *The child's construction of social inequality.* New York: Academic.

Kendall, F.E. (1996). *Diversity in the classroom: New approaches to the education of young children.* New York: Teachers College Press.

Kessler, S., & Swadener, B.B. (Eds.). (1992). *Reconceptualizing the early childhood curriculum: Beginning the dialogue.* New York: Teachers College Press.

Lay-Dopyera, M., & Dopyera, J.E. (1990). The child-centered curriculum. In C. Seefeldt (Ed.), *Continuing issues in early childhood education* (pp. 207–22). Columbus, OH: Merrill.

Linney, J.A., & Seidman, E. (1989). The future of schooling. *American Psychologist, 44,* 336–40.

Lubeck, S. (1994). The politics of developmentally appropriate practice: Exploring issues of culture, class, and curriculum. In B.L. Mallory and R.S. New (Eds.), *Diversity and developmentally appropriate practices* (pp. 17–43). New York: Teachers College Press.

Maxey, P.F. (1989). The many voices of multicultural education. In J.A. Braun (Ed.), *Reforming teacher education: Issues and new directions.* New York: Garland.

Moll, L.C. (1990). *Vygotsky and education: Instructional implications and applications of sociohistorical psychology.* New York: Cambridge University Press.

Noddings, N. (1993). *The challenge to care in schools: An alternative approach to education.* New York: Teachers College Press.

Paley, V.G. (1981). *Wally's stories: Conversations in the kindergarten.* Cambridge: Harvard University Press.

Paley, V.G. (1993). *You can't say you can't play.* Cambridge: Harvard University Press.

Porter, J. (1971). *Black child, white child: The development of racial attitudes.* Cambridge, MA: Harvard University Press.

Ramsey, P.G. (1987). *Teaching and learning in a diverse world: Multicultural education for young children.* New York: Teachers College Press.

Rogoff, B. (1986). Adult assistance of children's learning. In T.E. Raphael (Ed.), *The contexts of school-based literacy* (pp. 27–40). New York: Random House.

Rogoff, B. (1990). *Apprenticeship in thinking: Cognitive development in social context.* New York: Oxford University Press.

Rogoff, B., & Morelli, G. (1989). Perspectives on children's development from cultural psychology. *American Psychologist, 44,* 343–48.

Seefeldt, C. (Ed.). (1990). *Continuing issues in early childhood education.* Columbus, OH: Merrill.

Sleeter, C. (1991). Multicultural education and empowerment. In C.E. Sleeter (Ed.), *Empowerment through multicultural education.* Albany, NY: State University of New York Press.

Sleeter, C.E., & Grant, C.A. (1987). An analysis of multicultural education in the United States. *Harvard Educational Review, 57,* 421–44.

Smyth, J. (1992). Teachers' work and the politics of reflection. *American Educational Research Journal, 29,* 267–300.

Stremmel, A.J. (1993). Responsive teaching: A culturally appropriate approach. In *Multiculturalism in early childhood programs, Perspectives from ERIC/EECE: A Monograph Series, No. 3* (pp. 52–63). Urbana, IL: ERIC Clearinghouse on Elementary and Early Childhood Education.

Stremmel, A.J. (1996). Developing interpersonal understanding in teaching culturally diverse children. In V.R. Fu & A.J. Stremmel (Eds.), *Affirming diversity through democratic conversations.* Manuscript submitted for publication.

Stremmel, A.J., & Fu, V.R. (1993). Teaching in the zone of proximal development: Implications for responsive teaching practice. *Child and Youth Care Forum, 22* (5), 337–50.

Swadener, E.B. (1988). Implementation of education that is multicultural in early childhood settings: A case study of two day care programs. *The Urban Review, 20,* 8–27.

Tharp, R.G. (1989). Psychocultural variables and constants: Effects on teaching and learning in schools. *American Psychologist, 44,* 349–59.

Tharp, R.G., & Gallimore, R. (1988). *Rousing minds to life: Teaching, learning, and schooling in social context.* New York: Cambridge University Press.

Tizard, B., & Hughes, M. (1984). *Young children learning: Talking and thinking at home and at school.* London: Fontana.

Uzgiris, I.C. (1992). Fostering development in early childhood: An interactive approach. In *Proceedings of the Conference on New Directions in Child and Family Research: Shaping Head Start for the Nineties* (pp. 390–92). Washington, DC: The Administration on Children, Youth, and Families.

Van Manen, M. (1991). *The tact of teaching: The meaning of pedagogical thoughtfulness.* Albany, NY: State University of New York Press.

Vygotsky, L.S. (1978). *Mind in society: The development of higher psychological processes.* Eds. M. Cole, V. John-Steiner, S. Scribner, & E. Souberman. Cambridge, MA: Harvard University Press.

Wells, G. (1985). Preschool literacy-related activities and success in school. In D.R. Olson, N. Torrance, and A Hildyard (Eds.), *Literacy, language, and learning: The nature and consequences of reading and writing* (pp. 229–55). Cambridge: Cambridge University Press.

Williams, L.R. (1991). Curriculum making in two voices: Dilemmas of inclusion in early childhood education. *Early Childhood Research Quarterly, 6,* 303–11.

Williams, L.R. (1994). Developmentally appropriate practice and cultural values: A case in point. In B.L. Mallory and R.S. New (Eds.), *Diversity and developmentally appropriate practices* (pp. 155–65). New York: Teachers College Press.

Wood, D.J. (1988). *How children think and learn.* Oxford: Basil Blackwell.

Wurzel, J.S. (1988). Multiculturalism and multicultural education. In J.S. Wurzel (Ed.), *Toward multiculturalism* (pp. 1–13). Yarmouth, ME: Intercultural Press.

CHAPTER FIFTEEN

Integrating Home and School

Building a Partnership

JEAN M. LARSEN
JULIE H. HAUPT

Over the past two decades, an increasing amount of attention has been given to parents and the important role they play in the optimal development and learning of children (Berger, 1995; Powell, 1989, 1991). This mounting interest in the influence of parents, home, and family on children's education as well as their social, emotional, and cognitive development has been prompted by the rapid increases in maternal employment and nonfamilial child care. These societal changes have also caused general concern about children's readiness for school, the development of attitudes and values, and the establishment of familial and peer relationships. In order to meet the challenges facing families in today's rapidly changing society and to avoid the potential ill effects, a clarion call has gone out to all parents to provide learning opportunities for children in the home, to become more involved in their children's schooling, to form partnerships with their children's teachers, and to participate in parent education.

This chapter focuses on two avenues of integrating home and school to facilitate reaching each child's potential, academically as well as socially. The first avenue consists of the early childhood educator's responsibility to reach out to parents to assist them in fulfilling their role as the child's first and most important teacher through parent training efforts. Although parents do not generally view themselves (nor should they) as educators or professional teachers, in a very real sense parents are highly influential teachers, whether they recognize it or not. Indeed, parents are in the best position to positively influence their child's early learning and engender healthy dispositions that will enhance their child's school success.

The second avenue for integrating home and school focuses on parent involvement in the school. This aspect of the home–school partnership is reflected in current popular themes in the field of early childhood education referred to in the terms "parent involvement" or "parents as partners." Having parents involved in their children's formal education by understanding and being supportive of the under-lying philosophy and curriculum goals of the program, contributing to children's learning with follow-up activities at home, and even assisting in the classroom as volunteer teacher aides are significant elements of this dimension.

Assisting Parents as First Teachers

Although more than a decade ago, the landmark report "A Nation at Risk" alerted the American people to the importance of parents as a child's first teacher, the vital role that families play in the education of their children still hasn't received the attention it merits. In the mid-1960s Burton White (1990) and his associates at Harvard began an extensive study of young children in an effort to determine how to structure experiences during the first six years of life to help all children make the most of their potential. The initial insight emerging from their study was that by the time children reach 3 years of age, they have already undergone a great deal of "education." The researchers went on to find that a considerable number of 3-year-olds were remarkably able children and further that they exhibited the same pattern of special abilities found in outstanding 6-year-olds. As their study continued, the researchers were not only impressed by what some children could achieve and/or learn during these early years but also by the fact that informal learning experiences with their family seemed central to the outcome. The conclusions reached from their longitudinal observation of children for some thirteen years led White (1990) to proclaim that "the informal education that the family provides for their children *makes more of an impact on a child's total education than the formal education system. If a family does its job well, the professional can then provide effective training.* If not, there may be little a professional can do to save a child from mediocrity" (p. 4).

White's findings, along with indications from an increasing number of studies also attempting to identify factors contributing to early school success (Henderson, 1981, 1987; Henderson & Berla, 1994; Stevenson & Baker, 1987), demonstrate the importance of the home environment and informal learning in a family context prior to beginning school. It would seem that if parents were to provide a warm, stimulating environment, involve children in learning opportunities derived from the routines of day-to-day living in the home, and dedicate a period of time (even a few minutes) each day for interactive reading and/or discussion, children would be better prepared for and realize greater benefit from early school experience. In the event that children spend the greater part of their day in someone else's care, it is important that this setting be an extension of what is or should be happening at home. No matter who gives children their first formal lessons about letters and numbers, they have already learned from parents, other family members, and supplemental caregivers whether learning is a valued, exciting activity or not.

National Education Goal One

The readiness of America's children to profit from schooling was one of the major issues discussed by President Bush and the nation's governors at the 1989 education summit. The first of six national education goals announced by the president in 1990 was: "By the year 2000, all children in America will start school ready to learn (U.S. Department of Education, 1994). One may contemplate exactly what is meant by this goal statement since a vast amount of learning occurs from the earliest moments of life. For example, the fact that by 3 or 4 years of age most children can understand and use the language of those around them is just one example of the tremendous amount of learning that takes place long before children begin school. In other words, children are born ready to learn.

To facilitate efforts made toward achieving these goals, the various committees at the education summit formulated specific objectives related to each of the goals. The objective for the first readiness goal recommended that every parent in America will be a child's first teacher and devote time each day to helping his or her preschool child learn. The objective further recommended that parents would have access to the training and support they need. This objective acknowledged the fact that the knowledge, skills, and ability required to be an effective "teacher" of a child does not automatically come simply by virtue of giving birth. The notion that parents need assistance to fulfill their roles effectively is not new. Powell (1989) reminds us of Pestalozzi's postulation years ago that, for children, " the teaching of their parents will always be the core" and that the role of the teacher is to provide a "decent shell" around the core.

In more recent times there has been a general recognition of the need to enhance parental performance (Caldwell, 1980, 1989; Anastasiow, 1988). Further emphasis on this idea has been given by those who argue that every child deserves a parent with the skills that education can provide (Bell, 1975; Harris & Larsen, 1989; Rheingold, 1973). In today's world where responsibilities are often fragmented and highly demanding, perhaps there is greater need for parents to receive training and parenting information than in earlier times. Fortunately, more professional knowledge and resources are available to assist parents than at any other time in history. In addition to a current upsurge of printed material and electronic information (via the Internet) geared to meet the needs of parents, professional early childhood training programs are preparing human resources (teachers and caregivers) to work with parents in fulfilling their role as their child's first teacher.

While it is recognized that the home environment contributes significantly to the development of skills deemed important for successful formal learning, Powell (1991) cautions that parents should not be expected to assume total responsibility for either the success or failure of children's early school experience. For many years there has been an ongoing debate as to whether the child should be made ready for school or the school made ready for the child. While there may not be a definitive answer either way, the guidelines for developmentally appropriate practices in programs for young children (Bredekamp, 1987; Bredekamp & Copple, 1997) favor the view that the school experience as provided by the classroom teacher should be prepared to meet the children's individual and group learning needs. At the same time, parents have been admonished in the national education goals to have their children prepared to start school ready to learn.

Examples of Successful Parent Training Programs

To assist parents in preparing their children, access to training has been recommended in order to provide the needed education and support required to effectively meet the challenges of parenting. Who will be responsible for training and giving support to parents? While a plethora of church and community organizations play a significant role, school personnel, particularly the child's teacher, is a key player in this support network. Additionally, it should be noted that assistance to parents is crucial during the preschool years, prior to the child's entry into formal schooling. Therefore, one significant resource to draw on in accomplishing such an arduous task is the growing number of early childhood care and education professionals. This presupposes a parent component as an integral part of every quality care and education program for young children from their earliest out-of-home experience through their elementary school years. To accomplish this, preservice training and professional development efforts that emphasize the dual role of the early childhood professional—both to facilitate young children's development and learning and to assist parents in fulfilling their parental teaching role—should be provided routinely in early childhood teacher training course offerings and ongoing staff training. Brief descriptions of several exemplary parent programs that illustrate the variety of ways and the diversity of settings in which parent training can be implemented follow.

Head Start. A noteworthy and widely respected example of extensive efforts to provide parent education and involvement for parents of preschool children is the federally funded Head Start Movement, which began in 1965. While studies of early intervention programs initiated in the 1960s showed that parent involvement in their child's learning was a key to the child's success, Head Start was one of the relatively small number of programs that actually formalized a parenting component that would assist parents to be effective first teachers. It is well known that the basic objective of Head Start was to eradicate the possible limiting effects of a disadvantaged home environment on children by providing opportunities for optimal learning and socialization in an enriched environment. Additionally, a parent component was incorporated as an integral aspect of the Head Start program to encourage and empower parents to provide a rich and stimulating home environment that was more responsive to the needs of their child. Indeed, the parent component is viewed as essential to sustaining the positive impact of the Head Start program on the child (Lambie, Bond, & Weikart, 1974).

Parents as Teachers (PAT).   Another early parent program, *Saturday School,* was started in 1971 by a suburban middle-class Missouri school district that included some lower-income families with young children. Focusing on children's developmental characteristics, the program offered a preschool experience on Saturday as well as periodic home visits with parents. Later, the program was expanded to include a resource center that provided learning materials, speakers, short courses, and child care services, giving parents the opportunity to participate in and benefit from education sessions and enrichment activities (Wilson, 1991). Subsequently, a more extensive program originating in 1981, Parents as Teachers (PAT), continued the effort to provide an effective model of parent training. The PAT program was designed for all families with children from birth to kindergarten entry. It assists parents in acquiring the skills to help make the most of the crucial early learning years. The program covers child development and parent–child activities that encourage language and intellectual growth, curiosity, and social skills (Winter, 1993). (See table 15.1 for a more detailed program description.)

The program director's executive report (Winter, 1993) indicates that PAT has been shown to produce confident, competent parents

TABLE 15.1
Parents as Teachers Program

There are four components to this very functional program: (1) personal visits, which allow a professionally trained parent educator to personalize input to the family as well as give educational guidance that is relevant to the child's development and home environment; (2) group meetings, which provide opportunities for families to share successes and which serve as a vehicle for additional input from the staff as well as from outside speakers; (3) developmental screening, which reassures parents that the child is developing in a normal way or identifies problems early in order to assist parents with appropriate interventions; and (4) resource network, which identifies resource services such as speech and hearing clinics, diagnostic services, programs for children with special needs, which are beyond the scope of the PAT program. (Winter, 1993) and happy, well-rounded, academically able children. Evaluation studies conducted by independent research groups have provided empirical support for the beneficial claims of the program (Pfannenstiel & Selzer, 1985; U.S. Department of Education, 1987). Additional PAT program implementation and evaluation replications have been conducted with high-risk families in New York and California. Similar findings showed that PAT children were more ready to learn and were more advanced than comparison groups in language, social skills, problem solving and other intellectual abilities (Winter, 1993). Parents also credited the program with having increased their self-confidence as parents. Spanning a decade of field implementation, the program has demonstrated its adaptability potential for parents in a wide range of circumstances.

Parent Training Component of a University Preschool. Still another successful parent program was initiated over two decades ago as a mandatory component of a university-based preschool program. Since one of the purposes of the university preschool is teacher preparation, the parent training provided preservice teachers with experience in implementing parent education. The content information of the parent training program was designed to help parents gain a better understanding of the normal and/or typical behaviors of young children as well as how their child's behavior and development might differ from the norm. While the publication of the training materials (Cahoon, Price, & Scoresby, 1976, 1979) predated the concisely articulated NAEYC developmentally appropriate practice standards for working with young children (Bredekamp, 1987), an examination of the materials reveals that most of the practices recommended in the NAEYC standards were included in the content of the parent materials produced a decade earlier. This concordance of thought might be expected since both the parent training materials and the NAEYC standards were derived from long recognized ideas that an understanding of development and learning should be the philosophical foundation for educating young children (e.g. Dewey, 1938; Elkind, 1974, 1985; Erikson, 1962; Froebel, 1900; Gesell, 1923; Hymes, 1969; Katz, 1977; Katz & Chard, 1989; Piaget & Inhelder, 1969). As described in table 15.2, the parent program provides an opportunity to enhance teaching strategies and parent–child interaction skills as well.

Although participation in the parent training has been mandatory for both mothers and fathers of children attending the preschool,

TABLE 15.2
Parent Training Component of Preschool

Specifically parents were instructed in:
- Recognizing and appreciating developmental strides their children were making.
- Setting realistic goals.
- Making their teaching concrete, specific, and hands-on.
- Capitalizing on naturally occurring teaching opportunities.
- Integrating different types of instructional content for their children.
- Providing their children with both a variety and choice of activities.

Parents were also taught to:
- Give their full attention when their child is speaking to them.
- Get down on the child's level and look encouragingly at the child during conversation.
- Ask questions that encourage their child to share more information.
- Restate and clarify what their child said.
- Identify and restate emotional feelings that were being experienced by their child.

To promote positive affect parents were encouraged to:
- Comment briefly, pleasantly, and graciously when their child did something they wished to encourage.
- Use positive rather than negative phrasing in everyday conversation with their child.
- Share humorous experiences that their child could understand.

Adapted from *Supportive Teaching Behaviors* (Larsen, 1975).

parents have had several options about how they would receive the instructional component of the training program: (1) read selected sections from the parent education manual along with current articles and books that supported or supplemented the training manuals; (2) listen to dramatized cassette tapes based on the educational material; or (3) receive home visits, including a verbal presentation and discussion about the content material, from student teachers. Informational content is similar across dissemination modes. As part of the training program, parents were asked to spend a minimum of twenty minutes each week in a one-on-one activity with their preschool child practicing what they had learned in the training portion of the program.

The beneficial effects of the parent program have been documented through an ongoing longitudinal research project at the university preschool. Findings from one cohort group of parents in the study indicated that the majority of parents in the sample already possessed attitudes consistent with those espoused by the parent training program, yet significantly more parents, especially fathers, who had participated in parent training spent more time engaged in one-on-one activities with their preschool child than parents who did not have parent training (Harris & Larsen, 1989). Further analysis of these data along with that of succeeding groups included in the longitudinal study has shown that parent training seems to be linked to increases in parent–child interactions, positive family affect, and ultimately the child's social competence (Draper et al., 1993). Since the study was conducted with a low-risk population (educationally advantaged, middle-class, two-parent families), it gives support to the idea that all parents can benefit from parent education.

Outreach Efforts Targeting Specific Parenting Skills

While providing a broad understanding of child development principles is the necessary basis for an effective parent training program, outreach efforts directed toward enhancing specific parenting skills can create a strong partnership that ultimately benefits the child. For example, several recent outreach efforts have focused on enhancing parental skills in encouraging a child's language development and emerging literacy abilities (Rasinski, 1995). Parents can play an important role in their child's emergent literacy as demonstrated by research that strongly suggests that prior to formal literacy instruction young children learn many important concepts about written language through naturally occurring literacy events in the home (Debaryshe, 1993; Goldfield & Snow, 1984; Rowe, 1991; Sulzby, 1985; Taylor, 1983; Taylor & Strickland, 1986; Wells, 1985).

Research has further shown that young children's development of literacy skills is directly related to parent–child picture book reading (Chomsky, 1972; Greaney, 1986; Strickland & Morrow, 1989). More specifically, empirical study has identified the single most important activity for eventual success in reading to be reading aloud to children (Anderson et al., 1985). It is unfortunate that although children from low-SES homes experience many and varied literacy events, Teale (1986) found that these events mainly were centered around daily living routines and few if any were picture/story book reading.

Current research can be utilized to suggest pertinent parenting skills that can be enhanced through training, as illustrated in the two literacy studies highlighted here. The first study represented an effort to explore the effects of a home reading training strategy on the at-home reading behaviors of young children and their families. Two groups of pre-schoolers (Head Start and middle-class) participated in a study sponsored by a university early childhood program (Robinson, Larsen, & Haupt, 1995). One group of children enrolled in a Head Start class and one group of children attending a university laboratory preschool were given the opportunity to select and take home from their school a quality picture book each day. Cohort Head Start and university pre-school groups did not take books home. Child and family picture book reading behaviors were assessed on a weekly basis for all groups, using a telephone survey method. The findings indicated that both the Head Start and middle-class children who took picture books home from school each day more than doubled the number of books they read as compared to their counterparts who did not take books home. In addition, the Head Start children who took picture books home significantly increased the amount of time they were involved each day in reading with their parents and other family members.

Robinson and his associates further reported that in addition to significantly increasing home story time/reading behaviors for both the middle-class and the low-income families, there was a minimal amount of book damage or loss, and the enthusiasm of participants remained very high. This study highlights the fact that efforts by caregivers to enhance the child's home environment and increase parent–child interaction need not be restricted to formal training sessions. This simple procedure can be introduced into daily curriculum routines relatively inexpensively while demonstrating potentially very beneficial returns, especially for low-income children and their parents. In addition, storytime extender kits based around favorite books appropriate to the age and reading level of the children could be prepared and made available for check-out. For example, a kit based on Ruth Krauss's *The Carrot Seed* (1945) might have a packet of carrot seeds that can be planted along with a list of activities, such as looking through produce ads in the newspaper, purchasing carrots and following a simple carrot recipe, and sorting or comparing vegetable seeds of various kinds.

Another research project that suggests a training strategy for opti-mizing parental reading of picture books to children in the home was conducted by Whitehurst and his research associates (1988). Parents received videotaped instructions for using specific interactive reading procedures. The video training tape included examples of how to ask who, what, where, and when questions (not yes and no); follow the child's responses with additional questions; repeat what the child said; generally make the experience as enjoyable as possible by praising and encouraging the child; and expand the discussion based on the child's interests.

Results indicated significant increases in the expressive language ability of experimental children over control children (Whitehurst et al., 1988). Significant increases in language development were also shown in a subsequent study duplicating the training procedures with a disadvantaged sample (Whitehurst et al., 1994). Similar videotaped training approaches could be adapted and/or adopted by any early childhood teacher or child center interested in assisting parents to be more effective in a variety of specific parenting skills, such as reasoning and problem solving with children or utilizing daily routines as avenues for learning (i.e., sorting socks or setting the table).

Unfortunately, many parent programs developed with the best of intentions to enhance parents' informal teaching skills have not been successful (Rasinski, 1995). One reason some parent programs have been ineffective may be related to the fact that for the most part, programs admonish parents to do more, to be better, to spend more time, and so on. Many lack specific training in and/or demonstration of ways to facilitate learning as well as the appropriate use of materials in the home setting, unlike the two emergent literacy training examples cited above. In order for strategies and/or programs to be successful in assisting parents to fulfill their role as their child's first and most important teacher, the approach must have relevance, be functional, and be designed to meet the individual and group needs of parents.

Designing Effective Parent Training Programs

In planning and preparing a strategy for parent training, the needs and interests of the particular group of parents being served should carefully be considered. Administering a needs assessment is the first step in tailoring training to the parent group, either via a parent questionnaire or the teacher's observation of a particular need. A parent questionnaire at the beginning of the school year can ascertain what topics parents are most interested in and what kinds of scheduling would best encourage their participation (see samples in Berger, 1995; Brown, 1994). In this regard, technology can also play an important role in making available the information that parents may not be able to access due to time conflicts. Workshops, parent orientation meetings, and other parent gatherings can be videotaped and then checked out by parents to be viewed at a later date.

Once topics have been chosen or objectives have been formulated, the early childhood professional can begin to make plans for the most appropriate kind of training approach. Some may choose to create their own series of training workshops throughout the year. For others, a home visit format may best meet the needs of their particular parent population. Finally, others may adopt a more structured program already being successfully implemented in another area. Given the necessary resources, a home visit program has the advantage of greater personalization to the needs of each family. Additionally, the home environment provides an important degree of security that allows parents to ask questions and gives the trainer an opportunity to interact with both parent and child. The Mother-Child Home Program developed by Levenstein (1988) is a exemplary home-based program that encourages positive verbal interaction between the child and the parent via a toy, activity, or other material, which is brought and demonstrated by the home visitor. The goal of the program is to enhance mother–child interaction and extend the child's learning in the natural home environment. Significant improvement in parent–child interactions were realized from this type of parent training.

In the case of a school or community seeking a training program to meet the needs of a large group of parents, it is not necessary to go to the expense and effort of developing an entirely new program. A plethora of successful program models are already in existence and have proven effectiveness. A few examples include the Brookline Early Education Project (Pierson, Walker & Tivnan, 1984), the Minnesota Early Childhood Family Education Program (Berger, 1995), and Parents in Touch (Warner, 1991). To locate other programs throughout the United States, the most recent edition of *Educational Programs That Work* (National Dissemination Study Group, 1993) can provide an excellent resource.

Whatever the format, the following guidelines suggested by Berger (1995) should be carefully considered in order to optimize the success of parent training efforts:

- Establish a positive climate where risk is eliminated, positive feedback is generously used, and respect and encouragement are present.
- Plan curriculum that is relevant to parents and speaks to their concerns and needs.
- Use different approaches (role playing, short lectures, open discussions, debates, brainstorming, workshops) and a variety of sensory experiences (sight, sound, touch, taste, and smell) to allow parents to learn through an array of experiences.
- Ensure that parents are actively involved in their own education and that problem solving and analysis enable each participant to continue learning beyond the personal contact.
- Make sure that parents are considered to be an important part of the learning-teaching team and that they are recognized as having much of worth to contribute.

Parent Involvement

A second avenue for integrating home and school to improve the educational outcomes for today's children is parental involvement in the school. With national, state, and local leaders repeatedly emphasizing the importance of family involvement in the child's education, it is not surprising that the eighth National Education Goal reads: "Every school will promote partnerships that will increase parental involvement and participation in promoting the social, emotional, and academic growth of children" (U.S. Department of Education, 1994). At the ceremony commemorating the signing of Goals 2000, Secretary of Education Richard W. Riley emphasized that strong families make strong schools. Subsequently, the Department of Education formed a forty-five-member National Coalition for Parent Involvement in Education and issued a report entitled, *Strong Families, Strong Schools; Building Community Partnerships for Learning* (U.S. Department of Education, 1994) to foster parental involvement in children's education.

Beneficial Effects of Parent Involvement

Three decades of research confirm what parents and teachers sense intuitively, that is, that when parents are involved in their child's schooling, student learning dramatically improves. Henderson (1981, 1987) of the National Committee for Citizens in Education has compiled two comprehensive annotated bibliographies of studies linking parent involvement to student achievement. These studies show that programs designed with strong components of parental involvement produce students who perform better than those who have taken part in otherwise identical programs with little or no parental involvement. She concluded from her extensive review of the research literature in this area that "the evidence is now beyond dispute: parent involvement improves student achievement" (1987, p. 1). A recent third volume (Henderson & Berla, 1994) provides even stronger support for the beneficial outcomes when parents participate in their child's education.

While research confirms that families are integral to children's readiness for and success in school, true partnerships between families and schools exist more often in rhetoric than reality. In theory, parents and teachers seem to agree on the importance of parent involvement and home–school collaboration. Teachers across the spectrum feel that more home–school interaction would be beneficial (Moles, 1982) and almost all parents, even those from the most economically depressed communities, are committed to their children's education and say they want to help them succeed (Brandt, 1989). Indeed, one would think that with parents and teachers supporting the principle of home–school partnership and with such compelling data confirming its benefits, that family involvement would be thriving in schools across the country. Yet if an evaluation of the current status of home–school partnerships in this country were to be made it is likely the outcome would be discouraging. Although research evidence continues to mount (de Kanter et al., 1987; Epstein & Dauber, 1991; Henderson & Berla, 1994; Keith & Keith, 1993; Liontos, 1992; Stevenson & Baker, 1987) showing that children who do best in school are those whose families care about their education and are involved in their learning, the fact that there is minimal parent involvement in the schools leads to the inescapable conclusion that solutions must be sought on local levels to convert the rhetoric into a functioning partnership between families and schools.

Strategies for Involving Parents

As we attempt to bring the parent–school partnership rhetoric and reality closer together, it may be helpful to look at some of the barriers that inhibit parents' active participation in their children's school experience. Table 15.3 delineates four factors or aspects of modern life that a U.S. Education Report (1994) suggests may stand in the way. While the task of connecting families and schools must take into account the difficult conditions faced by many families today, it is encouraging to note that we have a greater knowledge base, more functional resources, and a growing body of skilled professionals available to assist in establishing a strong home–school integration. If we are to be successful, however, it will be necessary to address the barriers encountered "by parents and families with diverse backgrounds."

Meeting the challenge of involving uninvolved parents must surely become a high priority for early childhood professionals, teachers, and school administrators. Fredericks and Rasinski (1990) have suggested a number of procedures that have been successful in reaching non-

TABLE 15.3
Parent Participation Roadblocks

Time. Both parents and teachers want to do more but are having difficulties arranging the time. For example, two-thirds of employed parents with children under the age of 18 say they do not have enough time for their children.

Uncertainty about what to do and their own importance. Many parents say they would be willing to spend more time on activities with their children if teachers gave them more guidance. Teachers also need guidance, as very few colleges and school systems provide new and experienced teachers with coursework in working with families.

Cultural barriers. Language barriers of immigrant families and communication barriers of English-speaking families who have had little education or bad school experiences limit family-school contact.

Lack of supportive environment. A high rate of poverty and the concentrations of poverty by neighborhood limit student opportunities at home and after school. Many neighborhoods lack easy access to libraries, cultural institutions, health services, and recreation.

Excerpt from *Strong Families, Strong Schools* pp. 3–4 (U.S. Department of Education, 1994)

participating parents. Some of their ideas have been incorporated in the following:

- Flood parents with lots of written and visual information (as well as personal verbal invitations) over an extended period of time. One-time publicity announcements are not sufficient to provide parents with the information and motivation needed to become involved and/or stay involved.
- Give copious amounts of recognition (e.g., notes of appreciation, prizes, awards, certificates) to parents and students for their efforts. We all want to be recognized for our good deeds—both large and small.
- Make your classroom and your school a very comfortable place to be. Have an open-door policy and a willingness to meet parents on their terms. There should be a wide range of informational materials about the program curriculum and samples of children's work on display for parents to peruse.
- Telephone parents often. In addition, send home written notes to let parents know about a particular interest shown by their child and/or the progress their child is making. Too often communications are only made if there is a problem. Keeping parents advised of successful happenings is a good way to convey a spirit of optimism and inclusion to all families.
- Plan and implement relevant participatory projects in the classroom that may be extended to the home and motivate family involvement.
- Whenever a special event, such as a culminating activity in connection with project work is held, encourage parent attendance.

A simple example will illustrate how applying these ideas can create a higher level of success than previously experienced. Two student teachers working with a 2nd grade class in a Chapter I school had taken the children to visit the natural history museum as part of a unit of study on animal habitats. The children decided they wanted to make their own animal habitat museum in their classroom as a culminating activity for the unit and invite their families to come. The teacher had not been able to get more than a small number of parents to attend any school function up to that point and therefore was not optimistic about their participation. However, the children were extremely enthusiastic as they planned the various components of their museum and selected a committee to work on. When the day finally arrived to open their museum, every child had one or more family member attend.

Encouraging Parents' Unique Contributions

Henderson's research review (1981, 1987) revealed that although the results of parent involvement studies were uniformly positive (not a single negative study was found), the studies varied widely in approach, methodology, and subject matter. Similarly, parental involvement can and should take many forms, from taking advantage of informal learning opportunities in the home, to fostering educational readiness with a preschooler, to helping a school-age child with homework, to volunteering to help in the child's classroom or with special school projects, to taking an active interest in how the child performs in school. A higher order of parent involvement might include parents serving as members of strategic planning committees, representatives on policy-making or advisory boards, and/or members of other school auxiliary organizations. The rich diversity of forms that parent involvement can take illustrates the important point that there is no best way to involve parents. Indeed, as Henderson (1987) points out, what works is for parents to be involved in a variety of roles over a period of time (p. 2). Table 15.4 illustrates the variety of teaching and nonteaching tasks, as well as contributions from home that parents can make to a classroom.

Recognizing and Appreciating Diversity

Just as the recognition and appreciation of children's individual differences is a significant part of providing an appropriate educational experience for children, a knowledge and appreciation of children's families with their accompanying diversity is a key element in encouraging successful home–school partnerships. An open-door policy and a sincere interest in each child's family can create a nonthreatening climate that will invite more participation. Additionally, as parents share their diversity of talents, ideas, and cultural backgrounds, classroom teaching can be more developmentally appropriate and can more

TABLE 15.4
Suggestions of Ways Parents Can Assist

Teaching Tasks	Nonteaching Tasks
Involve children in creating, illustrating, and telling stories.	Make games.
Play math games.	Display children's art and/or project work.
Help children select library books.	Build and repair equipment.
Assist children in using computers.	Select and reproduce articles for parent use.
Help children conduct project fieldwork.	Conduct authentic assessment (i.e., observe, record, select work samples, etc.)
Support children's journal writing.	Prepare and rotate "take home" learning activity packets.
Take children on small-group or whole-class field trips.	
Participate in interactive reading.	**Contributions from Home**
Help children extend dramatic play.	Serve as telephone chairperson.
Supervise the making of books.	Collect recycling materials.
Assist in learning centers.	Furnish dress-up clothes and costumes.
Share talents, and interests.	Make art aprons.
Oversee a "messy" creative art activity.	Furnish resources for project work.
Supervise the production of a class newsletter or newspaper.	Care for another volunteer's children.
Help children in cooking and sensory activities.	Produce a parent newsletter.
Assist children's problem solving in cooperative learning groups.	

effectively meet the needs of all children—minority children as well as those of the dominant race and culture.

The diversity of cultural background that parents in any given classroom will represent insures varying opinions on issues pertinent to a cohesive partnership, that is, childrearing issues and parental philosophy regarding early academic experiences (Powell, 1994). Parents generally consider what they believe and do to be in the best interest of their children—as divergent as those views may be from one culture to another. Thus, in involving parents in schools, efforts should be made to recognize and appreciate the profound impact of ancestral worldviews, culturally defined childrearing practices, the level of acculturation of the family, and the particular stresses each family is coping with (Garcia Coll, Meyer, & Brillon, 1995). Just as the DAP philosophy underscores the significance of knowing individuals well, teachers will need to seek understanding of the families they serve to match parent involvement strategies to the particular needs of the parents they serve. Brand (1996) describes some simple, practical examples, such as hosting a parent evening that included an ethnic food potluck dinner or sending home wordless picture books to families who had limited English skills.

Meaningful Experiences for Parent Volunteers

Once parents have made an effort to become involved, teachers should do everything possible to encourage their continuing contribution to the classroom. Parents can be easily dissuaded from a return visit as volunteers in a classroom if they are confused about what is expected, given menial tasks, or feel their effort is unappreciated and ineffective. In general, providing ways for parents to be directly involved with children rather than performing mundane housekeeping tasks, such as cutting out bulletin board letters in the back of the classroom, will help most parents be more satisfied with their volunteering experience and help them feel their contribution has made a difference. Thus, it is critical to ensure that when parents volunteer, their desires and skills are considered. For parents who have agreed to assist in the classroom, especially those who intend to come in on a regular basis, a volunteer orientation meeting or training videotape may be an excellent way in which to clarify expectations and determine the specific interests of individual parents in helping in the classroom setting.

One Head Start teacher effectively used her volunteers to provide individualized instruction for the preschool children in her classroom. As a result of her ongoing assessment of children's skills, she was able to design specific one-on-one tasks that could be helpful to individual children. She wrote these mini-individualized activities on slips of papers, which she placed in a pocket. When parents came to volunteer, they pulled a slip out of the pocket and then worked for a few minutes with the child it named doing the activity that was suggested. For example, with a child who was struggling with scissors skills, the activity was to take a strip of green construction paper and have the child snip it all the way along in order to create some grass for a picture. The child successfully cut the snips to create the grass, completed the picture, and was proud of her accomplishment.

Meaningful volunteering experiences can also come through involving parents in the fieldwork for a project (see Katz & Chard, 1989 for an

overview of the Project Approach, a method for integrating curriculum). For example, in a project on fish, a volunteer could interact
with a small group of young children who are interested in dissecting a
real fish. The teacher could prepare the center with informational
books that have color plates and/or diagrams of the internal parts of a
fish, as well as paper and colored pencils for the children to do observational drawings. Such an activity integrates the curriculum in a
meaningful way as children measure, label, illustrate, question, speculate, and draw conclusions. The role of the volunteer in this situation
would be as a facilitator to the children's questions and ideas as they
discover and collect information about the fish. Although any parent
might assist in this kind of a hands-on fieldwork experience, a parent
with specific expertise or interest in fish might find this experience
particularly fulfilling.

In a classroom where this activity was done, one child in particular
was so fascinated by the dissecting experience that she was eager to
share her findings with her father when he came to pick her up. The
teacher reported to the father that she had been deeply engaged in this
activity. The father indicated that he was a pre-med student and often
worked in a lab as a part of his training. The teacher suggested that he
might consider taking his young child with him to the lab. The father
did take his daughter to the lab and as a result, the child was able to
follow up on her "budding" scientific interests as well as build a
deeper bond with her father. Other parents became involved with the
fish project as they accompanied their children on a field trip to a
fishing pond. Since each child was able to catch a fish to take home,
this provided a natural opportunity for parents to become involved
with their children in cleaning and preparing the fish for a meal. An
integrated curriculum can provide unusually rich opportunities to both
involve parents meaningfully as volunteers as well as to create wonderful developmentally appropriate learning activities in the home.

Summary

In conclusion, there seems to be mounting support for the thesis that
all schools and centers for young children would do well to work
toward offering both parent training and parent involvement opportunities as avenues for integrating home and school. Research during

the 1970s and 1980s documented the beneficial effects of parent training on children (Powell, 1986). Currently, parent participation continues to be highly valued as part of disadvantaged preschool programs and as mandatory for Head Start families. Additionally, the examples provided in this chapter of parent programs that have worked with middle-class families illustrates the notion that lower-risk families can and should be included in these partnership efforts. Thus, because of the important benefits accrued by the child, parent education and involvement should be integral components of early education programs regardless of the socioeconomic or educational status of the parent.

While much of the support research, program descriptions, and discussion presented in this chapter on integrating home and school resonates with common sense, the major points are worth reviewing again.

- A parent is the child's first and most important teacher.
- Thirty years of research show the importance of parents fulfilling this role.
- Early childhood professionals must assist parents in developing their role as their child's first teacher.
- All children in America should start school "ready to learn" and parents should have access to training and support in order to meet the "ready to learn" goal.
- Parent training programs have been successful in enhancing parental teaching skills.
- Effective parent training programs can be adapted from intervention research, as in the case of studies of emergent literacy.
- Training programs should be tailored to meet the needs of the parent group being served.
- Research confirms indisputably that parent involvement improves student achievement.
- Parent involvement can and should take a variety of forms based on the needs and interests of the parents.
- Teachers should be well prepared to help parents have a fulfilling experience when they volunteer.
- Parents from all socioeconomic levels should have opportunities to participate in training and volunteering.
- Every early childhood care and education program should have a parent training and/or involvement component.

In the final analysis, if teachers and caregivers hope to fulfill their commitment to provide meaningful learning experiences for children, they must enlist the support and cooperation of parents. Indeed, knowledge and skills may be introduced initially to children in the formal learning setting of the school, but the relevance and application of such skills and knowledge go beyond the classroom into the practical setting of the home and community. As teachers develop strategies for integrating curriculum in a developmentally appropriate classroom, they will find that including parents in classroom activities and providing parent training to enhance their effectiveness as parents will heighten the child's educational success in ways they never thought possible. Establishing a strong partnership with parents can thereby pave the way for children to reach their potential and become lifelong learners.

References

Anastasiow, N. (1988). Should parenting education be mandatory? *Topics in Early Childhood Special Education, 8* (1), 60–72.

Anderson, R.C., Hiebert, E.H., Scott, J.A., & Wilkinson, I.A.G. (1985). *Becoming a nation of readers: The report of the Commission on Reading.* Champaign, IL: Center for the Study of Reading.

Bell, T. (1975). The child's right to have a trained parent. *Elementary School Guidance and Counseling, 9,* 271.

Berger, E. (1995). *Parents as partners in education: Families and schools working together* (4th ed.). Englewood Cliffs, NJ: Prentice Hall.

Brand, S. (1996). Making parent involvement a reality: Helping teachers develop partnerships with parents. *Young Children, 51* (2), 76–81.

Brandt, R. (1989). On improving school and family connections: A conversation with Joyce Epstein. *Educational Leadership, 47* (2), 24–27.

Bredekamp, S. (Ed.). (1987). *Developmentally appropriate practice in early childhood programs serving children from birth through age 8.* Washington, DC: National Association for the Education of Young Children.

Bredekamp, S., & Copple, C. (Eds.). (1997). *Developmentally appropriate practice in early childhood programs: Revised*. Washington, DC: National Association for the Education of Young Children.

Brown, J. (1994). Parent workshops: Closing the gap between parents and teachers. *ACEI Focus on Early Childhood, 7* (1).

Cahoon, O.W., Price, A.H., & Scoresby, A.L. (1976). *Brushing Up on Parenthood*. Provo, UT: Institute of Family Home Education.

Cahoon, O.W., Price, A.H., & Scoresby, A.L. (1979). *Parents and the achieving child*. Provo, UT: Brigham Young University Press.

Caldwell, B.M. (1980). Balancing children's rights and parents' rights. In R. Haskins & J.J. Gallagher (Eds.), *Care and education of young children in America: Policy, politics and social science* (pp. 27–50). Norwood, NJ: Ablex.

Caldwell, B.M. (1989). Achieving rights for children: Role of the early childhood profession. *Childhood Education, 66* (1), 4–7.

Chomsky, C. (1972). Reading, writing, and phonology. *Harvard Education Review, 40*, 287–309.

Debaryshe, B.D. (1993, March). *Maternal reading-related beliefs and reading socialization practices in low-SES homes*. Paper presented at the biennial meeting of the Society for Research in Child Development, New Orleans, LA.

de Kanter, A., Ginsburg, A.L., & Milne, A.M. (1987). *Parent involvement strategies: A new emphasis on traditional parent roles*. Washington, DC: U.S. Department of Education.

Dewey, J. (1938). *Experience and education*. New York: Macmillan.

Draper, T.W., Larsen, J.M., Haupt, J.H., Robinson, C.C., & Hart, C.H. (1993, March). *Family emotional climate as a mediating variable between parent education and child social competence in an advantaged subculture*. Paper presented at the biennial meeting of the Society for Research in Child Development, New Orleans, LA.

Elkind, D. (1974). *A sympathetic understanding of the child: Birth to sixteen*. Boston: Allyn & Bacon.

Elkind, D. (1989). Developmentally appropriate practice: Philosophical and practical implications. *Phi Delta Kappan, 70* (10), 113–17.

Epstein, J.L., & Dauber, S.L. (1991). School programs and teacher practices of parent involvement in inner-city elementary and middle schools. *The Elementary School Journal, 91* (3), 289–305.

Erikson, E. H. (1962). *Childhood and society* (2nd ed.). New York: Norton.

Fredericks, A.D., & Rasinski, T.R. (1990). Working with parents: Involving the uninvolved. *The Reading Teacher, 43*, 424–25.

Froebel, F. (1900). *Pedagogics of the kindergarten.* Trans. J. Jarvis. New York: Appleton.

Garcia Coll, C.T., Meyer, E.C., & Brillon, L. (1995). Ethnic and minority parenting. In M.H. Bornstein (Ed.), *Handbook of parenting*, vol. 2, *Biology and ecology of parenting* (pp. 189–209). Mahwah, NJ: Erlbaum.

Gesell, A. (1923). *The preschool child.* New York: Houghton Mifflin.

Goldfield, B.A., & Snow, C.E. (1984). Reading books with children: The mechanics of parental influence on children's reading achievement. In J. Flood (Ed.), *Understanding reading comprehension* (pp. 204–18). Newark, DE: International Reading Association.

Greaney, V. (1986). Parental influences on reading. *The Reading Teacher, 39*, 813–18.

Harris, J.D., & Larsen J.M. (1989). Parent education as a mandatory component of preschool: Effects on middle-class, educationally advantaged parents and children. *Early Childhood Research Quarterly, 4*, 275–87.

Henderson, A. (1981). *Parent participation and student achievement: The evidence grows.* Columbia, MD: National Committee for Citizens in Education.

Henderson, A. (1987). *The evidence continues to grow: Parent involvement improves student achievement.* Columbia, MD: National Committee for Citizens in Education.

Henderson, A,. & Berla, N. (1994). *A new generation of evidence: The family is critical to student achievement.* Washington, DC: National Committee for Citizens in Education.

Hymes, J.L., Jr. (1969). *Early childhood education, and introduction to the profession.* Washington, DC: National Association for the Education of Young Children.

Katz, L.G. (1977). *Talks with teachers.* Washington, DC: National Association for the Education of Young Children.

Katz, L., & Chard, S. (1989). *Engaging children's minds: The project approach.* Norwood, NJ: Ablex.

Keith, T.Z., & Keith, P.B. (1993). Does parental involvement affect eighth-grade student achievement? Structural analysis of national data. *School Psychology Review, 22* (3), 474–96.

Krauss, R. (1945). *The Carrot Seed.* New York: Harper & Row.

Lambie, D.Z., Bond, J.T., & Weikart, D.P. (1974). *Home teaching with mothers and infants.* Monographs of the High/Scope Educational Research Foundation, No. 2. Ypsilanti, MI: High/Scope.

Larsen, J.M. (1975). Effects of increased teacher support on young children's learning. *Child Development, 46,* 631–37.

Levenstein, P. (1988). *Messages from home: The mother–child program.* Columbus, OH: Ohio State University Press.

Liontos, L.B. (1992). *At-risk families and schools becoming partners.* Eugene: University of Oregon, ERIC Clearinghouse on Educational Management.

Moles, O. (1982). Synthesis of recent research on parent participation in children's education. *Educational Leadership, 40* (2), 44–47.

National Dissemination Study Group. (1993). *Educational programs that work.* Longmount, CO: Sopris West.

Pfannenstiel, J., & Selzer, D. (1985). *New parents as teachers project.* Evaluation report prepared for the Missouri Department of Elementary and Secondary Education, Jefferson City, MO.

Piaget, J., & Inhelder, B. (1969). *The psychology of the child.* New York: Basic Books.

Pierson, D.E., Walker, D.D., & Tivnan, T. (1984). A school-based program from infancy to kindergarten for children and their parents. *The Personnel and Guidance Journal, 62* (8) 448–55.

Powell, D.R. (1986). Parent education and support programs. *Young Children, 41* (3), 47–53.

Powell, D.R. (1989). *Families and early childhood programs.* Washington, DC: National Association for the Education of Young Children.

Powell, D.R. (1991). *Strengthening parental contributions to school readiness and early school learning.* Paper prepared for the Office of Educational Research and Improvement, U.S. Department of Education.

Powell, D.R. (1994). Parents, pluralism, and the NAEYC statement on developmentally appropriate practice. In B.C. Mallory & R.S. New (Eds.), *Diversity and developmentally appropriate practices* (pp. 166–82). New York: Teachers College Press.

Rasinski, T.V. (1995). Teacher–parent partnerships. In T. Rasinski (Ed.), *Helping children learn to read and write.* Fort Worth, TX: Harcourt Brace.

Rheingold, H. (1973). To rear a child. *American Psychologist, 28,* 42–46.

Robinson, C.C., Larsen, J.M., & Haupt, J.H. (1995). Picture book reading at home: A comparison of Head Start and middle class preschoolers. *Early Education & Development, 6* (3), 241–52.

Rowe, K.J. (1991). The influence of reading activity at home on students' attitudes towards reading, classroom attentiveness and reading achievement: An application of structural equation modeling. *British Journal of Educational Psychology, 61,* 19–35.

Stevenson, D.L., & Baker, D.P. (1987). The family–school relation and the child's school performance. *Child Development, 58,* 1348–57.

Strickland, D.S., & Morrow, L.M. (Eds). (1989). *Emerging literacy: Young children learn to read and write.* Newark, DE: International Reading Association.

Sulzby, E. (1985). Children's emergent reading of favorite story books: A developmental study. *Reading Research Quarterly, 20,* 458–81.

Taylor, D. (1983). *Family literacy: Young children learning to read and write.* Portsmouth, NH: Heinemann.

Taylor, D., & Strickland, D.S. (1986). *Family storybook reading.* Portsmouth, NH: Heinemann.

Teale, W.H. (1986). Home background and young children's literacy development. In W.H. Teale & E. Sulzby (Eds.), *Emergent literacy: Writing and reading.* Norwood, NJ: Ablex.

U.S. Department of Education. (1987). *What works: Research about teaching and learning.* Washington, DC: Author.

U.S. Department of Education. (1994). *Strong families, strong schools.* Washington, DC: Author.

Warner, I. (1991). Parents in touch: District leadership for parent involvement. *Phi Delta Kappan, 73* (5), 372–75.

Wells, G. (1985). Preschool literacy-related activities and success in school. In D.R. Olson, N. Torrance, & A. Hildyard (Eds.), *Literacy, language, and learning* (pp. 229–55). Cambridge, MA: Harvard University Press.

White, B.L. (1990). *The first three years of life.* Englewood Cliffs, NJ: Prentice Hall.

Whitehurst, G.J., Falco, F.L., Lonigan, C.J., Fischel, J.E., DeBaryshe, D.B., Valdez-Menchaca, M.C., & Caulfield, M. (1988). Accelerating language development through picture book reading. *Developmental Psychology, 24,* 552–59.

Whitehurst, G.J., Arnold, D.S., Epstein, J.N., Angell, A.L., Smith, M., & Fischel, J.E. (1994). A picture book reading intervention in day care and home for children from low-income families. *Developmental Psychology, 30,* 679–89.

Wilson, M. (1991). Forging partnership with preschool parents: The road to school success begins in the home. *Principal, 70* (5), 25–26.

Winter, M. (1993, December). Parents as teachers: Invest in good beginnings for children. Presentation given at Harvard Forum on Schooling and Children, Cambridge, MA.

CHAPTER SIXTEEN

Informing Parents, Administrators, and Teachers about Developmentally Appropriate Practices

JULIE H. HAUPT
MARGARET F. OSTLUND

Early childhood educators embracing the principles of developmentally appropriate practices (DAP) (Bredekamp & Copple, 1997) note positive outcomes in their classrooms (Charlesworth et al., 1993a; Hart et al., this volume; Marcon, 1994). Children's engagement in learning tasks increases and desirable dispositions can be more effectively nurtured (Katz & Chard, 1989). Certainly, when curriculum becomes better suited to their current level of development and takes into account their individual needs, children will offer no complaints about these classroom modifications. However, adults, including administrators, parents, and other teachers, may question these classroom practices and challenge the teacher to justify certain educational decisions. More often than not, negative opinions are based on brief and infrequent encounters with the classroom setting without a thorough investigation of daily classroom life or child outcomes.

When a teacher's philosophical notions about teaching children comes in conflict with those of the administrator, Rusher, McGrevin, and Lambiotte (1992) suggest that there are three options available: (1) disregard the direction of the administrator; (2) teach in ways that are not consistent with the teacher's belief system; or (3) leave the profession. A fourth alternative may be available that would also apply when teachers meet resistance from parents and colleagues: continue to teach, modeling the best practices possible under the circumstances, while making a concerted effort to provide others with information that can broaden their perspectives about practices that are developmentally appropriate for young children. Even the best, most sensitive provision of information will not turn all critics into supporters. However, in the interest of providing young children with the most appropriate and effective educational experience, the effort to do so becomes an important responsibility of the early childhood educator (Granucci, 1990).

Making the change from a developmentally inappropriate philosophy and/or set of classroom practices to the developmental approach, as described by Krogh in chapter 2 in this volume, is an involved process. For those with less connection with the classroom, such as parents and administrators, understanding the value of the developmental approach can be even more elusive. Programs structured around developmentally inappropriate practice (DIP) can demonstrate quick, short-term gains, typically in achievement scores, which may be initially attractive and persuasive to administrators and parents. However, a careful look at the long-term effects is warranted to help educators make decisions based not only on what children can do in the early years, but what they should be expected to do based on their present level of development (Glascott, 1994; Katz & Chard, 1989). Currently, a growing body of research demonstrates positive long-term outcomes for children involved in developmentally appropriate programs, both in academic gains (Burts et al., 1993; Charlesworth et al., 1993a; Frede, Austin, & Lindauer, 1993; Frede & Barnett, 1992; Hart et al., this volume; Schweinhart & Hohmann, 1992) and desirable social outcomes (Charlesworth et al., 1993a; Weikart & Schweinhart, 1991).

While effective changes can be initiated at many levels (see Goffin & Stegelin, 1992), teachers are in a unique position to influence the parents they serve, the administrators they work with, and the colleagues with whom they interact. Though administrators can create a supportive climate for change, actual classroom practices will be affected only when teachers capture the vision of DAP, find ways to implement it in their classrooms (May, 1992), and uncover avenues for sharing that information with others. Many can testify that the process of effecting change can be frustrating and emotionally draining. However, there is a certain exhilaration that comes when teachers sense that they are part of something really worthwhile (Goffin & Stegelin, 1992) and find that they are teaching in ways that will make a significant difference in the lives of young children.

The purpose of this chapter is to suggest ways in which teachers can effectively educate parents and administrators about DAP, including an integrated curriculum, and how they and their colleagues can effectively work toward more developmentally appropriate classroom environments. Success will depend on how well teachers can build on the common goals they already share with parents and administrators, how well they can articulate and demonstrate through firsthand experiences the philosophy of DAP, and how sensitively and judiciously they respond to a plurality of educational views. Each section that follows offers specific suggestions for engaging other adults in a cooperative effort toward implementing developmentally appropriate practices in classrooms with young children.

Educating Parents

Parents care deeply about the kind of education their children receive. Indeed, their natural desire to champion the interests of their children makes a significant contribution to their child's development and should be encouraged. Additionally, engaging parents as partners in the educational process has long been acknowledged in the early childhood field as one of the most important ways to facilitate children's educational achievement, as discussed by Larsen and Haupt in the previous chapter of this volume. In doing so, a plurality of views should be expected as well as respected by classroom teachers in order to build the trust and communication necessary to form a basis for sharing ideas about educational practices.

In reviewing the literature, Powell (1994) notes the erosion of middle-class parental support for child-centered program philosophies in the 1980s and the preferences of lower-income and ethnic minority parents for didactic approaches to the education of their young children. This parental desire for strong academic skills, combined with societal pressures (see Elkind, 1986; and Carlson & Stenmalm-Sjoblom, 1989)—including voices from the popular press that often extol the virtues of early academics—can make parents particularly culpable to endorsing programs that utilize DIP (Stipek, Rosenblatt, & DiRocco, 1994).

While parents and teachers share the same general goals for children, such as academic and social success (Olmstead & Lockhart, 1995; Stipek, Rosenblatt, & DiRocco, 1994), differences often center around educational strategies and priorities. For example, several studies document the finding that parents tend to have higher expectations for academics than do their children's preschool and kindergarten teachers (Hyson, 1991; Olmstead & Lockhart, 1995; Rescorla, 1991), while kindergarten teachers rate curiosity and independence higher than do parents (Knudsen-Lindaur & Harris, 1989). Perhaps part of this discrepancy arises from the desire that parents have for their children to show early promise of academic success through readily visible indicators. For example, Hiebert and Adams (1987) found that fathers and mothers significantly overestimate their preschool children's performance on measures of emergent literacy, such as letter naming and writing. Parents of primary grade children also voice preferences for a strong academic approach with cries of "back to the basics."

When parents are approached with educational innovations that seem to downplay the reading and math work sheet approach that they are familiar with, they are likely to have questions (Healey, 1994). Some, perhaps, fear that their child may be subject to an educational experiment that will repeat some of the failures of past movements. Fortunately, however, practitioners as well as educational researchers are accumulating increasing evidence of the success of educational methods that promote a more child-centered approach, such as cooperative learning (Johnson & Johnson, 1991; Slavin, 1987), a balanced language approach (Goodman, 1987; Reutzel, this volume; Reutzel & Cooter, 1996), and integrated curriculum (Jacobs, 1989; Perkins, 1991).

Because parents and teachers are both concerned with the academic and social success of children, teachers can be more successful in introducing DAP to parents when they emphasize how these goals will be accomplished through an integrated curriculum. They can focus specifically on how skills will be learned and applied through many facets of the curriculum—for example, play, learning centers, systematic instruction, project work, and teacher-planned integrated units. As teachers describe the DAP philosophy to parents, it appears to be particularly significant that they are able to clearly articulate what DAP represents (Glascott, 1994; Granucci, 1990) in order to help parents avoid common misconceptions (Galen, 1994; Kostelnik, 1992).

As teachers implement a more child-centered and child-sensitive integrated curriculum, however, they would do well to insure that their classroom does not become subject to the "early childhood error" described by Bredekamp and Rosegrant (1992): inadequate attention to the content of the curriculum. An early childhood educator who understands and practices DAP at a superficial level, for example, may represent a DAP classroom as one in which a low-structure play environment is seen as a sufficient condition for learning. Though children are allowed to choose among toys or activities, they may be missing important learning opportunities. When teachers claim that their classroom practices are based on DAP, but insufficiently scaffold learning (in Vygotskian terms) by failing to provide appropriate levels of teacher guidance, their children do not achieve as well as they might (Charlesworth et al., 1993a; Kontos & Dunn, 1993; Mosley et al., 1996). Education that fails to respect the importance and intellectual integrity of curriculum content areas or properly assist the learner in the quest for knowledge demonstrates a lack of educational responsibility (Brophy & Alleman, 1991) and often does not sufficiently challenge and engage the capable minds of young learners (Katz & Chard, 1989). Parents, in this case, may justifiably be skeptical about these methods when learning goals are not being met. Therefore, careful planning and assessment coupled with good training in developmental philosophy and practice is the foundation on which effective advocacy efforts will be built.

Additionally, when parents are directly involved in and kept informed of changes taking place in the classroom, they are in a better position to understand and support them (Elkind, 1994). For example, an elementary school in Colorado, as reported by Kenney and Perry (1994), focused on creating a better assessment system that could report children's progress on learner outcomes, such as self-directed learner, community contributor, and complex thinker. They involved the parents in their initial deliberations about the problem and the preparation of a prototype. After initial approval to pilot the program, they called a special PTA meeting in which the parents who had been involved in the deliberations presented the new assessment format to the other parents.

When the first new assessment went home, it was accompanied by a brochure and a detailed survey. Though they received a positive response from the majority of the parents, they continued to use parental input to devise a friendlier version, which was explained to parents during their next parent–teacher conference. Involving parents in the process of change and being responsive to their suggestions in this instance created significant parental support for a more authentic and appropriate assessment format.

Informing parents about DAP classroom philosophy and the value of an integrated curriculum can best be accomplished through utilizing a variety of strategies across the school year. The final chapter of the initial DAP standards (Black & Puckett, 1987) includes many valuable suggestions for informing parents about developmental practices. Numerous articles have been written by practitioners since that time confirming these suggestions as successful in actual practice. Three general strategies appear to be the most widely discussed: (1) oral and written communication, (2) parent meetings, and (3) involvement in the classroom as a visitor or volunteer. These are essentially the same strategies typically listed to encourage parent involvement in the schools and echo some of the major themes of the previous chapter (see Larsen & Haupt, this volume). They can simultaneously provide an avenue for educating parents about classroom philosophy and integrated curriculum. In addition, a fourth strategy that consists of involving parents directly in DAP activities with their children at home can also be a valuable tool for educating parents.

Oral and Written Communication

Speaking directly with parents, whether in person or over the phone, can be a good time to discuss child progress and build relationships with parents, as well as field questions and respond to concerns regarding classroom practices. In conversations with parents, teachers can make it a point to share their child's successes, being sure to explain how a particular DAP activity nurtured the child's success in that instance. Making use of actual classroom experiences to illustrate the principles of DAP can make the ideology more understandable to parents, once they have been introduced to the basic tenets.

The more formal kind of oral communication that happens between teachers and parents generally comes in a parent–teacher conference setting (see Bjorklund & Burger, 1987; Ribas, 1992). Conferences have the potential to create a meaningful context for explaining how the appropriate activities within an integrated curriculum are strengthening the child's skills, especially when they include a review of the child's progress, time for setting goals, and open dialogue about how to work together (Bundy, 1991). Careful consideration of parental concerns and the use of appropriate assessment methods that meet the NAEYC guidelines can lead to discussions with a clear developmental focus that place the individual needs and strengths of the child in the forefront.

As teachers prepare written communication to go home, they should be aware of the value of clearly communicating how the activities they are describing help children build the knowledge and skills that parents value. While it might be quite obvious to a teacher that building a classroom store is helping children improve their literacy and social skills as well as strengthen their understanding of money, parents might not immediately recognize these benefits. Sending home curriculum plans that emphasize the reason for activities and suggest ways that parents can follow up at home in developmentally appropriate ways (Bundy, 1991) can strengthen parental support. Specific anecdotes documenting children's developing skills during key learning experiences and snippets of children's conversations that reveal their emerging insights may be appropriate to include as examples of ways children learn.

Newsletters can also include a broad scope of information and provide a discussion of issues that are suggested by parents or are of interest to them, particularly those relating to DAP and integrated curriculum (Healey, 1994; Passidomo, 1994). Maintaining current membership in national and/or local early childhood organizations that endorse developmental practices may introduce teachers to a wealth of current literature that can be shared with parents (Swick & McKnight, 1989). "Article boxes" with relevant readings that reflect a developmentally appropriate perspective can be provided as a resource for parents to check out or take home (Bundy, 1991).

Parent Meetings

Many early childhood programs sponsor parent meetings, such as Back-to-School Nights with the purpose of introducing parents to the teaching staff and the curriculum. Parent meetings that either involve parents directly in DAP activities (Healey, 1994) or feature slides and videotapes of the children in action in the classroom encourage better attendance (Passidomo, 1994; Stipek, Rosenblatt, & DiRocco, 1994). In addition, they provide excellent opportunities for teachers to explain how an integrated curriculum helps children develop a variety of valuable skills. For example, kindergarten teachers in one school entitled their orientation "Kindergarten Curriculum Night" and focused the event on helping parents understand developmentally appropriate philosophy (Passidomo, 1994). The meeting consisted of families participating in kindergarten activities together, such as painting and block play, along with a video of the program in action. Door prizes were given, and an atmosphere conducive to socializing with other parents was created.

In another instance, a preschool teacher, utilizing the Project Approach as an avenue for integrating the curriculum (see Chard, 1993, 1994; Katz & Chard, 1989), had just finished facilitating a project on shoes. She invited the parents to come for an evening meeting to celebrate the children's success and progress. While some parents had noted the immense interest that their children had demonstrated over the six-week project, others had questions about why the topic of shoes would merit so much attention. Through reviewing the classroom centers, the project display, and the experiences that the children had over the course of the project, the teacher was able to help the parents see that the topic of shoes had been the vehicle through which the children had applied their emerging literacy, numeracy, social, and large/small muscle skills in an integrated way.

Classroom Involvement

Inviting parents to participate in classroom activities gives them a firsthand opportunity to see the children's responsiveness to involvement in DAP activities. While time and scheduling constraints are prohibitive to many parents, helping them feel needed in the classroom and clear about how to best assist can encourage them to be more active participants (Finders & Lewis, 1994). For example, after warmly greeting a father volunteer, a well-prepared Head Start teacher provided him with a written activity description for the shaving cream finger painting that was planned for the sensory table. The sheet briefly described the purpose of the activity, summarized the rules for the sensory table, and suggested questions that could help make the children's experience more meaningful. Though he had no formal training in DAP, with the help of the written information he was asking very appropriate questions to which the children were responding enthusiastically.

While DAP classrooms are set up in child-centered ways with appropriately sized furniture, inviting learning centers, and bulletin boards at children's eye level, classrooms can also be enhanced to provide learning opportunities for parents. Whether a parent visits the classroom only for parent meetings and parent–teacher conferences or as a frequent volunteer, information at parent's eye level can be a helpful aid for understanding how children learn. For example, posting a brief list in each classroom learning center that describes what children typically do and what they learn while they are there can be helpful. Providing a parent bulletin board where children's work (Bundy, 1991) and handouts on DAP home activities are available (including recipes, suggested family outings, etc.) can become a good parent resource, especially if it is updated frequently.

Involving Parents in DAP Activities at Home

Some parents who are eager to help their children, but are unfamiliar with developmental approaches to learning, may use readily available educational materials, such as flash cards, workbooks, and other materials that can be used inappropriately and become less effective in nurturing their child's development and early education. Research indicates that parental beliefs about educational priorities in the school are translated into their interactions with their children at home (Powell, 1994). For example, Stipek, Rosenblatt, and DiRocco (1994) found that parents who endorsed DIP in educational settings reported engaging in more formal educational activities at home. However, another study (Campbell et al., 1991) found that for lower-SES parents, the involvement of their child in an appropriate, high-quality preschool program was associated with a shift away from traditional, authoritarian attitudes.

Teachers have the opportunity to wield an important influence in both home and school settings as they assist parents to become involved in appropriate educational experiences with their children. These hands-on experiences can help make the philosophy more concrete and perhaps more convincing to parents as well. For example, teachers can make parents aware of DAP activities that they can do at home in connection with current topics being studied in the integrated curriculum. They can send home books with children related to the topic being studied and provide suggestions to parents about DAP follow-up activities. Parents can also be invited to share ideas and materials in a classroom project, helping the learning extend beyond the walls of the classroom into the home.

Parent–teacher conferencing can be another place to make a concerted effort to form alliances with parents that encourage DAP activities in the home. For example, one kindergarten teacher who involves the child in the parent–teacher conferences invites the child to show the parents his or her portfolio. In preparing these portfolios, the teacher has been careful to avoid the temptation to build an "educational scrapbook." Rather, she includes "systematic collections of similar products constructed at regular intervals" that reflect children's progress over time, as Hills (1992, p. 60) suggests. As the parents peruse the dated work, they readily note their child's well-documented progress. This close look at children's writing, reading, and numeracy-related work leads into a conversation with the child about various academic skills. The child makes a decision about the skill he or she could work on to improve by the next conference. The teacher not only provides learning centers in the classroom that allow children to work in a self-motivated way on these skills through DAP activities, but has take-home materials, such as a "writer's briefcase," which encourage DAP follow-up activities at home as well. As a result, parents are able to use the DAP materials with their children and are given a hands-on experience in facilitating learning through exploration and experiences set in meaningful contexts.

In summary, as Galinsky (1988) notes, the parent–teacher alliance should provide a relationship in which the parent's own expertise is strengthened. Collaborative efforts with parents will require open lines of communication and proactive efforts to inform parents about DAP through many different avenues, including some that involve them directly in DAP activities. As Spiegel, Fitzgerald, and Cunningham (1993) found, parents have different preferences and perceptions of the learning process. Thus, providing a menu of choices will build a program more responsive to parents and will be more likely to prosper. Educating parents about DAP will be a continual opportunity for the teacher and a highly significant part of her or his work, because this information can impact the child's home life as well as maximize the benefits of the school experience.

Educating Program Administrators

Commitment on the part of administrators to support educational practice that is developmentally appropriate for children is undoubtedly a significant variable in a teacher's ability to implement DAP in the classroom. Although some teachers have managed to make changes in a climate hostile or indifferent to the developmental philosophy, teachers are best empowered to move forward when a supportive climate exists. For example, Horsch (1992) found that where administrative support was tentative or ambiguous, movement toward more developmentally appropriate practices in classrooms slowed or even reversed itself. Thus, though principals do not have the same direct impact on students that teachers do, they do have an important indirect impact (Heck, Larsen, & Marcoulides, 1990). In the final analysis, the relationship between teachers and principals and how they organize and coordinate the work life of the school affect the school environment as well as shape the learning experiences of students (Rusher, McGrevin, & Lambiotte, 1992).

Research on administrators beliefs demonstrates views reflecting both ends of the DAP-DIP spectrum. One study, for example, showed that about as many principals reported appropriate beliefs concerning kindergarten instruction as reported inappropriate beliefs (Charlesworth et al., 1993a). It is often assumed that principals and policy makers are knowledgeable about new curricular issues and trends, but this may not always be the case. Because of the magnitude of decisions and issues with which administrators deal on a daily basis, many may be only slightly aware of the implications of current research for best practice with young children, and may not be sufficiently informed to champion causes that counter public pressures (Rusher, McGrevin, & Lambiotte, 1992).

Indeed, limited training in early childhood education and a lack of information about developmentally appropriate practices are fairly common among both child care directors (Caruso, 1991; Kuykendall, 1990) and principals (Charlesworth et al., 1993a). As might be expected, Charlesworth, Hart, Burts, and DeWolf (1993a) found that principals who were certified as kindergarten teachers and/or had received training in early childhood education held stronger beliefs regarding the importance of DAP than those principals without certification and/or training. They also found that principals who lacked a knowledge of young children's needs and appropriate educational practices were more likely to value DIP and to have teachers who reported using more inappropriate practices. Evidence of a gender difference in the DAP beliefs of principals arose in one investigation (Rusher, McGrevin, & Lambiotte, 1992), with female principals more often supporting child-centered practices. The authors attributed the difference to the fact that male principals tended to have less time in the classroom before becoming a principal and were more likely to come from a secondary school background, thus being less aware of issues in the education of young children.

Also with regard to the impact of the administrative ambience, teachers reported that some of the strongest influences on classroom practices were school system policies and state regulations (Charlesworth et al., 1993a). Especially in the case of teachers who work in the public school system, widespread adoption of DAP will require the persistent and collaborative efforts of many early childhood educators, since systemic rather than cosmetic changes are required in order to affect policies and regulations that inhibit the implementation of DAP (Sykes, 1994). As Espinosa (1992) points out, transforming primary education in the United States from a transmission model to a constructivist, developmentally appropriate model may be one of the most difficult and challenging educational reforms to date. The challenges facing those promoting the universal implementation of DAP in the public school are corroborated and more specifically delineated by Schultz (1992) as follows: (1) the size and complexity of the public education system; (2) the complexity of decision making; (3) the scope of changes required in implementing DAP; (4) the current policy focus on accountability; (5) the shifting, never-ending demands placed on the education system, making it difficult for schools to focus on any one agenda; and (6) the competing ideas and "packages of curriculum" promoted for early childhood education.

Fortunately, however, current trends in educational reform have focused on "restructuring" education in ways that may open some doors to those advocating a developmental philosophy. For example, part of the restructuring movement includes site-based management, which invites teachers to participate on collaborative decision-making teams with administrators. When teachers have more training and experience in DAP than administrators, this joint effort can provide a prime opportunity for sharing information with their local teams that facilitates instructional decisions favoring DAP.

In addition, some of the classroom reforms currently being proposed, though not all, include practices congruent with developmental philosophy (Mitchell, 1993). For example, some of the factors that would qualify schools to be considered as research sites for studying comprehensive restructuring efforts (Newmann, 1993) include the following: Do teachers work with students as much in small groups and individual study as in whole-class instruction? Do students have substantial influence in the planning, conduct, and evaluation of their work? Are academic disciplines integrated in the curriculum? Do learning tasks aim for depth of understanding rather than broad exposure? Is school learning time flexibly organized rather than in periods of standard length? Does the school have a systematic program for parent involvement in the academic life of students that goes beyond normal activities?

Those administrators who are or become supportive of DAP are in a position to assist teachers in many ways. For example, May (1992) suggests that administrators can structure school policies to produce a favorable climate for DAP, provide time for teachers to discuss and share with one another, hire new personnel who value DAP, and provide monetary resources to implement the program successfully. Administrators can also write grants that lend monetary support to the implementation of DAP, thus providing resources such as additional teaching materials and professional development opportunities. Indeed, when all levels of administration, together with teachers, make the implementation of DAP a common goal, remarkable progress can be made.

Such was the experience of the teachers and administrators in a project undertaken in the District of Columbia public schools. The results of an empirical investigation into the effectiveness of the early childhood programs in the school system formed the impetus for the project (Marcon, 1994). As research evidence continued to mount in favor of the effectiveness of child-initiated preschools and kindergarten programs that valued socioemotional development, policy makers became increasingly convinced that most of the programs being offered for young children were not developmentally appropriate and thus were not resulting in the desired outcomes. With the research findings as a basis, their charismatic, energetic early childhood director found ways to turn these findings into significant policy changes that provided a climate for change (Marcon, 1994).

As Sykes (1994) reports, the first event centered around declaring the school year as "The Year of the Young Child" to focus attention on early childhood education as a top priority in the school system's reform agenda. Early on, an institute for all elementary principals was held to introduce them to DAP. This was done in a hands-on way by engaging the principals in the kinds of appropriate activities that the children might be involved in during the day (i.e., water play, hands-on mathematics, storytelling, etc.). Before large-scale changes were recommended, however, an intra-agency, early childhood collaborative was formed to seek common ground and to form a consensus around the definition of DAP. Once a shared vision was in place, an all-day citywide Early Childhood Institute for the staff of pre-K through 1st grade teachers and assistants was sponsored. Each year, the next grade level teachers were added to the list of those invited. Conference sessions helped participants learn about and implement DAP, with some of the sessions designed particularly to address the major areas of concern expressed by certain groups of teachers. For example, primary grade teachers were shown how skills can be taught effectively in DAP classrooms.

While good beginnings in reform efforts are quite common, many attempts are only partially successful because they fail to provide sufficient follow-up classroom support to create and sustain meaningful change (Wood, 1994). Follow-up support efforts in this project, however, came in a variety of formats to serve the diverse needs of the individuals involved. For example, groups of specialists provided technical assistance, demonstration centers were strategically located throughout the city, and consulting teachers were made available to help teachers in individual classrooms. Also, twenty special interest study groups were formed to provide forums focused on important topics in early childhood. While widespread interest and implementation have been the result, there are teachers in this system who did not desire to make changes and, therefore, have not. However, the system itself now invites change and provides a variety of resources for teachers as they make modifications in their classroom practices.

In summary, appropriate practice will flourish most effectively in schools where both teachers and administrators are fully informed about DAP and where both groups of educators collaboratively expend the necessary effort to implement DAP. Where such conditions do not exist, teachers who are convinced of the benefits of DAP must take the responsibility of informing administrators and providing visual models of best practices in their classrooms (Bredekamp, 1987). Principals and directors who recognize the value of DAP can provide a climate supportive of teachers who are in the process of applying principles and adopting practices that will better meet the educational needs of the children they teach (David, 1991).

Educating Teachers

Across roles and settings, early childhood educators experience a diversity of situations that both enhance and inhibit their opportunities to become aware of and implement DAP. A brief look at three distinct settings that span the developmental spectrum—center-based child care and preschool programs for under-5 children, kindergartens, and the primary grades in public schools, each of which have their own separate historical beginnings, distinct problems, and opportunities (Holloway & Fuller, 1992)—may elucidate some common barriers to change and suggest efforts that can be strengthened to make these settings more friendly to widespread adoption of DAP by teachers.

Center-Based Daycare/Preschool Programs.

Insuring program quality for the large number of America's under-5 children participating in child care and preschool programs depends on providing developmentally appropriate settings (Kagan, 1988). Specialized training of day care and preschool teachers is a significant factor in implementing DAP (Bredekamp, 1987; Cassidy et al., 1995). This is true even for teachers who have been in the field for many years, since work experience has been found to be a poor predictor of appropriate teacher behavior (Snider & Fu, 1990; Whitebook et al., 1989). Research consistently indicates that caregivers with specialized training in child development are more interactive, helpful, talkative, playful, positive, and affectionate in their relationships with young children (Howes, 1983; McCartney et al., 1982; Vandell & Powers, 1983). Studies also show that children who are cared for by trained caregivers are more involved, cooperative and persistent (Snider & Fu, 1990) and that caregivers who hold less authoritarian beliefs provide more positive caregiving (NICHD Early Child Care Research Network, 1996).

The demand for qualified professionals with relevant, specialized training in early childhood far exceeds the supply for this age group (Morgan et al., 1993). Not surprisingly, then, the National Child Care Staffing Study has assessed the overall quality of child care in America as barely adequate (Whitebook et al., 1989). Many early care and education practitioners are not required to have any early childhood training and typically have few incentives to invest in professional training (Morgan et al., 1994). Unfortunately, for example, child care workers are more likely to get information for improvement of their teaching from popular magazines than from professional journals (Powell & Stremmel, 1989). Finally, many directors of early childhood programs who could act as a resource for these teachers have little training in early childhood education themselves (Kuykendall, 1990).

Perhaps as a result of insufficient training, Goffin (1989) avers that many early childhood educators are unaware that their practices are developmentally inappropriate. Misinformation or lack of information can keep teachers bound to practices that are common or traditional for that center or program, but which do not effectively serve the needs of growing children. While good equipment and facilities can provide a better learning environment for children, the key factor is the teacher (Granucci, 1990; Snider & Fu, 1990).

Although training is a major barrier to the widespread adoption of DAP by child care/preschool teachers, the field generally offers teachers and directors the degree of flexibility as decision makers to choose their own objectives and curriculum, which is often not available in public school settings. As a result, child care and preschool settings across the country continue to be characterized by a wide diversity of program models (Goffin, 1989). Also, unlike the strong academic emphasis of the public schools, child care and preschool programs have historically been rooted in a philosophy more closely aligned to DAP that empha-sizes socioemotional issues, self-esteem, and a wider variety of domains of child development. As Jones (1986) points out, early childhood is the only educational level to have taken the developmental approach seriously enough to develop criteria for active learning.

National efforts by early childhood organizations have made strides to address the training issues and take advantage of the opportunity that teachers and directors have to implement DAP. For example, NAEYC provides on-the-job credentialing opportunities (such as the Child Development Associate or CDA) and accreditation (see Buck, 1987; Norris, 1994) in an effort to raise the quality of early childhood settings. Also, the Center for Career Development in Early Care and Education (located at Wheelock College) acts as a resource for states that are building professional development ladders for teachers of young children. Although there is much work to be done, strong national efforts are being made to address some of the issues that constrain teachers at this level from adopting appropriate practices.

Kindergarten Programs

Although changes in recent years have resulted in kindergartens that look much like the other grades, this level of schooling enjoyed a unique identity for many years (Walsh, 1989). From the initial Froebelian "child's garden" to its adoption in America and its early years as a part of the public school system, it has traditionally focused on preparing the child to learn successfully in a social setting (Bryant & Clifford, 1992). Fortunately, some kindergarten teachers, administrators, and parents continue to respect this important year in the child's education by encouraging a curriculum that incorporates play and social interaction as a highly valued part of the program. Unfortunately, societal changes (Elkind, 1986) and the increasing expectations for kindergarten to adopt an educational regimen similar to other grades in the public school system have tended to take many kindergarten programs in another direction. Hatch and Freeman (1988), for instance, found that the three most common changes reported in kindergarten by teachers over the past several years were a greater academic emphasis, increased grouping for instruction, and greater use of commercial materials.

Pressures from many different sources may be responsible for these changes. For example, the calls for excellence in education, back to basics, and strong emphasis on accountability have created pressure on kindergarten teachers (Hatch & Freeman, 1988). Also, the prevalence of mandated objectives, curriculum guides, and report cards encourages a more skill-centered orientation to reading instruction in kindergarten (Hatch & Freeman, 1988; Walsh, 1989). Related to this is the use of standardized testing in schools that promotes more DIP (Charlesworth et al., 1993b; Kamii, 1990). In addition, some teachers report that pressure comes from parents who want kindergarten to be more academic than the pre-K programs their children were coming from (Walsh, 1989).

Perceptions of the expectations of the next grade level teacher may also cause teachers to place more emphasis on a lock-step, drill-and-practice methodology with these young children (Hatch & Freeman, 1988). In one investigation of teacher attitudes, however, the expectations preschool teachers had for exiting preschool children went dramatically beyond the expectations of teachers for entering kindergartners (Hains et al., 1989). This suggests that assumptions of teachers about their colleagues at the next grade level may not always be completely accurate, especially when they teach in different educational systems. Love and Logue's (1992) extensive study corroborates this proposition, finding that a lack of communication between preschool and kindergarten teachers about students, curriculum issues, and other important matters is very common.

In the same study, Love and Logue found that most schools considered themselves "developmental," yet rated themselves relatively low on some of the key classroom activities that would characterize a DAP classroom, suggesting that a lack of understanding of DAP was rather pervasive in this large sample. Thus, the pressure that kindergarten teachers feel from parents and from other teachers, along with a lack of understanding of what "developmental" means in terms of the appropriate practices outlined by Bredekamp & Copple (1997), pose significant challenges for change in today's kindergarten classrooms.

Both kindergarten and primary grade teachers, however, enjoy the advantages of advanced training and generally have greater access to resources and opportunities for professional development than other teachers in the early childhood field. In terms of implementing integrated curriculum within a developmentally appropriate approach, it is the presence of mandated curriculum requirements that typically restricts the amount of flexibility teachers have to make changes in their classrooms. This lack of opportunity to make an informed, professional decision due to organizational constraints is a very real and compelling challenge (Goffin, 1989).

Primary Grade Programs

The primary grades are viewed by most as a highly significant window of opportunity for helping young children gain proficiency in literacy and numeracy skills. Pressure from administrators and parents to ensure that children are actively pursuing achievement in these areas makes providing tangible products (i.e., completed work sheets) a sort-of proof of a strong academic program. In addition, the widespread use of standardized testing, the desire to prepare children well for the next level of school, the use of report cards, and mandated programs for individual curriculum areas all contribute to the challenge. For some teachers, reliance on whole-group teaching and a preplanned, compartmentalized curriculum provides a sense that everything has been "covered" and that the teacher has fulfilled her or his mandated responsibility.

However, organizations that represent well-respected educational circles, such as the National Association of Elementary School Principals (1990), the National Education Association (1990), the National Association of State Boards of Education (Schultz & Lombardi, 1989), the International Reading Association (1986), and the National Council of Teachers of Mathematics (1991) are currently emphasizing goals and strategies that are supportive of DAP. Indeed, national standards reflecting a transformation in the nature of curriculum expectations from a narrow focus on knowledge and facts to a broader scope that also encompasses processes and dispositions is evident in the major subject area standards for K-3 children (Bredekamp & Rosegrant, 1995). In addition, widely publicized educational movements, such as emergent literacy and cooperative learning, open doors for increased appropriate practice in primary grade classrooms. Although local mandates that promote DIP may limit full implementation of DAP, reforms in elementary education today are providing good opportunities for kindergarten and primary grade teachers to align themselves more closely with DAP.

Strategies for Nurturing the Change Process

For any teacher, the first step of the change process is an awareness of DAP and an internal sense of motivation to make a change in teaching practices (Passidomo, 1994). The eventual goal of developmentally appropriate classrooms is children who have a better, more effective educational experience. However, the actual process of shifting from a developmentally inappropriate to a developmentally appropriate classroom was aptly described by one district's director of early childhood as "wrenching" (Passidomo, 1994). In another project involving a large number of teachers, Sykes (1994) astutely observed that the change process is often bumpy and messy, with each teacher progressing at his or her own pace. She also noted that, ultimately, some teachers become more proficient at teaching in a democratic developmentally appropriate way than others.

Indeed, those who have studied teacher practices posit the notion that a continuum of developmental appropriateness is the best way to describe early childhood educators (Mangione & Maniates, 1993; Oakes & Caruso, 1990). They find that few teachers have classrooms that are entirely developmentally inappropriate. Likewise, few teachers have a fully developmentally appropriate classroom. Most seem to fall somewhere along the continuum between these two extremes (Charlesworth et al., 1993b; Love & Logue, 1992; Mangione & Maniates, 1993; Oakes & Caruso, 1990). Studies also document a tendency for teachers to exhibit more appropriate beliefs than they report using in actual practice (Charlesworth et al., 1993a; Hatch & Freeman, 1988; Hitz & Wright, 1988). However, inservice training can make a significant difference in developmental beliefs and practices for teachers who are interested in learning about and implementing DAP (Haupt et al., 1995) and can encourage their subsequent advocacy efforts with administrators and colleagues (Mangione & Maniates, 1993).

Because teachers will begin at different levels and proceed at different rates, Mangione and Maniates (1993) suggest that professional development offerings provide a variety of formats for participants, including group meetings, individual consultation with trainers, trainer visits to classrooms, visits by participants to other teachers' classrooms, readings, reflective writing, and team planning with administrators. May (1992) suggests that through this training process, beneficial changes will result as teachers are provided with opportunities to acquire and refine new knowledge, learn necessary skills, develop a sense of ownership in the idea, and nurture the disposition to implement a developmentally appropriate way of educating children.

This variety of training experiences coupled with the provision of adequate time for change to occur is essential since DAP is an educational approach that demands reflection and complex implementation (Goffin & Stegelin, 1992). After their experiences facilitating change in public schools, both Horsch (1992) and Gronlund (1995) recommend that school change projects should expect at least a five-year commitment to the process. Given time, teachers will have the opportunity to experiment and evaluate their implementation of the developmental philosophy in activities, themes, projects, and classroom routines. While many teachers might desire a more "recipe-oriented" approach than the DAP standards provide, the developmental philosophy empowers teachers to understand the children they work with and fashion the curriculum and classroom environment so that the particular needs of the children and their relevant sociocultural surroundings are taken into consideration. A well-founded understanding of developmental philosophy and child development, therefore, is an essential component to a teacher's success in implementing DAP, since it will be the responsibility of each individual teacher to use this knowledge to make the plethora of decisions that are required in everyday classroom life (Gronlund, 1995).

Indeed, moving from a developmentally inappropriate classroom in which large-group instruction is the dominant teaching method and subject matter is taught in a nonintegrated manner to a classroom that embraces wholeheartedly the developmental approach will require significant modifications. For many teachers, changes in classroom practice will likely include some of the following: a reworking of the curriculum to include more integrated, child-oriented/teacher-facilitated activities; the rearrangement of the classroom environment into spaces where children can work in small groups and on individual projects; and the adjustment of assessment methods from a unidimensional approach that relies on tests (such as achievement tests and end-of-the-chapter quizzes) to the use of more authentic assessments, such as the Work Sampling System, which includes developmental checklists, portfolios, and summary reports (Meisels, 1993).

Finally, teachers need support from both mentors and colleagues, since they cannot be expected to construct a new method of teaching without assistance (Burchfield & Burchfield, 1992; David, 1991). Peer support and effective mentoring prove to be particularly helpful in the important work of translating DAP from theory into classroom practice (Bryant, Clifford, & Peisner, 1991). As some have cautioned, unless teachers are educated to teach within a strong theoretical framework that is closely attached to specific classroom practices, teachers' beliefs will not likely be congruent with practices (Charlesworth et al., 1991; Glascott, 1994). Teachers need opportunities to see DAP programs in action, to reflect on new practices, and to design and implement appropriate curriculum. Horsch (1992) cogently notes that achieving these results requires granting teachers permission to collaborate with one another, to inquire, and to plan. Indeed, we must give teachers the very permission we hope they will grant to children in a constructivist classroom setting.

Thus, as several teacher training projects have shown (Horsch, 1992; Mangione & Maniates, 1993; Marcon, 1994), certain strategies appear to successfully nurture changes in teachers and their classrooms. Clearly, personal commitment by teachers to change is the crucial first step. Second, successful training experiences need to provide a variety of formats, focus on both theory and implementation, and recognize that teachers follow their own path through the change process. Third, lasting change is created over time (David, 1991; Elkind, 1994; Healey, 1994; Wood, 1994) and with the support of administrators, mentors, and peers (Cassidy et al., 1995). Finally, a certain degree of persistence is necessary, since frustrations and setbacks are likely to be part of the process. The combination of clear vision, determination, time, and a great deal of support can eventually bring about the desired changes (Horsch, 1992).

Conclusion

In summary, early childhood educators can serve as important advocates for developmentally appropriate classroom practices. Implementing an integrated, developmentally appropriate curriculum and informing parents and administrators tabout this educational approach begins with a well-articulated philosophy. From there, transforming curriculum to meet DAP standards is an involved process requiring a concerted effort over several years. Long-term change can result when all involved—teachers, parents, and administrators—agree on common goals, foster strong relationships, circulate relevant information, learn from practical classroom experiences, and devote time to shared inquiry in a professional development setting.

Teachers are in a unique position to help parents recognize that although inappropriate practices may provide quick, short-term gains, a growing body of research demonstrates positive long-term academic and social gains for students involved in DAP classrooms. Advocacy efforts with parents will be most successful when teachers can both demonstrate and document how the educational goals parents have for their children are being accomplished through an integrated curriculum. Involving parents in the DAP classroom environment and in related educational activities at home, as recommended in this chapter, provides firsthand demonstrations of the advantages of child-sensitive teaching strategies. Combined with ongoing formal and informal communication between parents and teachers about appropriate practices over the course of the school year, a productive dialogue can be fostered.

Administrators, likewise, can become more fully informed about DAP by teachers who provide child-centered practices in the classroom and who share readings and stimulate discussions about DAP principles and current research results. Informing administrators about the benefits of developmentally appropriate curriculum can result in much needed support for those attempting to effectively integrate their curriculum. Administrators who are supportive of DAP, for example, can structure school policies to support integrated learning along with providing some of the essential resources, such as grant monies and time for teachers to reflect on and improve classroom practices.

In conclusion, nothing in the literature or in the real experiences of teachers seems to point toward easy, quick, or simple avenues for either making changes in classrooms or helping others understand and support DAP and integrated curriculum methods. However, many teachers have noted a genuine sense of satisfaction that has resulted as they more effectively meet the varied needs of the children they teach (Horsch, 1992). Persistence, energy, effort, and sensitivity characterize those who have become excellent advocates for developmentally appropriate practices and who are thereby creating a better learning environment for children now and in the future.

References

Bjorklund, G., & Burger, C. (1987). Making conferences work for parents, teachers and children. *Young Children, 42* (2), 26–31.

Black, J.K., & Puckett, M.B. (1987). Informing others about developmentally appropriate practice. In S. Bredekamp (Ed.), *Develop-*

mentally appropriate practice in early childhood programs serving children from birth though age 8. Washington, DC: National Association for the Education of Young Children.

Bredekamp, S. (Ed.). (1987). *Developmentally appropriate practice in early childhood programs serving children from birth though age 8.* Washington, DC: National Association for the Education of Young Children.

Bredekamp, S., & Copple, C. (Eds.). (1997). *Developmentally appro-prite practice in early childhood programs: Revised.* Washington, DC: National Association for the Education of Young Children.

Bredekamp, S., & Rosegrant, T. (Eds.). (1992). *Reaching potentials: Appropriate curriculum and assessment for young children* (Vol. 1). Washington, DC: National Association for the Education of Young Children.

Bredekamp, S., & Rosegrant, T. (Eds.). (1995). *Reaching potentials: Transforming early childhood curriculum and assessment* (Vol. 2). Washington, DC: National Association for the Education of Young Children.

Brophy, J., & Alleman, J. (1991). A caveat: Curriculum integration isn't always a good idea. *Educational Leadership, 49* (2), 66.

Bryant, D.M., & Clifford, R.M. (1992). 150 years of kindergarten: How far have we come? *Early Childhood Research Quarterly, 7,* 147–54.

Bryant, D.M., Clifford, R.M., & Peisner, E.S. (1991). Best practices for beginners: Developmental appropriateness in kindergarten. *American Educational Research Journal, 28* (4), 783–803.

Buck, L. (1987). Directors: How to sell accreditation to staff, board and parents. *Young Children, 42* (2), 46–49.

Bundy, B.F. (1991). Fostering communication between parents and preschools. *Young Children, 46* (2), 12–17.

Burchfield, D.W., & Burchfield, B.C. (1992). Two primary teachers learn and discover through a process of change. In S. Bredekamp & T. Rosegrant (Eds.), *Reaching potentials: Appropriate curriculum and assessment for young children* (Vol. 1, pp. 150–58). Washington, DC: National Association for the Education of Young Children.

Burts, D.C., Hart, C.H., Charlesworth, R., DeWolf, D.M., Ray, J., Manuel, K., & Fleege, P.O. (1993). Developmental appropriateness of kindergarten programs and academic outcomes in first grade. *Journal of Research in Childhood Education, 3* (1), 23–31.

Campbell, F.A., Goldstein, S., Schaefer, E.S., & Ramey, C.T. (1991). Parental beliefs and values related to family risk, educational intervention, and child academic competence. *Early Childhood Research Quarterly, 6,* 167–82.

Carlson, H.L., & Stenmalm-Sjoblom, L. (1989). A cross-cultural study of parents' perceptions of early childhood programs. *Early Childhood Research Quarterly, 4,* 505–22.

Caruso, J.J. (1991). Supervisors in early childhood programs: An emerging profile. *Young Children, 46* (6), 20–26.

Cassidy, D.J., Buell, M.J., Pugh-Hoese, S., & Russell, S. (1995). The effect of education on child care teachers beliefs and classroom quality: Year one evaluation of the TEACH Early Childhood Associate Degree Scholarship Program. *Early Childhood Research Quarterly, 10,* 171–83.

Chard, S. (1993). *The project approach: A practical guide for teachers.* Edmonton, Alberta: University of Alberta.

Chard, S. (1994). *The project approach: A second practical guide for teachers.* Edmonton, Alberta: University of Alberta.

Charlesworth, R., Hart, C.H., Burts, D.C., DeWolf, M. (1993a). The LSU Studies: Building a research base for developmentally appropriate practice. In S. Reifel (Ed.), *Advances in early education and day care, vol. 5, Perspectives in developmentally appropriate practice* (pp. 3–28). Greenwich, CT: JAI.

Charlesworth, R., Hart, C.H., Burts, D.C., & Hernandez, S. (1991). Kindergarten teachers' beliefs and practices. *Early Child Development and Care, 70,* 17–35.

Charlesworth, R., Hart, C.H., Burts, D.C., Thomasson, R.H., Mosley, J., Fleege, P.O. (1993b). Measuring the developmental appropriateness of kindergarten teachers' beliefs and practices. *Early Childhood Research Quarterly, 8,* 255–76.

David, J.L. (1991). What it takes to restructure education. *Educational Leadership, 48* (8), 11–15.

Elkind, D. (1986). Formal education and early childhood education: An essential difference. *Phi Delta Kappan, 67,* 631–36.

Elkind, D. (1994). Early childhood education and the postmodern world. *Principal, 73* (5), 6–7.

Espinosa, L. (1992). The process of change: The Redwood City story. In S. Bredekamp & T. Rosegrant (Eds.), *Reaching potentials: Appropriate curriculum and assessment for young children* (Vol. 1, pp. 159–66). Washington, DC: National Association for the Education of Young Children.

Finders, M., & Lewis, C. (1994). Why some parents don't come to school. *Educational Leadership, 51* (8), 50–54.

Frede, E., Austin, A., & Lindauer, S. (1993). The relationship of specific developmentally appropriate teaching practices in preschool to children's skills in first grade. In S. Reifel (Ed.), *Advances in early education and day care, vol. 5, Perspectives in developmentally appropriate practice* (pp. 95–111). Greenwich, CT: JAI.

Frede, E., & Barnett, W.S. (1992). Developmentally appropriate public school preschool: A study of implementation of the High/Scope curriculum and its effects on disadvantaged children's skills at first grade. *Early Childhood Research Quarterly, 7,* 483–99.

Galen, H. (1994). Developmentally appropriate practice: Myths and facts. *Principal, 73* (5), 20–22.

Galinsky, E. (1988). Parents and teacher-caregivers: Sources of tension, sources of support. *Young Children, 43* (3), 4–12.

Glascott, K. (1994). A problem of theory for early childhood professionals. *Childhood Education, 70* (3), 131–32.

Goffin, S.G. (1989). Developing a research agenda for early childhood education: What can be learned from the research on teaching? *Early Childhood Research Quarterly, 4,* 187–204.

Goffin, S.G., & Stegelin, D.A. (1992). *Changing kindergartens: Four success stories.* Washington, DC: National Association for the Education of Young Children.

Goodman, K.S. (1987). *Language and thinking in school: A whole language curriculum.* New York: Richard C. Owen.

Granucci, P.L. (1990). Kindergarten teachers: Working through our identity crisis. *Young Children, 45* (3), 6–11.

Gronlund, G. (1995). Bringing the DAP message to kindergarten and primary teachers. *Young Children, 50* (5), 4–13.

Hains, A.H., Fowler, S.A., Schwartz, I.S., Kottwitz, E., & Rosenkoetter, S. (1989). A comparison of preschool and kindergarten teacher expectations for school readiness. *Early Childhood Research Quarterly, 4,* 75–88.

Hatch, J.A., & Freeman, E.B. (1988). Kindergarten philosophies and practices: Perspectives of teachers, principals, and supervisors. *Early Childhood Research Quarterly, 3*, 151–66.

Haupt, J.H., Larsen, J.M., Robinson, C.C., & Hart, C.H. (1995). The impact of DAP inservice training on the beliefs and practices of kindergarten teachers. *Journal of Early Childhood Teacher Education, 16* (2), 12–18.

Healey, P.M. (1994). Parent education: Going from defense to offense. *Principal, 73* (4), 30–31.

Heck, R.H., Larsen, T.J., & Marcoulides, G.A. (1990). Instructional leadership and school achievement: Validation of a causal model. *Educational Administration Quarterly, 26* (2), 94–125.

Hiebert, E.H., & Adams, C.S. (1987). Fathers' and mothers' perceptions of their preschool children's emergent literacy. *Journal of Experimental Child Psychology, 44*, 25–37.

Hills, T.W. (1992). Reaching potentials through appropriate assessment. In S. Bredekamp & T. Rosegrant (Eds.), *Reaching potentials: Appropriate curriculum and assessment for young children* (Vol. 1, pp. 43–63). Washington, DC: National Association for the Education of Young Children.

Hitz, R., & Wright, D. (1988). Kindergarten issues: A practitioners' survey. *Principal, 67* (5), 28–30.

Holloway, S.D., & Fuller, B. (1992). The great child-care experiment: What are the lessons for school improvement? *Educational Researcher, 21* (7), 12–19.

Horsch, P.D. (1992). School change: A partnership approach. *Early Education and Development, 3*, 128–38.

Howes, C. (1983). Caregiver behavior in center and family care. *Journal of Applied Developmental Psychology, 4*, 99–107.

Hyson, M.C. (1991). The characteristics and origins of the academic preschool. In L. Rescorla, M.C. Hyson, & K. Hirsh-Pasek (Eds.), *Academic instruction in early childhood: Challenge or pressure?* (pp. 21–29). San Francisco: Jossey-Bass.

International Reading Association. (1986). Literacy development and pre-first grade: A joint statement of concerns about present practices in pre-first grade reading instruction and recommendations for improvement. *Young Children, 41* (4), 10–13.

Jacobs, H.H. (Ed.). (1989). *Interdisciplinary curriculum: Design and implementation.* Alexandria, VA: Association for Supervision and Curriculum Development.

Johnson, D.W., & Johnson, R.T. (1991). *Learning together and alone: Cooperative, competitive and individualistic learning* (3rd ed.). Englewood Cliffs, NJ: Allyn & Bacon.

Jones, E. (1986). Perspectives on teacher education: Some relations between theory and practice. In L. Katz (Ed.), *Current topics in early childhood education* (Vol. 6, pp. 123–41). Norwood, NJ: Ablex.

Kagan, S.L. (1988). Current reforms in early childhood education: Are we addressing the issues? *Young Children, 43* (2), 27–32.

Kamii, C. (Ed.). (1990). *Achievement testing in the early grades.* Washington, DC: National Association for the Education of Young Children.

Katz, L.G., & Chard, S.C. (1989). *Engaging children's minds: The project approach.* Norwood, NJ: Ablex.

Kenney, E., & Perry, S. (1994). Talking with parents about performance-based report cards. *Educational Leadership, 52* (2), 24–27.

Knudsen-Lindauer, S., & Harris, K. (1989). Priorities for kindergarten curricula: Views of parents and teachers. *Journal of Research on Childhood Education, 4* (1) 51–61.

Kontos, S., & Dunn, L. (1993). Caregiver practices and beliefs in child care varying in developmental appropriateness and quality. In S. Reifel (Ed.), *Advances in early education and day care, vol. 5, Perspectives in developmentally appropriate practice* (pp. 53–74). Greenwich, CT: JAI.

Kostelnik, M.J. (1992). Myths associated with developmentally appropriate programs. *Young Children, 47* (4), 17–23.

Kuykendall, J.M. (1990). Child development: Directors shouldn't leave home without it! *Young Children, 45* (5), 47–50.

Love, J.M., & Logue, M.E. (1992). *Transitions to kindergarten in American schools.* (Contract No. LC88089001). Washington, DC: U.S. Department of Education, Office of Policy and Planning.

Mangione, P.L., & Maniates, H. (1993). Training teachers to implement developmentally appropriate practice. In S. Reifel (Ed.), *Advances in early education and day care, vol. 5, Perspectives in developmentally appropriate practice* (pp. 145–66). Greenwich, CT: JAI.

Marcon, R.A. (1994). Doing the right thing for children: Linking research and policy reform in the District of Columbia public schools. *Young Children, 50* (1), 8–20.

May, L. (1992). Developing appropriate practices in the kindergarten: A district-level perspective. In S.G. Goffin, & D.A. Stegelin (Eds.), *Changing kindergartens: Four success stories* (pp. 51–72). Washington, DC: National Association for the Education of Young Children.

McCartney, K., Scarr, S., Phillips, D., Grajeck, S., & Schwartz, J.C. (1982). Environmental differences among day care centers and their effects on children's development. In E.F. Zigler & E.W. Gordon (Eds.), *Day care: Scientific and social policy issues* (pp. 126–51). Boston: Auburn Plouse.

Meisels, S.J. (1993). The work sampling system: An authentic performance assessment. *Principal, 72* (5), 5–7.

Mitchell, A.L. (1993). Shouldn't preschool people advocate for better elementary schools, too? *Young Children, 48* (5), 58–62.

Morgan, G., Azer, S.L., Costley, J.B., Elliott, K., Genser, A., Goodman, I.F., & McGimsey, B. (1994). Future pursuits: Building early care and education careers. *Young Children, 49* (3), 80–83.

Morgan, G., Azer, S.L., Costley, J.B., Genser, A., Goodman, I.F., Lombardi, J., & McGimsey, B. (1993). *Making a career of it: The state of the states report on career development in early care and education.* Boston: The Center for Career Development in Early Care and Education at Wheelock College.

Mosley, J., Charlesworth, R., Hart, C.H., Burts, D.C., & Norris, J. (1996). *A comparison of writing, drawing, and storytelling in kindergarten children from classrooms differing in degrees of developmentally appropriateness.* Manuscript submitted for publication.

National Association of Elementary School Principals. (1990). *Early childhood education and the elementary school principal: Standards for quality programs for young children.* Alexandria, VA: Author.

National Council of Teachers of Mathematics. (1991). *Professional standards for teaching mathematics.* Reston, VA: Author.

National Education Association. (1990). *Early childhood education and the public schools.* Washington, DC: Author.

Newmann, F.M. (1993). What is a restructured school? *Principal, 72* (3), 5–8.

NICHD Early Child Care Research Network. (1996). Characteristics of infant care: Factors contributing to positive caregiving. *Early Childhood Research Quarterly, II,* 269–306.

Norris, N.C. (1994). The NAEYC accreditation process isn't really so scary—Why not try it? *Young Children, 49* (6), 72–74.

Oakes, P.B., & Caruso, D.A. (1990). Kindergarten teachers' use of developmentally appropriate practices and attitudes about authority. *Early Education and Development, 1* (6), 445–57.

Olmstead, P.P., & Lockhart, S. (1995). Do parents and teachers agree? What should young children be learning? *High Scope Resource, 14* (1), 7–9.

Passidomo, M. (1994). Moving from traditional to developmentally appropriate education: A work in progress. *Young Children, 49* (6), 75–78.

Perkins, D.N. (1991). Educating for insight. *Educational Leadership, 49* (2), 4–8.

Powell, D.R. (1994). Parents, pluralism, and the NAEYC statement on developmentally appropriate practice. In B.C. Mallory and R.S. New (Eds.), *Diversity and developmentally appropriate practices* (pp. 166–82). New York: Teachers College Press.

Powell, D.R., & Stremmel, A.J. (1989). The relation of early childhood training and experience to the professional development of child care workers. *Early Childhood Research Quarterly, 4,* 339–55.

Rescorla, L. (1991). Parent and teacher attitudes about early academics. In L. Rescorla, M.C. Hyson, & K. Hirsh-Pasek (Eds.), *Academic instruction in early childhood: Challenge or pressure?* (pp. 13–19). San Francisco: Jossey-Bass.

Reutzel, D.R., & Cooter, R.B. , Jr. (1996). *Teaching children to read: From basals to books* (2nd ed). Columbus, OH: Merrill-Prentice Hall.

Ribas, W.B. (1992). Helping teachers communicate with parents. *Principal, 72* (2), 19–20.

Rusher, A.S., McGrevin, C.Z., & Lambiotte, J.G. (1992). Belief systems of early childhood teachers and their principals regarding early childhood education. *Early Childhood Research Quarterly, 7,* 277–96.

Schultz, T. (1992). Developmentally appropriate practice and the challenge of public school reform. In D. Stegelin (Ed.), *Early childhood education: Policy issues for the 1990s.* Norwood, NJ: Ablex.

Schultz, T., & Lombardi, J. (1989). Right from the start: A report on the NASBE Task Force on Early Childhood Education. *Young Children, 44* (2), 6–10.

Schweinhart, L.J., & Hohmann, C.F. (1992). The High/Scope K–3 curriculum: A new approach. *Principal, 71* (5), 16–19.

Slavin, R. (1987). *Cooperative learning: Student teams.* Washington, DC: National Education Association.

Snider, M.H., & Fu, V.R. (1990). The effects of specialized education and job experience on early childhood teachers' knowledge of developmentally appropriate practice. *Early Childhood Research Quarterly, 5,* 69–78.

Spiegel, D.L., Fitzgerald, J., & Cunningham, J.W. (1993). Parental perceptions of preschoolers' literacy development: Implications for home-school partnerships. *Young Children, 48* (5), 74–79.

Stipek, D., Rosenblatt, L., & DiRocco, L. (1994). Making parents your allies. *Young Children, 49* (3), 4–9.

Swick, K.J., & McKnight, S. (1989). Characteristics of kindergarten teachers who promote parent involvement. *Early Childhood Research Quarterly, 4,* 19–29.

Sykes, M. (1994). Creating a climate for change in a major urban school system. *Young Children, 50* (1), 4–7.

Vandell, D.L., & Powers, C. (1983). Day care quality and children's free play activities. *American Journal of Orthopsychiatry, 53,* 493–500.

Walsh, D.J. (1989). Changes in kindergarten: Why here? Why now? *Early Childhood Research Quarterly, 4,* 377–91.

Weikart, D.P., & Schweinhart, L.J. (1991). Disadvantaged children and curriculum effects. In L. Rescorla, M.C. Hyson, & K. Hirsh-Pasek (Eds.), *Academic instruction in early childhood: Challenge or pressure?* (pp. 57–64). San Francisco: Jossey-Bass.

Whitebook, M., Howes, C., Phillips, D., & Pemberton, C. (1989). Who cares? Child care teachers and the quality of care in America. *Young Children, 45* (1), 41–45.

Wood, C. (1994). Responsive teaching: Creating partnerships for systemic change. *Young Children, 50* (1), 21–28.

Contributors

Joan H. Benedict is Director of the Northwestern Laboratory School Child Development Center in Alexandria, Louisiana and Assistant Professor, Northwestern State University, Family and Consumer Sciences Department. She administers several grants involving the training of child care workers and the parents of special needs children. Dr. Benedict teaches college level child development/early childhood education courses. She previously was Director of the Human Ecology Laboratory Preschool and instructor at Louisiana State University. She has taught children ages 2 years through 8 years. Dr. Benedict recently completed her dissertation on the comparison of the oral language of kindergarten students in basal based and whole language kindergartens.

Sue Bredekamp is the Director of Professional Development of the National Association for the Education of Young Children. Her major contributions to the work of NAEYC have been developing and directing a national, voluntary accreditation system for early childhood programs. Dr. Bredekamp also researched and wrote NAEYC's position statements on early childhood teacher education, developmentally appropriate practice, and appropriate curriculum and assessment. Dr. Bredekamp's professional experience includes teaching and directing early childhood programs, serving on a four-year college faculty, and in the Head Start Bureau at the Administration for Children, Youth, and Families.

Diane C. Burts is Professor of Human Ecology at Louisiana State University. She served as the Director of the Human Ecology Preschool Laboratory for 15 years and previously taught preschool, kindergarten, and primary school children. Dr. Burts is the recipient of several teaching awards including the University Excellence in Teaching Award and the National Association of State Universities and Land-Grant Colleges (NASULGC) Southern Regional Award. Her research focus is in the area of developmentally appropriate practices. She is the author of several book chapters and has published in journals including *Early Childhood Research Quarterly, Child Development, Journal of Research in Childhood Education*, and *Journal of Early Childhood Teacher Education*. Dr. Burts presents frequently at professional meetings including AERA, SRCD, NAEYC, and NAECTE.

Rosalind Charlesworth teaches Child Development and Early Childhood Education courses at Weber State University in Utah and was formerly a Professor in the Department of Curriculum and Instruction at Louisiana State University. Her special interests are developmentally appropriate practices, integrated curriculum, teachers' beliefs and practices, and young children's concept development. Dr. Charlesworth is the author of numerous articles and book chapters and has published the fourth edition of her book, *Understanding Child Development*, and the second edition of *Math and Science for Young Children* with Karen Lind. She is a consulting editor for *Early Childhood Research Quarterly* and is Region 8 Representative on the Governing Board for the National Association of Early Childhood Teacher Educators.

Shawn L. Christiansen is a doctoral student at the University of Delaware in the Department of Individual and Family Studies. His research interests include fathering, child development, and Japanese family life. He has published and presented papers on the sharing of housework and child care by dual-earner couples, the relationship between fathers' involvement in child care and adult development, and gender bias in Erikson's theory of psychosocial development.

Cynthia Colbert is Professor of Art and Chair of Art Education at the University of South Carolina. She teaches courses on children's artistic and aesthetic development, a graduate research seminar, and an elementary methods course for art education majors. Her special interests are young children's artistic development, particularly their attempts to represent three-dimensional space on a two dimensional plane; developmentally appropriate practice; integrated curriculum; issues of gender and education; and using the visual arts as a way to help children construct concepts. Dr. Colbert is completing a new integrated visual arts textbook for grades 1–3. She is the author of numerous book chapters and articles and frequently writes for the National Art Education Association.

Michele DeWolf currently works as a graduate assistant in Louisiana State University's School of Human Ecology while she completes requirements for her Ph.D. Prior to this experience she was employed as a research associate at Louisiana State University. In this position, she directed research on developmentally appropriate practice and children's social development. She has worked with young children in a variety of settings (e.g., day care, public schools, lab preschool, therapeutic horseback riding centers), taught child development courses for child care personnel, served as a consultant for a hospital developing a short-term child care facility, and currently serves on the Louisiana Early Childhood Association (LAECA) State Board. She has coauthored articles on developmentally appropriate practice and parental influences on children's peer relationships in journals such as *Early Childhood Research Quarterly* and *Child Development.*

Pamela O. Fleege is Assistant Professor of early childhood education at the University of South Florida. She received her doctoral degree from Louisiana State University. Dr. Fleege's areas of interest include assessment, developmentally appropriate practices in the primary grades, and integrated mathematics and science for young children. Her publications include several book chapters and articles in journals including the *Journal of Research in Childhood Education, Early Childhood Research Quarterly,* and *Early Education and Development.*

Craig H. Hart is Associate Professor of Family Sciences at Brigham Young University and was formerly an Associate Professor in the School of Human Ecology at Louisiana State University. He has authored and coauthored numerous research papers on developmentally appropriate practices in early childhood and on parenting/familial linkages with children's social development and peer relations. These have appeared in well known journals such as *Child Develop-*

ment, Developmental Psychology, and *Early Childhood Research Quarterly.* He recently published an edited volume entitled *Children on Playgrounds: Research Perspectives and Applications* and is associate editor for *Early Childhood Research Quarterly.*

Julie H. Haupt, is an Instructor of Family Sciences at Brigham Young University. She has been the administrator of the University preschool and a CDA National Representative. Her teaching and research interests include integrated curriculum, emergent literacy, and parent education. Recent publications include articles on emergent literacy in *Early Education and Development* and *Reading Research and Instruction,* an article on an inservice training program for kindergarten teachers on developmentally appropriate practices published in *Journal of Early Childhood Teacher Education,* and an article on parent education in *Early Childhood Research Quarterly.* She is the mother of two young children.

Marion C. Hyson is Professor and Chair of the Department of Individual and Family Studies at the University of Delaware. Her interests include the study of early emotional development, parents' and teachers' beliefs about development and educational practices, and the effects of academic environments on young children. Dr. Hyson was the guest editor of a special issue of *Early Education and Development* on "Emotional Development and Early Education" (January 1996). She is the author of *The Emotional Development of Young Children: Building an Emotion-Centered Curriculum,* published in 1994. Dr. Hyson serves as editor of *Early Childhood Research Quarterly.*

Susan H. Kenney is Associate Professor of Music at Brigham Young University, where she is Elementary Music Education Coordinator. She founded the Parent-Toddler Music Program at the University and served as its director. In 1984, she and Barbara Andress co-chaired the Music in Early Childhood International Conference held at BYU. She was a contributing writer to the Holt, Rinehart and Winston music textbook series *Music,* grades K–3 and has articles in several music education publications. Active in professional music education organizations, she has served as national chair of the Music Educators National Conference Society for General Music and was a consultant for the writing of pre-kindergarten national standards in music. Her articles and numerous presentations at professional meetings have focused on creating developmentally appropriate music environments in early childhood education settings.

Suzanne Krogh teaches courses in early childhood and elementary education Western Washington University. Dr. Krogh is the former chairperson of her department. Her research and writing focus is on integrating the curriculum and on inservice-learning. She recently published the second edition of *The Integrated Early Childhood Curriculum*.

Jean M. Larsen is Professor of Child Development/Early Childhood Education in the Department of Family Sciences at Brigham Young University. She has been on the faculty for 36 years and for the past 15 years has served as ECE program coordinator and director of the BYU preschool longitudinal research study. Her research publications (appearing in journals such as *Early Childhood Research Quarterly* and *Child Development*) and numerous conference presentations (at NAEYC, SRCD, and AERA) have primarily focused on preschool effects, parent education, and teacher behaviors. Dr. Larsen has been active in NAEYC, served as president of UAEYC, headed the Utah Early Childhood Inter-Institutional Consortium, and was appointed to the advisory board for the Utah State Office of Child Care. She has also been instrumental in developing and implementing two parent/provider training programs, *Because You Care for Young Children* and *To Those Who Care for Infants and Toddlers*.

Karen K. Lind is an Associate Professor in the Department of Early and Middle Childhood Education at the University of Louisville, Kentucky, where she is the recipient of the 1993 Distinguished Teaching Professor award from the university. Dr. Lind spent one and one half years at the National Science Foundation as a program director in the Teacher Enhancement and Instructional Materials Development programs. She is past president of the Counsel for Elementary Science International (CESI). She is Early Childhood column editor of *Science & Children*, a publication of the National Science Teacher's Association (NSTA). She is also a member of the NSTA Preschool-Elementary Committee. Her research publications and inservice programs focus on integrating science into preschool and primary classroom settings. Dr. Lind's most recent publications include the second editions of *Math & Science for Young Children* with Rosalind Charlesworth and *Exploring Science in Early Childhood*, both with Delmar Publishers.

Margaret F. Ostlund is Undergraduate Coordinator of Elementary Education at Brigham Young University and a faculty member in the area of Social Studies. She has taught all elementary grades in the public schools, directed a preschool, and taught multi-age (K-2) classes for several years in a private school for gifted children. Recently her interests have included the simultaneous renewal of teacher education and professional development schools. She served for five years as District Liaison in the Brigham Young University/Public School Partnership. Her publications include articles on restructuring teacher education and clustering of schools as an organizational plan for school-university partnerships.

Greg Payne is a Professor in the Department of Human Performance at San Jose State University where he is a specialist in human motor development with interest in aging and physical activity. He has produced over 70 publications including numerous refereed articles and books. He recently published the third edition of *Human Motor Development: A Lifespan Approach*. Dr. Payne is the recipient of numerous awards including The Distinguished Honorary Professor of the Sheyang Institute of Physical Education and the distinguished alumni award from Western Illinois University. He also received the *Research Quarterly for Exercise and Sport* Research Writing Award for research involving children's physical training and VO2 max. Dr. Payne has served as President of the California Association for Health, Physical Education, Recreation, and Dance and was recently elected President of the National Association for Sports and Physical Education (NASPE). He has chaired two editorial boards and currently reviews for major journals in the field.

D. Ray Reutzel is a Karl G. Maeser Research and Creative Arts Distinguished Professor of Elementary Education and Associate Dean of the David O. McKay School of Education at Brigham Young University. He has been a classroom teacher in kindergarten, 1st, 3rd, 5th, and 6th grades. Dr. Reutzel is the author of over 90 articles, book chapters, and books related to reading instructional practices with early childhood and elementary students as well as program author for the Scholastic Literacy Place school-based instructional program. He co-authored the text *Teaching Children to Read: From Basals to Books*, now in its second edition.

Judith E. Rink is a Professor and department chair in the Department of Physical Education, University of South Carolina, Columbia. Her research interests are in the area of research on teaching and teacher education in physical education. Judy has been an elementary school physical education teacher in the public schools of New York and North Carolina. Her early career was heavily involved in teacher development in movement education. She is the author of several text books in the curriculum and instruction area, has authored many research studies, and has been co-editor of the *Journal for Teaching Physical Education*. Dr. Rink is presently a co-section editor for pedagogy for the *Research Quarterly for Exercise and Sport*. She was the chairperson of the committee that developed the national standards for physical education for the National Association of Sport and Physical Education.

Carol Seefeldt is Professor of Human Development in the Institute for Child Study at the University of Maryland where she received the Distinguished Scholar/Teacher Award. She has worked in the field for over 40 years and has taught 2-year-olds through graduate school. She is active in the National Association for the Education of Young Children and the Association for Childhood Education International. She is the author of numerous books, book chapters, and articles, some of which have focused on social studies during the early childhood years. Her research emphasizes early childhood curriculum, intergenerational attitudes, and the effects of competition on child growth and development.

Andrew J. Stremmel is Associate Professor in Family & Child Development and Director of the Child Development Laboratories at Virginia Polytechnic Institute & State University. He received his B.A. from the Pennsylvania State University in 1978 and his M.S. and Ph.D. degrees from Purdue University in 1981 and 1989. In between graduate degrees, he was a head teacher in the Purdue Child Development Laboratories. His research interests and publications have focused on issues of early childhood teacher education and professional development; the use of Vygotsky's theory in teacher education and the classroom; teacher job satisfaction; and more recently, intergenerational exchanges between preschool children and older adults. He is co-editing a book on diversity entitled, *Affirming Diversity Through Democratic Conversations*, which is currently under review.

Donna E. Dugger Wadsworth is Assistant Professor at the University of Southwestern Louisiana. She recently received her Ph.D. from Louisiana State University in Early Childhood Education. Dr. Wadsworth teaches early childhood special education/intervention and behavior management courses. Her special interests are young children with special needs and their families. She has published articles in journals including *Childhood Education, Early Childhood Education Journal,* and *Intervention in School and Clinic.*

Author Index

457

Subject Index